THE CLASSICAL PAPERS
OF GILBERT HIGHET

GILBERT HIGHET

THE CLASSICAL PAPERS
OF GILBERT HIGHET

edited by ROBERT J. BALL

COLUMBIA UNIVERSITY PRESS
New York
1983

Publication of this book was made possible by support from the Frank Diehl Fackenthal Fund of the Press.

Library of Congress Cataloging in Publication Data
Highet, Gilbert, 1906–1978.
  The classical papers of Gilbert Highet.

  Bibliography: p.
  Includes index.
  1. Classical literature—History and criticism—
Collected works.   I. Ball, Robert J.   II. Title.
PA3003.H5   1983   880'.09   83-7181
ISBN 0-231-05104-2

Columbia University Press
New York   Guildford, Surrey

Clothbound editions of Columbia University Press books are Smyth-sewn and printed on permanent and durable acid-free paper.

067162

PERMISSIONS

FOR GILBERT HIGHET AND HELEN MACINNES

et quasi cursores uitai lampada tradunt

(*Lucretius* 2.79)

CONTENTS

* Unpublished, appearing here for the first time.

PREFACE

I OFFER this book as a memorial for a great teacher and scholar, who taught at Columbia University for thirty-five years. It is intended for both the professional classicist and the literary-minded layman, the double audience for whom Dr. Highet wrote during his long and distinguished career. The volume consists of three parts—a biographical essay, a collection of his classical papers, and a bibliography of all his publications.

The biographical essay focuses on his professional career, from his student days in Glasgow to his retirement from Columbia. I have gathered most of my information from Dr. Highet's files, from a number of his publications, and from articles that have appeared about him. The word "allegedly" has been used to refer to several of the apocryphal anecdotes with which he became associated during his years as a teacher. I have occasionally drawn upon personal recollections of his activities on the Columbia campus in the hope that others will remember him in the same way. There appears at the end of the essay a bibliography of all substantial publications about his life and his work (arranged chronologically).

The classical papers included in this volume range from scholarly articles to those of a less technical nature. They consist of articles that Dr. Highet published in journals and periodicals, and several that he had put into finished form and was planning to publish. They do not include articles that he published in books or as introductions to books, since he himself opposed republishing articles on such a basis. They have been arranged in three groups, corresponding to his three central interests—Greek Literature, Latin Literature, and the Classical Tradition. Within each group they have been arranged chronologically by authors treated in order to demonstrate the vast period of time and large number of writers encompassed by his genius.

The bibliography of his publications includes everything that he published, as far as I have been able to determine. Although Dr. Highet left a great deal of material related to his teaching and research, he did not leave a complete bibliography (only short lists for various years). I have examined all his files, the standard bibliographical reference works, and indexes to the periodicals themselves for additional locations. His publications have been arranged in chronological order, in groups that should benefit readers of different literary backgrounds, classicists and nonclassicists. I have annotated the entries wherever possible and have provided extensive cross-references in order to make the bibliography a truly valuable one.

University of Hawaii   ROBERT J. BALL

ACKNOWLEDGMENTS

I wish to thank the following individuals for accommodating my various requests during the period I was working on this project:

Helen MacInnes, Dr. Highet's lifetime companion, for allowing me to honor her late husband with this volume—a debt that I also have acknowledged in the dedication;

William F. Bernhardt, Associate Editor of Columbia University Press, for his warm reception of the project and for enabling me to produce the kind of memorial I envisioned;

Kenneth A. Lohf, Librarian for Rare Books and Manuscripts in Columbia University, and his excellent staff, for assisting me during my examination of Dr. Highet's files;

Ellen L. Chapman, Head of the General Reference Department in the University of Hawaii, and her efficient colleagues, for providing me with their expert bibliographical knowledge;

Al Silverman, President of the Book-of-the-Month Club, and his professional staff, for assisting me during my examination of the records of Dr. Highet's book reviews;

Jeffrey Norton, President of Jeffrey Norton Publishers, for providing me with information related to the reproduction on audio-cassettes of Dr. Highet's radio talks;

P. G. Walsh, Professor of Humanity in Glasgow University, for furnishing me with material on Dr. Highet's contributions as a student to the *Glasgow University Magazine*;

James Diggle, Fellow of Queens' College (Cambridge), for furnishing me with material on Dr. Highet's contributions as a student to Oxford University's *Isis*.

ABBREVIATIONS

THE FOLLOWING list contains all the abbreviations used in this volume for journals and books in which Dr. Highet published. Abbreviations for journals correspond to those found in *L'Année Philologique*, except for several that I have created for items of a nonclassical nature. Abbreviations for authors and texts correspond to those found in the *Oxford Classical Dictionary*, except for Vergil's *Eclogues*, which Dr. Highet always called *Bucolics*.

AHR	*American Historical Review*
AJPh	*American Journal of Philology*
BMCN	*Book-of-the-Month Club News*
BMCT	*Book-of-the-Month Club Transcripts*
CJ	*Classical Journal*
Clerk	*A Clerk of Oxenford*
CPh	*Classical Philology*
CR	*Classical Review*
CW	*Classical World* (née *Classical Weekly*)
GRBS	*Greek, Roman, and Byzantine Studies*
GUM	*Glasgow University Magazine*
HSPh	*Harvard Studies in Classical Philology*
People	*People, Places, and Books*
Powers	*The Powers of Poetry*
SEJ	*Scottish Educational Journal*

SPh	*Studies in Philology*
Talents	*Talents and Geniuses*
TAPhA	*Transactions of the American Philological Association*

THE CLASSICAL PAPERS
OF GILBERT HIGHET

GILBERT HIGHET
AND THE CLASSICAL TRADITION

GILBERT HIGHET was born on June 22, 1906 in Glasgow, Scotland, the only child of Gilbert and Elizabeth Boyle Highet. He lived with his parents, educated people, on Byres Road in Hillhead; his father worked as Superintendent of Telegraphs for the West of Scotland. He grew up in comfortable surroundings, in which he learned that one could succeed by combining hard work with a good character. He attended Hillhead High School from 1913 to 1924, which from the outset had a fine reputation as an excellent Scottish school, especially in foreign languages. At Hillhead his peers regarded him as something of a genius, and the school awarded the youthful prodigy a number of its coveted scholarships. At eleven he began learning French and Latin, and soon afterward Greek, when James Buchanan, the schoolmaster, tutored him during the lunch hour. By fourteen he could read Homer and Vergil with ease and for pleasure, and by sixteen Aeschylus's *Prometheus Bound*, which he found difficult but exciting. At sixteen he read and analyzed ten plays of Shakespeare and wrote his first poem after reading George Meredith's "Lucifer in Starlight." Greek, Latin, and English became the hallmarks of his existence, except for his editing the school magazine (the first in a series of editorships). One former classmate[1] remembers him as a gifted pianist, who used to invite his friends to his home on Friday afternoons for a jazz session. Before he began playing he would remove his wristwatch and place it on top of the piano—an early example of his tendency to do everything by the clock.

He attended Glasgow University from 1925 to 1928 and became the

---

[1] J. H. Rhynd, a member of the Institute of Chartered Accountants of Scotland, who kindly provided me with this recollection of Highet as a student at Hillhead.

most well-known classical scholar in Scotland. Studying partly under
J. S. Phillimore, he earned an M.A. in Greek and Latin with the highest
honors in 1928, and a Diploma in Ancient History and Archaeology in
1929. He received the Logan Memorial Medal and Prize (for the most
distinguished graduate) and the Snell Exhibition and Newlands Scholarship (entitling him to four years of study at Oxford). He edited the *Glasgow University Magazine,* to which he contributed numerous articles,
poems, and short stories under the pseudonym of "Cyrano." Soon after
his editorship a fellow Scotsman published a tribute, filled with caustic
wit, which testified to his amazing and enviable accomplishments.[2] Highet
served as President of the Dialectic Society (the debating team), which
enabled him to visit other campuses, such as Trinity College in Dublin.
At that time he developed his interest in oratory and his riveting style of
speaking, which would become famous and admired by generations of
students. He doubled in piano and trumpet for the Glasgow University
Band and composed (and sang) lighthearted songs for "College Pudding"
(the students' annual review). He gave private recitals of the piano music
of Alexander Scriabin and played saxophone in the band of a cruise ship
that sailed to Canada. During his first year at the university he met Helen
MacInnes, who would become his lifetime companion and famous in
her own right as a novelist. They were inseparable and shared everything
during this period of intense study, including mountain-climbing and
long-distance walking around the island of Arran.

From 1929 to 1932 he attended Balliol College (Oxford); the college
was founded by a Scottish prince and bred many famous Scotsmen. He
earned a B.A. in Classics in 1932 with a double first in Mods and Greats
(the upper and lower divisions of the curriculum), and several university
distinctions. He received the Ferguson Scholarship, the Craven Scholarship, the Jenkyns Exhibition, and the Chancellor's Prize for Latin Prose
Composition. At Oxford he studied under three great teachers—Cyril
Bailey, C. M. Bowra, and Gilbert Murray—who all exerted a strong
influence on his career. He loved and respected these three men, for
their devotion to teaching and for the depth and breadth of their scholarly
accomplishments. He contributed articles, reviews, and poetry to *Isis,
Farrago, Oxford Poetry,* and *Oxford Outlook* (popular literary journals
published by the university). At Oxford his writing revealed a penchant
for satire and an incisive critical acumen, and it contained a number of

---

[2] See W. A. Smellie, "Gilbert Arthur Highet: Editor 'G.U.M.,' 1928–29," *GUM* 41.5
(December 18, 1929) 134 for this early appreciation by the classmate who became a min-
ister.

tantalizing allusions to the American scene. He cofounded the Oxford Experimental Theatre Society and composed two verse-dramas, produced in the private theater of the Poet Laureate, John Masefield. He called them "The Apple" (on Joseph in Egypt) and "Acts of Faith" (on Scottish witch-trials)—both of them performed at Hillcrest, the second broadcast to Scotland from Glasgow.[3] For seven years Highet and the young Miss MacInnes remained engaged, because of the rules prohibiting Oxford students from marrying. Finally the university gave in, and on September 22, 1932 they were married and may have been the first couple to break through that barrier.

He taught in St. John's College (Oxford) from 1933 to 1937 as Fellow and Tutor, and received an M.A. in Classics in 1936. Having passed through the tutorial system as a student, he now did so as a teacher and regarded it as one of the best experiences of his life. He taught on a campus whose architecture he much admired, especially the graceful Canterbury Quadrangle with its Gothic and Renaissance elements. He coedited the *New Oxford Outlook*, to which he contributed a long literary essay and his first review of a major American author, William Faulkner. To the *Oxford Book of Greek Verse in Translation* he contributed translations of a dozen poets, which Bowra later characterized as brilliantly adventurous.[4] Working together, he and Helen translated from the German Otto Kiefer's *Sexual Life in Ancient Rome*, which may have raised a few eyebrows at insular Oxbridge. They also collaborated on translating from the German Gustav Mayer's *Friedrich Engels: A Biography*, about the friend and compatriot of Karl Marx. He published *An Outline of Homer*, a commentary on twenty-three passages from the *Iliad* and the *Odyssey*, chosen so as to form a microcosm of Homer's poetry. He also completed *Beginning Latin*, a textbook consisting of seventy-two lessons, displaying his talent for presenting difficult material clearly and crisply. During this period his wife gave birth to their only child, Keith, who had Bowra for his godfather and who would become a successful lawyer. And they entertained friends, like Jimmy Wardrop, the calligrapher, who had designed Highet's bookplate, of a youth in profile in the style of early Italian Renaissance (see reproduction at end of essay).

Highet came to Columbia University in 1937 as a Visiting Associate on a one-year appointment, which soon became permanent. Nicholas

---

[3] See G. Highet, "The Apple," *Farrago* 1.2 (June 1930) 100–106 and "Acts of Faith," *Farrago* 2.2 (February 1931) 91–98 for the published versions of these two verse-dramas.

[4] See C. M. Bowra, *Memories: 1898–1939* (London, 1966) 261 for Bowra's evaluation of Highet's contribution to this important anthology.

Murray Butler, President of Columbia, invited him at Bowra's suggestion after attempting to woo Bowra himself with an attractive salary. Bowra allegedly told Butler that he (Butler) would never be able to lure an Englishman to America but that he might be able to lure a Scotsman for the money. The Scotsman met the seventy-five-year-old Butler during his first year at Columbia, when the Board of Trustees was already pressuring Butler to resign. He used to recall how Butler later mentioned to him with undisguised amusement that he had just attended the funeral of the last of the members of the Board.[5] When the Scotsman arrived at Columbia, he joined a faculty including such senior scholars as Frank Gardner Moore, La Rue Van Hook, and Kurt von Fritz. He also became acquainted with a congenial instructor named Moses Hadas, with whom he would share over the years a good professional relationship. In 1938, within one year of his appointment, he became Professor of Greek and Latin—an amazing achievement for a man just turning thirty-two. In 1950 he became Anthon Professor of the Latin Language and Literature (named after the eminent nineteenth-century Columbia professor Charles Anthon). When he first joined the Columbia faculty, he worked with Hadas at rejuvenating undergraduate and graduate instruction in Greek and Latin. He also recognized the pressing importance of the Humanities course, with educators like Jacques Barzun, Lionel Trilling, and Mark Van Doren.

Highet taught at Columbia for thirty-five years, except during World War II when he served in the British Army. When war broke out in Europe, he was already writing reviews on classical and nonclassical subjects for the *Nation*, the *Saturday Review*, and the *New York Times*. In the *Nation* they appeared in the form of parodies, on authors such as Ezra Pound and Ernest Hemingway; one even satirized the British High Command. From 1941 to 1946 he served in the British Mission to the United States, in the British Intelligence Center in New York, and in the British Zone of occupied Berlin. In Germany he became partly responsible for appropriating the property of the Nazis and for recovering the treasures that they had taken from occupied countries. While serving under Sir William Stephenson, he drew up psychological profiles of the German general staff, based on his psychoanalysis of the Roman emperors. He succeeded in predicting, with only limited information on their backgrounds, how certain hostile leaders would react to differing

[5] See A. Marrin, *Nicholas Murray Butler* (Boston, 1976) 50–52 for Butler's struggle with the Board of Trustees and his announcement of his intention to "die on the job."

circumstances.[6] He used to tell his students how in occupied Berlin he once angered a Russian general during a performance of Jacques Offenbach's opera *Tales of Hoffmann*. He risked arrest by accidentally sitting in a section of the stalls reserved for the general and his girlfriend—an unintentional breach of Russian military etiquette. At the end of the war he received the rank of Lieutenant Colonel and returned to the United States, where five years later he and his wife became American citizens. During the war years he published his translation of Werner Jaeger's *Paideia* (in three volumes), which still serves as a model of the translator's art.

In appearance, not surprisingly, he reminded students of a British Army officer or the actor Jack Hawkins (who portrayed one). He was tall, erect, handsome, clean-shaven, and always impeccably dressed, with a taste for pin-striped shirts and unusually colorful tweeds. He took great pride in himself and in his attire, and once remarked that he wanted to see classes, or at least doctoral defenses, conducted in academic regalia. In Philosophy Hall he furnished his office with rugs, drapes, flowers, a coffee-table, and a huge iron safe, in which he kept all his valuable papers. On his wall he had a portrait of A. E. Housman and Pieter Bruegel's *Peasant Wedding*, the painting in which he claimed to have identified the bridegroom.[7] On campus he would frequently have lunch in John Jay Hall, the graduate men's dormitory, although he asked his students not to approach him in the cafeteria. Even there, while dining, he would be reading some book or article, or reshaping his ideas for one of his late-afternoon graduate classes. He would remind his students about Martin J. Routh, President of Magdalen College (Oxford), who at ninety-two uttered the precept "verify your references." In Butler Library one might see him scanning the shelves, or documenting his lectures with Pauly-Wissowa, or preparing bibliographies from *L'Année Philologique*. Even in his later years Highet displayed the posture of a much younger man, always walking briskly on the campus or in midtown Manhattan. When he first arrived in New York, he explored every quarter of Manhattan Island on foot, at a time when he regarded the city as friendly, peaceful, and safe.

When Gilbert Highet entered the classroom, one felt as though the

[6] See W. Stevenson, A Man Called Intrepid (New York, 1976) 348–49 for Highet's part in developing these "proso-profiles" for the British Intelligence Center.

[7] See G. Highet, "Bruegel's Rustic Wedding," *Magazine of Art* 38 (1945) 274–76 and "Where Is the Bridegroom?," *Horizon* 9.2 (Spring 1967) 112–15 for his solution to the problem.

curtain were going up on a Broadway play. On the first day he began: "Good afternoon, ladies and gentlemen. The name is Highet"; on one occasion he uttered: "I was reading Toynbee this morning while shaving." He would set down his notes, removed from a loose-leaf book, and a small clock, which rang halfway through a two-hour class and signified a short break. He stood and walked during most of the period, with the presence of a Sir Laurence Olivier, and when he turned, he moved his entire body all at once. He wrote with a flourish, in a small, elegant script, with chalk in a metal holder, and occasionally removed a linen handkerchief from the left sleeve of his jacket. He loved Vergil and taught the Aeneid every year to enormous classes; he loved his "darling" Juvenal and the Roman satirists, because they exposed decadence. He hated Plato and Julius Caesar, the one for setting out the principles of dictatorship, the other because he became dictatorship's most accomplished practitioner.[8] With his Scottish-English burr and his riveting, rapid-fire delivery, he gave the most dazzling, the most brilliant, and the most organized lectures imaginable. The inspired anecdotes, the poignant pauses, and the sudden bursts of laughter would all form part of a magnificent, comprehensible structure. He laughed like Homer's Zeus ('Ω πόποι), hissed like Vergil's Dido ("dissimulare etiam sperasti"), and wielded a window-pole when imitating a Roman legionnaire. He gave his students, above all, an overwhelmingly intellectual experience, through a showmanship perhaps unparalleled in the American classroom.

To his students and his colleagues he gave constant personal attention, whatever the time and whatever their needs. He asked his "pupils" to visit his office, where they could talk "eyeball to eyeball," and went out of his way to help those who worked hard and with integrity. After every final examination he sent his students a typed, mimeographed letter in which he analyzed the results and provided valuable suggestions.[9] He urged his graduate students to call him at any time, at school or at home, and set for them the same rigorous pace that he set for himself. He sponsored numerous dissertations in Greek and Latin, and he would invite doctoral candidates to oysters and champagne after a successful defense. He talked with his colleagues about new theories and new developments in Classics, and served them for several years as Chairman of the Department. He did not set out to compete with his colleagues, nor

---

[8] See "The Ides of March Betray Scholars," New York Times (March 15, 1956) 33 for an anecdote connected with the 2000th (or 1999th) anniversary of Caesar's assassination.

[9] See G. Highet, "Her Sons—'Alert and Grateful,' " Life 36 (February 15, 1954) 126–31 for his appreciation of Columbia's undergraduates during Columbia's bicentennial.

did he mean for them to compete with him, and always made himself accessible for consultation. He kept up a lively correspondence with several members of the Department and with classical scholars elsewhere, and always answered letters promptly. Only a few colleagues turned away from him, men perhaps jealous of his achievements, who accused him of popularizing their serious and elitist discipline. They could not understand that no single person had done more to revitalize the study of Classics on the Columbia campus and in the United States. A frequent focus of media-attention both here and abroad, Highet became the most talked-about classical scholar in American history since Thomas Jefferson.

In his thirty-five years of teaching at Columbia, Highet never found anything as painful as the student riots of 1968. He detested the student radicals, especially those who wanted to destroy Columbia during the Vietnam War and who threatened to burn down Butler Library tier by tier. Possibly he recalled the Dark Ages, which almost extinguished the Greek and Roman classics, for him minds alive on the shelves, each with its own voice.[10] During this period he maintained the highest standards of teaching, thus vindicating himself and setting an example for others who were wavering in their resolve. Of the anarchists, whom he described as dirty and dizzy with drugs, he allegedly uttered his famous paraphrase of Matthew 7.6: "I shall not cast pearls before swine." He recalled a doctoral examination, disrupted by the inflamed oratory and rhythmic shouts of a protest rally, which reminded him of a Nazi demonstration. When demonstrators blockaded the entrance to his building, he told them that after teaching at Columbia for thirty years, he would be damned if he would leave by the window. Although he strode out unharmed, he could not forget the violence that swept over the campus and that eventually led President Grayson L. Kirk to resign. He wrote to Kirk that he blamed him no more than he would the director of a great museum if a gang of hoodlums suddenly began slashing the paintings or fire-bombing the library. He deplored what happened at Columbia during the late 1960s—a far cry from the mood of the campus fourteen years earlier during its bicentennial celebration. For that occasion he had written *Man's Unconquerable Mind*, on the powers of the intellect, and in the same year *The Migration of Ideas*, on the influence of great thoughts upon human affairs.

During his long and illustrious association with Columbia, Highet wrote a phenomenal number of articles, reviews, and books. His com-

---

[10] See G. Highet, *Explorations* (New York, 1971) 222–23 and *The Immortal Profession* (New York, 1976) 126–28 for his recollections of the student revolutionaries.

plete bibliography, spanning a fifty-year period, consists of nearly a thousand items—a truly extraordinary achievement for a classical scholar. Yet he took the greatest pride in his books, which fell into three categories: pedagogy; scholarly literary criticism; essays of a more general nature. He wrote two pedagogical works, *The Art of Teaching* (dedicated to his teacher Cyril Bailey) and *The Immortal Profession* (dedicated to his students of forty years). In *The Art of Teaching* he set out his methods of teaching; in *The Immortal Profession* he considered what teaching had meant to him and what it could mean to others. His scholarly books consisted of *The Classical Tradition, Juvenal the Satirist, Poets in a Landscape, The Anatomy of Satire,* and *The Speeches in Vergil's Aeneid. Poets in a Land-scape* received the ENIT Prize from the Italian Government; *The Anatomy of Satire,* the Award of Merit from the American Philological Association.[11] He published five volumes of essays: *People, Places, and Books, A Clerk of Oxenford, Talents and Geniuses, The Powers of Poetry,* and *Explorations.* For these he revised and enlarged many of the talks that he presented on his weekly radio program during the 1950s (a subject to be considered shortly). In his books he revealed himself as the master of organization, making them extremely readable by outlining his central points in the table of contents. With his powerful and speculative mind he made a colossal contribution to classical scholarship, while making that contribution comprehensible to the educated public.

He served in a number of editorial capacities, through which he exercised his talent for judicious discrimination. In 1952 he became chief literary critic for *Harper's Magazine* (the magazine's "arbiter elegantiae") and held the title for two years. In it he reviewed new books every month in his own column, and he also contributed several poems and the chilling short story "Another Solution." In 1954 the Book-of-the-Month Club appointed him to its Board of Judges, a position that he held for twenty-three years, until his death. He followed in the tradition of the original quintet: Heywood Campbell Broun, Henry Seidel Canby, Dorothy Canfield Fisher, Christopher Morley, and William Allen White. Clifton Fadiman, a fellow judge, regarded him as the most learned member of the Board, equally at home in classical and contemporary literature. Fadiman characterized him as a charming man, with a remarkable histrionic talent for anecdote, which would rescue their meetings from excessive sobriety.[12] During his twenty-three years as a judge, Highet wrote over

---

[11] See C. M. Bowra, "The Classical Tradition," *Sewanee Review* 58.3 (1950) 495–504, especially 502–4, for Bowra's evaluation of Highet's first great scholarly book.

[12] See C. Fadiman, "The Most Exclusive Lunch Club in Town," *BMCN* (April 1976) 6–8 (Special Fiftieth Anniversary Supplement) for Fadiman's retrospect of the judges.

four hundred book reviews that appeared in *Book-of-the-Month Club News*. And he maintained an active correspondence with authors such as Maxwell Anderson, James Michener, Ogden Nash, James Thurber, and Edmund Wilson. In 1958 he became Chairman of the Editorial Advisory Board for *Horizon Magazine*, whose founders were seeking an audience in the literary-minded layman. To it he contributed numerous articles and reviews, including his verse-translation (in the original meters) of Menander's newly discovered comedy, the *Dyskolos*.

Yet he captured the public eye most of all through his radio program of the 1950s, "People, Places, and Books." In 1952, under the auspices of Oxford University Press, he began to speak once a week on the subject of literature over a local radio station in New York. By 1959 his talks were carried by over three hundred stations in the United States and Canada, and by the British Broadcasting Company and Voice of America. His program evoked an enthusiastic response from the critics and the public, who enjoyed his magnificent voice and his understanding of the world of books. The formidable critic John Crosby described the talks as scholarly, flavorsome, and filled with exquisite detail, which deserved publication in book form.[13] The talks focused on classical and contemporary books, and they covered an unusually broad spectrum—prose and poetry, language and literature, music and art. Regarding these urbane and witty presentations Highet once remarked: "When the three goldfish in the control room are laughing, I know that my little talk is a good one." Responding to popular demand, Oxford issued transcriptions of 188 of the 283 radio broadcasts, exactly as he had delivered them over the air. He also published a great number of them in the five volumes of essays mentioned earlier, although he revised and enlarged everything for these volumes. He later gave permission to Jeffrey Norton Publishers to reproduce for classroom use a large selection of the original broadcasts on audio-cassettes. For the classroom as well, Encyclopaedia Britannica asked him to write two filmscripts on the Greek myths and to narrate three films on Homer's *Odyssey*.

His profession honored him on numerous occasions during his lifetime, both before and after his retirement. He received two earned degrees: D.Litt. (Glasgow) 1951 and D.Litt. (Oxford) 1956—both awarded for substantial contributions to knowledge. He also received five honorary degrees: L.H.D. (Case Institute) 1952, D.Litt. (Syracuse) 1960, L.H.D. (Adelphi) 1964, L.H.D. (Massachusetts) 1973, and D.Litt. (Columbia)

---

[13] See J. Crosby, "Mr. Highet Talks on Books," *New York Herald Tribune* (May 21, 1952) 25 for Crosby's evaluation of the first season of the radio talks.

1977. He served as President of the New York Classical Club, Fellow of the Royal Society of Literature (London), and Trustee of the American Academy in Rome. He studied Juvenal on a Guggenheim Fellowship, lectured for the North Foundation (Franklin and Marshall), and spoke on satire as Spencer Trask Lecturer (Princeton). When he retired in 1972 as Anthon Professor Emeritus, Mayor John V. Lindsay wrote to him, expressing regrets over his decision to leave New York City. Although Highet replied that Manhattan had lost its charm and friendliness, he and Helen continued to alternate between their apartment on Park Avenue and their home in East Hampton.[14] During his retirement he continued to write as productively and as energetically as ever, while his wife continued to write novels of mystery and intrigue. In 1973, for their combined literary achievements, they shared the Wallace Award, presented annually by the American-Scottish Foundation to distinguished Americans of Scottish heritage. They continued to travel extensively, to Europe and the American West, and the year before his death to Hawaii, where I saw him for the last time. When I identified our waitress at the Kahala Hilton as one of my students, he alluded with a chuckle to the passing of the torch from one generation to another.

Gilbert Highet died on January 20, 1978, of cancer, and as he had requested, his ashes were scattered over the Atlantic. Columbia held a Memorial Service for him on the Ides of March in St. Paul's Chapel, where eleven years earlier he had delivered the eulogy for Moses Hadas. The speakers included President William J. McGill, Professor Peter R. Pouncey, and Alan Cameron, his successor as Anthon Professor. Cameron remarked that probably never again would the profession see the entire field of Classics surveyed through the perspective of one man's vision. The assemblage also listened to tributes from Clifton Fadiman, his fellow judge, and Julian P. Muller, the publisher, who brought a special tribute from Sir William Stephenson. At the end of the service, at the playing of Henry Purcell's "Trumpet Voluntary," one former student[15] remembered how Highet used to say: "Leave them on a high note!" He was gone—the consummate teacher and scholar, who had electrified students for over forty years with his encyclopedic knowledge of classical civilization. All his life he passionately believed that he had as his mission to convey the values and standards of excellence communi-

---

[14] See W. K. Zinsser, "Far Out on Long Island," *Horizon* 5.5 (May 1963) 4–27, especially 22–23, for a glance at the Highets as residents of East Hampton.

[15] Ann R. L. Dewey, who provided me with this recollection and who informed me that she found the service itself as carefully balanced and polished as any of Highet's lectures.

cated by the Classics. In awarding him the D.Litt. a year before his death, McGill described him not only as the defender of the classical tradition but also as the embodiment of it. Indeed, in his own life and work he provided the model for the strength, the vitality, and the brilliance that he found in the world's greatest literature. And in doing so, he profoundly influenced the lives of those who believed, as he did, in the immortal profession and in the joys of teaching and learning.

Gilbert Highet's bookplate designed by Jimmy Wardrop

BIBLIOGRAPHY OF PUBLICATIONS ON GILBERT HIGHET

W. A. Smellie, "Gilbert Arthur Highet: Editor 'G.U.M.,' 1928–29," *GUM* 41.5 (December 18, 1929) 134 and photograph opposite 134.

"Gilbert Arthur Highet," *Directory of American Scholars* (New York, every edition since 1942 until his death in 1978).

C. Taylor, "They Take the High Road," *New York World-Telegram* (October 11, 1949) 27.

J. K. Hutchens, "On an Author," *New York Herald Tribune* (December 25, 1949) section 7, p. 2.

"Teaching Is an Art," *Newsweek* 36 (September 25, 1950) 86.

"How to Be an Artist," *Time* 56 (October 9, 1950) 71–72.

"Gilbert Highet," *Who's Who in America* (Chicago, every edition since 1950 until his death in 1978).

H. Breit, "Talk with the Highets," *New York Times* (April 8, 1951) section 7, p. 25. See also *The Writer Observed* (London, 1956) 187–89.

J. Crosby, "Mr. Highet Talks on Books," *New York Herald Tribune* (May 21, 1952) 25.

J. House, "The Fearless Professor," *Glasgow Evening News Saturday Supplement* (June 7, 1952) 3.

"Beginning Next Month," *Harper's* 205 (August 1952) 96.

T. Dewhurst, "Gilbert Highet: Conversationalist Deluxe," *New York Times* (March 14, 1954) section 2, p. 13.

"Professor at Large," *Newsweek* 44 (November 15, 1954) 114 and 116.

"A New Judge: Gilbert Highet," *BMCN* (December 1954) 6.

"Gilbert Arthur Highet," *Who's Who* (New York, every edition since 1954 until his death in 1978).

"Gilbert Highet," *International Who's Who* (London, every edition since 1960 until his death in 1978).

"Gilbert Arthur Highet," *Current Biography* (New York, 1964) 192–94.

"Highet Is Appointed Classics Chairman," *New York Times* (July 26, 1965) 25.

P. Bovie, "Highet and the Classical Tradition," *Arion* 6 (Spring 1967) 98–115.

M. A. Farber, "Columbia's Highet Is Retiring Today," *New York Times* (June 30, 1972) 12. See also *New York Times Biographical Edition* (January–June 1972) 1178–79.

W. M. Calder III, "Gilbert Highet, Anthon Professor of Latin, Emeritus," *CW* 66 (1973) 385–87.

"Gilbert Highet," *Men of Achievement* (Cambridge, 1974) 449.

J. F. Baker, "Gilbert Highet," *Publishers' Weekly* 209 (1976) 6–7. See also *The Author Speaks: Selected PW Interviews (1967–1976)* (New York, 1977) 363–66.

B. Campbell, "Gilbert Highet, Scholar and Poet, Dies of Cancer at the Age of 71," *New York Times* (January 21, 1978) 24. See also *New York Times Biographical Service* 9 (January–May 1978) 59.

"Gilbert Highet," *San Francisco Chronicle* (January 21, 1978) 14, based on the obituary appearing in the *New York Times*.

"Gilbert Highet, 71, Dies, Teacher, Author, Critic," *Washington Post* (January 23, 1978) section C, p. 6.

"Professor Gilbert Highet: Teacher and Popularizer of the Classics," *Times*, London (January 26, 1978) 16.

"Gilbert Highet," *Newsweek* 91 (January 30, 1978) 37.

"Gilbert Arthur Highet," *Time* 111 (January 30, 1978) 65.

C. McCarthy, "Gilbert Highet: A Teaching Career of Lifelong Delights," *Washington Post* (January 31, 1978) section A, p. 19. See also *Los Angeles Times* (February 3, 1978) section 2, p. 7.

W. T. Levy, "Gilbert Highet," *Los Angeles Times* (February 16, 1978) section 2, p. 8.

"Gilbert Highet: 1906–1978," *BMCN* (June 1978) 29.

M. Crosby, "Gilbert Highet: A Remembrance," *College Board Review* 108 (Summer 1978) 28–30.

W. M. Calder III, "Gilbert Highet," *Gnomon* 50 (1978) 430–32.

O. Jensen, "Gilbert Highet: 1906–1978," *Century Yearbook* (New York, 1979) 244–48. Published by the Century Association.

GREEK LITERATURE

Diogenes and Alexander:
The Dog Has His Day

LYING ON the bare earth, shoeless, bearded, half-naked, he looked like a
beggar or a lunatic. He was one, but not the other. He had opened his
eyes with the sun at dawn, scratched, done his business like a dog at the
roadside, washed at the public fountain, begged a piece of breakfast bread
and a few olives, eaten them squatting on the ground, and washed them
down with a few handfuls of water scooped from the spring. (Long ago
he had owned a rough wooden cup, but he threw it away when he saw
a boy drinking out of his hollowed hands.) Having no work to go to and
no family to provide for, he was free. As the market place filled up with
shoppers and merchants and gossipers and sharpers and slaves and foreigners, he had strolled through it for an hour or two. Everybody knew
him, or knew of him. They would throw sharp questions at him, and get
sharper answers. Sometimes they threw jeers, and got jibes; sometimes
bits of food, and got scant thanks; sometimes a mischievous pebble, and
got a shower of stones and abuse. They were not quite sure whether he
was mad or not. He knew they were mad, all mad, each in a different
way; they amused him. Now he was back at his home.

It was not a house, not even a squatter's hut. He thought everybody
lived far too elaborately, expensively, anxiously. What good is a house?
No one needs privacy: natural acts are not shameful; we all do the same
things, and need not hide them. No one needs beds and chairs and such
furniture: the animals live healthy lives and sleep on the ground. All we
require, since nature did not dress us properly, is one garment to keep us
warm, and some shelter from rain and wind. So he had one blanket—to
dress him in the daytime and cover him at night—and he slept in a cask.

Reprinted from *Horizon* 5.4 (March 1963) 10–13.

His name was Diogenes. He was the founder of the creed called Cynicism (the word means "doggishness"); he spent much of his life in the rich, lazy, corrupt Greek city of Corinth, mocking and satirizing its people, and occasionally converting one of them.

His home was not a barrel made of wood: too expensive. It was a storage jar made of earthenware, something like a modern fuel tank—no doubt discarded because a break had made it useless. He was not the first to inhabit such a thing: the refugees driven into Athens by the Spartan invasion had been forced to sleep in casks. But he was the first who ever did so by choice, out of principle.

Diogenes was not a degenerate or a maniac. He was a philosopher who wrote plays and poems and essays expounding his doctrine; he talked to those who cared to listen; he had pupils who admired him. But he taught chiefly by example. All should live naturally, he said, for what is natural is normal and cannot possibly be evil or shameful. Live without conventions, which are artificial and false; escape complexities and superfluities and extravagances: only so can you live a free life. The rich man believes he possesses his big house with its many rooms and its elaborate furniture, his pictures and his expensive clothes, his horses and his servants and his bank accounts. He does not. He depends on them, he worries about them, he spends most of his life's energy looking after them; the thought of losing them makes him sick with anxiety. They possess him. He is their slave. In order to procure a quantity of false, perishable goods he has sold the only true, lasting good, his own independence.

There have been many men who grew tired of human society with its complications, and went away to live simply—on a small farm, in a quiet village, in a hermit's cave, or in the darkness of anonymity. Not so Diogenes. He was not a recluse, or a stylite, or a beatnik. He was a missionary. His life's aim was clear to him: it was "to restamp the currency." (He and his father had once been convicted for counterfeiting, long before he turned to philosophy, and this phrase was Diogenes' bold, unembarrassed joke on the subject.) To restamp the currency: to take the clean metal of human life, to erase the old false conventional markings, and to imprint it with its true values.

The other great philosophers of the fourth century before Christ taught mainly their own private pupils. In the shady groves and cool sanctuaries of the Academy, Plato discoursed to a chosen few on the unreality of this contingent existence. Aristotle, among the books and instruments and specimens and archives and research-workers of his Lyceum, pursued investigations and gave lectures that were rightly named *esoteric*, "for those within the walls." But for Diogenes, laboratory and specimens and lecture halls and pupils were all to be found in a crowd of ordinary people. Therefore he chose to live in Athens or in the rich city of Corinth, where travelers from all over the Mediterranean world constantly came and went. And, by design, he publicly behaved in such ways as to show people what real life was. He would constantly take up their spiritual coin, ring it on a stone, and laugh at its false superscription.

He thought most people were only half-alive, most men only half-men. At bright noonday he walked through the market place carrying a lighted lamp and inspecting the face of everyone he met. They asked him why. Diogenes answered, "I am trying to find a *man*."

To a gentleman whose servant was putting on his shoes for him, Diogenes said, "You won't be really happy until he wipes your nose for you: that will come after you lose the use of your hands."

Once there was a war scare so serious that it stirred even the lazy, profit-happy Corinthians. They began to drill, clean their weapons, and rebuild their neglected fortifications. Diogenes took his old cask and began to roll it up and down, back and forward. "When you are all so busy," he said, "I felt I ought to do *something!*"

And so he lived—like a dog, some said, because he cared nothing for privacy and other human conventions, and because he showed his teeth and barked at those whom he disliked. Now he was lying in the sunlight, as contented as a dog on the warm ground, happier (he himself used to boast) than the Shah of Persia. Although he knew he was going to have an important visitor, he would not move.

The little square began to fill with people. Page boys elegantly dressed, spearmen speaking a rough foreign dialect, discreet secretaries, hard-browed officers, suave diplomats, they all gradually formed a circle centered on Diogenes. He looked them over, as a sober man looks at a crowd of tottering drunks, and shook his head. He knew who they were. They were the attendants of the conqueror of Greece, the servants of Alexander, the Macedonian king, who was visiting his newly subdued realm.

Only twenty, Alexander was far older and wiser than his years. Like all Macedonians he loved drinking, but he could usually handle it; and toward women he was nobly restrained and chivalrous. Like all Macedonians he loved fighting; he was a magnificent commander, but he was not merely a military automaton. He could think. At thirteen he had

become a pupil of the greatest mind in Greece, Aristotle. No exact record
of his schooling survives. It is clear, though, that Aristotle took the passionate, half-barbarous boy and gave him the best of Greek culture. He
taught Alexander poetry: the young prince slept with the *Iliad* under his
pillow and longed to emulate Achilles, who brought the mighty power of
Asia to ruin. He taught him philosophy, in particular the shapes and
uses of political power: a few years later Alexander was to create a su-
pranational empire that was not merely a power system but a vehicle for
the exchange of Greek and Middle Eastern cultures.

Aristotle taught him the principles of scientific research: during his
invasion of the Persian domains Alexander took with him a large corps
of scientists, and shipped hundreds of zoological specimens back to Greece
for study. Indeed, it was from Aristotle that Alexander learned to seek out
everything strange which might be instructive. Jugglers and stunt artists
and virtuosos of the absurd he dismissed with a shrug; but on reaching
India he was to spend hours discussing the problems of life and death
with naked Hindu mystics, and later to see one demonstrate Yoga self-
command by burning himself impassively to death.

Now, Alexander was in Corinth to take command of the League of
Greek States which, after conquering them, his father Philip had created
as a disguise for the New Macedonian Order. He was welcomed and
honored and flattered. He was the man of the hour, of the century: he
was unanimously appointed commander-in-chief of a new expedition
against old, rich, corrupt Asia. Nearly everyone crowded to Corinth in
order to congratulate him, to seek employment with him, even simply to
see him: soldiers and statesmen, artists and merchants, poets and philosophers. He received their compliments graciously. Only Diogenes, although he lived in Corinth, did not visit the new monarch. With that
generosity which Aristotle had taught him was a quality of the truly mag-
nanimous man, Alexander determined to call upon Diogenes. Surely
Dio·genes, the God-born, would acknowledge the conqueror's power by
some gift of hoarded wisdom.

With his handsome face, his fiery glance, his strong supple body,
his purple and gold cloak, and his air of destiny, he moved through the
parting crowd, toward the Dog's kennel. When a king approaches, all
rise in respect. Diogenes did not rise, he merely sat up on one elbow.
When a monarch enters a precinct, all greet him with a bow or an acclamation. Diogenes said nothing.

There was a silence. Some years later Alexander speared his best
friend to the wall, for objecting to the exaggerated honors paid to His
Majesty; but now he was still young and civil. He spoke first, with a

kindly greeting. Looking at the poor broken cask, the single ragged garment, and the rough figure lying on the ground, he said, "Is there anything I can do for you, Diogenes?"

"Yes," said the Dog. "Stand to one side. You're blocking the sunlight."

There was silence, not the ominous silence preceding a burst of fury, but a hush of amazement. Slowly, Alexander turned away. A titter broke out from the elegant Greeks, who were already beginning to make jokes about the Cur that looked at the King. The Macedonian officers, after deciding that Diogenes was not worth the trouble of kicking, were starting to guffaw and nudge one another. Alexander was still silent. To those nearest him he said quietly, "If I were not Alexander, I should be Diogenes." They took it as a paradox, designed to close the awkward little scene with a polite curtain line. But Alexander meant it. He understood Cynicism as the others could not. Later he took one of Diogenes' pupils with him to India as a philosophical interpreter (it was he who spoke to the naked *saddhus*). He was what Diogenes called himself, a *cosmopolitēs*, "citizen of the world." Like Diogenes, he admired the heroic figure of Hercules, the mighty conqueror who labors to help mankind while all others toil and sweat only for themselves. He knew that of all men then alive in the world only Alexander the conqueror and Diogenes the beggar were truly free.

The *Dyskolos* of Menander

SCENE

*Harsh mountain country twenty miles from Athens, with a few lonely
farms scattered on the slopes of the wooded hills.*
*In center background the stage shows a cave—shrine of Pan and the
Nymphs.*
Far right, a poor farmhouse, the home of Cnemon.
Far left, a still poorer farmhouse, the home of Gorgias.
*Downstage, a road running left to right, with paths leading off to the
shrine and to either of the farmhouses.*

CHARACTERS

CNEMON, *the curmudgeon; a hard-fisted farmer, about fifty.*
HIS DAUGHTER, *who has no name, because he never thought of giving
her one; frail, beautiful, fifteen.*
SIMIKÉ, *his old housekeeper; barefooted, in a ragged black dress.*
CALLIPPIDES, *a rich Athenian landowner; about fifty, handsome.*
SOSTRATUS, *his son, handsome and easy-going; luxurious dress.*
PYRRHIAS, *servant of* SOSTRATUS.
GETA, *servant of* CALLIPPIDES, *young, pert, energetic.*
DONAX, *servant of* CALLIPPIDES, *a musician at the party.*
MYRRHINÉ, CNEMON'S *wife, and mother of his daughter; she lives apart
from* CNEMON *with*
GORGIAS, *son of* MYRRHINÉ *by a previous marriage; poor, serious.*
DAVUS, *servant of* GORGIAS, *middle-aged and gloomy.*
CHAEREAS, *a friend of* SOSTRATUS; *an incidental figure.*
SICON, *a cook; large, pompous, eloquent.*
PAN, *the god of wild nature.*

Reprinted from *Horizon* 1.6 (July 1959) 78–89.

ACT ONE

Enter Pan, from his sacred cave.
PAN Imagine this to be the Athenian countryside—
the place called Phylé—and the grotto here behind me
a local sanctuary for these hard-rock farmers
who live in Phylé: this is a very famous shrine.
The farm you see here on the right is owned and worked
by a man called Cnemon. He hates all his fellow men.
He treats them all like a curmudgeon. He loathes people.
Loathes people? Why, though he is well into middle age,
never in all his life has he said an agreeable word,
not one. He's never given anyone "Good morning,"
except to Pan (that's me), his neighbor—when he's forced
to pass my shrine; and then, he's sorry he opened his mouth,
I'm sure of that. Well, though he's such a character,
he married a wife! He chose a woman lately widowed,
whose first husband had died not very long before,
leaving her with one son, still almost a baby.
But he quarreled with his new wife the whole day long,
and went on bickering afterwards nearly the whole night,
and lived a wretched life. Then a daughter was born.
This made him worse.[1] His wife suffered unspeakably,
found her existence full of hard labor and sourness,
and left him. She went away to find a home with her son—
the son of her first marriage. He has a tiny farm,
only a field or two, here in the neighborhood
close by; and there he just contrives to scratch a living
for his mother, and himself, and a single faithful servant
left him by his father. The boy is now in his teens,
but has a mind far more mature than youths of his age:
for we progress through learning to face difficulties.
Meanwhile, the old man lives alone with just his daughter
and one old servant-woman: carrying logs, digging,
always digging and slaving, and—starting with his neighbors
and his own wife, right down as far as the walls of Athens—
hating the whole world, each and every one. The girl
has grown to be just what he's made her, ignorant

---

[1] Because a girl could not do as much farm-work as a son, and would have to be given a dowry when the time came for her to be married.

but innocent of evil. She is quite devoted
to my sisters here, the Nymphs: she honors them sedulously;
and so she has persuaded us to show some favor
to her. There is a youth, who has a wealthy father,
a landowner in this place, with enormous estates
worth many thousands: he is a young man about town.
Well, he came out to hunt, with his servant and his dogs,
and he happened to stop off at this place, by pure chance.
I used my power as a god. He fell in love with the girl.
There are the main facts. Now you shall see the story
worked out in detail, if you like. I hope you will.
For here I think I see, coming toward us now,
the young man in love, with his friend and boon companion,
deep in conversation about his love affair.
Exit Pan into his grotto.
Enter Sostratus, the young lover, with Chaereas.
CHAEREAS No, you're not serious! You say you saw a girl
crowning the statues of the Nymphs here, Sostratus,
you fell in love, and went away at once?
SOSTRATUS   At once.
CHAEREAS You came out here on purpose, just to fall in love?
SOSTRATUS You're laughing at me, Chaereas, but I'm unhappy.
CHAEREAS Oh, I believe you.
SOSTRATUS   That's why I have brought you here
to help in my affair. You are a trusty friend,
and very practical.
CHAEREAS   Sostratus, here is my line
in love affairs. A friend who loves a party girl
asks me for help. Without delay, I kidnap her;
I drink, set fire to the house, rave, shout everyone down.
(First get hold of the girl, before asking questions:
for long delays exasperate a young man's love,
but quick possession means that he'll soon tire of her.)
Marriage, says someone else, to a nice young lady of birth.
At once I change my tactics, ask about her family,
her life and character, as a permanent investment.
(For then, you see, my friend can never, never forget
my technique in these delicate matters.)
SOSTRATUS   Very good:
and yet, for me, not satisfactory.
CHAEREAS   So now
we must go over all your adventure.

SOSTRATUS   Early this morning
I sent my servant Pyrrhias, who hunts with me,
up here.
CHAEREAS And why?
SOSTRATUS   Because I thought he might perhaps
happen to meet the girl's father, or else the head
of her family, whoever he might be.
CHAEREAS   Good heavens,
what an absurd idea!
SOSTRATUS   Yes, I was wrong. A servant
is probably bad for such a mission. Yet it's hard,
when one's in love, to see where one's best interests lie.
And now, his long delay, with no apparent reason,
surprises me. I told him to come home at once,
and tell me all he'd learned about this family here.
Enter Pyrrhias, running and shouting.
PYRRHIAS Look out! watch it! clear out, everybody! make way!
A lunatic is chasing me, he's mad!
SOSTRATUS   What's wrong?
PYRRHIAS Run, run!
SOSTRATUS   What is it?
PYRRHIAS   Showers of rocks and flying clods!
Help, murder!
SOSTRATUS   Who's attacking you, you fool?
PYRRHIAS   Perhaps
he's stopped chasing me now.
SOSTRATUS   Of course!
PYRRHIAS   You're sure?
SOSTRATUS   What rubbish
is this?
PYRRHIAS Please, sir, let's move away, I beg you!
SOSTRATUS   Where?
PYRRHIAS Away from the door of that house, as far as we possibly can.
He's surely a son of sorrow, a man of misery,
a serious mental case, the fellow who lives in that house,
the one you sent me to see. Oh, what a criminal
and brute he is! I nearly fractured all my toes,
stumbling against the rocks as I bolted for safety.
He dashed at me like a raving drunk! He'll attack again,
that's obvious.
SOSTRATUS   Good God, he must be out of his mind.
PYRRHIAS We're done for, Sostratus: we must take every precaution.

Oh, I can scarcely talk, my breathing's stopped cold
in my throat . . . I went to the door of the farm, and knocked, and said
I wished to see the master. I waited, and out came
a miserable old hag. From here—just where I stand
talking to you—she showed me the old man, on the hill,
gathering fruit from wild pear-trees, and picking up
armfuls of twisted logs.

SOSTRATUS   Quite an angry old man!

PYRRHIAS Wait, my dear sir. I then walked to the farmland,
and made my way toward him. From quite a long distance off,
wishing to emphasize my admirable manners
and diplomatic approach, I greeted him, and said,
"Old gentleman, I've come to see you, in connection
with something that concerns you." Right away, "Damn you,"
says he, "what's your idea in trespassing upon
my property like this?" and he picks up a clod,
and fires it straight into my face, right here, like that!

CHAEREAS Confound his impudence!

PYRRHIAS   I blinked my eyes, and started
to say "For heaven's sake—" but he picked up a vine-pole
and parted my hair with it, saying "What's your business
with me, hey? This is not a public highway, is it?"
He bawled at the pitch of his lungs.

CHAEREAS   Mad, completely mad,
this country clown.

PYRRHIAS   The finish was this. I bolted, and
he chased me, oh, perhaps a matter of two miles,
first of all round the hill, and then, hard on my tracks,
down here into the woods, bombarding me with clods
and stones, and, when he had nothing else, with pears.

SOSTRATUS What utter savagery! What a detestable
old man!

PYRRHIAS I beg you, please, let's go.

SOSTRATUS   That's cowardice!

PYRRHIAS No, you don't know how terrible he is. He'll eat us,
and raw!

CHAEREAS (suavely) Perhaps he has some personal distress
on his mind. Therefore I think we should postpone our plan
to approach him, Sostratus. You can be sure of this:
in all negotiations, the one effective thing
is choosing the right time.

PYRRHIAS   That's true.
CHAEREAS   Bitter as acid
are these poor farmers, bitter! not this man alone,
but almost all of them! Well: tomorrow morning
I'll come and see him myself, alone, now that I know
his home here. Meanwhile, Sostratus, go back to town
and just relax. Wait. This will turn out all right.
PYRRHIAS Yes, let's do that.
SOSTRATUS (*bitterly, to himself*) Any excuse! He jumps at it
quickly and gladly. I can see he didn't like
coming out here with me, and never really approved
this project of mine for marriage. (*To Chaereas*) Confound and blast
and damn your miserable soul for ever to hell!
CHAEREAS Oh, heavens above, Sostratus, what have I done wrong?
SOSTRATUS Suppose that I'd gone up to his farm, what do you think
he would have done to me, eh?
CHAEREAS   You'd have got a beating
if you'd tried that.
SOSTRATUS   Oh look there, there he comes himself!
CHAEREAS Let's go, and quickly, please, my friend.
SOSTRATUS   You talk to him.
CHAEREAS Oh, no, indeed; I am not a good negotiator,
no gift of the gab, what can I say to such a man?
SOSTRATUS He isn't brimming over with the milk of human kindness,
charging down here like that! Quick, quick, move away
from the door, for safety! Why, he's shouting out aloud,
as he marches down all alone: he must be *very* sick!
And yet, I swear to heaven, I am terrified
of him . . . to tell the truth . . . one ought to tell the truth . . .
Sostratus, Chaereas, and Pyrrhias move to the side of the stage.
Enter Cnemon, growling and talking to himself.
CNEMON Oh, he was a happy man, the hero Perseus, happy
for two reasons! First, he had miraculous wings
and didn't have to meet the people walking on earth;
and secondly, he had a gadget that turned to stone
every human being who bothered him. Oh, if I
could only get one! There would be a rich supply
of statues made of stone, standing everywhere.
But as things are, I swear that life is not worth living.
They invade my little place and walk around chattering.
For some time now, I've been compelled to let this land

lie idle here beside the highway: I can't work it,
it's quite impossible; I had to evacuate it,
because of the people passing by. And now they chase me
right up into the hills. The crowds keep multiplying.
Oh God, again! Look, here is still another stranger
standing in front of my door!
SOSTRATUS (*aside*) I wonder if he'll attack me?
CNEMON It seems to be impossible to find a crowd-free spot
even if you want to take a rope and hang yourself.
SOSTRATUS (*to himself*) He's angry with me. (*To Cnemon*) Sir, I'm wait-
ing to meet someone
here. I have an appointment with him.
CNEMON (*to himself*)   Didn't I say so?
They all think this is a public park, or an open square.
(*To Sostratus*)
Look, if you want to see someone here outside
my front door, organize the whole thing thoroughly
and build a lounge: that will be the sensible notion—
or even better, a public hall. (*Goes into his house.*)
SOSTRATUS (*backs away and speaks reflectively to himself*)
This is frightful:
I think he has a chronic case of ingrown spite.
This problem will demand no ordinary effort
to solve it: no, it needs sustained concentration:
that's obvious right away. I think I should consult
my father's servant Geta on this matter. Yes,
I shall. He has a brain as quick and hot as fire,
and he has vast experience. He is just the man
to tackle this curmudgeon here, and to outface him.
For I reject the notion of procrastinating
in this affair. Within a single day, a lot
can happen. Hey, what's that? a noise at the farmer's door!
Enter the Daughter of Cnemon, in great distress.
DAUGHTER Oh dear, oh lord have mercy, oh, what a disaster!-
What shall I do now? Nurse was in there drawing water,
and dropped the bucket into the well.
SOSTRATUS (*to himself*)   Great God above,
and all you heavenly protecting deities,
what irresistible beauty!
DAUGHTER   Daddy told her, when he
went out, to have hot water ready.

SOSTRATUS (*to Chaereas and Pyrrhias*) Isn't she lovely?
DAUGHTER If he finds out about this, he'll flog the poor old thing
within an inch of her life. I cannot lose a moment:
oh, dearest Nymphs, I'll take some water from your shrine.
And yet, I'm too embarrassed, if people are sacrificing,
to go in and disturb them. (*She hesitates. Sostratus comes forward.*)
SOSTRATUS   Well, give me your bucket,
and I shall dip it in and bring it out to you.
(*To himself*) By Jove, that old man is no gentleman, that's sure,
but a coarse country bumpkin. (*Exit Sostratus into the shrine.*)
DAUGHTER   Heaven bless me,
and save me from my toil and trouble. Oh, what's that,
that noise at the door? Can that be Daddy coming out?
Now *I* will get a thrashing, if he catches me
outdoors.
Enter Davus from the house of Cnemon.
DAVUS (*to Daughter*) I have been working for you now, for hours,
in there. He's digging in the field alone: I must
go up and join him. (*Points toward his master Gorgias's farm.*)
                      Damn you, damn you again and again,
Poverty! why did we ever adopt you fully grown?
why do you live with us uninterruptedly,
like a guest that never leaves the house?
Reenter Sostratus from the shrine.
SOSTRATUS (*to Daughter*)   Here it is,
your bucket.
DAVUS (*interposing*) Give it here. (*To himself*) Now, what on earth does *he*
want, this fellow?
(*To Daughter, as he hands her the bucket.*)
                      Good-bye now, and mind your father.
Exit the Daughter, into Cnemon's house.
SOSTRATUS (*walking over to join Pyrrhias and Chaereas*)
                      How miserable I feel!
PYRRHIAS   Don't grieve so, Sostratus,
it will be all right.
SOSTRATUS   How?
PYRRHIAS   Now, don't you be so anxious,
but do as you proposed. Go and get hold of Geta,
explain the whole affair clearly, and bring him back.
Exeunt Sostratus, Pyrrhias, and Chaereas toward the city.
DAVUS Now, what the devil does that mean? I don't like it at all,

not the slightest, this young man dancing attendance
on the girl, the rascal. As for you, Cnemon, I hope
you die and go to hell just as you deserve—
leaving an innocent girl deserted and alone
this way, without a soul to guard her, like an orphan
abandoned. So perhaps the youngster, learning of this,
scraped up a quick acquaintance with her, thinking she'd be
a treasure trove. I see. I must inform her brother
about this situation instantly, so that
we two can keep a watch and ward over the girl.
I think I'd better go immediately and do it.
And here I see a group of jolly worshipers,
all drunk in honor of Pan, approaching the shrine:
I shall be tactful and not interrupt their party.
Exit Davus toward the fields. Enter Chorus of revelers. Song and Dance.

ACT TWO

After some minutes' interval, enter Gorgias and Davus.
GORGIAS Look here, now, did you *have* to be so casual
and stupid about this problem?
DAVUS   What do you mean?
GORGIAS   You should
have found out right away who this young fellow was,
the man who spoke to my sister; and then told him outright
that we don't wish to see him at any time in the future
near her. Instead, you hung back and ignored the matter
as no concern of yours. But there are family duties,
Davus, which no one can ignore. My sister matters.
Suppose her father wishes to behave to us as though
he were a stranger, still, we must not imitate
his churlish manners. For suppose the girl's involved
in some disgrace, then I too would be bound to suffer
shame. For the general public does not see the cause
(whatever it may be), but only the result:
be sure of that.
DAVUS   Yes, Gorgias, but, sir, I'm scared

of the old man. If he ever catches me at his door,
at once he throws a tantrum.
GORGIAS   He's rather hard to handle
when he picks a quarrel. And I can't see any method
either of forcing him to make a change for the better
or of reforming him by giving him advice.
The law is on his side, so that we can't *compel* him
to change. His nature makes him proof against persuasion.
Enter Sostratus from the city.
DAVUS Hold on a moment: now we're getting some result.
Just as I said, he has returned; and here he is.
GORGIAS This fellow with the fancy coat—is he the one?
DAVUS That's him.
GORGIAS   A scoundrel: I can tell at a single glance.
SOSTRATUS (*to himself and the audience*)
              I did not manage to discover Geta at home.
My mother plans to offer sacrifice to some god—
I don't know which, she does this every single day,
making a crazy pilgrim's progress round our district
incessantly—and she dispatched him off to market,
to find a cook and hire him. I paid no attention
to the sacrificial rites, but came straight back here;
and now I think I'll abandon all this coming and going,
and speak up on my own behalf. So, right away,
I'll knock at the front door, and hesitate no longer.
GORGIAS Young man, would you consent to hear a speech from me
on a matter of importance?
SOSTRATUS   Yes, with pleasure. Speak.
GORGIAS I hold that every man upon this earth of ours—
whether he is fortunate or miserable—
has a fixed terminus, a moment of decision.
As far as that point, the lucky and prosperous man
can well maintain the even tenor of his fortune,
provided only that he can endure his luck
without committing a sin. But if he yields to evil
through confidence in his prosperity, ah, then
the change begins. His happiness starts down the slope.
While as for those whose means are limited, if they
just keep their heads, commit no wrong, and endure
their fate with honor, they may well be confident
that in the course of time they will see happiness.

My point is this. Although you may be most distinguished,
put not your trust in rank, and even if we are beggars,
do not despise us. To retain prosperity,
show those who watch you that you really do deserve it.
SOSTRATUS Why, do you think I am doing something irregular?
GORGIAS Yes: I believe that you have formed a shameful plan:
you hope you will persuade a girl to go astray,
a decent girl; or find an opportunity
in which you can commit a foul and criminal act,
an outrage.
SOSTRATUS God forbid!
GORGIAS   You have time on your hands.
You should not use it to annoy and injure others
who have to work. Remember this. If you wrong a beggar,
he is, of all men, the most harsh and difficult.
At first he is a pitiable victim; then
he blames his misery, not on crime, but on luck.
SOSTRATUS Young man, I ask you earnestly to listen to me
for a moment.
DAVUS (*to Gorgias*) Good for you, sir, that was splendid stuff,
that speech of yours!
SOSTRATUS   You too, stop chattering, and listen.
I saw a girl, who is a beauty; and I love her.
If that's a crime, perhaps I am a criminal.
But where's the harm in it? I've come around today,
not to wrong her, but because I want to interview
her father. I am a freeborn gentleman, with money
sufficient for my needs. I am prepared to take her
in marriage, with no dowry, and undertake to love her
for ever. If I came here with an evil purpose
or with some underhand plot in my mind against you
and your family,
(*turns toward the shrine of the deities*)
          then I pray that the god Pan and the Nymphs
may strike me dumb and paralyzed, beside her home,
here and now. It gives me great distress, believe me,
to think that you could ever believe me such a man.
GORGIAS Ah, if I spoke to you with too much vehemence,
just now, then please dismiss it from your memory.
You have convinced me, and you've made a friend of me.
I say this to you, my dear fellow, not as a stranger,

but as the girl's own brother born of one mother.

SOSTRATUS Good; and you will be helpful to me, in the future.

GORGIAS Helpful: how?

SOSTRATUS I see you have a generous heart.

GORGIAS I shall not send you away from here with empty promises,
but tell you the true facts. The girl has a father
who is not like any human being, either in history
or now in modern times.

SOSTRATUS The difficult old man?
I think I know.

GORGIAS It is a painful situation.
He owns a farm here worth a moderate amount
of money. But he will insist on farming it
alone. He will not have a single fellow worker,
neither a slave of his own, nor a hired laborer
from round about, nor a neighbor: he works all himself.
His greatest pleasure is to see no human being,
not one. He keeps the girl beside him most of the time,
and works incessantly. He talks only to her;
he'd find it difficult to speak to anyone else.
He says the only husband he'll accept for the girl
is a man exactly like himself.

SOSTRATUS That means a man
who doesn't exist!

GORGIAS Now, please don't worry about this,
my friend; it would be pointless. Just let us endure
the relatives who are allotted to us by fate.

SOSTRATUS In heaven's name, my lad, have you never been in love
with anyone?

GORGIAS I've never had the chance.

SOSTRATUS How's that?
What could prevent you?

GORGIAS Night and day, incessantly,
I am haunted by the consciousness of poverty.

SOSTRATUS Ah yes, I think that you have little experience
in love. You tell me to forget her. That depends
not upon me, but upon God.

GORGIAS If that is the case,
you are not wronging us, but distressing yourself in vain.

SOSTRATUS How can I get the girl?

GORGIAS You certainly won't get her

by doing nothing, just by following me about
or standing idly by. The old man works in the valley
beside my property.
SOSTRATUS   What then?
GORGIAS   Suppose I mention
my sister's marriage to him: when he understands
the situation, right away, with great delight
he'll launch out into long tirades against all men
as lazy good-for-nothings. And if he sees you
dressed like a gentleman of leisure, he'll be furious.
SOSTRATUS Is he there now?
GORGIAS   No, not yet; wait; a little later
he'll go up by his usual route.
SOSTRATUS   Will he take the girl
with him? Tell me! My friend, if I could only see her
somehow, I'd gladly go wherever you might take me.
I do implore you, give me your assistance.
GORGIAS   How?
SOSTRATUS You ask me how? By taking me up there!
GORGIAS   But why?
While he and I are working, will you stand about
wearing those elegant clothes?
SOSTRATUS   Why not?
GORGIAS   He'd surely pelt you
with clods of earth and call you a lazy beast. Oh no,
you'll have to dig along with us. If he once sees that,
perhaps he'll be receptive, and listen to what you say,
because he believes that you are poor and support yourself
by your own labor.
SOSTRATUS   I'll do anything. Come on!
GORGIAS But why are you so keen on suffering?
DAVUS (aside)   I hope
that we put in a long exhausting day's labor,
so that this fellow breaks his back, and then at last
he'll give up visiting us and getting in our hair.
SOSTRATUS (in exultation) Bring out a mattock.
GORGIAS   Here, take mine, and off
                                                        you go.
I have to stay here meanwhile and repair this wall:
the job is urgent, I must do it now.
Sostratus puts on a rough sheepskin coat over his
fine clothes, and shoulders the heavy mattock.

SOSTRATUS   Thank you.
You've saved my life.
DAVUS   I'll take him, master; meet us there.
SOSTRATUS Know how I feel? Either I'll work myself to death,
or win the girl, and live!
GORGIAS   Well, if you really mean
all that you say, good luck.
SOSTRATUS   As God is my witness,
the facts which you imagine will discourage me
just make me doubly keen to carry out my resolve.
For, if the girl has really not been brought up among
other women, and has not learned the sordid side
of life from some old aunt or chattering grandmother,
but by good fortune has been reared like a decent girl
with a father who is harsh but detests the thought of vice,
then it is marvelous good luck for me to find her.
Oh my, this mattock weighs at least four hundredweight:
it will wear me down to nothing. Courage, don't grow soft,
now that you have begun your sentence at hard labor!
Exeunt Sostratus and Davus, carrying mattocks on their shoulders,
toward the fields. Exit Gorgias into his house. Enter, from the
city, Sicon the cook, followed by the slave Geta. Sicon is carrying
a live sheep, and Geta a large number of bundles.
SICON This sheep here is no ordinary animal.
It's a damned nuisance. If I try to carry it,
it bites at the branches and hangs in the air by its jaws,
eating the young leaves, ripping and tearing them off.
If I put it down on the ground, it will not walk forward,
but turns and heads backwards. I'm too exhausted to cook,
worn to a frazzle hauling this beast along the road.
Ah, here at last I see the famous shrine of the Nymphs,
where we're to sacrifice. I greet you, Pan! (*kissing his hand*) Geta!
You're awfully slow.
GETA   You see why. These confounded women
loaded me up with more stuff than half a dozen
mules could carry.
SICON   It really looks as though we'd have
a huge crowd of guests. You've got an indescribable
number of bundles there.
GETA   Well, what now?
SICON   Drop them.
GETA   Right.

(*He drops them, and soliloquizes while rubbing his shoulders.*)
Whenever the old lady dreams a dream about Pan
whose shrine is out in the country, off we go at once
to sacrifice there.
SICON (*nudging him*) Here, who dreamed a dream?
GETA Don't hit me, you!
SICON Oh, all right, then, but tell me, Geta,
who dreamed a dream?
GETA The mistress.
SICON What about, for God's sake?
GETA Oh, bosh. She thought that she saw Pan—
SICON Who? This Pan here?
GETA Yes, this one.
SICON Doing what?
GETA He took young Sostratus—
SICON A fine young man.
GETA —and fastened shackles on his feet.
SICON Good heavens!
GETA Then he gave him a poor sheepskin coat
and a mattock, and ordered him to dig the field right here
beside us.
SICON What a curious dream!
GETA We're sacrificing
so that the frightful dream may turn out harmlessly.
SICON I understand. Now, lift your bundles and bring them in
to the shrine. We must make proper couches of clean straw
and have everything ready. We don't want a hitch
to spoil the ceremony when they come, God bless it.
He's raised his eyebrows in despair. Poor wretch, come on,
I'll give you a good belly-stuffing presently.
Exit Sicon into the shrine.
GETA (*lifting his burdens*) I am a great admirer of you and of your art,
and ever shall be; but I'll never trust your promises.
Exit Geta in the shrine. Interlude by the Chorus: Song and Dance.

ACT THREE

*Enter Cnemon from his farmhouse. He speaks to the old
slave-woman inside.*

CNEMON Old woman, bolt the door, and open it to no one
till I return again this evening. That will be
quite late at night, I think, long after dark has come.
Enter Geta from the city, leading a crowd of servants toward the shrine.
GETA Come, Plangon, hurry up; the sacrifice should have
been finished by this time.
CNEMON   Now, what the devil is this?
Who are this mob of people, damn them?
GETA   Parthenis,
play a tune for Pan. They say we shouldn't approach him
in silence.
Enter Sicon from the shrine.
SICON Here you are! You've finally arrived!
This has been God-damned boring, to sit on our hands here
and wait for such an endless time. Everything
is ready and prepared.
GETA   Prepared and ready for hours.
The sheep has nearly died of pure old age.
SICON   Poor creature,
it won't wait for ever, to please you. In you go.
The barley-basket, the boxes, the towels and cakes of incense,
lay them all out. (*He shoves one of the boys.*)
                    What are you gaping at, you clown?
Exeunt Sicon, Geta, and the servants into the shrine.
CNEMON (*shaking his fist*) Damn you all, every one, damn you to hell!
                                                    They've ruined
my working day: for now I dare not leave the house
unguarded. Nothing but a pest to me, these Nymphs.
In fact, they are such wretched neighbors that I think
I'll have to tear my house right down, and move away
altogether. Look at the crooks who visit the shrine
to sacrifice, and bring bottles of wine and couches,
not for the gods, but themselves. Incense is holy enough,
and the little cake put on the altar-fire and burnt,
the god gets that. But these folk offer the backbone
and the spleen of the beast, all uneatable stuff, to the gods.
They themselves gobble up all the rest. Woman!
Hurry up, open the door! Something must be wrong
with my household in here, I feel certain of that.
Exit Cnemon into his house. Enter Geta from the shrine.
GETA So you forgot to bring the cooking-pot! You people

behave as though you were drunk. What do we do now?
Well, I suppose we'll have to go and bother the neighbors
who live next door to the god.
Geta crosses to Cnemon's house, and begins to knock on the
front door, soliloquizing meanwhile.
                                    Hello, there! (Damn it,
I never saw a sloppier set of servant-girls
in any house.) Hello, inside there! (They don't care
for anything but swinging their backsides.) Hey, there!
(And calling you a liar if you notice.) Hey!
What the hell's wrong here? Isn't anyone at home
inside? Ah ah, I think I hear them running up.
Cnemon opens his front door.
CNEMON Will you stop banging on my door, you filthy rascal?
GETA Hey, there, don't bite me!
CNEMON   Yes, by God, I will, with pleasure,
and eat you alive too!
GETA   No, please don't, for heaven's sake!
CNEMON Why not, you scoundrel? Eh? Have we got some agreement,
you and I?
GETA No, we haven't got any agreement,
so I've not come to claim a debt, or serve a summons
on you, but to request the loan of a cooking-pot.
CNEMON A cooking-pot?
GETA   A cooking-pot.
CNEMON   You stinking crook,
do you think that I can afford to sacrifice whole oxen,
as you do?
GETA (*to himself*) Oxen? No, not even a single snail.
(*Aloud*) Well, good luck to you anyhow, kind sir. The women,
they told me I should knock at your door and ask for a pot.
I've done so. No result. Now I'll go back again
and give them your reply, sir. (*Aside*) Merciful God above,
that old man is nothing but a hoary-headed viper.
Exit Geta into the shrine.
CNEMON Arrh, these bloodsucking beasts, they come right to my door
as though I was their friend. When I catch any of you
near my gate, if I don't make an example of him
to shock the countryside, put me down for a lout
and a common coward. That last fellow got away:

he made a lucky escape, whoever the devil he was.
Exit Cnemon into his house, bolting the door. Enter
Sicon from the shrine, with Geta.
SICON Confound your clumsiness! He scolded you? I'll bet
you asked him in a lousy offhand way. Most people
do not know how to borrow; but I have got the knack.
You see, in the city, I serve many thousands of people;
I take advantage of their neighbors, borrowing stuff
from everybody. When you want to borrow something,
you must use diplomacy. If an old man opens the door,
when you knock, always call him "Papa" or "Granddaddy";
call an old woman "Mother"; a woman of middle age,
say "Reverend lady"; if it's a servant, call him "Sir."
That always works. But you're not worth the rope to hang you:
such crass stupidity! (*Knocking at Cnemon's door.*)
               Hello, in there, hello,
hello, come out, old fellow, hear me calling you?
Cnemon opens his door and sees Geta first.
CNEMON What, you again!
GETA   Again, for the same reason.
CNEMON   Are you
annoying me on purpose? Didn't I tell you to stay
away from this door? Woman, fetch a strap.
GETA   Oh no!
No, let me go, please sir, I beg you, in heaven's name.
Geta runs off. Sicon advances to the door, grandly.
CNEMON Now here's another!
SICON   Bless you, sir.
CNEMON   And still talking?
SICON I came to you to request the loan of a caldron.
CNEMON (*with forced calm*)   I
do not possess a caldron, nor an axe, nor salt,
nor vinegar, nor anything. I have explained
to everyone that I just want to be left alone.
SICON You didn't explain to me.
CNEMON   Well, now I have explained.
SICON Yes, very rudely. Could you tell me, if you please,
where I might find a pot?
CNEMON   No, I cannot. I've said so.
Now shut up.

SICON   Good-bye, sir, and all good wishes.

CNEMON   No!
I don't want your good wishes.

SICON   All right, then, bad luck.

CNEMON (*in agony*) What misery, what abject misery! (*Shuts his door.*)

SICON   By Jove,
he dusted me off neatly. What an art it is
to borrow gracefully! It makes a difference
whose door you knock at. Well, if all the people here
are so handy with their fists, I'll have a tough job.
I think I'd better roast or fry, and give up boiling.
I have a frying-pan. To the devil with you all,
you country bumpkins. I shall use the gear I've got.
Exit Sicon into the shrine. Enter Sostratus, limping and bent.

SOSTRATUS If anyone wants trouble, let him come out to Phylé
on a hunting trip, like me. I am a mass of aches and pains:
my neck, my back, my sides, my bottom, and in fact
my entire body. I jumped straight at the job,
young and enthusiastic. I heaved up the mattock
with a tremendous effort like a powerful workman,
and went hard at it like a man who loves to labor—
but not for long. I kept turning around, to see
when the old man would arrive, bringing the girl with him.
I watched; and then by Jove, I felt it in the loins,
quite quietly at first; then as time lengthened out,
hour after hour, I found my backbone bent into a curve,
my body stiff as a log. It was quiet. No one came.
The sun burned down upon me. Gorgias looked at me,
just like a swingbeam on a water-pump, moving up
with a huge effort, then, with all my body straining,
moving down again. He said, "I don't believe
the man will come now after all." I said, "So what
should we do now?" "Tomorrow, let's look out for him;
meanwhile let's give this up." Davus was ready at hand
to take my heavy spade and carry on. Well, then,
that was my debut as a digger. Now I've come back,
although I swear to heaven I don't know why I've come:
as though I had no will-power, just like a machine.
Enter Geta from the shrine, complaining of overwork.

GETA Oh really, what I need is thirty pairs of hands
to help you people. Blow the coals red-hot for you,

my dear, sprinkle the barley here, slice up the innards,
knead the dough, set out the dishes, blind myself
stooping over a smoky fire, and so enjoy
our gay festivity.
SOSTRATUS   Hey, you there, Geta. Hi!
GETA Who wants me?
SOSTRATUS   I.
GETA   And who's that?
SOSTRATUS   Can't you see?
GETA   Why, yes,
it's master.
SOSTRATUS What are you all doing here?
GETA   Well, sir,
we've just done sacrifice; and now we're getting ready
lunch for the guests.
SOSTRATUS   Is Mother there?
GETA   Been here for hours.
SOSTRATUS And Father?
GETA   We expect him.
SOSTRATUS   Now come here a moment,
out of their hearing. This banquet and sacrifice
come somehow at a lucky moment. I'll go over,
just as I am, and invite the young man from this farm
with his servant. Once they've shared a sacrificial meal
with us, then they will be far more cooperative,
and give assistance to me in my plans for marriage.
GETA What's that, sir? Are you going over specially
to invite more guests to the party? As far as I am concerned,
ask fifty thousand. I am perfectly certain of this,
that I won't get a single mouthful. Bring them all,
without exception. That was a fine beast you slaughtered,
a worthy sacrifice. Only, the womenfolk—
they're very nice, but they wouldn't share with anyone:
no, not so much as a tiny grain of salt.
SOSTRATUS (not listening to him)   Today
everything will turn out for the best. This I foresee
with my own vision, Pan. I'll always give you a greeting
whenever I pass your shrine, and treat you courteously.
Exit Sostratus into the house of Gorgias.
From the house of Cnemon, enter Simiké, crying.
SIMIKÉ Oh misery, oh misery, oh misery!

GETA To blazes with her, it's only an old woman-servant
of that curmudgeon.
SIMIKÉ   Oh, what shall I do? The bucket,
the bucket from the well, the master told me to get it,
I was trying to fish it out, and without letting him know,
I tied the mattock onto a cord, and the cord was weak
and thin and rotten, and it all came apart
at once!
GETA   That's perfect.
SIMIKÉ   Oh, God help me, now I've lost
the mattock too in the well, together with the bucket.
GETA Jump in the well yourself, there is no other solution.
SIMIKÉ As it so happens, the master wants to shift some dung
that's lying in the yard, and now he's running around
searching for his mattock, yelling and banging the door.
GETA Well, run, you poor old creature, run! He'll surely kill you.
At least, defend yourself.
Enter Cnemon, furious.
CNEMON   Where is the criminal?
SIMIKÉ (*crying*) Oh sir, it was an accident.
CNEMON   Get on there, move:
inside!
SIMIKÉ Why, sir, what will you do to me?
CNEMON   Do? Do?
I'll tie you up and drop you into the well.
SIMIKÉ   Oh no!
CNEMON Oh yes, by God, and with the same identical rope:
that's a good notion: it's all rotten anyhow.
SIMIKÉ I'll call for Davus to help me from the neighbors' house!
CNEMON You would call Davus, you old monster, you foul devil!
Get in there, don't you hear me? Move! Get in there quickly!
SIMIKÉ Oh mercy on me, I'm alone and helpless!
GETA   Here,
I shall go down, as well as anyone else could, to fetch
the bucket or anything else. And we'll gladly provide
the rope, too.
CNEMON   You? I hope you die and go to hell
and burn for ever, if you provide me with anything,
for you'll deserve damnation.
Exit Cnemon into his house, driving off Simiké.
GETA   Off he goes again,

poor hopeless miserable wretch. Oh, what a life!
That old man is a genuine Athenian farmer,
fighting the stones that bear nothing but thyme and lichen,
enduring hard privations, and never enjoying himself.
But there I see the master coming across to the party,
and bringing with him his two extra guests. They look
like workmen from the neighborhood. How very tactless!
I wonder why on earth he invited them, and how
he ever made their acquaintance.
Enter Sostratus, with Gorgias and Davus.
SOSTRATUS   I'll take no refusal.
Come on, I beg you, it's all ready. No, no, please!
Nobody in the world would ever think of refusing
to go and share the meal, when a friend had sacrificed.
And, speaking accurately, I have been a friend of yours
for long before I met you.
(*To Davus, handing him the mattock and sheepskin coat.*)
                          Take this, and carry it in,
and then come back.
GORGIAS   No, no, I cannot leave my mother
alone at home.
SOSTRATUS   Well, then, go and make sure that she
has all that she requires. I shall be out in a moment.
*Exeunt, Gorgias and Davus to the house of Gorgias, Sostratus into the
shrine. Interlude by the Chorus: Song and Dance.*

ACT FOUR

Enter Simiké, crying, from Cnemon's house.
SIMIKÉ Help, help, I'm desperate! Oh, help me, someone, please,
please help me, somebody!
Enter Sicon from the shrine.
SICON   Oh, God preserve us all,
for heaven's sweet sake, will you not leave us alone for a moment,
to pass the loving-cup around and drink? You shout,
you thrash people, you scream for help: you live in a madhouse.
SIMIKÉ The master's in the well!
SICON   And how did he get there?

SIMIKÉ He wanted to fish out the mattock and the bucket,
so he went down, and then he lost his footing, and
fell in!
SICON For once in his life the surly old curmudgeon
did something properly! That was really perfect!
And now, old lady, you complete the job.
SIMIKÉ   But how?
SICON Get a large block of stone, or a rock, or anything heavy,
carry it to the well, and drop it in.
SIMIKÉ   Oh please,
go down and save him!
SICON   I? I'd be the man in the fable,
who fought a dog inside a well. Not on your life!
SIMIKÉ Oh Gorgias, oh Gorgias, where are you?
Enter Gorgias.
GORGIAS   Here.
What is it, Simiké?
SIMIKÉ   Oh, must I say it again?
The master's in the well!
GORGIAS (*shouting into the shrine*)
                      Hi there, friend Sostratus,
come out here, please!
Sostratus runs in.
SOSTRATUS   Lead on, I'm coming right away.
*Exeunt Gorgias and Sostratus, running, into Cnemon's house.
Old Simiké follows them.*
SICON (*meditatively*) There *is* divine justice, after all. You won't
lend a cooking-pot to people sacrificing,
you atheist! All right, then, drink up all the well,
so that no one can borrow even a drop of water.
Well, now at last the Nymphs have punished his mistreatment
of me, and given him what he deserves. No man
may wrong a Chef, and hope his crime will go unpunished.
Ours is a sacred art, connected with religion.
But anyone can do whatever he likes to a waiter.
Cnemon's Daughter is heard crying inside.
DAUGHTER Oh dear, don't say he's dead! Save him, my poor dear daddy,
save him!
SICON   I hear somebody screaming; but that won't
do any good. They need a little organization.
The technique's obvious. First they make fast a rope—

a strong rope this time—then they lower it down the well;
and then the old grouch can tie it round his waist.
At least two men are needed, to pull both strong and steady:
together they'll haul him up, dripping and spluttering.
Oh, what a sight he'll be, when he reaches terra firma!
They'll bring him out of the house, all trembles and shivers,
a real figure of fun. I can hardly wait to see
the spectacle that he'll present, by Jove, can you? (*To the audience.*)
(*To the girls inside the shrine.*)
And you, girls, fill the wine-cups, pour out wine to the gods,
pray that the old man will be saved—but badly injured,
say, with a broken leg. That will make him a cripple,
and more respectful toward the god Pan. He is a neighbor
to me and all Pan's worshipers; he's my concern
whenever anyone hires me to superintend a feast.
Enter Sostratus from the house of Cnemon.
SOSTRATUS Upon my word, upon my oath, upon my soul,
upon my life, I never saw or heard of a man
who came so close to giving up the ghost by drowning,
and stopped just one step short of the gate of heaven.
The moment Gorgias got inside the house with me,
he jumped immediately into the well, while I
stayed above ground with the girl, helpless. After all,
what could we do? She wept, of course, and kept tearing
her long hair and beating her young breast with her fists.
And meanwhile I stood by, noble and useless, like
a guardian angel watching the girl. I begged her
not to hurt herself. I beseeched her, gazing at her
as though she were some lovely statue. I didn't give a damn
for the injured man in the well—or rather I found it boring
to keep hauling away at the rope to fetch him up.
In fact, I very nearly killed him by carelessness:
while I looked at the girl, three times or maybe more,
I dropped the rope. But Gorgias, down below,
stood there as firm as Atlas, caught his falling body,
and finally brought him up. As soon as he appeared,
I had to come out here. I really couldn't manage
to restrain myself any longer from going up to the girl
and kissing her on the lips. I'm desperately eager
to marry her. And I'm getting ready—Here they come.
Good God, just look at that! What a fantastic sight!

Enter Cnemon, leaning on Gorgias and his Daughter.
GORGIAS Do you need anything, Cnemon? Tell me.
CNEMON   Oh, shut up.
I'm a sick man.
GORGIAS   Cheer up.
CNEMON   Well, once I'm dead and gone,
you won't have anyone to bother you thereafter,
like Cnemon.
GORGIAS   See how wretched it is to live alone.
You very nearly perished there, just now, you know.
At your advanced age, you cannot live without
someone who will look after you.
CNEMON   I'm difficult,
I know it, Gorgias. Please call your mother to me.
As a general rule, we never learn the lessons we need
except from suffering misfortune. Here, my girl,
do you want to help me to stand up?
SOSTRATUS (*aside*)   Oh, lucky man!
I envy you!
CNEMON (*to Sostratus*) Well, why are you standing there like a fool?
GORGIAS Just move away a little, Sostratus; let's not
provoke him while he's still in a state of shock.
(*Calling his mother out of his house.*)
                                          Oh, Mother!
Cnemon has had an accident: he wants to see you.
Enter Myrrhiné, Cnemon's wife and Gorgias's mother, from
Gorgias's house. She does not speak.
CNEMON Myrrhiné, you see me weak and ailing, only just alive.
I'd be dead this moment, lying at the bottom of a well,
if your son here had not saved me, risking his own life for me.
Now I have a thing to tell you, Myrrhiné and Gorgias.
Rather than accept a kindness, I would once have gladly died
with no hope of rescue: no, no; don't attempt to contradict.
On this point you must believe me: grant that what I say is true.
But I made one fearful blunder. I believed that I alone
could live wholly independent, needing help from nobody.
Now I've seen how rapidly, yes, and unforeseeably,
life can end in death; and now I recognize how wrong I was.
Every woman should have someone near to help her and protect.
Yet I swear my mind was so embittered, twisted out of shape,
when I watched men living meanly, calculating all the time,

thinking of their private profit: I concluded that not one
human being could be kind to any other. I was wrong,
badly wrong; and Gorgias has demonstrated how I erred.
He has acted nobly toward me, like a truly generous soul.
Though I never would permit him even to approach my door,
though I gave him no assistance, totally ignoring him,
never speaking to him, still he rescued me, and willingly.
GORGIAS Well, when you felt justified in saying "Keep away from me,"
then I stayed away. You couldn't be of any use to us,
no, nor I to you.
CNEMON   But listen, now it's different, so, my boy,
if I die—and well I may, for I feel pretty miserable—
yes, and even if I live, I now adopt you as my son.
All the property I own is yours; and take my daughter too—
find a husband for her. Even if I should get back my health,
I shall never find one, never; they'll disgust me, every one,
that I'm sure of. So just let me live as I prefer to live.
You take over all my business. With God's help you'll manage it.
And you ought to be your sister's guardian: so you calculate
half my property and give it for a dowry to the girl.
Take the other half and use it to support your mother and me.
Now, girl, help me. I'll lie down a little. No one ought to speak
more than what is strictly needful: just a few more words, my boy.
I have something still to say, on human life and character.
If all men were just kind-hearted, there would be no courts of law,
no police, and no one carried off to prison for long years;
there would be no wars, for each would live contented with a little.
But you seem to like it this way, go on, people, live as you like!
Soon this cross-grained old curmudgeon will not trouble you any more.
GORGIAS I accept all your proposals. But we ought to look at once
for a bridegroom for my sister, one whom you will not dislike.
CNEMON Here, I've told you my ideas. Now, by God, stop pestering me!
GORGIAS There's a youth who wants to meet you—
CNEMON   No, no, no, for God's sake, no!
GORGIAS —he would like to marry my sister.
CNEMON   I've no interest in all that.
GORGIAS He's the man who helped to save you.
CNEMON   Who is he?
GORGIAS   (To Sostratus, brusquely.)
                              Come forward, you.
CNEMON Why, he's sunburned, he's a farmer!

GORGIAS   Oh yes, Father, yes, indeed.
He is not a man of leisure, strolling about with nothing to do:
he can't boast of birth and breeding, he's a common man like us.
CNEMON All the same, I can't be bothered. Take him if you think he's
                                                              right.
Now get me indoors.
GORGIAS   Yes, Father; just you think of getting well:
that's your main concern.
CNEMON   Good-bye, then, Gorgias, I leave to you
your young sister.
Exit Cnemon, into his house.
GORGIAS   He'll recover. Now he's left all this to me.
He will not oppose me. Therefore I betroth this girl to you,
here before these witnesses,[2] and give you, to endow the bride,
all that you think fair and just of my property, Sostratus.
You did not approach this marriage wearing a deceitful mask,
but with frankness. You had courage. Though you've lived in luxury,
still you worked to win the girl, swinging a mattock, toiling hard.
Bravo, friend. In such a trial, there's a proof of character,
when a man is brave enough, though he is rich, to share the life
of the poor: for then he knows that he can face vicissitudes
in the future, without flinching. So you've proved your strength of mind.
Never lose your new-found will-power.
SOSTRATUS   Now at last, I'm really a man.
Still, it is a little tactless when one starts to praise oneself.
Enter Callippides, from the city, exhausted with the long walk.
SOSTRATUS Here's my father. Oh, how splendid!
GORGIAS   Isn't that Callippides?
He's your father?
SOSTRATUS   Yes, indeed.
GORGIAS   Why, he's a very wealthy man,
and deserves it, for he is a splendid farmer.
CALLIPPIDES   I'm worn out!
I'll be bound they've eaten all the sacrificial meat by now,
and gone off again.
SOSTRATUS   Oh careful, he is almost starving to death.
Shall we broach the subject?
GORGIAS   No, no. Let him have his luncheon first.
He'll be gentler after that.

---

[2] The witnesses are the members of the audience.

CALLIPPIDES   Ah, Sostratus, is luncheon over?
SOSTRATUS Yes, but we kept some for you, Father, come.
CALLIPPIDES   With pleasure, son.
GORGIAS You go with him, talk to him, say what you like, as man to
                                 man
confidently.
SOSTRATUS You will wait here, won't you?
GORGIAS   Yes, I'll be inside,
at home.
SOSTRATUS That's right. Wait a little. Then I'll come and call you in.
*Exeunt Sostratus with Callippides into the shrine, Gorgias with his
mother Myrrhiné and his sister into his house.
Interlude by the Chorus: Song and Dance.*

ACT FIVE

Enter, from the shrine, Sostratus and his father Callippides.
SOSTRATUS No, Father, frankly, this is not quite what I wanted,
nor what I had expected from you.
CALLIPPIDES   What do you mean?
I am permitting you to marry the girl you love:
that is my wish—in fact, my order.
SOSTRATUS   I doubt that.
CALLIPPIDES Oh yes, indeed, I know exactly what I'm saying.
A young man is most likely to build a lasting marriage
if love persuades him to take on the marriage-bond.
SOSTRATUS Yes, Father. Now when I am marrying the sister
of this young man, because I think he's suitable
as a relation, then why not reciprocate
and give my sister to him for his wife?
CALLIPPIDES   Absurd!
To take a bridegroom and a bride into our family,
both paupers, that's too much! One at a time's enough!
SOSTRATUS Oh, money! That is not a thing of lasting value.
For, if you know your wealth will always remain your own
throughout eternity, then guard it, never share it
with any human being. But what you do not own
in perpetuity, but hold by the whim of chance,

then, Father, do not grudge to share it with anyone.
For chance may choose to strip you arbitrarily
of all your wealth, and give it to a worthless man.
Money is transitory. So, while it is yours,
why try to hoard it, Father? Use it generously
and wisely, so that you may benefit as many
as you can reach through liberality. That is
true immortality. And if misfortune hits you,
you'll find your kindnesses returned to you with interest.
It really is far better to have an acknowledged friend
than any amount of money hidden away in the cellar.
CALLIPPIDES You know me, Sostratus. I'd never bury my money
in a secret hiding-place as a private hoard. Oh, no!
It's yours, my boy. Do you want to use it to acquire
a friend? Well, test him out, and go ahead: good luck.
Don't preach me sermons! Hand it out, just hand it out!
Give it away and share it freely! I'll support you.
SOSTRATUS Honestly, Father?
CALLIPPIDES   Yes, and gladly. Don't you worry,
not for a moment.
SOSTRATUS   Oh, then, I'll call Gorgias.
Enter Gorgias from his farmhouse.
GORGIAS I was just coming out; and here, behind the door,
I overheard your conversation right from the start.
I must say this. You are a good and faithful friend,
Sostratus, I believe: I like you amazingly well.
Nevertheless, I do not wish to live a life
above my rank; and I know I simply couldn't endure it.
SOSTRATUS I don't know what you mean.
GORGIAS   I'm giving you my sister
to be your wife; but as for my marrying yours,
no, thank you very much!
SOSTRATUS   Why not?
GORGIAS   I can't enjoy
the luxury that other men have toiled to make:
I'd rather earn it for myself.
SOSTRATUS   Oh, stuff and nonsense!
Don't you believe you're good enough to marry her?
GORGIAS I know for certain that I'm good enough for her,
but still it's wrong for a poor man to marry wealth.
CALLIPPIDES Good God! Young fellow, you have all the finest feelings
but you are crazy.

GORGIAS   How?
CALLIPPIDES   Because, though you have nothing,
you *will* be independent. All right. I believe you.
Now let me give you something.
GORGIAS   You persuade me, doubly.
If I refused, I'd be both a pauper and a fool.
Your generosity saves my integrity.
SOSTRATUS (*eagerly*) Now all we have to do is make the marriage con-
tract.

CALLIPPIDES (*formally*) I now betroth my daughter to you, Gorgias,
to be the mother of your children: with a dowry
of three gold talents.
GORGIAS   Right; and in return I offer
a dowry of one talent with my sister.
CALLIPPIDES   Oh!
You mustn't give too much!
GORGIAS   Yes, yes.
CALLIPPIDES   No, Gorgias,
keep the farm all for yourself. Now go and fetch your mother '
together with your sister; we want them to meet
the ladies of our house.
GORGIAS   Of course, I'll go at once.
SOSTRATUS Tonight, we shall stay here and have a jolly party,
all friends together; then tomorrow we can have
the weddings. Oh yes, Gorgias, there's your stepfather:
go and fetch him; he'll be more comfortable
among us all.
GORGIAS   My friend, he will refuse to come.
SOSTRATUS Try to persuade him.
GORGIAS   Well, I'll try.
Exit Gorgias into his farmhouse.
SOSTRATUS   Now, let's arrange,
first, a men's drinking-party, honoring the two grandpas,
then for the women a moonlight dance.
CALLIPPIDES   Oh yes; and yet
they'll do the drinking, that I know; while we stay up
and look at the moon. However, I'll go in and start things
moving.
Exit Callippides into the shrine.
SOSTRATUS Yes, do. (*To himself*) If you only have common sense,
you never will despair of anything in the world.
There's no prize you can't win with work and application,

not one! Now I have an excellent proof of that.
In just one single day I have achieved a marriage
that everybody would have called simply impossible.
Enter Gorgias with his mother and sister.
GORGIAS Come on there, you two, don't hang back.
SOSTRATUS   Welcome! Come in!
(*Speaking into the shrine.*)
Mother, here are our guests. (*The women enter the shrine.*)
GORGIAS   But Cnemon, he won't budge.
He begged us to take out his elderly housekeeper,
so that he could be all alone at last.
SOSTRATUS   He is
a champion! Well, that's his nature. Let him stay,
while we go on to the party.
GORGIAS   I am awfully nervous
about my mother and sister.
SOSTRATUS   Nonsense! Go ahead!
Remember, from now on, we're all one family.
Exeunt Gorgias and Sostratus into the shrine.
Enter Simiké, talking over her shoulder to Cnemon inside.
SIMIKÉ All right, then, I'll go too, for heaven's sake. Stay there
alone on your sickbed. You enjoy suffering.
Although the people wanted you to come to the shrine,
you *would* refuse. Oh well, you'll pay for it one day,
and suffer worse than you do now. And serve you right!
Enter Geta from the shrine, followed by a young musician, Donax.
GETA I'll just walk out to see that everything's in order.
Donax plays a dance-tune on the clarinet.
GETA No, no! No music now, you idiot! Can't you see I'm busy?
They've sent me out to see the patient, suffering on his sickbed.
SIMIKÉ Oh yes, please let someone else go in and sit beside him;
for I must go and take my leave of my young mistress, kiss her
and talk with her, and say good-bye.
GETA   Of course you must. Go right in.
Let me be his attendant meanwhile.
Exit Simiké into the shrine.
                        I still owe him something.
I never thought I'd find the chance, but here it is, and perfect.
Revenge is sweet; and all the more when you must wait to get it.
He'll be quite helpless.
(*Shouting into the shrine.*)

Hey there, cook! Come out here, cook, a mo-
ment!
Sicon, come out here, can't you hear me, what's the matter, cookie?
Are you asleep there, lazybones?
Enter Sicon from the shrine.
SICON   You want me, Geta?
GETA   Yes, yes!
Look, would you like to get revenge for all those frightful insults?
SICON For all *what* frightful insults? What's this balderdash you're talk-
ing?
GETA The old curmudgeon's fast asleep inside there.
SICON   Oh? How is he?
GETA (*significantly*) He might be worse; might be *much* worse.
SICON   But couldn't he wake up,
and attack us with his fists?
GETA   Oh no, he can't stand up, they tell me.
SICON Oh dear, how marvelous! Let me go in and borrow something.
He'll really go insane with fury.
GETA   Yes, but first, old fellow,
suppose we drag him out of the house, and then, after we dump him,
let's go and bang on all his doors, and ask for things, and madden him.
Oh, it will be delightful!
SICON   Yes, but how about his stepson?
Young Gorgias might catch us; he would tan our hides.
GETA   Just listen!
You hear the noise. They're drinking. Who would hear us? And, more-
over,
young Gorgias will not be touchy now: he's a relation:
you know, a member of the family by marriage. (What a burden
for us to carry!)
SICON   Yes, I see.
GETA   Let's just make no disturbance,
but carry him out here gently. Now then, go ahead, get in there.
SICON Well, stick with me, for God's sake, Geta, don't back out and
leave me,
and don't make any noise, God damn it!
GETA   No, I won't, God damn it!
Sicon and Geta tiptoe into Cnemon's house, and reappear,
carrying Cnemon, lying on a light pallet-bed, fast asleep.
To the right, now.
SICON   Check.

GETA   Here. Down with him. At last, the golden
                                                      moment!
SICON Let me start off.
GETA   All right.
SICON   Then you. Make sure to keep the
                                                      rhythm.
*Sicon bangs on the door of Cnemon's house and shouts at the top of
his voice.*
Hello! Hello inside there! Hey! Hello there!
Cnemon wakes with a start.
CNEMON   Oh, I'm dying.
Geta joins Sicon in banging on the door.
GETA Hey, hey! Hello! Inside, hello! Who's there? Hey!
CNEMON   Oh, I'm dying!
Who's that? You must be somebody from hereabouts. What is it?
SICON I want to borrow cooking-pots from you, and a basin.
CNEMON   Help me
up on my feet!
SICON   I'm sure you have them, that I know for certain.
GETA And seven cooking-tripods, and twelve dining-tables.
                    (*Shouting at Cnemon's door.*) Hey, there!
Tell them inside there what we need. I'm waiting!
CNEMON   I've got nothing.
SICON What, nothing?
CNEMON   No! I've told you twenty thousand times.
SICON   I'll go,
                                                      then.
Sicon walks away from Cnemon's house as though rebuffed.
CNEMON Oh, help, what misery this is! Whoever brought me out here?
Who took me from my bed inside my house?
Sicon returns as though he were a new borrower.
                              Get out, you!
SICON   Wait, now.
Sicon hammers at the door again.
Hey, boy, hey, women, hey, men, doorman, hey, inside!
CNEMON   You're crazy!
You there, you'll smash the door in pieces!
SICON   Here, we need nine carpets
from you.
CNEMON From me?

SICON   Oh yes, and one rich oriental curtain
about a hundred feet in length.
CNEMON   I wish I'd ever owned one.
SICON You've got one!
CNEMON   Nonsense.
Cnemon starts calling for Simiké.
                              Woman! Hey, come out!
SICON   I'll knock
                                           again, then,
on *this* door.
Sicon moves to a side-door and starts pounding on that.
CNEMON   Go to blazes, you. (Hey, Simiké!) Confound you,
and damn your rotten soul to hell, what do you want there, blast you?
SICON I want to borrow one large mixing-bowl of bronze.
CNEMON   Oh, who the
                                                devil
will help me to my feet?
SICON   Come on, old boy, I know you have it:
I know you have that curtain.
CNEMON   Where's that woman?
SICON   And the bowl, too.
CNEMON I'll murder Simiké.
Geta and Sicon return from the house, and stand over Cnemon.
GETA   Now, Cnemon, rest and stop your shout-
                                                        ing.
You don't like crowds, and you hate women; you won't join a party
whenever there's a sacrifice? You'll do all that, and like it!
You haven't anyone to help you now, we're all around you.
So listen, Cnemon, let me tell you all about the party.
Your wife and daughter needed no compulsion: they enjoyed it.
CNEMON My womenfolk—how could they ever take such treatment from
                                                              you?
SICON Your wife and daughter? They've gone through a thorough trans-
                                                          formation.
They're both really happy, and they thought our family party
delightful. Now let me describe it. I poured out the wine for
the gentlemen. You hear me, don't you? You're not sleeping?
CNEMON (*with his eyes closed in disgust*)   No, no.
I wish I was.
SICON   You'd like to join the revels? Pay attention.

I hurried everywhere: I laid the couches, decorated
the tables—that, you know, is my particular profession:
for I'm a party-manager, remember? (He's a half-wit!)
Among the guests, one poured the ancient venerable Bacchus
into a hollow bowl with water from the Nymphs' clear fountain.
Another pledged the ladies, passing round the merry goblet.
Wine disappeared as though into the sand. D'you understand me?
And then a handmaid, flown with wine, veiling the flowerlike beauty
of her young features, rose and stepped out, happily though shyly,
into a merry dance, and sang melodiously in cadence.
Another linked her hand with hers to start a dancing circle.
(*Donax begins to play a dance-tune on the clarinet.*
Geta pulls at Cnemon's hands, as though to drag him into a dance.)
GETA You poor old miserable wretch, come on now, rise and dance too!
CNEMON What do you want, you beasts?
GETA   Get up and join our merry
                                                              dance, now!
You rude old creature!
CNEMON   Please don't, please!
SICON   Or shall we take you in there
to the party?
CNEMON   What's to do?
GETA (*pulling at his hands*) Or dance, then?
CNEMON   No, perhaps it's better
to face the music. Carry me. I'll join them.
GETA   Now you're talking!
    Hurrah, we've won! Now, Donax, and you too, Sicon,
    hoist up old Cnemon here and carry him in. And you,
    remember, Cnemon, if we catch you misbehaving
    just once, we shall be quick, drastic, and merciless
    in setting you to rights. Here, bring out wreaths of flowers
    for us to wear, and a torch too.
SICON   Here is one. Take this.
Geta and Sicon crown old Cnemon with a wreath of fresh flowers, and
then put wreaths on their own heads. Sicon and Donax pick up the bed
with Cnemon on it and start toward the shrine with dancing steps. Geta
waves a torch, and just before he follows the little procession into the
shrine, he turns and says to the audience:
GETA Now you have shared our trials and our final triumph
    over this truculent old man. So show your friendship,

children, and boys, and men; applaud our comedy!
And may that noble lady with the laughing face,
kind Victory, be our companion now and always.
Exeunt with music, song, and dancing.

The Huntsman and the Castaway

IN ONE of his most lively and apparently original speeches (the *Euboean*, No. 7) Dio Chrysostom describes an adventure which he says happened to him during his years of exile and penury. Crossing the Aegean from Chios to mainland Greece, he was caught in a storm and cast ashore in the Hollows of Euboea. It was a desolate place. He set out to try to find another ship. After a time he saw a hunted deer, which had leapt off the cliff and was dying on the beach. When the huntsman appeared, Dio showed him the quarry, helped him to skin it and cut it up, and was invited to his home for dinner.

As they walked (slowly enough, carrying half a deer) the man—Dio does not give him a name, but let us call him Demeas—described his life. It was poor: he lived mostly by hunting, dressed in skins (§ 62), and grew only a little grain (§§ 11 and 45). It was simple: there were only two families in the settlement (his own and that of his brother-in-law), not big enough to form a village (§ 42). The land over which he hunted game had formerly been part of a large estate, with horses and cattle; but its owner had been put to death by the emperor because of his wealth, the cattle and horses driven off, the land abandoned, legally, although not actually, reverting to the nearest city-community, Carystus.[1]

[1] The brother-in-law of Demeas is fifty years old (§ 21); the adventure takes place in the last years of Domitian's reign, say about A.D. 95: therefore the brother-in-law was born in 45 or so. Therefore his father was born in 20 or 25: he died an old man in about 94 (§ 20). The estate was confiscated well before Demeas was married (§ 20), indeed while he was still a boy (§ 21): therefore during the sixties. This means that the emperor responsible was not, as some have thought, Domitian, but Nero (with whom the last Flavian was often compared, e.g. by Juvenal 4.38). The occasion will have been Nero's tour of Greece in 66–67,

The father of Demeas had been one of two freeborn herdsmen on the estate, who had remained after the confiscation as squatters and had taken to hunting in order to live. Each had one son and one daughter. They joined the families by marrying the daughters to the sons; and now, by the time of Dio's visit, the third generation was growing up, one granddaughter having already married and left home (§68). Demeas's brother-in-law had never visited the city.[2] Demeas had been there twice, once as a boy, and once later on, when the fathers were dead and he represented the little group (§21). He was summoned by a man sent by the magistrates. He was taken into the citizens' assembly. There, says he, recollecting the episode, he is accused of enriching himself by trespassing on public land without a title and without paying rent, and in addition of being a wrecker, luring ships onto the rocky coast by false beacons, like the mythical king Nauplius. A prominent citizen then comes forward to defend Demeas, saying that too much land is derelict, and that anyone willing to work it should be given title, with a small rent to be paid in kind. Bidden to make a statement, Demeas explains how miserably poor he and his people are, and yet conveys the impression that they are content with what they have. Eloquent in his indignation, he denies that he has ever made any profit out of shipwrecks: on the contrary, he has often helped castaways (as in fact he succored Dio).

At this a man rises in the assembly, accompanied by a neighbor, and testifies that two years earlier they were both shipwrecked with heavy loss off Cape Caphereus and cast ashore destitute. Demeas (he declares) took them in, warmed them at a fire, rubbed them with tallow (having no olive-oil), poured hot water over them, clothed them and fed them, and kept them for three days to recover: he saved their lives. Demeas recognizes him, greets him by his name as Sotades, and naively kisses him.

The original defender now proposes that Demeas be honored with a dinner in the prytaneum, given regular clothes, granted the use of the

---

when he swallowed up enormous properties and executed their owners (Dio Cassius 62.11, a report interpreted as "imposing taxation on the rich" by A. Momigliano in the relevant section of *CAH* 10.21.6 and called "exaggeration" by E. Hohl in "Domitius," *RE Suppl.* 3 [1918] 349–94, especially 389). If the proprietor was Tib. Claudius Hipparchus (grandfather of Herodes Atticus), then his execution cannot be attributed to Domitian, as suggested by M. P. Charlesworth in *CAH* 11.1.5, p. 29 n. 1, and Wilamowitz must be mistaken in commenting "Dies zielt auf das Missregiment Domitians" (*Griechisches Lesebuch*[5] 2.1 [Berlin, 1910] p. 10). The whole thing happened a generation before Dio visited Euboea and heard the story.

[2] The city is not named; but since the huntsmen live on the foothills of Mount Ocha in southern Euboea (§38), it must be Carystus: Chalcis is too far distant to be concerned.

land, and awarded a hundred drachmas. This is passed by acclamation. Demeas accepts the dinner, refuses the money, and goes home, to remain undisturbed thenceforward.

As he ends his story, he and Dio reach his cottage. Dio dines on the venison with Demeas and his wife, served by a daughter and two sons. During the meal Demeas's brother-in-law (for convenience we may call him Simon) enters with his son, who brings a gift for his girl cousin. (The young couple might be named Gorgias and Glycera.) Tactfully Dio asks when the girl will be married and to whom. The father answers that the bridegroom is present. Then why the delay? First, says Simon (§70), to choose an auspicious day—at which Gorgias observes that the moon is full and the air clear (§71)—and second, says Demeas, because Simon has to go and purchase a sacrificial victim (§72)—which Gorgias counters by saying that he has got hold of a pig and has been fattening it up (§§73–74). The pig is brought in and approved, the wedding is fixed for the day after the morrow, and Dio is invited to be a guest. He accepts, thinking how much happier and more natural such weddings are than the marriages of the rich, encumbered by the work of matchmakers, by the legal problems of settlements and dowries, and by arguments during the celebration itself (§80).

Now, as Dio himself says (§81), I have not told this story without meaning to make a point. I suggest that these two episodes, the trial in the city and the wedding in the country, may have been inspired by a play, one of the lost works of New Comedy, and that in the play they were connected much more closely as parts of a single intrigue. It is really quite artificial that two kinsmen living in a tiny community should wait for the arrival of a benevolent stranger to make the final arrangements for a wedding between their children. It is also rather artificial to have the hunstman tell a long tale about a legal adventure in the city to a poor barefooted vagabond while they walk home carrying their dinner.

The story narrated by Demeas (§§21–63) has several predecessors in scenes from Attic drama. In each of them a person who has attended a meeting of an assembly describes it on stage to an interested auditor. They are Aristophanes' *Knights* 624–82, Euripides' *Orestes* 852–956, Aristophanes' *Women's Assembly* 395–457, and Menander's *Sicyonian* (ed. R. Kassel, Berlin, 1965) 169–271.[3]

---

[3] Links between some or all of these scenes have been examined by several scholars: notably E. W. Handley, "Notes on the *Sikyonios*," *BICS* 12 (1965) 38–62; R. Kassel, "Menanders Sikyonier," *Eranos* 63 (1965) 1–21; H. Lloyd-Jones, "Menander's *Sikyonios*," *GRBS* 7 (1966) 131–57; and G. A. Ricciardelli, "Osservazioni sulla *rhesis* del Sicionio di Menandro," *RCCM* 8 (1966) 210–14. Evidently Menander is gently parodying (or, as Lloyd-Jones prefers, lightly alluding to) the speech in *Orestes*, and also in certain details

In *The Sicyonian* a messenger describes to Smicrines an assembly at which the citizenship of a girl kidnapped in childhood was debated. It was a noisy meeting. The messenger not only gives the speeches and verbal fencing of the debaters in direct speech, but even reports the shouts of the crowd (244–45). The just cause triumphs—with the help of a good man, who is described as ἀνδρικὸς πάνυ (215), as the defender of Orestes was ἀνδρεῖος ἀνήρ (*Or.* 918).

In the *Euboean Discourse* Demeas describes to Dio an assembly at which his entire livelihood and even his life were endangered, until—thanks to the unexpected intervention of someone apparently a stranger to him—he was vindicated and rewarded by the favor of the citizens.

It is possible that Demeas's tale in Dio is based on a passage in a lost comedy, of the type known to us from *The Sicyonian*.[4] Its central theme is particularly common in New Comedy: an important character is saved from misfortune by the appearance of some person or thing from the past, which leads into a recognition-scene (Dio § 59). Suppose that in the comedy Demeas was a poor huntsman or farmer, living on the bare subsistence level (like Cnemon in *The Curmudgeon*) and strange to the ways of the city (like the speaker of *Georgos* fr. 3); that he was falsely accused of trespassing, and threatened with eviction or worse; and that Sotades appeared out of his past, to justify him, so that the right cause, as it must do in comedy, triumphed.

Can that adventure be connected with the other episode in Dio's narrative, the preparations for the wedding of Demeas's daughter Glycera? This also is a favorite comic theme, e.g. *Curmudgeon* 935–53, *Samian Woman* 325–32. A wedding often occurs at the end of a play, just after some obstacle to it has been removed by an unexpected twist of fortune; and it was just such a happy *peripeteia* that brought about the acquittal of the bride's father Demeas. In Dio's story the two impediments which have held up the marriage—the need to fix an auspicious day and the requirement of procuring a sacrificial animal—are too trivial to have been part of a comic intrigue. In New Comedy the commonest external obstacles to a marriage are lack of a dowry and dubiety about the

copying both the Aristophanic scenes. Kassel (21 n. 43) points out that "der Bravour-stück der Euripidesparodie" was a stylistic triumph for Menander, and was also a fine opportunity for the actor, who had to evoke the whole of a noisy debate filled with different types of voice. The opening of the *Orestes* speech was also parodied by the Middle Comedy poet Alcaeus (fr. 19 Kock).

[4] Dio admires and praises Menander (18.6–7) and quotes him at least once (32.16 = *Plocium* fr. 335.6–7). He refers to plots and productions of New Comedy (old by his time) in 15.7, 19.5, 32.94, and 57.11. He also likes paraphrasing Attic drama: e.g. in 52 and 59.

bride's citizenship and status. Suppose that Demeas had been involved in a legal case concerning money or citizenship or both;[5] that this had prevented his daughter's marriage; that Sotades unexpectedly appeared to give the evidence that saved him; and that in recognition of an earlier benefaction (such as his rescue after shipwreck) Sotades had presented him with a sum of money.[6] The wedding could then proceed. The guest of honor would be, not the shipwrecked philosopher Dio, but the former castaway Sotades.

I have failed to find a title which would clearly indicate the existence of such a play, or any group of fragments which might belong to it. No *Kynagos* or *Kynegos* is known.[7] Only one line remains of the *Kynegetai* of Anaxandrides (Middle Comedy) and it tells us nothing.[8] Two titles involve shipwreck. One is *Dis Nauagos* or *Dionysus Nauagos*, falsely attributed to Aristophanes and held to be by his imitator Archippus: this can scarcely be relevant.[9] The other comes from the Middle Comedy, the *Nauagos* of Ephippus;[10] but the only fragment from it is a witty speech mocking the members of Plato's Academy, and it is hard to fit it into such a comedy as we have imagined. Only one word of the *Naukleros* by Eudoxus survives;[11] and the fragments of Menander's *Naukleros* are not encouraging. Menander's *Halieus* may have contained a shipwreck and a rescue (see fr. 15); fragment 14 expresses a sentiment rather like that which Dio voices in §§ 109–26;[12] but the other fragments will not fit into any intrigue such as has been suggested above. The connection between the *Euboean Discourse* and a play of the New Comedy is therefore, at least for the present, purely conjectural. Yet many dramas of which we know virtually nothing were familiar to Dio and to scholars of his era: for example, in 32.23 he quotes what appears to be a fragment from a wholly unknown comedy.

[5] In §49 he tells the assembly with considerable emphasis that his father was legally a citizen.

[6] Dio makes the huntsman refuse the hundred drachmas (§63), but this is part of the general philosophical doctrine expressed in this discourse, that money is evil (§§104–6, 109).

[7] Philetaerus of the Middle Comedy wrote a *Kynagis* or *Kynegis* (Kock, *CAF* II, pp. 231–33, frr. 6–9), but the hunting girl was no doubt a harlot, and the play was sexy and sophisticated.

[8] Kock, *CAF* II, p. 144, fr. 24.

[9] Kock, *CAF* I, p. 459, fr. 266; and pp. 679–89.

[10] Kock, *CAF* II, pp. 257–58, fr. 14.

[11] Kock, *CAF* III, p. 332, fr. 1.

[12] Similarly the little speech in Menander's *Hydria* (fr. 401 Koerte) would go quite well in the mouth of Demeas. So would the speech on farming from Philemon's *Pyrrhus* (Kock, *CAF* II, pp. 496–97, fr. 71).

Lexical Notes on Dio Chrysostom

IN A BRIEF article proposing certain emendations in the text of Dio Chrysostom's *Euboean Discourse*, W. B. Anderson concluded by remarking, "I may perhaps express the hope that the forthcoming revision of Liddell and Scott's Greek Lexicon will take more account of Dion than preceding editions have done. It is easy to point to words or to notable constructions which the Lexicon ignores."[1] That was written some seventy years ago. Unfortunately, even after the appearance of the latest edition in 1940 (with its many Addenda et Corrigenda on pp. 2043–111) and the *Supplement* in 1968, it is still true.

Dio is often an attractive writer. His Greek, lively, copious, and varied, deserves study for its own sake. A good number of words and locutions appear first in his work, to be taken up later by his admirers, such as Julian; but not enough of these are given in LSJ. No doubt it is natural that Plutarch, a more famous and more important author, should be cited without mention of Dio for words used by both men. Such, for example, are: ἀθέατος II, 'not seeing' (Dio Chrys. 4.113); ἀκάθεκτος, 'ungovernable' (Dio 7.138); διάτορος, neut. as adv., 'piercingly' (Dio

Reprinted from *GRBS* 15 (1974) 247–53.

[1] *CR* 19 (1905) 347. The following abbreviations are used: Arnim = *Dionis Prusaensis* (sic) . . . *quae extant omnia, edidit apparatu critico instruxit* J. de Arnim (2 vols., Berlin, 1893 and 1896, repr. 1962); Dio and Budé = *Dionis Chrysostomi orationes . . . edidit* Guy de Budé (2 vols., Leipzig, 1916 and 1919); Schmid = W. Schmid, "Der Atticismus des Dio Chrysostomus," ch. 3 of Vol. I (Stuttgart, 1887) of *Der Atticismus in seinen Hauptvertretern*; Schwyzer = E. Schwyzer, *Griechische Grammatik* (3 vols., Munich: I, 1959³; II, ed. A. Debrunner, 1959²; III, index by D. Georgacas, 1960²); *Suppl.* = Liddell, Scott, Jones, *Greek-English Lexicon, a Supplement*, edited by E. A. Barber with the assistance of P. Maas, M. Scheller, and M. L. West (Oxford, 1968).

4.108); ἐπίκωμος, 'reveling' (Dio 33.14); στρατήγημα 2, 'trick' (Dio 11.148); ὑπηνέμιος 1.2, 'swift as the wind' (Dio 4.117); ὑστερίζω 1 abs., 'hang back' from battle (Dio 2.30). It is, however, anomalous that some words used by Dio should have no other authority in LSJ than the *Septuagint* or late writers such as Oppian, and that others again (for example, Ἰλιεύς, 'Trojan') should be wholly omitted. On pp. ix–x of his preface, Stuart Jones thanks Herbert W. Greene of Magdalen for his contributions to the lexicography of later Greek literature, "including the works of practically every non-technical writer of importance from Polybius to Procopius." But among the authors whom Greene and others named with him read and excerpted, Dio Chrysostom is not mentioned; and it is difficult to escape the impression that his work has never been thoroughly examined for the *Lexicon*. Although a few omissions were repaired in the *Supplement*—for instance, εὐθύτης II, 'rightness' (Dio 36.23) and κουρική (sc. τέχνη) 'haircutting' (Dio 7.117)—many still exist. The following list is representative but does not claim to be nearly complete.[2]

ἀγράφως, 'without an official record' (Dio 31.132). LSJ cite *P. Oxy.* 267.19 (I cent.).

ἀκούω IV, 'understand,' 'take' in a certain sense (Dio 36.29). LSJ quote Julian.

ἀκτήμων, 'without property,' of animals (i.e. not simply 'poor') (Dio 10.16): an unusual application, perhaps worth noting.

ἅλλομαι, aor. 2 inf. ἀλέσθαι (Dio 7.4). LSJ give "Oppian, etc."

*'Αμουσία personified (Dio 32.61). Cf. LSJ s.v. ἀρετή IV.

ἀμφιγνοέω τινά, 'to be doubtful about' someone (Dio 7.54). LSJ cite Plato, Isocrates, and others, but not with personal objects.

†ἀνανήφω (in Dio 4.77), not 'recover from a swoon' but metaph. 'sober up.'

ἀνάπηρος, "sts. spelt ἀνάπειρος in codd.": add Dio 3.21 Arnim. LSJ give *LXX* and *Ev.Luc.*

*ἀναφέρω I.2 med. abs., 'heave a deep sigh,' impf. ἀνεφερόμην (Dio 36.29). LSJ quote only the aorist.

ἀνελλιπής, 'unfailing' (Dio 2.68, 4.104). LSJ mention an inscription, Aelian, and Pollux.

*ἀνέξοδος II, of wealth, 'not circulating' (Dio 4.100).

ἀνεπίγραφος, 'without inscription,' of statues (Dio 31.90). LSJ cite only inscriptions in this sense.

---

[2] An asterisk means that the word, or a particular form of the word, or a particular meaning of the word, does not appear in LSJ. A dagger shows that the interpretation in LSJ is erroneous.

ἀνήκοος 2.c abs., 'ignorant'—a favorite word of Dio, e.g. 11.150, 25.4, 32.7, 32.24, 42.4, and with a double meaning in 3.105, 'not hearing' and 'uninformed'; in 31.154 c.gen. LSJ cite Dem. 19.312 and Sallustius.

ἀντιγράφω II.3, 'issue a rescript' (Dio 45.6). Inscriptional authority only in LSJ.

*ἀπάρχομαι III.2, 'give charity' to a beggar (Dio 11.16).

*ἀπελπίζω I c.acc. et inf., 'feel no confidence that' (Dio 31.91). As Schmid 170 remarks, Dio likes litotes.

ἀπονίναμαι: later aor. 1 ἀπωνάμην (Dio 1.46, 66.26). LSJ quote Lucian and Proclus.

ἀποσχεδιάζω 3, 'say offhand' (Dio 31:116). Schmid 156 is too strong, translating it 'thöricht reden.' LSJ have 'extemporize' (sc. a poem), citing Ath. 3.125c, which should probably read "Callistratus of Alexandria ap. Ath. &c."

*ἀραιός IV adv., 'rarely' (Dio 18.18).

*ἀρκέω I.2 c.dat., 'defend,' with πρό (Dio 36.49).

*ἀρρενικός, 'with men,' of sexual intercourse (Dio 4.102).

*αὖθις II.4, of past time, 'later' (Dio 30.2).

ἄφρακτος, of ships, 'not decked' (Dio 31.103). LSJ mention only an inscription; but see also Polyb. 4.53.1, D.S. 17.95.5, Plut. Cat. Min. 54.

βλάστημα II, 'offspring, youngling' (Dio 36.59): "also in late Prose, Jul. Or. 7.232d," LSJ.

δημιούργημα, 'creation,' of the universe (Dio 12.34). LSJ cite Zaleucus (7th cent. B.C., ap. Stobaeus) and Philo.

διαπνέω III, 'evaporate,' of drugs (Dio 13.15). LSJ refer to Aristotle.

*διαυγής, comparative (Dio 30.44, 33.23). LSJ give only superlative (as a v.l. in Aristotle).

διοίκησις, 'government' (Dio 1.42, 3.43). Plato and others in LSJ.

ἐγγίζω II.2, 'be of close kin' (Dio 3.120, in MSS U and B). LSJ quote only LXX; and there is no other example in Stephanus.

ἐγείρω I.4 'erect' a tent (Dio 12.18), a city (Dio 32.62).

*εἰσψύχω (so MSS and Budé), 'send coolness into' (Dio 12.31).

*ἐκδέχομαι, 'admit' the sea, of the Syrtes (Dio 5.9).

ἐκμελῶς, 'unmusically' (Dio 32.46). For the adverbial form LSJ cite only Pollux, while Stephanus quotes it from John of Antioch and Zosimus.

ἐλαφρύνω, 'lighten' (Dio 13.3). LSJ give Julian.

ἐλεέω, impf. ἠλέουν (Dio 8.28). For this tense-form LSJ quote only the comic poet Apollodorus.

*ἐλευθερία, 'nobility' of style (Dio 36.27). So H. L. Crosby in the Loeb translation and W. Elliger in his version (Zurich, 1967). It could mean 'frankness'; but the speaker is thinking of the lofty style of Plato's myths, which Dio proceeds to emulate in §§ 39–60.

*ἕλιξ III.6, 'arabesque' on a wine-bowl (Dio 30.37); not 'vine-tendril,' since it is paired with τορεία.

*ἐμφράσσω, pf.pass. ἐμπέφρακται (Dio 32.26).

*ἔνσπονδος, metaph., 'tame,' of a speaker's audience (Dio 32.8). Note that the marginal paragraph numbers on p. 269 of Arnim's text are wrong.

*ἐπαυλίζομαι, dep. with aor.pass., 'encamp on the field' (Dio 11.111).

*ἐπαφίημι, 'leave alone,' 'refrain from plucking,' of vines (Dio 7.46).

ἐπίσταμαι II.3, 'know' a person (Dio 30.1). LSJ cite Aristophanes, Musonius, Lucian, and Act. Ap.

ἐποίνιος, sung 'over the wine' (Dio 2.63). The MSS have ἐποίνων, corrected by Dindorf. LSJ cite this form from Nonnus, ἐπιοίνιος from Theognis.

*ἑταιρέω I.2, 'prostitute oneself,' of a woman (Dio 5.25, Plut. Per. 24).

*εὐδιεινός, 'having a mild climate,' superlative εὐδιεινότατος (Dio 6.1: εὐδινοτάτοις V, εὐδινωτάτοις U B).

*εὔληπτος 2, 'easy to understand,' comparative (Dio 18.11). LSJ cite only Iamblichus for this sense and give no instance of the comparative.

εὔρεμα = εὔρημα (Dio 3.135). LSJ offer a mixed bag of references. Schwyzer, I p. 523 §1, says the change from a long to a short vowel before -μα is typical of the Koine, giving many examples. Cf. πόμα in Dio 30.36.

*θηλυκός, 'with women,' of sexual intercourse (Dio 4.102); cf. ἀρρενικός above.

ἰκμάς, 'moisture' in the soil (Dio 12.30). LSJ quote only Ev. Luc.

ἱλαστήριον II.2, 'propitiatory offering' (Dio 11.121). LSJ cite Ep. Rom. and an inscription.

*'Ἰλιεύς, 'Trojan' (Lycophron 1167, Dio 11.4, 33.8).

κάματος I, 'toil' (Dio 3.124). The end of the article in LSJ is slightly disordered; the citations should be rearranged thus: Aristotle, Dio, Lucian, and so on.

*καμπή, 'detour' (Dio 12.43).

*κατανυστάζω, metaph., 'be neglectful' (Dio 12.27).

κατανύω II, 'accomplish' (Dio 3.127). LSJ quote only Euripides.

*καταπονέω, 'wear out' by running, 'run down' a deer (Dio 7.71).

*καταφρονέω 2, pass.pf. καταπεφρονῆσθαι (Dio 31.158).

κίβδηλος I, of a ἱμάτιον (Dio 10.14; κερμάτιον cj. Wilhelm). LSJ cite LXX, also of a ἱμάτιον.

κόρος (B), "rare in Prose, Pl. *Lg.* 772a"; add Dio 7.149.

κοῦφος 3, of persons = κουφόνους (Dio 3.20). LSJ refer to Herodian.

κωθωνίζω, pass., 'drink hard' (Dio 33.7). This might be added to LSJ's references.

λιχμάω II *med.*, 'lick up' (Dio 12.30). LSJ cite Nicander.

*λυπρός II.2, 'painful,' comparative (Dio 31.135; λυπηρότερον **B**). LSJ refer to Aeschylus and Euripides, giving only the positive.

*μάχλος neut. as adv., 'lewdly,' of a man (Dio 4.112). LSJ should say "later also of men," as in the article dealing with μέθυσος.

μετανάστης, 'migrant' (Dio 11.50; μεταναστᾶσι cj. Cobet). LSJ refer to Homer, Herodotus, Priscian, and papyri.

μέχρι III.2 with ἄν and subj., 'as long as' (Dio 4.56). LSJ cite Menander and Aeneas Tacticus, in that order.

μή B.3 after ὅτι ('that') (Dio 31.26). LSJ refer to the astronomer Cleomedes and Lucian.

*νωθρός 1, 'sluggish,' of horses (Dio 8.3).

οἰνάριον III, colloq. for οἶνος (Dio 7.76). The reference to Alexis and Diphilus in LSJ should be transferred from I to III, since they use the word colloquially or affectionately, not pejoratively.

†ὀκλάζων 1 (Dio 1.78), 'giving way, wobbling,' not 'folding-seat.' Schmid p. 161 has it right, 'wanken.'

* ὀργίζω II pass. πρὸς τινά (Dio 7.39).

*ὄρουσις, 'charge,' of a warrior (Dio 36.13).

†παλίμπρατος, 'sold more than once,' of honors bestowed on several different men in succession (Dio 31.37). LSJ have this reference in §2 with the interpretation 'good-for-nothing'; but the context refers to selling (κάπηλοι, καπηλεύειν).

*παραλαμβάνω, 'catch, contract' a disease (Dio 4.103).

παραφέρω III.3 pass., 'stagger,' of a drunken man (Dio 32.94, cf. 32.56). LSJ cite only Diogenes Laertius.

*περιαγκωνίζω, pf. inf. pass. περιηγκωνίσθαι (Dio 32.90). For the verb LSJ refer to LXX, Eustathius, and (in the *Suppl.*) Aesop.

†περίδημα, 'girdle, corset' to improve the figure (Dio 31.116). LSJ say only 'band,' but the context implies the wearer is an effeminate dandy.

περιέλκω 2, metaph., 'push around, put off balance' (Dio 4.77).

LSJ cite Julian in a different metaphorical sense.

*πλήσιος III, superlative -ώτατος (Dio 36.45).

προσαιτέω II, 'be a beggar' (Dio 11.15). LSJ quote Plato, a papyrus, and a probable reading in Plutarch.

ῥίπτω IV, 'throw away' money (Dio 3.15).

*σαίρω (A), plup. with impf. sense, ἐσεσήρει, 'was grinning' (Dio 1.79).

†σελήνιον (Dio 7.70), not 'little moon' but 'friend moon, dear moon.' 'Volkstümlich,' like βοίδιον (7.12) and οἰνάριον, says Schmid p. 162.

σκύμνος, of the monstrous 'offspring' of snake-women (Dio 5.19).

στίλπνος, comparative (Dio 36.58). LSJ cite the superlative from Dio 35.23, the comparative only from Julian.

*στρυφνός II, 'sour,' of the face (Dio 4.72).

συμβάλλω II.4 act., 'meet,' with dat. (Dio 1.56). LSJ cite Arrian and papyri.

συναγρυπνέω, 'keep awake with' (Dio 1.28). LSJ give Aristaenetus and Philostratus.

σύρω, pass.aor.inf. συρῆναι (Dio 11.104). "Spät," says Schwyzer I p. 714. LSJ cite Pausanias.

*ταμιεύω II.4 med.abs., 'husband one's strength' (Dio 11.95).

*Ταρσεύς, 'man of Tarsus' (Act. Ap. 21.39, Dio 33.57, 34.1, al). This word is given by Ruge in RE 4A (1932) 2414, and (with examples from coins and inscriptions) in 2421, 2426, 2433–34; he also cites 2 Macc. 4.30 (col. 2420) and Lucian, Macr. 21 (col. 2423). He may be mistaken in attributing the form Ταρσικός to Dio (col. 2414): it appears in the titles of Dio's 33rd and 34th speeches, but was perhaps added by editors.

*ταώς, acc. ταῶ (Dio 12.2). LSJ give ταών or ταῶν.

τερέτισμα, 'humming, twanging' (Dio 32.62, cf. 32.69). LSJ quote Diogenes ap. Diogenes Laertius, Lucian, and Agathias.

*τέφρα, 'splinters' of wrecked ships (Dio 7.51). This is the sense apparently required: so W. Elliger in his translation has "ein paar Splitter." But there is no parallel, and the word may be corrupt like its neighbor λάρους.

τηλαυγής II, 'conspicuous,' of footprints in snow (Dio 7.19). LSJ refer only to poets and LXX.

τρυγήτρια, fem. of τρυγητήρ, 'grape-gatherer,' is scarcely worth listing, except that Dio uses it in 7.114, which is evidently inspired by Demosthenes 57.45 (note ἔριθος). LSJ gives only Demosthenes and Pollux.

*ὑπαίτιος, 'open to criticism, questionable,' of coinage (Dio 31.24).

ὑπόβλητος, 'substitute' (Dio 11.102). LSJ give Sophocles.

†φθείρω I.3.b pass., 'rape' (Dio 11.153). LSJ translate it as 'seduce,' but the woman mentioned is Cassandra.

φιλάοιδος, superl. -ότατος, "Epic, ap.D.Chr. 32.84." The poem in which the word occurs is a parody of epic, which deserves to be in P. Brandt's *Parodorum epicorum Graecorum reliquiae* (Leipzig, 1888), and which is likely to be by Dio himself. In the *Suppl.* this adjective is cited from Sappho fr. 58.12 (Lobel-Page); the papyrus (P. Oxy. 1787 fr. 1.11) reads]φιλ'άοιδον.

φροντίζω II.1, 'take thought' that, c.acc. et inf. (Dio 36.43). LSJ give only *Ep. Tit.* and a reference to *BGU* (III cent.).

*χαράσσω II, 'stamp, paw with the hoof' (of Pegasus, Dio 36.46).

*χράω (B).c. med. χράομαι v abs. 2, 'masturbate' (Dio 6.17). Schmid p. 140 hints at this meaning, which is apparently unique.

Lexical and Critical Notes on Dio Chrysostom

In a previous issue of this periodical I gave a short list of words and of special senses of words occurring in Dio Chrysostom which were not attributed to him in Liddell-Scott-Jones but were usually supported by references to later authors.[1] The following should be added to the brief catalog.[2]

ADDENDA

* ἀγγεῖον I, metaph. of the human body, ἀ. φρονήσεως καὶ λόγου (Dio 12.59).

ἀπομαραίνω, 'cause to waste away' (Dio 3.83). The passive occurs in Plato, but for the active LSJ cite only Soranus and other late authors.

ἀριστεύς, 'champion' (Dio 29.11, 32.48).

ἄτοπος 3, of things, 'bad, harmful' (Dio 16.5).

* διαίρω med., 'stand up straight' (Dio 40.9).

* διακρίνω med., 'part one's hair' (Dio 21.7).

δυσαπαλλάκτως ἔχειν, 'be reluctant to abandon' (Dio 38.50). LSJ quote only Eustathius.

* δυστυχής, 'foolish, misguided' (Dem. 14.32, Dio 35.8).

ἐνειλέω, 'wrap in' (Dio 23.3). For the active LSJ cite Dioscorides.

* ἐρέπτω, 'roof' (Dio 79.1).

Reprinted from GRBS 17 (1976) 153–56.

[1] GRBS 15 (1974) 247–53. I should like to correct an oversight. On pp. 252–53 I said that the epic parody in Dio 32.82f. ought to be in P. Brandt's *Parodorum epicorum Graecorum reliquiae* (Leipzig, 1888). It is there, with a valuable commentary, among the "incertorum fragmenta" on pp. 100–107.

[2] An asterisk means that the word, or a particular form of the word, or a particular significance of the word, does not appear in LSJ.

ἴκρια II.3, 'benches' in a theater (Dio 33.9).

* ἱστορία, 'sightseeing' (Dio 27.5).

κατανοέω I.5, 'look at, view' (Dio 28.3).

κενοδοξέω 2, 'to be vainglorious' (Dio 38.29).

μέρος IV.2.b. ἐκ τοῦ πλείονος μέρους, 'for the most part' (Dio 31.22).

* μίσθαρνος, adj., 'working for wages' (Dio 22.1).

* ὀλίγος IV. πρὸς ὀλίγον, 'for a short time' (Dio 32.89, 34.18, 34.37, Lucian, Nigr. 23, Hdn. 3.7.8 [p. 90 Stavenhagen]).

ὁράω II.2, 'see to' (Dio 34.49).

* παντοδαπός, 'trying every method' (Dio 4.76). The regular word is παντοῖος 2.

* πωλεύω pass., 'be suckled,' of a colt (Dio 21.6).

ῥαιστήρ, 'hammer' (Dio 40.9).

* ταχύς C.I.2: θᾶττον, 'earlier, previously' (Dio 31.30, 31.33, Diog. Laert. 6.56).

* ὑψηλός I, of a man, 'tall' (Dio 21.1).

* χρῆμα I: χρημάτων alone, 'for money' (Dio 17.11).

CORRIGENDA

Here are a few suggestions for the improvement of von Arnim's text of Dio Chrysostom (2 vols., Berlin, 1893 and 1896, repr. 1962).

3.86. The emperor (Dio tells Trajan) considers friendship the finest of his possessions. It is not so disgraceful or so dangerous to lack money as to lack friends: οὐ γὰρ οὕτως τῇ χορηγίᾳ καὶ τοῖς στρατοπέδοις . . . διαφυλάττειν τὴν εὐδαιμονίαν ὡς τῇ πίστει τῶν φίλων. The adverb οὕτως hangs in the air. Read οὕτως ⟨ἀσφαλὲς⟩, comparing a repetition of the idea in 3.96: ἄνευ δὲ φιλίας οὐδ' ἐν εἰρήνῃ ζῆν ἀσφαλές.

7.50. Addressing the assembly of city-folk, the Euboean home-steader offers, if they wish it, to pull down his cabins, but adds that the Urban Housing Committee must give his family a home in the city: ἢ πῶς ὑπενεγκεῖν δυνησόμεθα τοῦ χειμῶνος; The verb requires an object: read τοὺς χειμῶνας, which is more graphic.

8.8. Diogenes declared that if he professed medicine people would flock to him, but when he offered to cure them of ignorance and other vices, nobody would consult him, οὐδ' ἂν εἰ πολὺ προσλήψεσθαι ἀργύριον ἔμελλεν. But Diogenes never suggested that his spiritual cures would make his patients rich: he would have scorned the idea. Delete ἀργύριον as an addition by a reader who did not know that προσλαμβάμω can be used without an object, as in Dem. 2.7.

8.34. Diogenes praised Hercules for choosing death by fire, δείξας ὅτι οὐδὲν ἄξιον ἐφρόντιζε τοῦ πυρετοῦ. Von Arnim says in his *apparatus criticus* that he does not understand the clause, and (with Wilamowitz) believes it to be lacunose. The meaning is clear if ἄξιον is excised: οὐδὲν φροντίζω is a common idiom meaning 'despise.'

11.96. Explaining to the Trojans that the Greeks were really defeated in the Trojan war, Dio asserts that Hector killed Achilles and (as Homer says) captured his armor; he then pursued Achilles' chariot-team, οὐ λαβεῖν δέ, κἀκείνων ἁλόντων. Self-contradictory. The horses, like Hector himself, were tired; Dio remembers *Iliad* 17.75–78 and rationalizes it. Read καμνόντων.

11.114. After this (Dio continues) the Greeks sailed away to the Chersonese and stayed there in the hope of concluding the war without a Trojan counterattack on Greece, εἴ πως τῷ Πάριδι κάμνοντι διαλλάξειαν αὐτούς. But the Achaeans' chief enemies in Troy were Priam and Hector, mentioned a few lines below. Read τῷ Πριάμῳ.

18.7. Dio declares Menander best of all the comedians: ἥ τε γὰρ τοῦ Μ. μίμησις ἅπαντος ἤθους καὶ χάριτος πᾶσαν ὑπερβέβληκε τὴν δεινότητα τῶν παλαιῶν κωμικῶν. Menander does indeed excel in character-drawing, but μίμησις χάριτος is not a dramatic virtue. Read καὶ ⟨ἐπίδειξις παντοδαπῆς⟩ χάριτος, or something of the sort.

18.8. Lyric, elegiac, iambic, and dithyrambic poems are well worth reading if one has the leisure; but not for a busy man, τῷ πράττειν τε καὶ ἅμα τὰς πράξεις καὶ τοὺς λόγους αὔξειν διανοουμένῳ. Von Arnim, followed faithfully by Budé, excises τὰς πράξεις. But Dio's friend is trying to enlarge his command of literature while engaged in politics (18.1), so we should read ἅμα ταῖς πράξεσι.

24.2. Men excel in different pursuits. Some are better than others at wrestling and boxing and running, καὶ τοῦ σπόρου μὴ διαμαρτεῖν, καὶ πλέοντες μὴ διαφθεῖραι τὴν ναῦν. Not all men are sowers, just as not all are sailors. Here ⟨γεωργοῦντες⟩ is required to parallel πλέοντες.

25.1. Dio and a pupil discuss what is meant by a *daemon*. Dio asks, "Is a *daemon* something within a man, ἢ ἔξωθεν ὂν ἄρχον τι καὶ κύριον τοῦ ἀνθρώπου;" The pupil answers " Ἔγωγε." But ἔγωγε cannot be employed to reply to a disjunctive question and to mean "The latter." Read Ἔξωθεν.

30.4. In his final illness Charidemus retained his intellectual powers, τὸ συνεῖναι . . . καὶ διαλέγεσθαι. So the editors, von Arnim and Budé. But the infinitive of συνίημι (= 'understand') is shown, for instance by Herodotus 3.46.1, 3.63.4, and 5.80.1, to be συνιέναι.

30.18. Charidemus describes the world as a prison in which all men are fettered body and soul. Some are small and some tall, some ugly and some handsome, but all are bound by necessity. Just as they differ in physique, ὁμοίως καὶ ταῖς τύχαις τε καὶ δόξαις καὶ τιμαῖς ἀλλήλων ὑπερέχειν. All men cannot be superior to one another: read ἄλλους ἄλλων ὑπερέχειν.

30.26. In another interpretation of man's fate, Charidemus says we are akin to the gods, who placed us in this earth as a great city plants a small colony, ἐφ᾽ ἥττοσι τιμαῖς καὶ ὄλβῳ, δικαίοις δὲ καὶ νόμοις τοῖς αὐτοῖς. The adjectival δικαίοις breaks the symmetry and is anyhow too imprecise. Read δίκαις.

31.27. Lecturing the Rhodians, Dio tells them it is absurd to omit honoring benefactors, ἀτόπου γε ὄντος τοῦ τινα παρεῖναι τῶν ἀξίων τιμῆς. The infinitive of πάρειμι = 'pass over' is παριέναι.

32.90. The Alexandrians, says Dio, should realize that not only an individual but a whole city can be made a captive, αἱρεθεῖσα ὑπὸ μέθης ἢ ᾠδῆς γυναικῶν ἢ ἁρμάτων. Alexandria had lots of singing girls (Dio 32.62) but no singing chariots. Read ἢ ⟨τάχους⟩ ἁρμάτων.

33.1. In a long and involved exordium Dio tells the Tarsians he wonders why they want to listen to orators. It is because of their sweet voices? ἔπειτα ὥσπερ ὀρνέων ποθεῖτε ἀκούειν μελῳδούντων ὑμῖν; The adverb of sequence, ἔπειτα, makes no sense. A subordinate clause of explanation is needed, introduced by ἐπειδή γε.

36.5. The city of Borysthenes is small and poor because of barbarian attacks. The Greek settlements on the western Black Sea coast have not yet recovered from being overrun by the Getae over a century ago. (In *CAH IX*, ch. 5, p. 228 Rostovtzeff places this incursion between 67 and 50 B.C.) Πολλαὶ γὰρ δή τινες ἁλώσεις κατὰ πολλὰ μέρη γεγόνασι τῆς Ἑλλάδος, ἅτε ἐν πολλοῖς τόποις διεσπαρμένης. This remark is of course true of the Greek lands and colonies before they became part of the Roman empire; but it is not relevant here, and may well be a marginal comment added by a reader who lived in the chaotic centuries after Dio's death.

48.14. Dio begs his fellow citizens to be calm and orderly for their own sakes and for his. For, if a philosopher enters politics and cannot produce concord in his city, τοῦτο δεινὸν ἤδη καὶ ἄφυκτον, as though a shipbuilder neglected the seaworthiness of his vessel. Such a failure is distressing but not literally inescapable, ἄφυκτον. Read ἀφόρητον.

Mutilations in the Text
of Dio Chrysostom

IT IS a curious experience to read Dio Chrysostom's works with a close
eye to their structure. The reader is often left hanging in mid-air, or let
down with a bump. The thought is seldom difficult to follow, but not
many of the speeches come to an emphatic, or even a satisfactory, conclusion.[1]

Consider, for instance, his third discourse, "On Kingship." Addressing the emperor Trajan, he begins what may well have been a birthday
address[2] by declaring that—all flattery aside—Trajan is truly happy because he is truly good (1–24). Then he embarks on a description of the
ideal monarch as contrasted with the tyrant, citing as his authority Socrates (25–42).[3] He follows this with a definition of the three types of good
polity, paired with the three bad (42–49),[4] which leads him into a discussion of the imperial government of Rome, τῆς νῦν ἐπικρατούσης:

Unpublished, appearing here for the first time.

[1] My warm thanks go to Professor C. P. Jones of Toronto, who read a draft of this
paper and made useful suggestions. A brief bibliography: H. von Arnim, "Entstehung und
Anordnung der Schriftensammlung Dios von Prusa," *Hermes* 26 (1891) 366–407 (= Arnim,
"Entstehung"); H. von Arnim, *Dionis Prusaensis . . . quae extant omnia* (2 vols., Berlin,
1893 and 1896, repr. Berlin, 1962) (= Arnim, Text); H. von Arnim, *Leben und Werke des
Dio von Prusa* (Berlin, 1898) (= Arnim, *Leben*); W. Elliger (tr.), *Dion Chrysostomos, Sämt-
liche Reden* (Zurich, 1967) (= Elliger); A. Emperius, *Dionis Chrysostomi Opera Completa*
(2 vols., Brunswick, 1844) (= Emperius); J. Geel, *Dionis Chrysostomi Olympikos* (Leyden,
1840) (= Geel); W. Schmid, "Dion Cocceianus," *RE* 5.1 (1903) 848–77 (= Schmid); A.
Sonny, *Ad Dionem Chrysostomum Analecta* (Kiev University, 1897) (= Sonny).

[2] Arnim, *Leben* 404–5.

[3] He is thinking of Plato, *Grg.* 470c–479e, but he has anachronistically changed Plato's
Archelaus to Xerxes.

[4] This is based on Plato, *Resp.* books 8–9, and Aristotle, *Pol.* 3.7.

he calls it happy and divine (50). After a gap in the argument,[5] Dio goes on to a lengthy description of the ideal monarch and his happiness (50–85). Next, certain special aspects of the ideal monarch's life and character are examined: he treasures his friends (86–118) and his kinsmen and wife (119–22). Here a few paragraphs about the energetic and toilsome life of the ruler (123–27) break the continuity, and seem to have intruded from an earlier section.[6] They are followed by a final disquisition on friends and friendship (128–32). Then Dio turns to the ideal monarch's recreations—not foolish and despicable tricks such as Nero's acting and Ptolemy's piping, but the vigorous sport of hunting. That is, real hunting, which involves exertion and danger, rather than the safe but ignoble Persian method of keeping wild animals in game-parks and shooting them down in safety. . . .

And there Dio suddenly stops talking; or so it seems.[7] Yet he still has plenty to say. He has not even finished his praise of real hunting. From that he could have proceeded to other recreations of the ideal monarch—also chosen with specific reference to Trajan's tastes. Surely, to counterbalance the emperor's riding and running and facing the charge of big game, Dio would have brought in his presumed interest in literature and philosophy. However meager it may have been in reality, Dio had alluded to it in the opening of his discourse (3), and would fitly close by passing from exercises of the body to those of the mind. After that, a general survey of the monarch's character, and a conclusion. The speech cannot have stopped dead on a relatively unimportant point, a criticism of Persian big-game hunting. It must have run on, for at least thirty paragraphs.

Turn to another work, even more ambitious (Or. 12). Speaking at the great festival at Olympia, Dio chooses a subject which is both lofty and appropriate: Phidias's statue of Zeus as a representation of the nature of the highest divinity. He starts with a long exordium heavy with autobiographical detail and protestations of modesty, ending with an awkward transition: "Would you prefer me to describe the climate and inhabitants of the Danubian regions, or commemorate the nature and power of Zeus, patron of this place?" (21–22). Now follows a second exordium, more serious, and decorated with quotations from Hesiod and Homer (23–26):

[5] The content of the missing part is apparently summed up by the editor (or by Dio himself?) in the phrase τὰ περὶ τοῦ Διός (50 fin.). Arnim (Leben 419) conjectures that it contained the same ideas as the parallel of monarch and deity in 1.37–47.

[6] They would fit in fairly well after paragraph 85.

[7] It would be frivolous to suggest that Trajan, restless under this long lecture, had suddenly called for his horse and galloped off, preferring a wild boar to a tame one.

after which Dio proceeds to analyze the origins of religious feeling in mankind (26–43), and then passes on (44–48) to introduce Phidias and his statue of Zeus. In a prosopopoeia he imagines the sculptor defending his work and explaining why he presented God in human form—largely by drawing a parallel between his own work and the poetry of Homer (49–84).

And then, in a much more daring prosopopoeia (84–85), Dio fancies that the statue itself speaks. Zeus, from his throne, gazes down kindly on his worshipers, felicitating them on their conduct of the festival held in his honor. "But," he goes on, addressing Greece, "I view this with concern, that

> thyself art sore neglected: grim old age
> besets thee, squalid is thy form and mean thy garb."

These are the words spoken by Odysseus when he sees his old father dressed in poor patched garments digging in a vineyard like a slave.[8] It is an allusion full of pathos. Impoverished, lacking nearly all her former grandeur, reduced to the status of a subject province, Greece is a pitiful spectacle.

But is that all Zeus has to say? Would Dio, after inventing a speech occupying twenty-eight paragraphs for the sculptor Phidias, have cut the god himself short after half a dozen lines? And would he have permitted his own oration, which contained such fine compliments to the men of Elis and the visitors to Olympia (25, 49, 74), to conclude with an agonizingly pessimistic description of the Greeks as little better than beggars and slaves? Would he have made Zeus, the all-powerful, the all-knowing, the beneficent, say "I view this with anxiety, ἐκεῖνο φροντίζων σκοπῶ," and not go on to give some wise counsel, appropriate to his attributes (listed in 75–76), to the assembled Greeks, together with some noble words of comfort? Dio himself is never reluctant to offer advice to the Greeks on how to manage their lives more wisely, often lecturing them at great length; and in another speech he gives a prosopopoeia of Socrates which runs to several pages filled with moral exhortations (13.16–27). No, the quotation from the *Odyssey* cannot be (as the German translator calls it) an "ironic conclusion."[9] It must have been the opening of a long discourse put in the mouth of Zeus, which, together with Dio's own conclusion following it, has been lost. To bring the speech to an end

---

[8] *Od.* 24.249–50. For Homer's αὐτόν, contrasting old Laertes with his well-kept garden, Dio substitutes αὐτήν, referring to σύμπασα Ἑλλάς.

[9] Elliger 804.

proportionate to those parts which are extant, forty further paragraphs would scarcely suffice.

Here is an outline of the *Olympicus*, with conjectural supplements to complete the work.

Arnim sensed that something must be wrong with the end of the *Olympicus* as it stands.[10] Noting that Dio promises to call artists, poets, and philosophers to account for their influence on religion (48), he asserted that the greatest poet and the greatest sculptor were compared and criticized, while the philosopher (like the lawgiver) was simply pushed aside. Yet in 55–83 Homer makes no defense of poetry: Phidias simply uses him as a glorious example to defend the visual arts. Therefore, in a later section of the speech, either a poet would vindicate poetry in its presentation of the divine powers, or else Dio himself would speak to defend both the poets and the philosophers.

Arnim, who calls both the *Olympicus* and the *Euboicus* "ächte Ste-

---

[10] *Leben* 474–75.

greifreden,"[11] implies that the omission of this defense is due to Dio's carelessness. Yet, in spite of all we hear from Philostratus about Dio's gifts as an improviser,[12] it is impossible to believe that a speech on such a theme as this, delivered before such an eagerly attentive audience, would be literally improvised, without premeditation or plan.[13] The defense of poetry and philosophy was not simply thrust aside through Dio's improvisatory negligence, but has been lost for another reason.

In his text (p. 178) Arnim shows his uneasiness by athetizing all but the first sentence of paragraph 84, saying simply "spuria esse, docet sententiarum conexus." He is followed by L. Lemarchand, who terms the passage a flat recapitulation.[14] It is indeed a recapitulation and a transition, but it is neither spurious nor irrelevant. It prepares, by the mention of Zeus (line 26), for the address of the deity to the assembled Greeks. Remove this section, and πάνυ εὔνους καὶ κηδόμενος must apply to Phidias: which is absurd. Lemarchand saw this absurdity and amputated everything after στεφανῶσαι ἄν in line 20: which is too arbitrary to be borne.

Other scholars who have read the Olympicus, some of them analyzing its text with minute attention, have made no comment on the ending of the speech, and appear not to suspect that it is seriously truncated.[15] To me, the Olympicus is like a finely carved statue, from which one arm and the head have been, through some misfortune, broken off and destroyed.

One of the longest and most deservedly popular of Dio's discourses is the seventh, inaccurately titled "The Euboean Speech; or, The Hunter." As we have it, it opens with a romantic narrative of Dio's adventures as

[11] Leben 474.

[12] Philostr. VA 5.37; Arnim, Leben 179–81.

[13] So Arnim, Leben 464: "Es widerstrebt dem natürlichen Gefühl, solche kunstreiche Gebilde, wie etwa die Olympica und den Euboicus, als Eingebungen des Augenblicks zu betrachten."

[14] "Dion de Pruse: observations critiques sur le texte des discours LXVI et XII," RPh 55 (1929) 13–29, esp. 28.

[15] E.g. T. Christofferson, "Bemerkungen zu Dion von Prusa," Kungliga Humanistiska Vetenskapssamfundet i Lund, Årsberättelse (Lund, 1933–34), who on p. 6 calls paragraphs 84–85 a "conclusio": he does however reject Arnim's and Lemarchand's excisions (pp. 22–23); Emperius, who produced the first usable modern text; Geel, who edited the speech with great care; B. F. Harris, "The Olympian Oration," JRH 2 (1962) 85–97; Schmid; and (in spite of his learning and acumen) Sonny. The mutilation of Or. 12 (and Or. 4 and Or. 21) is mentioned but not discussed by J. R. Asmus, "Synesius und Dio Chrysostomus," ByzZ 9 (1900) 85–151, esp. 121.

a castaway given shelter and hospitality by a poor family living as farmers and hunters in the lonely wilds of Euboea (1–80), and then moves smoothly into moral reflections on the hospitality of the poor, particularly poor folk living in country districts (81–102). Thence to an allied topic, the life of the poor in cities (103–52). How ought such people to live? Some occupations are unhealthy or dishonorable, while others are honorable or at least unobjectionable (109–13). Dio leads off by describing and denouncing the inadmissible vocations: dyers, perfumers, hairdressers, interior decorators, actors, dancers, auctioneers, journalists, lawyers (114–26); and then, after a brief Platonic digression (126–32), launches into a strong invective against pimping and prostitution, which have the effect of spreading corruption outside the brothels into family life, so that wives are seduced, and unmarried girls too, and boys (133–52). . . .

There the speech breaks sharply off. But Dio would surely go on from there, to contrast the vicious sexual habits of the corrupt city folk with the healthy love-life of the rustics (as described in 67–80), and thus complete his survey of dishonorable ways of living. Then, after that, moving in a leisurely way (as he admits in 127–32), he still has to list and commend the *honest* occupations open to the urban poor. That would be (as he remarks in 127) a subject needing much careful analysis.[16] Thereafter a conclusion, summing up the contrasts of city and country, wealth and poverty, vice and virtue. Much, very much, has been lost.[17] And, to judge by the extremely energetic and highly individual diatribe against prostitution, it would not all have been rehearsal of ethical commonplaces.

As for the opening of the *Euboicus*, it seems to start briskly and clearly: "I shall describe something which I did not hear about from others, but saw for myself." Reading this without close attention, one might easily believe it to be the first words of the speech, like Κατέβην χθὲς εἰς Πειραιᾶ at the beginning of the *Republic*. However, Arnim saw that it was not.[18] The first sentence starts Τόδε μήν, which is not a tolerable opening phrase for a long discourse, but implies that something else has preceded it. Dio adds that it is natural for an old man to *follow up* any subject that comes into his mind—which shows that he has already been talking for some time. Later, after closing his adventure narrative, he explains that he has told the tale to illustrate *both* his own way of living *and* the existence of the poor (81). Therefore the "Euboean"

---

[16]The Roman Umbricius gave it up as impossible: Juv. 3.29–57.
[17]Arnim, *Leben* 502–3.
[18]Arnim, "Entstehung" 397–404; *Leben* 492.

discourse is mutilated both at its beginning and at its end: it must have been far longer than the existing remnant.

This phenomenon is often repeated in Dio's works. Again and again he starts a discourse on a subject which sounds important or at least enticing. He moves into an argument that promises to be both ample and intricate; and then the speech breaks off or peters out—without any hint from Dio himself that he has approached his conclusion, and sometimes with several questions in the body of the work left unanswered. Arnim perceived something of this. Discussing the last words of Or. 4, he says he was led to the conclusion "dass hier wie bei mehreren anderen dionischen Reden der Schluss verloren gegangen sei."[19] But he did not usually look out for it or emphasize it; nor—although he analyzed the text of many speeches with fine critical judgment—did he always observe their truncated ends and speculate how much had been lost.

Here are some examples.

The thirteenth discourse has a clear structure, so far as it goes:

(1) Dio recalls how he was an exile (1–8);
(2) On the advice of an oracle he became a philosopher, like "a certain Socrates" (9–15);
(3) Socrates used to criticize the education of the Athenians (16–28);
(4) So Dio criticized the education of the Romans (29–37);
(5) The Romans (he told them) were corrupted by their wealth; yet during their earlier history they had learned much, for instance fighting in armor (34–37)—

—and therefore (he would surely continue) they can still learn, and can improve both their state and themselves by studying philosophy: a discipline whose merits Dio would explain to them. Thirty or forty paragraphs are missing.[20]

In the nineteenth speech Dio narrates a personal experience from the years of his banishment; or rather, begins to narrate it. Debarred from his home province of Bithynia, he arranged to meet some of his friends outside it, in Cyzicus. To Cyzicus at the same time came one of the greatest singers of the day. Dio went eagerly to hear him because of his

[19] *Leben* 401, with a reference to "Entstehung" 372.

[20] In "Entstehung" 380–81 and Text 1, pref. xxxiv–xxxv, Arnim proposes that *Or.* 13 stood at the end of one section of the archetype and was accidentally mutilated. Yet in his analysis of the discourse (*Leben* 255–60) he does not even mention the fact that it lacks its ending. Later, almost casually, he calls it "die . . . leider kaum zur Hälfte erhaltene Rede," but on the same page speaks of its "hochpathetischen Schluss" (334).

passion for music. Also (Dio adds) he loves dramatic poetry . . . and in the midst of an irrelevant digression about thin men and fat men, the speech is discontinued.[21]

The twenty-first piece is longer than that, but it also is truncated. It is a dialogue about beauty, centering on a handsome youth, whom Dio and his interlocutor are apparently admiring in the gymnasium (21.14). Such good looks (says Dio) are rare nowadays; and this youth is purely Greek in his beauty. Are there then different types of beauty in different races? asks his friend; and off goes Dio to distinguish between the handsome Greeks and the handsome Trojans, and indeed the Ethiopian Memnon. . . . That is all we have. Clearly, after expatiating on types of beauty differentiated by race, Dio intended to return to the other and more important aspect of the young Greek's good looks, namely, that they were an expression of the nobility of his soul. Virtue and beauty are paired in paragraph 2; the youth's modesty is praised in 13–14, and his gentleness and humanity in 15. Dio has even planted a little puzzle, to be solved later in the speech. He tells his interlocutor (15) that the handsome youth is nobody's son.[22] Nobody's? Later this riddle would be solved; but the continuation is lost. We possess merely the first section of this discourse, I shall not even say the first half.

The twenty-second discourse as we have it covers only five paragraphs; yet it begins with a large comparison between philosophers and statesmen, rich in historical examples; and then introduces an important problem, which still exercises us today: εἰ πολεμητέον, should men make war? Nothing beside remains. We have therefore only a fragment of the introduction to a philosophical treatise which—to judge by the amplitude of its opening—would cover many centuries and many pages. This little initiatory section ends with a contrast between philosophers, who "have deliberated about everything far in advance," and politicians, "who know no more than others and have not examined these problems beforehand" (4–5). Surely this contrast would have been developed at length in the rest of the speech. Of course it derives from Plato, and goes straight back to *Gorgias* and the *Republic*.

[21] "Verstümmelt am Schluss," Schmid 870. Arnim laconically observes (Text 2, p. 258), "In fine multa deesse vidit Selden." He does not tell us who Selden is. The illustrious English jurist is the only Selden in the *DNB*, and Dio is not cited in his biography there. However, Emperius p. XX informs us that Christian Freiherr von Wolff (1679–1754) found some manuscript notes on Dio by John Selden in the Bodleian Library, and published them in an eighty-page volume of *Seldeni Castigationes*, full of sharp attacks on Casaubon. Selden was so learned that the book must contain something of value, but I have never seen it mentioned in modern times.

[22] υἱός secl. Emperius.

Two little dialogues, numbered 25 and 26 in Dio's works, are no sooner begun than they are ended; or amputated. In the twenty-fifth, Dio—after a cursory glance at the Stoic doctrine that only the wise man is happy[23]—launches into a brief lecture about the *daemon*, or ruling spirit, of individuals. Then, rapidly and speciously, he alters the frame of reference to interpret *daemon* as meaning "ruler" or "controller" of a large number of people, whether that connotes slaveowner or politician; he lists a number of statesmen from Lycurgus to Numa; and then, declaring that he has said enough, invites his interlocutor to pursue the subject of ruling spirits. There the conversation leaves off, almost before it has got started. It is merely a fragment, says Arnim,[24] picked out of a discussion intended to prove the Stoic paradox, simply because Dio's comparison of lawgivers, generals, and monarchs to *daemones* interested an editor—or should we say an anthologist?

Like the twenty-second, the twenty-sixth raises an important question and drops it before arriving at the desired conclusion. It starts off like a little Socratic dialogue.[25] Dio wonders what is meant by "deliberation." The problem is in part epistemological: do we debate, or deliberate, about things which we know or things which we do not know? things which exist or things which do not exist? In either case the process of deliberation seems to be useless. This is a superficial and ridiculous discussion: it omits the real-life examples which might have clarified the question. "It is useless," says Dio, "to deliberate about things which already exist." Therefore the Athenians ought not to have deliberated about the invading Spartan army encamped outside the city. And we cannot deliberate about the future, since it does not exist: therefore it is pointless to plan for next year's harvest.[26] Dio can never have read, or at least understood, Aristotle's discussion of deliberation in *Nicomachean Ethics* 3.3; nor has he recalled what he himself says in 22.4. This flimsy idea-spinning passes into two paragraphs (6–7) extolling intelligence and culture—and why? Because they can help us to deliberate: although we have just been told that deliberation is impracticable and infertile. And to deliberate about what? Περὶ τῶν ἰδίων, says Dio; and then proceeds to

[23] This looks like a bridge-passage connecting the twenty-fifth discourse with the twenty-fourth—a very brief monologue proving that real happiness is to be won only through knowledge of essentials.

[24] *Leben* 291.

[25] In fact, it is close to *Sisyphus*, wrongly attributed to Plato. See J. Pavlu, "Der pseudoplatonische Sisyphus," *Mitteilungen des Vereins klassischer Philologen in Wien* (Vienna, 1926) 19–36: who however is mistaken in adducing Quint. 2.17.30f., which concerns a different problem, whether rhetoric is or is not an art.

[26] Contrast 24.2: τοῦ σπόρου μὴ διαμαρτεῖν.

give, as examples of such problems, political alliances, war and peace, and colonialism. Apparently he was endeavoring to prove that we need philosophical wisdom in all fields of human life; perhaps, later in the discourse, he would have distinguished public from private affairs. But it is all left hanging in the air.[27]

Among Dio's works appear several long and complex speeches made to the citizens of Greek-speaking cities: Rhodes (31), Alexandria (32), and Tarsus (33 and 34). Their structure is intricate, but they do not (at least at first sight) seem to be distorted or mutilated. However, after them comes the thirty-fifth, an address to the people of the Phrygian city Celaenae. As it stands, it amounts to twenty-five paragraphs, and is clearly only a small part of what Dio originally said. Consider its outline:

(1) *Exordium*, full of self-depreciation (1–12);
(2) *Praise* of Celaenae (13–17);
(3) *Comparison* of Celaenae with other lands and peoples rich in material goods: Indians, Scythians, Byzantines (18–25). . . .

Evidently this comparison would continue until Dio had established the point that the Celaenians should not be proud of their material wealth alone.[28] And then he would explain to them that *phronesis* and *paideia* were the true riches on which a city such as theirs should pride itself, riches to be attained through disciplining themselves and accepting the guidance of wise Roman governors and sage Greek philosophical teachers. Thirty paragraphs at least would be required for this development, even without digressions.[29]

That speech is cut off before it really gets going. Dio's exhortation to the men of Prusa, recommending peace and cooperation with their rivals and neighbors of Apamea (40), is perhaps half-complete. Its structure is simple enough:

Exordium: why Dio is reentering politics (1–15);
Proposition: harmony between the cities must be maintained (16–19);
Argument: (a) discord is painful to all (20–34);
(b) the cosmos is harmonious, except for human beings:

---

[27] Briefly noted by H. v. Herwerden in "Ad Dionem Prusaensem ed. v. Arnim," *Mnemosyne* 37 (1909) 310–21, especially 321: "XXVI. Huic quoque orationi finis deesse videtur."

[28] Another such *synkrisis* (also bringing in Byzantium) appears in the first Tarsian speech (33.25–27). It proceeds to eulogize σωφροσύνη καὶ νοῦς (28), purity and moderation (29).

[29] Arnim, "Entstehung" 380–81, notices the break in this speech and attributes it to a mutilation in the archetype. Schmid notes it without comment (870).

they are more contentious than animals. Consider
parents and children (35–41). . . .[30]

That is all we have. But it is very far from being a conclusion. The theme
would surely be developed further thus:

>   (c) discord within families is evil: so is discord between
>   social classes and adjacent communities;
>   (d) the ideal for neighboring cities is harmony, under
>   the benevolent tutelage of the emperor, who is my
>   friend.

And so to a peroration: all that I can do, trust me to do on your behalf;
but you yourselves must put away your hostile emotions and attitudes.
The entire speech might cover sixty or seventy paragraphs.[31]

The next oration, the forty-first, addressed to the neighboring Apameans, is on a smaller scale, but also halts during the argumentation.

>   *Exordium:* Dio is friendly to both Prusa and Apamea (1–8);
>   *Proposition:* emulate Rome in showing friendship to your neighbors
>   (9–10);
>   *Argument:* (a) discord is foolish and painful (11–14). . . .

No orator would conclude such a speech of positive exhortation with such
a gloom-ridden tricolon as χαλεπόν, λυπηρόν, βλαβερώτατον. Dio's
argument would move forward from this threat to deal with the advan-
tages of inter-city concord, and then end with positive advice on how to
realize it.

The forty-second piece, filled with mock-modesty, is a little overture
or part of an overture to a speech which has vanished. The title says it
was delivered "in his native city," which is nonsense: Dio is addressing
people who have never heard him speak (2, 4), and warns them that they
may be disappointed (2). He observes, however, that his speeches are very
popular, being learned by his audiences and repeated and distributed
broadcast, and frequently altered and rearranged—spoilt in the process,
like fine pottery smashed up while being shipped abroad. . . . The rest
of this introduction and the connecting links with the speech itself are
gone. But what we have is a valuable datum on the dissemination of
Dio's work.

The forty-third also is an overture, to a speech delivered in his own
defense. Dio compares himself to Epaminondas and Socrates facing trial.
The actual speech is lost—although its content can be partly conjectured
from paragraphs 11–12, and its tone from the mutilated forty-sixth speech.

---

[30] Dio illustrates this idea with some parallels from the animal world, which show how
little he cared for close observation. Birds nesting near one another, he declares (40), do
not quarrel over food and twigs; and colonies of ants do not compete.

[31] Schmid 870 notes that it is mutilated at the end.

The discourses numbered 44, 45, 46, and 47 are all heads without bodies. All concern Dio's relations with his fellow citizens.

In the forty-fourth, after thanking the Prusans for offering him certain honors (which he declines), Dio urges them to achieve social order and self-discipline, which mean *paideia*. This adjuration he proposes to support by reading a letter of his to the emperor, followed by the emperor's reply. Vanished, these valuable documents, together with the conclusion of the speech.

After a brief proem, the forty-fifth sails straight into a narrative of Dio's relations with the emperors Domitian, Nerva, and Trajan (1–3); then to an argument expounding the value of Rome's concessions to the city of Prusa (4–6); thereafter into a *refutatio* (7–16), striking down several charges against him and incidentally comparing himself with Odysseus, Epaminondas, and Theseus. While he is still in the midst of his defense, the threat is cut. He has outlined two charges against him: first, that he wished to improve and enlarge the public buildings of Prusa (12); second, that he hoped to make Prusa the chief city of the province (13). But he has only started to defend himself against the former charge, and is still attempting to shift or share the responsibility, when the fragment stops.[32]

Peculiar, though trivial, is Dio's forty-sixth speech. Trivial, because it concerns a petty disturbance in a provincial city; peculiar, because in it class-conflict is described by one of its victims. Such hostilities were not uncommon in the Roman empire, but infrequently reported from this point of view. The incident was like one of the riots one reads of nowadays in India or the Philippines, in regions where there is scarcely any middle class, and the very poor hate the very rich. Dio was rich— although (he explains) far less rich than other Prusans; he had been erecting new buildings in important parts of the city, obviously as an investment, although the public would benefit from them; and the price of grain had risen. So a mob from the city came out to attack Dio's house, threatening to burn it down and stone its inmates to death. Before doing any real harm, they turned back. Now Dio addresses an assembly of his fellow citizens, some of whom were recently part of the mob.

Exordium: give me a hearing (1);
Argument: injustice is rampant in Prusa (2–6);
Refutation: but Dio is blameless (7–13);
Proposition: be careful: Rome is watching (14). . . .
The address closes unexpectedly with a paragraph of three fairly long sentences (14). The first two warn the Prusans to refrain from illegal

---

[32] Nevertheless, the Loeb translator, H. L. Crosby, remarks on p. 204, "Dio concludes his address with a vigorous defence of his programme." Schmid 870 declares briefly that both 43 and 45 are "verstümmelt am Schluss."

disturbances, since any such actions will be reported to the Roman governor: a scarcely veiled threat. In the last, Dio declares it is reasonable to elect a price-control board. We now expect at least ten paragraphs more, in which Dio would develop a peaceful solution for the other grievances of the citizenry, calm down the protesters who had threatened to lynch him and who had been shouting him down only a few minutes earlier (πάλιν αὖ θορυβεῖτε, 10), and in a peroration assure them of his own innocence, his own patriotism. Perhaps not much has been lost, but some important sections of the address have vanished: Dio could not simply stop dead after suggesting the creation of an office of price-control.

The forty-seventh speech is the most unappealing in the whole corpus, and shows clear signs of senile decay. Dio often rambles, and frequently compares himself to heroes, Nestor and Odysseus and such great names as these, but never so extravagantly as here. Indeed, as sufferers from senescence sometimes do, he shows that he is conscious of the danger: ἵνα δ᾽ οὖν μὴ ἐπιλάθωμαι οὗ χάριν ἀνέστην (12); ἢ ἐγὼ τετύφωμαι καὶ ἀνόητός εἰμι; (18). The proem is absurdly long, covering nearly half of the extant speech (1–11). Then, having cited some famous men who were injured by their fellow citizens (Zeno, Chrysippus, Cleanthes, Hercules, Homer, Pythagoras, Aristotle), he launches into a refutation, admitting a mistake (something to do with clearance of old buildings and the erection of new, 12 and 15) and asking how he should make amends (12–20: μόνον ἕν τι προστάξατε, 19). Next he turns to answer two individuals who have criticized him, one telling him to desist from his public activities or else leave home and go on a celebrity tour (20–24), and the other denouncing him as a home-town tyrant (23–25). A tyrant! Paradoxical and ridiculous, cries Dio, declaring that he is not like the terrible tyrants known in rhetoric, who boiled people alive (24). "With my long hair and beard, and the ingratitude I suffer, I am more like a king!" (25).

That is no place to stop a speech of self-defense. Dio evidently went on to complete his vindication of his behavior as well as his public acts, and then (doubtless after a few digressions comparing himself with Socrates and Pericles) to produce a suitably lenitive peroration. Unless, perhaps, the Prusans were provoked into creating a θόρυβος and driving him off the speaker's platform, on hearing the almost insanely arrogant word βασιλικόν.

In their present state, Dio's collected works end with a group of brief pieces on literary and ethical topics, numbered 52–80. Few of them have

a strong logical structure, for that is not Dio's forte. But even apart from
that, many are clearly mutilated, with their final thoughts and final words
left unexpressed.

In *Or.* 69 Dio is going to speak on Virtue: a noble subject indeed.
In his first paragraph he explains that we all admire virtue; but (2–3) that
we aim at other ends—a grave error. For only reasoning men are happy
("happiness" meaning "being dear to the gods"). Whence the error? It
arises because most people are fools (5–8) and by nature evil (9). And
there, on a profoundly hopeless thought, the speech is interrupted. This
is not even the torso of a philosophical discussion. Arnim glances at the
fragment,[33] but does not mention the fact that it closes with the equation
men = wild beasts, which is not even a logical conclusion.

Wealth: the wealth of a city. Is it a desirable and admirable thing?
No, says Dio in *Or.* 79. Ivory is cheap in India, amber in Celtic countries; and yet we buy these things from abroad in exchange for our good
silver and gold. But such material goods are trash, not worth a penny:
only intelligence matters. . . . The piece has no sooner begun than it
appears to end. Evidently it was intended to lead into a larger discussion
of one of Dio's favorite themes:

> *either* (a) how foolish it is for the citizens of any city to set great store
> by its wealth (cf. *Or.* 35) or by the magnificence of its public
> buildings (cf. *Or.* 48.9 and 12);
>
> *or* (b) that the unphilosophical life is not worth living (cf. *Or.* 13.31–
> 36);
>
> *or* the two combined, with the moral that the citizens should not
> strain their communal finances or make excessive demands of their
> fellow citizens, but rather concentrate on living a reasonable, or-
> derly, peaceful life under the guidance of a philosopher.

What we have is the introduction, or part of the introduction, to a
preachment half-political and half-philosophical.

Another short talk approaches the same theme from a different direction. In *Or.* 80 Dio begins by praising the philosopher (whom others,
poor fools, think eccentric) as being truly free. Men living in communi-
ties are not free, because they obey man-made laws (3–6); and in addition
nearly all are enslaved by their own follies (7–10), such as their obedi-
ence to Fortune, who fetters them with elaborate chains; "but let us not
go too far afield pursuing our metaphor: ἱκανῶς ἔχει." And yet much
remains to be said about the slavish condition of the ordinary man. Fortune (Dio tells us) is only the first of the many slaveowners ruling many

[33] *Leben* 273.

prisons (πάσας τὰς εἰρκτάς, 11) whom he could describe. We await a description of the others; but he stops without developing the image.

Still less satisfying is the little piece numbered 56 and labeled "Agamemnon; or, On Kingship." This is a dialogue in the Platonic manner between Dio and a docile but anonymous pupil. It centers on a point which may not have been so obvious in Dio's time as it is now: the distinction between absolute and limited monarchy. From history and myth Dio cites examples of limited monarchy: the Spartan kings (5–7) and Agamemnon, "supervised" or at least advised by Nestor, and accountable to the council of Greek chiefs (8–15). Now he says, "Let us drop the subject, since it was adequately dealt with yesterday"; his pupil replies, "No, please go on discussing kingship" (16); and there the piece terminates. It is as though Plato's *Charmides* had been broken off just at the angry intervention of Critias (162d) which ushers in the main theme of the dialogue.

This work Arnim discusses at some length.[34] In *Der Dialog* (Leipzig, 1895) Rudolf Hirzel criticized the dialogues of Dio as empty and artificial imitations of Plato, which were never actually spoken but were simply cut out of whole cloth by the sophist at his writing-desk. Arnim sets out to controvert this. So here, "the subject was adequately dealt with yesterday" may, according to Hirzel, be pure fiction, aimed at proving that Dio and his notional pupil have had many discussions with each other; or it may refer to another of Dio's invented dialogues (now lost), part of a connected group like certain works of Plato. Both these explanations (says Arnim) are unlikely and unacceptable. The little conversation, he suggests, is part of an actual stenographic transcript of one of Dio's real tutorials, picked up at some later period by an editor (without the other conversation to which it refers) and inserted in a collection of Dio's works.

The sixty-second discourse is like the Stoic divinity in Seneca's *Apocolocyntosis* 8.1: *nec cor nec caput habet*. It begins with καὶ μήν, which (whatever its precise implications in each context) introduces a fresh section of a speech already well begun.[35] It has one principal theme: self-control as the essential virtue of the ideal monarch (1–2; cf. *Or.* 1.12–14), which is closely attached to the other cardinal virtues—wisdom, justice, and courage (3–4; cf. *Or.* 1.74–75, 3.7, 3.9–10, 3.58)—and which was emphatically not possessed by one of the worst conceivable monarchs, Sardanapalus (3–4; cf. *Or.* 4.135). It has no peroration, but—after a rhetorical question closely comparable to those in *Or.* 1.34–35—stops

[34] *Leben* 285–88.
[35] J. D. Denniston, *The Greek Particles* (Oxford, 1966²) 351–58.

dead (7). Evidently this is a fragment of a speech on kingship addressed to Trajan (ὥσπερ σύ, 1 and 3; cf. Or. 1.36): the kind of thing that Dio, after delivering it in the imperial court, recited to his fellow citizens of Prusa (and possibly to other audiences such as the envious Apameans) after giving them a preface comparing himself to Nestor advising Agamemnon (Or. 57). In a long discussion Arnim proposes that it is a collection of extracts from one speech, or even from several speeches, on kingship;[36] but the argument seems to me no looser or less continuous than in some of Dio's complete discourses.

A special problem is presented by the Praise of Hair.[37] It is not found among Dio's works as they have been transmitted to us; never mentioned by Dio, or by Philostratus, or by Photius. It appears only in the Praise of Baldness by Synesius, who quotes it in order to refute it at length. It is remarkably brief. First, a proem, closely resembling the introduction to Dio, Or. 52. Then—after a self-depreciatory aside about his own matted hair—Dio praises (1) dandies who love and tend their elegant locks, (2) the Spartans who combed their hair at Thermopylae, (3) Homer, who often spoke of the hair of heroes and gods. There the little jeu d'esprit stops, without a comparison, climax, or conclusion. Dio could say much more. He could very well have mentioned those Greeks who, in his own time, still wore full hair and flowing beards—such as the Euboean hunter (7.4) and the Borysthenites (36.17); he could have said that philosophers were notably hirsute; surely he would at least (in order to give his discourse a broad application) have drawn a moral, similar to those which appear in 12.15 and 72.1–2, 5–6; bolder, perhaps, than that in 35.1–4.

Possibly he did. But Synesius begins his quotation by declaring that the piece is so short that he has memorized it; and ends emphatically ταυτὶ μέν σοι τὰ Δίωνος. These few paragraphs therefore are all that Synesius had of Dio's writing on this theme. He believed the piece to be complete, for later, alluding to the citation of Il. 1.529 which comes at the end, he writes Ὁμήρου δὲ ἐξάψαμενος, ὥσπερ ἱερᾶς ἀγκύρας, ἔχεται μέχρι τελευτῆς τοῦ βιβλίου (c. 19, 82B).

Modern critics have resisted the idea that the Praise of Hair is truncated. Arnim admits that we should believe it a fragment or an excerpt, if Synesius had not thought it complete: he suggests that Synesius's copyists made their work easy by reproducing only the beginning and the

---

[36] "Entstehung" 387–92.

[37] For the text see Synesii Cyrenensis Opuscula, ed. N. Terzaghi (Rome, 1944) 193–95; and Arnim, Text 2, pp. 307–8; for a discussion, perhaps oversubtle, Asmus (note 15 above) 119–34.

end.[38] Asmus thinks Synesius forged it, in order to write a refutation of it aimed against the long-haired Cynics.[39] Both ingenious, but unconvincing. The piece, like so many of Dio's works, is merely a head and part of a torso.

Quite a large number, then, of Dio's surviving discourses are truncated, and lack part of their development, or their conclusion, or both.

However, a few of his works were designed to be incomplete. They were composed as prefaces to other speeches (now lost), or as preliminary talks on occasions which demanded no more. These are merely introductions, and do not pretend to be artistic wholes.

For example, *Or.* 53 starts by rehearsing the opinions of a few philosophers about Homer (1–5). It then proceeds to eulogize the poet for several rather superficial reasons—because his poetry was translated into the language of India (6–8), because he lived as a wandering beggar and never mentions his own name (9–10), and because he advises kings to model themselves on Minos, first of monarchs, and on Zeus, king and all-father (11–12). There is no conclusion. Clearly these few hundred words were intended to introduce a reading of Homer to an auditor or auditors who knew some elementary facts about the Greek philosophers and historians, and who had a particular interest in the problems of kingship.[40] Dio here does not touch on the fact that the king of gods and men and the supreme kings of both the Trojans and the Achaeans are shown in Homer as capricious and vacillating, infirm of purpose, very far removed from the faultless monarch Dio envisages. That faultless monarch is no doubt Dio's chief auditor: Trajan, who is superficially acquainted with Greek culture (*Or.* 3.3), and who can be persuaded to listen to Homer because Homer teaches the ideals of monarchy.

In the few paragraphs on Socrates which compose his fifty-fourth discourse Dio begins by contemptuously dismissing the sophists Hippias, Gorgias, Polus, and Prodicus as talkative fools who made lots of money (1–2).[41] Then he lauds Socrates as uninterested in wealth, although poor

---

[38] *Leben* 154–55.

[39] Note 15 above.

[40] Crosby the Loeb translator suggests this on his p. 355, but without attempting to specify the audience.

[41] He shows even more contempt for "a man from Abdera" who made no money out of philosophy but lost all his own riches (2). Here he has confused Protagoras of Abdera, wealthiest of all the sophists, with Anaxagoras (ps. Plato, *Hp. Ma.* 283a). This is a typical Dionean digression, spoiling his own point. He started out to contrast rich sophists with the poor philosopher Socrates, and then, incurably discursive and inaccurate, brought in a

(3); and ends by saying that although Socrates wrote nothing, his friends recorded his words—which will endure even if few people read them (4). This is at least rather better put than his remarks in *Or.* 55.12–13, where he compares Socrates with Homer as a dramatic author filled with moral purpose, illustrating the point by alluding to half a dozen of Plato's dialogues. But what is the purpose of this little talk? As Arnim reminds us, Synesius knew of "many" Socratic pieces among Dio's works. So he proposes that this was a preface to a collection of discourses centering on Socrates—just as *Or.* 6, 8, 9, and 10 (and others now lost) center on Diogenes.[42] This may well be the case. Yet Dio concludes by referring to the *words* of Socrates. That looks as though this were a preliminary to the public reading of one or more extracts from the Platonic dialogues and other "Socratic" writings: comparable to *Or.* 53, introducing a reading from Homer. In each case the audience is assumed to be respectful but unscholarly and unsophisticated.[43] It is also an audience which Dio wishes to alienate from the contemporary "sophists," so that he may focus its admiration on himself as a reincarnation of Socrates.

Another preface, beginning in a lively informal manner, is *Or.* 57, a little disquisition on Nestor. The Greeks loved to hear Homer recited, and Dio loved to quote him verbatim. So he starts by repeating part of Nestor's admonitory speech to Agamemnon and Achilles (*Il.* 1.260–68 + 273–74). He points out that Nestor was not bragging about his past experience in diplomacy, and that the two haughty princes really needed his advice (2–9). Therefore, if someone such as Dio were to tell an audience about his own diplomatic successes, he should not be considered vain; and the audience should profit from his words: words which Dio uttered in the presence of the emperor (10–12). And with that Dio begins the recital of a speech he made to Trajan—perhaps, as Arnim[44] and others suggest, one of the discourses on kingship.

After one of the innumerable and apparently endemic outbreaks of social disorder in Prusa, the proconsul of Bithynia, Varenus Rufus, visited the city to address a public meeting. At the time, Dio himself held no official position (although his *auctoritas* was considerable), but his son, though young and inexperienced, was the archon or one of the

---

thinker who sacrificed all his fortune to philosophy, and therefore should be even more admired than Socrates.

[42] "Entstehung" 374–75; Synesius, Arnim, Text 2, p. 317, lines 17–18.

[43] It is impossible to imagine Dio's contemporary Plutarch listening to either of these speeches without indignation. On Plutarch's knowledge of Plato see K. Ziegler, "Plutarchos," *RE* 21.1 (1951) 636–962, especially 749–51.

[44] "Entstehung" 392–93; *Leben* 410–11.

archons.[45] In the short speech handed down as *Or.* 48, Dio commends the distinguished and powerful guest. He exhorts the Prusans not to shout him down or make a disturbance (1–5); he produces calm and reasonable grounds for solving the disputes which have racked the city (once again the public buildings and once more the price-control bureau, 6–12); and then, with a warning about the power of Rome to control local disorders (13) and a mild appeal for sympathy and attention (14–16), he presents the archon (17)—who will thereafter officially introduce the proconsul.[46] A short conciliatory utterance, this is not a complete oration, merely a brief introductory statement.

Who wrote the titles under which Dio's discourses now appear, we cannot tell; but he was the same kind of fellow as now writes headlines in the newspapers: he glanced at the first few paragraphs, and then stuck down a phrase. So the twenty-seventh discourse is called "An informal talk about drinking-parties." But in fact Dio is setting out to discuss the great national festivals of Greece; and the nub of his talk, or what remains of it, is that people come to festivals in order to see and hear exhibitions of skill (athletic, literary, etc.), while a moral philosopher—like a sober man at a carousal—can scarcely make himself heard. Clearly Dio is heading into a lecture on ethics, to be delivered at a festival, to the audience (fit though few) which will listen; and this is his introductory chat. The lecture itself is lost, although any experienced reader of Dio will find its themes easy to reconstruct.

The fourth speech, "On Kingship," is a special case. It is fairly long (139 paragraphs) and carefully wrought. Beginning with a conversation between Diogenes and Alexander (14–74), it passes on into a continuous harangue by Diogenes, analyzing the three commonest types of bad character, the avaricious, the sensual, and the ambitious (70–138). This we expect to be preparation for a concluding description of the perfectly good man, an ideal which Alexander himself may still attain (65, 75, 79–80). But no such description appears. The speech breaks off with a brief exhortation (139): let us change to a purer and better harmony, and τὸν ἀγαθὸν καὶ σώφρονα ὑμνῶμεν δαίμονα καὶ θεὸν, οἷς ποτε ἐκείνου τυχεῖν ἐπέκλωσαν ἀγαθαὶ Μοῖραι παιδείας ὑγιοῦς καὶ λόγου μεταλαβοῦσι.

Now, this may be a deliberately speeded-up ending: a single sentence compressing all the positive advice Diogenes might give at length. Plato's *Theaetetus* ends briefly too (210b11–d4); the conclusion of *Gorgias*

---

[45] This is Arnim's conjecture (*Leben* 386–88).

[46] Later to be impeached for corruption by representatives of the turbulent province.

(527a5–e7) is terse; and Dio likes sharp cutoffs, particularly in his pieces about Diogenes. In that case, ὑμνῶμεν will be vague, meaning "let us praise and revere"; and Diogenes will be associating himself with Alexander rather like Socrates with Lysimachus at the end of *Laches* and with Callicles at the end of *Gorgias* (τούτῳ οὖν ἐπώμεθα, 527e5). Yet ὑμνεῖν always implies speech, and usually poetic speech or song. Therefore ὑμνῶμεν here must announce an actual eulogy of the good spirit, a eulogy spoken or sung, which does not appear in Dio's text. Wilamowitz conjectured that the discourse contained (and doubtless closed with) a glorification of Zeus similar to those in *Or.* 1.39–41 and 12.75–77. But Arnim pointed out that Dio speaks, not of the king of the universe, but of the "good spirit" of the individual (as in 79–80).[47] Therefore, since the speech is addressed to Trajan, its final paragraph led into a real hymn, sung to honor the genius, the good spirit, of the emperor on his birthday.

This speech and several others of Dio's appear incomplete because they are merely prefaces: prooemia like those attributed to Demosthenes.[48] They are not mutilated: they are hilts without blades.

Some of the discourses of Dio have unexpected endings, but are not therefore necessarily incomplete. He often likes to begin briskly, with a question, a proverb, a challenge, or a combination of these devices.[49] In this he is following Plato, and also working within the tradition of teaching informally through the living word. But Plato likes to end his dialogues in a quiet measured tone; whereas Dio, even in those conversations which are apparently complete, sometimes ceases very sharply, as though to take his audience by surprise. Thus he makes Diogenes cut short a sermon (*Or.* 6) with a brief eulogy of his own poverty (6.60–62), and he terminates his description of Diogenes at the Isthmian Games (*Or.* 8) with a startling παρὰ προσδοκίαν. Diogenes, recounting Hercules' various labors, at last mentions the Augean stables, which the hero cleared of dung; and then, apropos, squats down and defecates in public, on the Cynic principle that *naturalia non sunt turpia*. And there Dio leaves him (8.36), with the "sophists" croaking all around like frogs in a pond. The Cynics despised most men as fools, or as invalids all but

[47]*Leben* 401–4.

[48]F. Blass, *Die attische Beredsamkeit* 3.1 (Leipzig, 1893³, repr. Hildesheim, 1962) 322–28; A. Rupprecht, "Die demosthenische Prooemiensammlung," *Philologus* 82 (1927) 365–432.

[49]Questions: 20.1; 23.1; 56.1; 67.1; 70.1; 72.1; 73.1; 74.1; 77.1; 79.1. Proverbs: 12.1; 43.1. A challenge: 60.1.

incurably sick. Therefore it was appropriate for a Cynic to show his contempt for them by abrupt shocking actions, such as crowning the winner of a horse-fight (Or. 9.22, to which Dio adds quite a good final joke of his own). It was also right for Dio when talking about Cynics to terminate his discourses curtly, with a silencer like the end of Or. 10. A number of Plato's dialogues conclude with the opponent reduced to silence, unable or unwilling to carry the discussion on any further. So do Dio's two dialogues on slavery (14 and 15).

Three of Dio's longest speeches close naturally enough, apparently without distortion or mutilation, yet with a surprise ending which does not look in the least like a peroration. In the second of two speeches delivered in Tarsus (Or. 34), after a highly personal proem (1–6), he gives the Tarsians much salutary advice on politics and morals (6–42); then announces the approaching conclusion of his speech (43); hints that the discussion may take too long (51); and, after two harsh words for his audience, φιλαργυρία and ἀκρασία, says (53) "Like a swimmer in calm weather, I am going out too far." No more: no apology, no self-justification, no summing-up, no memorable aphorism for his hearers to take away; but a "throwaway" ending.[50]

In the thirty-second discourse, he lectures the people of Alexandria at great length, belaboring them with hard words: ἐξεστηκότες καὶ παρανοοῦντες (42), ἐοίκατε κραιπαλῶσιν (56), μίμους καὶ γελωτοποιούς (86), κόπρον βαθεῖαν (87), and so on for many paragraphs (1–95). Then comes an emphatic warning: preserve public order, you are watched by the agents of the emperor (95–96). After this, we might expect a concluding section in which Dio would reconcile himself with his audience and sum up his teaching. What we find is the reverse. Wise though he was, the philosopher Theophilus (says Dio, 97) never once addressed you and never tried to teach you: you would not care to listen to him, just as dung-beetles will not taste honey. And I? Once there was a musician who dreamed he was fated to sing to a donkey: he performed for a visiting monarch who scorned his music; he recalled the dream; the monarch heard of his comment and had him flogged (101). So I (the implication is) am like a skilled artist performing before a stupid and cruel audience, resembling both a donkey and a tyrant.[51] No peroration, not even the briefest; but a dark and minatory phrase as conclusion: καὶ τοῦ-

---

[50] Arnim thinks Dio concluded his speech in such a quick offhand manner because he was improvising and found his time running short (Leben 475–76). But it would be a very unskillful orator who could not improvise a few minutes' peroration; and when did audiences ever give an improviser a time-limit?

[51] In this speech (25–28) the demos is explicitly compared to a potentate who can be either king or tyrant.

τὸ πολέμου λέγουσιν αἴτιον γένεσθαι (101). War. The Romans are the greatest warriors in the world and their emperor is a victorious commander: you Alexandrians are δειλοὶ καὶ ἀστράτευτοι (43): in a recent riot when the troops faced you, you had a taste of war, and suffered (72). To be highhanded with the representative of Roman power is dangerous. Beware. That is the meaning of this unusual and striking conclusion.[52]

The first speech to the Tarsians (Or. 33) Dio seems to end with a shout of scorn, hatred, and rage. In a rambling discourse he has accused them of habitually making curious noises—snorts or snuffles—which sound like the heavy breathing of men engaged in sexual intercourse.[53] He goes on to accuse their women of being sexually corrupt, although heavily veiled (48–49), and their menfolk of being effeminate (58–61), even shaving off their bodily hair (61–66) in the effort to become ἀνδρόγυνοι. Did this injurious word end the speech? If so, Dio must have turned away in contempt and walked off the platform among the shouts of a hostile crowd.[54] He would therefore conceive his relation to the men of Tarsus as like that of the Cynic who thought it essential to speak frankly to his crazy hearers, even when *parrhesia* became *loidoria*.[55]

Yet it is hard to imagine what positive effect Dio wished to produce on the Tarsians by this speech. It is hard also to conceive how he could address an audience in the same city in a more civil and diplomatic tone (Or. 34). Was he, in the thirty-fourth speech, speaking to the solid bour-

---

[52] E. Wilmes, *Beiträge zur Alexandrinerrede des Dio Chrysostomos* (Bonn, 1970), suggests that Dio concludes this oration sourly and pessimistically because he knows that immediately after he quits the platform the audience will shout "Bring on the conjurers!" (as in paragraph 7).

[53] ῥέγκουσι, 33.18. This is the only passage in pagan literature known to me where the sound of snorting or snuffling is given an explicitly sexual connotation. The verb, and nouns allied to it (ῥέγκος, *rhonchus* in Latin, ῥέγξις, ῥωχμός), are used of (1) snoring in sleep: Aesch. *Eum.* 53, Ar. *Nub.* 5; (2) the wheezing of persons stuffed with food: Clem. Al. p. 219; (3) a sniff expressing disdain and hostility: Mart. 1.3.5, 4.86.7; cf. *sanna* in Juv. 6.306, and see Amm. Marc. 14.6.25: *turpi sono fragosis naribus introrsum reducto spiritu concrepantes.* However, C. Bonner, "A Tarsian Peculiarity," *HThR* 35 (1942) 1–8, cites two passages from Christian authors in which snuffling or nasal speech and sexual perversion are clearly associated: Tatianus, *Ad Gr.* 22 and Clem. Al., *Paed.* 3.29.2–3. C. B. Welles, "Hellenistic Tarsus," *MUB* 38 (1962) 65–68, thinks Dio's denunciation is "a monstrous jest" designed to carry the true charge that the men of Tarsus were shaving their beards and neglecting philosophy. It is difficult to read the vivid description of homosexual behavior in paragraphs 52 and 63–64 (cf. Epict. 3.1) and accept Welles' kindly interpretation.

[54] Ἀλλ' ἀπελεύσεσθε ἀγανακτοῦντες (56). Dio was accustomed to one of the hardest ordeals of the orator, confronting an angry audience: see 32.22–24, 34.6.

[55] So 9.20; 9.22; 33.16; Diog. Laert. 6.32. Dio portrays himself as the lonely Cynic in 33.6–7 and 44 (the Cynic as physician) and 33.14; not infrequently elsewhere.

geoisie, and in the other oration delivering a challenge to "alienated" groups? No, scarcely. In Or. 33 the evil seems to be city-wide, and there is no hint that only the rich or the poor or the outcasts are affected by it.

One further dubious ending. Or. 16 is an elegant little discourse on pain—emphasizing emotional distress caused by illness or loss of money or damage to reputation (3), although including the pains of the body (7). Live, if only for a day, free of pain and fear and such afflictions, says Dio (9). How? Jason protected himself by Medea's magic ointment, and so he suffered nothing from the dragon and the fire-breathing bulls. We must use the salve of Intelligence, which makes us emotionally invulnerable. And then, a wonderful little sentence, one of the finest in all Dio's work: εἰ δὲ μή, πάντα πῦρ ἡμῖν καὶ πάντα ἄυπνοι δράκοντες. A perfect ending: unforgettable.

However, in the manuscripts another paragraph follows, disappointingly trivial in thought: just as men are physically strong or weak, so they are more or less able to endure pain. . . . Obvious and banal. Of these lines, Arnim says, "Neque cum antecedentibus satis cohaerent, neque sententiam plenam et absolutam continent," dismissing the final sentence as "aut valde corrupta aut a Dione aliena."[56] Similarly, Sonny (p. 191) remarks, "Ultima verba male cohaerent cum antecedentibus. Neque tamen a Dione abjudicanda sunt. Frustulum enim esse videntur ex commentariis scriptoris protractum." But neither scholar considers another possibility, that paragraph 11 may be the opening of a new line of argument, still on the same topic (τῶν λυπουμένων); and that the rest of the development may, as so often in other discourses, have been lost. Although the sentence about fire and sleepless dragons would make a superb conclusion, we must admit that Dio is seldom so laconic, so Tacitean: that, in fact, he rarely knows when to stop; and we may well conclude that with καίτοι (as so often)[57] he launched into an objection to his last point, followed by another series of arguments, now lost.

CONCLUSION

The discourses of Dio are very various in structure and purpose. Some of them are brief dialogues between teacher and pupil; some are short essays, some prefatory talks introducing a speech or a reading; some

[56] Text 2, p. 244.

[57] καίτοι: see 3.14; 6.40; 20.11; 31.30, 32, 43, 58, 69, 96, 101, 109, 115, 120; 32.47, 51, 56, 91; and many other passages. This is καίτοι adversative (Denniston, note 35 above, 556–57).

are large and serious political orations, others again ambitious philosophical disquisitions. Photius, the patriarch of Constantinople, read the eighty pieces which have come down to us under Dio's name, and wrote a summary of them, briefly outlining their subjects and commenting on Dio's style.[58] One of his remarks is particularly revealing.

> Dio never abandons his habit of stretching out the exordium or quasi-exordium, so that he slips from a political and literary style into the tone of conversation, and makes the head, so to speak, larger than the rest of the body.[59]

Now, Photius read quickly and sometimes superficially.[60] Even so, it seems clear that he read Dio's discourses in the same condition as we do; and that he was struck by the malformation in their structure. If only twenty-five paragraphs of a speech have survived, and twelve of these are occupied by the exordium, it is natural to suppose that the exordium is disproportionately large.[61]

We have suggested, then, that many of the speeches are incomplete, and were incomplete when they came into the hands of Photius. The question is, what brought them into this condition?

Before we try to answer it, one point must be made. There are no variations in the manuscript tradition affecting the beginnings and endings of the speeches. Some manuscripts omit a few sections inside a speech;[62] some omit whole speeches;[63] there are occasional repetitions of paragraphs. But no manuscript contains, at the opening or close of the speeches as they now exist, material which is unknown to all other witnesses. Therefore, when the collection now extant was formed, its editor (or editors) had, for a number of speeches, only mutilated copies, or, it may well be, only one mutilated copy available.

Exactly when he worked it is hard to tell. Obviously before Photius read the collection—that is, at some time earlier than A.D. 858.[64] Ob-

---

[58] Arnim reprints his remarks on Dio in Text 2, pp. 320–25.

[59] Arnim, Text 2, p. 321, lines 1–5.

[60] Witness his comments on *Or.* 13, where he summarizes approximately the first sixteen paragraphs, omits the rest (including the opening of Dio's important sermon to the Romans), and invents a false point, the mutability of fortune; on *Or.* 35, he talks chiefly about long hair (paragraphs 1–12) and misses the moral lesson; on *Or.* 27, he overlooks the parallel between symposium and panegyris; and on the fine Olympic speech his comment is perfectly vapid. Schmid's comment on p. 874 needs severe qualification: "Gründliche Kenntnis seiner Schriften [zeigt] Photios."

[61] Such is *Or.* 35.

[62] U and the books copied from it have a large gap in *Or.* 31, beginning at paragraph 32: see Arnim, Text 1, p. x.

[63] Arnim, Text 1, p. v; p. xxv.

[64] K. Krumbacher, *Geschichte der byzantinischen Litteratur* (Munich, 1897²) 517.

viously after Synesius wrote his essay on Dio (that is, about A.D. 403), since Synesius mentions many works by Dio which did not enter the present corpus and have vanished.[65] And, it is likely, before the middle of the seventh century, when Byzantine culture sank into a dark age which was to last far into the ninth.[66]

He used three types of material. First, complete and (although sometimes interpolated and lacunose) authoritative manuscripts of some of Dio's most characteristic speeches and essays: most of the big city-speeches, the *Borystheniticus*, the *Troicus*, some of the political orations delivered in or near his home, the two *Melancomas* pieces, *Charidemus*, and others.

Second, a large number of excerpts from Dio's verbal teaching: short discussions of general themes, *Law*, *Pain*, *Virtue*, and so on. Apparently Dio's pupils had taken down these monologues and conversations piece-meal in the same way as Arrian took down the discourses of Epictetus. But either Dio's pupils were less intelligent than Arrian (as Dio was a less considerable thinker than Epictetus) so that they sometimes recorded in-complete and intellectually unsatisfying extracts of his talk; or else, when the collection came into the hands of the editor, some of the individual pieces had already suffered damage.

Third, the editor had some important works of Dio which were in-complete. One, the *Euboicus*, lacked both its beginning and its ending. Others had lost their conclusions; some indeed were deprived of the de-velopment of their main theme as well as their peroration.

The last book of Juvenal's satires consists of four complete poems and one fragment. The fragment is the beginning of what was announced by the poet as a satire on a large important subject. To judge by the opening, it was two or three hundred lines long; but it stops dead in the middle of a sentence at line 60. There are several hundred manuscripts of Juvenal, but in every one the sixteenth satire breaks off at the sixtieth line. (The scholia have petered out fifteen lines earlier.) Therefore only one copy of the satires survived through the centuries after Juvenal's death, to reach the editors who, about A.D. 400, produced a text and a com-mentary and made him a classic.[67]

Similar mutilations appear in the text of Plutarch's *Moralia*. *De glo-ria Atheniensium*, *An uitiositas ad infelicitatem sufficiat*, *De inuidia et odio*, *De tribus r.p. generibus*, and one or two others lack both their beginnings and their endings. Material is missing at the opening of *De*

---

[65] His essay appears in Terzaghi's edition (note 37 above).

[66] Krumbacher (note 64 above) 12.

[67] G. Highet, *Juvenal the Satirist* (Oxford, 1954) 156–58, 186–87, and notes.

facie in orbe lunae. Several others break off sharply, with some of the argument still to be completed: *An uirtus doceri possit, Animine an corporis affectiones sint peiores,* the two discourses *De esu carnium; Bruta animalia ratione uti* stops with a question left unanswered, and *Ad principem indoctum* with an abrupt break; *De amore prolis* is likewise unfinished, and also, it would seem, *De cupiditate diuitiarum.*

Some of these may have been left as unfinished sketches by Plutarch himself, and published from his files after his death.[68] Others, more drastically mutilated, were apparently preserved through the Greek Dark Age only in physically damaged copies.[69] The essay *De anima procreatione in Timaeo* has two large sections interchanged, "also jedenfalls in der Zeit der Codices."[70]

The same sort of thing evidently happened to some of Dio's speeches. Although he says they were widely copied and disseminated, not under his supervision,[71] it is apparent that much later, when the collection which we have was being formed, the editor could find only one exemplar of certain orations, and that one damaged. Since a papyrus roll is more likely to suffer loss at the beginning than at the end, and since most of these mutilated works are cut short at the end, they must have been written, not on rolls, but on codices. Recent research has shown that the papyrus codex was a format which could be used to preserve works that were, so to speak, not officially in circulation: τοὺς ἐμοὺς λόγους σχεδὸν πάντες ἀλλήλοις ἀπαγγέλλουσιν, οὐχ ὅπως ἐρρήθησαν, ἀλλ' ἔτι βελτίους ποιήσαντες (42.4). C. H. Roberts has suggested that the earliest Gospel, that attributed to St. Mark, was first written down and circulated in this form (it seems to have lost its ending); and a fairly large number of papyrus codices written in the second, third, and fourth centuries A.D. have been discovered.[72]

The conclusion is therefore that the extant collection of Dio's works was made long after his death, at a time when many of his once famous speeches had disappeared and when others survived in only a single copy, and that mutilated.

[68] So Pohlenz quoted by K. Ziegler (note 43 above) 779.

[69] Nothing is heard of Plutarch in the Greek East between Agathias and Photius (Ziegler, note 43 above, 949).

[70] Ziegler (note 43 above) 745.

[71] *Or.* 42.4–5.

[72] C. H. Roberts, "The Codex," *PBA* 40 (1955) 169–204, esp. 184–85, 187–90; E. G. Turner, *Greek Papyri* (Princeton, 1968) 10–12.

LATIN LITERATURE

The Shipwrecked Slaver

THE TWO villains of Plautus's *Rudens*, Labrax the greedy pander and his disreputable accomplice Charmides, do not appear until line 485. Then they come up the cliff, still dripping and shivering from their shipwreck. The scene begins and ends with ordinary dramatic conversation: they curse their luck and each other, they lament their losses, and they fit the end of their conversation neatly into the plot by remarking that things would not be so bad if the girls had not been drowned. (The girls have of course escaped; and thirty seconds later Sceparnio enters, loudly asking the audience what has come over the two girls who are weeping in the temple.)

The middle of the scene, however, has nothing to do with the plot. It is a series of disjointed jokes, usually just two lines long. Both Labrax and Charmides step quite out of character when they exchange remarks like:

535 LA. Suppose I joined a circus, as an ogre!
CH. Why?
LA. Why, because my teeth keep clashing loudly!

At the beginning and end of the scene, Labrax is much too miserable to offer jokes for Charmides' amusement, and, even if he were not, Charmides is much too miserable to ask him to explain them. Both the matter and the form of this particular joke are Roman anyhow, not Greek—the ogre (*Manducus*) was the clown who walked in processions wearing a big head with movable jaws. The other jokes in this section too are fairly obviously Roman. Fraenkel[1] describes the whole passage (516–39) as a

Reprinted from *AJPh* 63 (1942) 462–66.

[1] E. Fraenkel, *Plautinisches im Plautus* (Berlin, 1922) 112.

"coarse expansion" of the original, made by Plautus himself. If it is cut
out, he says, the scene will run straight on from 515 to 540.

That is probably true. But we must not be led by this to imagine
that a poet so versatile as Plautus was content merely to translate the rest
of the scene phrase by phrase from his Greek original and to add nothing
of his own until he came to a place where twenty-five lines of "gagging"
could be inserted. For instance, the first speech of Labrax opens with a
gentle joke about the dangers of associating with Neptune (485–88), and
goes on to a stronger one, which no one now understands because the
myth is lost (489–90):

> How smart of you, Liberty, to refuse
> ever to go to sea with Hercules!

(This is a double-edged joke. In the first place, the comparison between
the miserable human castaway and the wise if somewhat abstract deity is
funny; and, secondly, it is ridiculous to hear the slave-dealer praising
Liberty.)

A little later there is another joke which has always seemed rather
pointless. Labrax suddenly says:

> 510 LA. Oh dear, I feel so bad. Please hold my head!
> CH. I really wish you'd spew out all your lungs.

Evidently, Labrax is sick on the stage, suddenly and very briefly. In the
very next line, however, he has recovered, and is, like Shylock, lament-
ing his ducats and his daughters:

> 512 LA. Palaestra, Ampelisca, where are you now?

Now, what is the point of line 510? Line 511 accepts the fact that
Labrax is being sick and makes a little cruel fun of the fact. But line 510
looks as though it were meant to be funnier than it is.

In the first place, Plautus and his audiences (and doubtless his originals) did not think it was funny to see people being sick on the stage.
Aristophanes is full of gross jokes about such acts—they are described, or
actually performed, in elaborate detail. But throughout Plautus and the
fragments of Roman comedy there is not one other scene in which a
character is actually seen performing one of the coarser physical functions. There are in fact only nine or ten indirect references to vomiting
in the plays;[2] and they are mostly brief scurrilous threats, like *Cas.* 732:

---

[2] *Amph.* 329, *Curc.* 74 and 688, *Merc.* 389 and 575, *Mostell.* 652. Mimes, of course,
are different: cf. Pomponius, fr. 130 (Ribbeck).

        potin a me abeas
        nisi me uis
        uomere hodie?

The nearest thing to the incident in the *Rudens* is *Pseudolus* 952:

    Ps.   credo, animo malest
            aedibus.
    SIM.   quid iam?
    Ps.   quia edepol ipsum lenonem euomunt.

Still, although that is not a drawing-room joke, it is not a physical act.

Second, it is not even very appropriate for Labrax to be suddenly seasick, and as suddenly to recover, in the middle of a conversation. He has been out of the water for about twenty minutes—long enough to climb up the cliff and speak the first lines of the scene. If he were seriously sick from the effects of the wreck (as Sosia says he is from the voyage in *Amph.* 329), more would be made of it; both Labrax and Charmides make a great deal of the dampness and chills which afflict them, from 523 to 536.

Therefore there may be something more in the joke than meets the eye. Let us look at the lines before it. Charmides tops off a rather random exchange of well-earned abuse by an allusion to the dinner at which (497, 501) he became the guest-friend of Labrax:

    508 CH.   scelestiorem cenam cenaui tuam
               quam quae Thyestae quondam aut posita est Tereo.
         LA.   perii, animo male fit. contine quaeso caput.

Now, the feast of Thyestes (like the feast of Tereus), at which he ate the corpses of his own children, was the climax of the saga. Both banquets were often described by poets and portrayed by tragedians. The scene is always conceived in the same way: Thyestes (or Tereus) dines in state, encouraged by his treacherous host. Immediately after the feast, he is told that he has eaten his own children's flesh. At once he leaps up, and either vomits it out or tries to do so. The poets describe this act with varying degrees of realism, according as they are grandly truthful like Aeschylus, or subtly sophisticated like Seneca. Here are the most notable descriptions of it.

        κἄπειτ' ἐπιγνοὺς ἔργον οὐ καταίσιον
        ᾤμωξεν, ἀμπίπτει δ' ἀπὸ σφαγὴν ἐρῶν.
                                    Aeschylus, *Ag.* 1598

quis hic tumultus uiscera exagitat mea? . . .
uoluuntur intus uiscera, et clusum nefas
sine exitu luctatur et quaerit fugam.

Seneca, *Thy.* 999, 1041–42

et modo, si posset, reserato pectore diras
egerere inde dapes immersaque uiscera gestit.

Ovid, *Met.* 6.663 (of Tereus)

Ovid and Seneca, of course, could not say anything so drastic as Aeschylus's ἀπὸ σφαγὴν ἐρῶν, and they have converted it into the victim's wish to cut himself open: Seneca in a peculiarly digusting epigram says "ferro liberis detur uia." But it is perfectly clear what the original dénouement was. Neither Thyestes nor Tereus committed suicide; they could not calmly continue with the process of digestion: they must therefore have behaved as Aeschylus says.

Parodies of tragedy are of course extremely frequent in Plautus.[3] They are mainly verbal reminiscences.[4] But sometimes they are allusions to the plot and stage effects of a recently produced tragedy: as in this very play (line 86), where Sceparnio explains to the audience how violent was the storm which knocked the tiles off his master's roof (and caused the shipwreck), by saying

non uentus fuit, uerum Alcumena Euripidi.

I suggest that the rather flat line 510, with the imitation vomiting which accompanied it, was a parodic allusion to the feast of Thyestes or Tereus. As soon as Labrax hears the monstrous banquet mentioned, he vomits—as the unhappy father had done in the tragedy. Of course the tragic poet would not show anything like this on the stage; but he would have it described by a messenger; while for Plautus's audience the joke of seeing what the tragedian had only described would justify its coarseness.

It is unfortunately impossible to tell what tragedy Plautus was parodying in this passage. Livius Andronicus wrote a *Tereus*, which must have been produced before his death *ca.* 204. Ennius's *Thyestes* appeared in 169 (Cicero, *Brut.* 78), which is too late for Plautus to have parodied

---

[3] A. G. Kiessling thought the parodies were all in Plautus's originals: *Analecta Plautina* (Progr., Greifswald, 1878 and 1882) I.14; II.ix. F. Leo, *Plautinische Forschungen zur Kritik und Geschichte der Kömodie* (Berlin, 1912) 132. Fraenkel (note 1 above) 67f., 88f.

[4] *Bacch.* 933 and 1053, *Cas.* 621, *Pseud.* 703, *Rud.* 523, *Stich.* 365, and *Truc.* 931 are some of the more notable examples, with, of course, the prologue to the *Poenulus.* See O. Ribbeck, *Scaenicae Romanorum Poesis Fragmenta* (Leipzig, 1871 and 1873) 2 vols., especially vol. 1, pp. 269–70.

it here.[5] There is no surviving fragment of Roman tragedy describing this
scene. But both Plautus and his audiences knew the legends (that of
Tereus is alluded to once again in the *Rudens*, at 604), and it can only
have been from Roman tragedies that they knew them. Even as explained, the joke is not very good; but it is rather better than it has hitherto been thought to be.

[5] O. Ribbeck, *Die Römische Tragödie im Zeitalter der Republik* (Leipzig, 1875) 202
suggests that its climax was the entry of Thyestes after the feast (fragments II and VIII).

Lucretius

THE MATERIAL of the world is not what it seems to be. A solid, like rock, or a fluid, like water, is only apparently solid or fluid. Both the rock and the water are composed of myriads of invisible particles which are associated by laws of their own and are in constant movement.

This earth and the sun and moon and planets, all our universe, in fact, is made up of atoms. The atoms came together to form them, as tiny drops of water come together to form a huge river. In time the atoms will separate again, and our universe will cease to exist, as a river does when it runs into the desert and evaporates. But the atoms will never cease to exist. They, and they alone, are eternal.

Earthquakes, volcanic eruptions, epidemics, and such disasters are not caused by God's anger. They are natural phenomena and can be explained scientifically.

Sensation and thought are functions of the body. The soul is not immortal, but is born in the body, develops with it, and will cease to exist when the other physical functions, such as respiration and heartbeat, stop.

Of these four propositions, most civilized people in the Western world nowadays believe the first and the third. Many believe the second. Some believe the fourth. All four were accepted as unquestionable truth by many Greeks and Romans; they became the theme of a magnificent Latin poem; they were maintained for at least five centuries; and thereafter, for a thousand years, they were buried in oblivion. The first and second, if anyone had even thought of them in the Middle Ages, would have been dismissed as ridiculous; the third and fourth as blasphemous.

Reprinted from *Horizon* 6.2 (Spring 1964) 28–32.

And yet the Latin poem built on these statements somehow survived. That such a book, opposed to all the tenets of medieval Christianity and common sense, should have been laboriously copied out in the ninth century, obviously by monks who understood some of what they read and transcribed, is truly surprising. The poem itself, and the character of its author, are something of a mystery, too. But one thing is certain: it is a superb poem and it was written by a great poet. His name was Lucretius. He wrote it about sixty years before the birth of Jesus, and he called it *The Nature of Things*, i.e. *The Nature of the Universe*.

Who Lucretius was, where he lived, how he learned (or taught himself) to write so well, who his friends were, and even what social status he held, we have no way of knowing. None of his contemporaries ever mentions him by name—except Cicero, who remarks that his poetry is full not only of genius but also of technical skill, and Nepos, who refers in passing to his death. Several centuries later, in a historical survey, a sort of World Almanac, St. Jerome states that Lucretius was born in 94 B.C. and died at the age of forty-three; another late writer places his death in 55 B.C., but the discrepancy is small. He was evidently about a dozen years younger than Julius Caesar and more than twenty years older than Vergil. This agrees, also, with the historical allusions in his poem. Clearly he lived through many of the desperate wars and revolutionary outbreaks that devastated the Roman world in the early first century before Christ, and died not long before they came to their climax in Caesar's successful attack on the Republic. He speaks of himself as a Roman born and bred; obviously he was well educated in literature and philosophy, both Latin and Greek; probably he was a gentleman of independent means and retiring nature; certainly he was a genius.

Lucretius did not invent the doctrines that are the body of his poem. What he did was to clothe them in noble verse of a power and subtlety previously unknown in Latin, devise lucid and eloquent illustrations for them, and infuse them with such a perfectly unmistakable and all but irresistible personal emotion that he often seems—over the gulf of time and through the barrier of language—to speak directly to us from heart to heart. The poetry is his. The doctrines are those of Epicurus.

Epicurus was an Athenian schoolmaster's son who founded a philosophical college in Athens in 306 B.C., and taught his own system of philosophy quietly and successfully there for nearly forty years. It was not merely a place of instruction, but a community of friends. Although Epicurus was a prodigiously energetic writer, the center of his school was not thought of as the library, but as the garden; and perhaps the Hindu word *ashram* would best describe the serenity and dedication of the place.

Although he was a mild, pure-hearted man, his name has become the Hebrew word for an unbeliever or renegade, *apikoros*; and although he was scrupulously moderate in diet and called a pot of cheese a luxurious treat, an "epicure" in English and French is a devoted gourmet like Brillat-Savarin.

Epicurus claimed to have originated his entire philosophy, but he owed much to his predecessors. The theory that the physical universe is composed of an infinite number of variously shaped atoms constantly moving in void space was worked out a century before his birth by two brilliant philosophical thinkers, Leucippus and his pupil Democritus. By anticipating some of the most advanced scientific discoveries of our own era, and by doing so without complex apparatus, almost wholly through pure speculative reasoning, these two men gave one of those demonstrations of penetrating and comprehensive thought that justify us in calling the Greeks the founders of Western civilization.

Epicurus took their description of the structure of matter and united it with ethical, psychological, social, and religious teachings of his own. Among the four propositions stated at the beginning of this article, Leucippus and Democritus enunciated the first and second; they would have accepted the third and fourth, and perhaps they actually set them down, although their books are now lost. But it was Epicurus who built all four into a coherent system which, with its many ramifications and its subtle analyses, claimed to solve all the important problems of the world, and in particular to show mankind the secret of true happiness.

The secret, Epicurus maintained, was easy to understand. Only mental sloth, or superstition, or timidity, or evil custom kept everyone from grasping it. It could be stated in a series of interlocking propositions, and, memorized, could become an ever-present guide through life. Its basis was . . . but let Lucretius explain it.

> The terror and the darkness in the mind must yield
> not to the sun or to the glittering shafts of day
> but to the knowledge and analysis of nature.
> Now, first, the great initial principle is this:
> *nothing is made from nothing by the power of God.*
> This is the fear that grips the hearts of all mankind:
> many events they see on earth and in the sky
> and cannot understand the causes there at work:
> so therefore they believe the will of God controls them.

The second principle corresponds to this. As nothing is created out of nothing,

so further, nature causes all things to dissolve
into their atoms, but does not annihilate them.
The atoms are immortal, indestructible,
and so they cannot ever be obliterated.
No thing can be reduced to nothing; every thing
reverts by dissolution to the basic atoms.

Having laid down this double principle, Lucretius (following the lost work of his master, Epicurus) goes on to give arguments to support it and to demonstrate how it explains many of the phenomena that puzzle minds untrained in logic and science. Sensation, perception, thought, and such psychical events as dreams and visions—he explains them all. But although most of his analysis is scientific, his purpose lies beyond pure science. The real beauty of Epicureanism, he repeats again and again, is that it sets us free from the two great fears: fear of God and fear of death. It does not deny the existence of a divinity. There *are* gods, superhuman in power, supernal in beauty, but they exist far away from our world, illimitably far. Since they are perfectly happy, they do not busy themselves with interfering in mundane affairs: they do not slash the earth with a trident to cause earthquakes, or hurl the thunderbolts that sometimes hit their own temples, or send epidemic diseases among their worshipers. Nor do they answer prayers; nor even hear prayers. We can honor them; we need not fear them. We know of their existence only through visions. They themselves know nothing of our world, and exist far off in outer space.

There are the dwellings of the gods, remote, serene,
which never windblasts shake, or darkling tempests drench
with rain, or cold gray crystal snow and freezing hail
besmirch, but always in a cloudless firmament
poised, they remain in spacious smiling radiance.

And death? It is this fear, the greatest of all human fears, that is the most central and most urgent theme of Lucretius's poem. Again and again with passionate emphasis he explains that death is nothing to be feared because it means—nothingness. It is cessation. A man fears death, he explains, because he illogically thinks of himself as *being* the dead corpse that is put away in the ground or burned to ashes on the pyre. But this is absurd. When the functions of life cease, sensation and thought come to an end, total and final. The body dissolves into dust and then into primordial atoms—and where is the man? He is where he was a thousand years before his birth.

Consider how the ages of eternal time
meant nothing to us while we did not yet exist.
This is a mirror held for us by nature, showing
all that the future means after we meet our death.
Is any horror there, or any sense of sadness?
Is it not all as peaceful and as calm as sleep?

As for hell and its torments—all that is an old wives' tale. Or rather, it is a projection of this life. Sisyphus, rolling the huge stone forever up the mountain and doomed to see it roll back, exemplifies insatiate ambition. The Danaides, condemned to draw water in leaky vessels, are those restless spirits who in this life constantly seek for pleasures and are never satisfied. Cerberus, and the Furies, and the demons of punishment—they exist, but they are the torments of fear and remorse that the guilty suffer in this existence, which is for each of us the only one. Therefore, be tranquil. Enjoy your life, which nature has made so pleasant; and do not sit on and on at the table, but make way for others when, for you, the feast is over.

Such is the doctrine of Epicurus, as presented by Lucretius in more than seven thousand lines of superb poetry. Epicurus himself wrote three hundred books; all but three letters to pupils giving summaries of parts of his teaching, two collections of aphorisms, and some few fragments of his works have been destroyed. However, other writers, who record his career and analyze his work, tell us enough of it to make it clear that Lucretius's *Nature of the Universe* is not a flat verse transcription of the founder's theory, but a highly personal document which must be handled sensitively and imaginatively if we are to understand it.

The difference between the doctrine of Epicurus and the poem of Lucretius is far more than the difference between prose (crabbed technical Greek prose) and verse (rolling melodious Latin hexameters). It is the difference between assured serenity and repressed excitement; between cool conviction and eager persuasion; and, ultimately, between certainty and doubt. Epicurus teaches like a man who never felt a tremor in his heart or a shadow fall on his intellect. Lucretius argues with a tense urgency that ranges all the way from the exultation of a triumphal hymn, through the slangy bitterness of social satire, to the hopeless melancholy of a dirge.

And why? Whom is he trying to convince?

Lucretius dedicates *The Nature of the Universe* to a Roman nobleman called Memmius, whom he treats as a friend and a potential convert:

It is your merit, and the pleasure I shall reap
from your sweet friendship, which persuade me to endure
this toilsome effort, spending many peaceful nights
in search of phrases and poetic melody
to kindle a bright light within your intellect
and show you all the secrets of the universe.

Yet Memmius appears only a dozen times throughout the poem: in the first, second, and fifth books. In the last book he is not even mentioned. From a private letter of Cicero we learn that, having acquired the old house of Epicurus in Athens, Memmius proposed to tear it down and build a palace for himself on the site—although it was a shrine revered by all Epicurus's followers. Does this not mean that he remained unconverted to Epicureanism (which indeed was alien to his restless, greedy character), and that Lucretius dedicated the work to him merely as a conventional civility?

The poem seems rather to be aimed at you, the sympathetic reader. "You must have noticed," says Lucretius, and we assent; or he says, "Come, let me tell you," and we follow his argument. This is a didactic poem, then, meant not for one man but for all who wish to understand the nature of the universe.

Yet, if we read the poem carefully, not simply as a nexus of scientific theorems but as a series of emotional experiences, we shall notice something else. It is profoundly pessimistic. Epicurus's teaching is, on the whole, optimistic. Life, it holds, is easy to enjoy if you are sensible about it: a few friends, a retired garden, simple food, a tranquil mind, these are the sum of human welfare. Excitement—sexual passion, the intoxication of wine, or any emotional outburst—is highly dangerous; gloomy forebodings and dismal sights should naturally be shunned. Now consider the shape of Lucretius's poem. It opens with a magnificent, full-chorded paean to Venus, mother of the Romans, bringer of peace, personification of pleasure, spirit of spring and love and creative Nature—a wonderful passage which inspired Botticelli to paint *Mars and Venus*.

Kind lady Venus, cause the savage work of war
to rest in calm surcease throughout the sea and land.
For you, and you alone, can bless mankind with quiet
peace: all the savage work of war is ruled by Mars
the warrior, who often sinks upon your breast
a helpless victim of the quenchless wound of love;
with supple neck supine, he gazes up to you,
feasting his greedy eyes and drinking in your beauty,

a captive hanging helpless on your breathing lips.
Embrace him with your sacred body, lady Venus,
and while he lies enraptured, speak sweet pleading words
beseeching him to grant the Romans rest and peace.

Some seven thousand lines later it ends with a detailed clinical and so-
ciological account of the fearful epidemic of typhus which devastated
Athens during the Peloponnesian War four centuries before. This description comes in logically enough. Lucretius is explaining a number of
curious phenomena which seem to be incomprehensible—lightning
strokes, earthquakes, volcanic eruptions—and thereby demonstrating that
the atomic theory makes them all intelligible. In due time he reaches
epidemics. These, he says, are caused by tiny invisible particles inimical
to human and animal life, which are carried by the air and taken in
through breathing, and which sometimes corrupt water, grass, and green
crops. This is an intelligent anticipation of the germ theory. Lucretius
might have stopped there. Instead, he goes on to turn into somber poetry
the description of the plague at Athens given by the historian Thucydides. Detail after grisly detail is given, with an emotional fervor quite
different from that of a historian: the throat closed by swollen ulcers, the
tongue dripping with blood, the breath as foul as the stench of a decaying
corpse, burning fever, insanity, interrupted breathing, at last the signs of
death in the hollowed cheeks and nostrils and bared teeth. Enough? No.
Lucretius does not stop there; he goes on, still with the same febrile,
fascinated attention, to describe the disintegration of society, the sick dying
in the streets, the many corpses lying unburied, and the sad rites of burial
thus perverted.

Panic and hideous poverty persuaded them
to run amok and seize the pyres built up by others
and lay the corpses of their own kinsfolk upon them
and kindle them forthwith: they came to blows and bloodshed,
fighting in fury, rather than desert the corpses.

These are the last words. This is the end of a poem designed to free
mankind from fear, to teach that life can be understood and lived out in
a state of tranquil happiness.

You will at once say that this passage is unfinished; that the description has not been completed. It breaks off in the midst of a scene of
demoralization, with no paragraph to round out and emphasize the initial purpose of the whole discussion: the argument that epidemic diseases,
however horrible, have a logical explanation. True. Writing long afterward, St. Jerome states that Cicero "emended" the poem. This may

mean that he corrected a few faults of diction; or it may mean that he (or his brother Quintus, who also read it) actually prepared the poem for publication. If so, Lucretius died leaving it incomplete. There remains, unresolved, the hideous discord between the opening of the poem and its present close; between the Epicurean doctrine of tranquil pleasure enjoyed by individuals and this overattentive description of the physical and moral collapse of a civilization.

We find the same dissonance elsewhere. The poem is set out in six books. Each of the six opens with a grand, confident invocation, glorifying the godlike genius of Epicurus, extolling the freedom from fear given by true philosophy, and so forth. Of the six, only one closes optimistically, with a rising curve; one has a neutral and apparently imperfect conclusion; the other four end in thoughts of gloom, dissolution, and death. Book 2, for instance, fades out with a picture of a despairing farmer trying to wring crops out of our aging and exhausted earth—a picture that makes an irreconcilable antithesis to Book 1, with its glorification of Nature ever young and fresh. Book 3, after calmly explaining that, since the soul is mortal, death is nothing to be feared, moves into this grim final chord:

> Prolong your life for many years, for centuries;
> yet none the less eternal death will still be waiting,
> and he who ends his life before sunset today
> will be no more through the same vast eternity
> as he who perished many months or years before.

I emphasize these structural contrasts because Roman writers paid special attention to the preludes and finales of their poems and of each main section of their poems, and because I do not believe critics have paid adequate attention to these discords in Lucretius. The last book opens with a glorification of Athens as the birthplace of agriculture and civilization and the supreme philosopher Epicurus, and breaks off in a description of the devastating plague of Athens.

On a smaller scale the same clash of major and minor keys can be heard throughout the poem. Again and again, in a passage that opens with serene confidence in Epicurean logic and the liberating power of the intellect, Lucretius will falter, and flag, and begin to brood, while the firmness of his reasoning seems to be overborne by the dark, confused power of his imagination. What begins as a clear-brained, optimistic analysis of a problem changes into something more like the cloudy, melancholy monologues of Hamlet.

And on a far larger scale there is another problem. Admitting that the last book is imperfect, and supposing that we could somehow reconstruct its lost or unwritten conclusion—would the poem then be complete? Most critics seem to fancy it would. They consider that these six books—which give us a reasonably complete Epicurean analysis of the physical universe, the body-and-soul unity, the inception of this world and the evolution of mankind, the sexual instinct, the origins of religious belief, and certain major scientific questions such as volcanic activity— were all that Lucretius intended to write; yet I think they are mistaken. The central purpose of Epicurus's teaching was not to explain atoms and earthquakes, but to teach men how to live. The motive for understanding physics and cosmology and psychophysical interaction and so forth was, says Lucretius, to escape from fear—and then to learn how to live rightly. And it was Epicurus's highly individual ethical system that made the greatest impression on Greek and Roman thinkers. Therefore I believe that Lucretius, having explained the physical universe in his first six books, meant to go on to analyze moral and social problems in his second six books: to give us the Epicurean method of attaining and preserving happiness, to explain the true meaning of "pleasure" as a state of calm well-being, to show why the wise man will shun social duties and responsibilities, prefer the status of a resident alien, and "live in secret." These essential teachings, more than any amount of knowledge about cosmology, would really bring happiness to his readers, to Memmius (if Lucretius still remembered him), and to himself.

To himself. Is that not the key to all these problems of poetic structure and imagination?

One curious statement about Lucretius appears, not in any contemporary or near-contemporary writer, but in the Christian chronicle of St. Jerome: that he was driven mad by a love philter administered by his wife, wrote the poem in his lucid intervals, and committed suicide. A distinguished English poet who had affinities with both Vergil and Lucretius, Alfred Tennyson, accepted this statement and converted it into a remarkable dramatic monologue called *Lucretius*—a soliloquy of great power and passion spoken by a thinker who finds himself struggling against the terrible visions of madness. We have no way of judging whether it is true or not: love philters were often used by Roman women, sometimes with dire effects. And certainly there is, both in the fourth book of Lucretius's poem and in Tennyson's re-creation of his troubled mind, an unusual, un-Roman, unphilosophical interest in sex and its aberrations. In Book 4 is a passage which looks as though it had been developed from Epicurus's simple warning, "Sexual intercourse has never done anyone any good and may well have done harm," into the idea that sexual activity was either a disagreeable routine, or a dangerous form of insanity, or . . . and again Lucretius drifts inconclusively away.

If we were to read the poem without knowledge of Jerome's report, we might reach a similar, but simpler, conclusion. A poet who vacillates between lofty confidence in reason and feverish fascination with decay and death, whose arguments are often compulsively repetitive and sometimes trail away into half-comprehensible reveries, and whose final lines describe, with gruesome intensity, mania and death—was he not endeavoring, through meditation upon those doctrines which with great technical and linguistic skill he turned from hard Greek prose into rich Latin poetry, to liberate, not Memmius or his other readers, but himself, from the horror of great darkness? And did he succeed, or fail?

Performances of Vergil's *Bucolics*

THE BUCOLICS were publicly recited, or chanted, or sung, in theaters during Vergil's lifetime. So says the Donatus life (ed. Hardie 91–92): *Bucolica eo successu edidit, ut in scena quoque per cantores crebro pronuntiarentur.* In a recent essay on the methods by which poetry was publicly delivered or performed by the Romans, Dr. W. Allen says that the phrase *per cantores* requires elucidation: adding, "My interpretation is that only one *cantor* performed at a time, although possibly several successively on the same occasion."[1]

The matter can be elucidated by a close look at the *Bucolics.* Three of them are duets: 1, 5, and 9. Three others are duets attended by a third person as auditor or umpire: 3, 7, and 8. Two are plain solos: 2 and 4. Two are solos with other voices heard within them: 6 and 10.

It would be neither difficult nor unattractive for a single performer to deliver the solos: Dr. Allen reminds us that, according to Servius on *Buc.* 6.11, the famous Cytheris performed (*cantare* is the verb used) *Buc.* 6 in the theater. But a sensitive audience would find it intolerable to have the duets spoken or sung or chanted by a soloist, however versatile he or she might be. The main point of Vergil's duets—amoebean or other—is the contrast in mood between the two singers. To have *Buc.* 7.53–60 (for instance) uttered by the same man would ruin the pointed conflicts—or else make the poem sound like a dialogue between a ventriloquist and his dummy. Similarly, where there are three characters, the appropriate performing cast would be three *cantores.* Consider *Buc.* 3.55–63. One voice says "Incipe, Damoeta; tu deinde sequere Menalca.

Reprinted from *Vergilius* 20 (1974) 24–25.
[1] "Ovid's *cantare* and Cicero's *cantores Euphorionis*," TAPhA 103 (1972) 5.

. . ." It should then be a second voice (already heard in lines 2, 7–9, etc.) that proclaims "Ab Ioue principium . . ." while a third takes up the pattern of thought with "Et me Phoebus amat. . . ."

As for the two poems in which there is one principal speaker but other utterances than his are heard, we might think of Eliot's *Waste Land*—which the poet originally called (with an allusion to a boy in Dickens reading a newspaper aloud) *He Do the Police in Different Voices*.[2] *The Waste Land* gains enormously in force and clarity if it is read aloud by a group of people, each representing one of the many personages whose voices are heard: e.g. the Baltic-German noblewoman in the first section. In the same way the effect of both *Buc.* 6 and *Buc.* 10 would be greatly enhanced, and the emotional values of their various phases or movements much intensified, if several different speakers were used, with a change at each change of voice: for example, when Gallus speaks of his sufferings in *Buc.* 10.31–69. This may have been done, or may not. At least it seems likely that when the *Bucolics* were publicly performed, those written in dialogue were spoken (or sung) in dialogue, *per cantores*.

[2] See Valerie Eliot, ed., *The Waste Land: A Facsimile and Transcript of the Original Drafts* (New York, 1971) 5, 11, 17, and 125.

A Lacuna in the *Aeneid*

THERE IS a small problem in Vergil's account of Amata's madness (*Aen.* 7.373–405). After rushing wildly through the streets, the queen flees into the woods and mountains. All the married women leave their homes and follow her as shrieking bacchantes, loosening their hair, donning animal skins, and carrying *thyrsi* wreathed with vine leaves. In their midst Amata holds a flaming torch.

The problem is a matter of two adjectives. Vergil writes:

> fama uolat, furiisque accensas pectore matres
> idem *omnis* simul ardor agit noua quaerere tecta.
> deseruere domos, uentis dant colla comasque.
> ast *aliae* tremulis ululatibus aethera complent
> pampineasque gerunt incinctae pellibus hastas.
> ipsa inter medias flagrantem feruida pinum
> sustinet. . . . (392–98)

They *all* left their homes. But *others* filled the air with shrieks. The logic is wrong.

This was noticed in antiquity by a corrector in the Medicean manuscript, who changed *aliae* to *illae*.[1] And indeed *ast* occurs six times in the *Aeneid* juxtaposed to a form of *ille*. However, in each case a strong opposition is implied: 1.116 *ast illam (nauem)* × *magister*; 3.330 *ast illum (Pyrrhum)* × *me (Andromachen)*; 5.468 *ast illum (Dareta)* × *Aeneas et Entellus*; 5.676 *ast illae (matres Troianae)* × *Aeneas et agmina Teucrum*; 9.162 *ast illos (bis septem)* × *centeni*; 12.951 *ast illi (Turno)* ×

Reprinted from *CPh* 71 (1976) 337–38.
[1] Given as ᴀLLAE in O. Ribbeck's apparatus, in *P. Vergili Maronis Opera*, vol. 3 (Leipzig, 1895). Servius, by the way, makes no comment.

Aeneas. But in the passage from the seventh book there is no such opposition between *omnis* (*matres*) and *aliae* (*matres*). How to explain *ast aliae?*

Peerlkamp, in his edition of 1843, printed the text as given above, but, in a note, suggested transposing lines 395 and 396. "Prius vestitum aliarum mulierum descripsit, tum dixit, quid illae facerent, mox quid ipsa, princeps, regina mater." Ribbeck printed the lines transposed, crediting Peerlkamp in the apparatus.[2] Yet this transposition does nothing to solve the problem: it still makes Vergil write *omnis* followed by *ast aliae.*

Forms of *alius* appear with *ast* elsewhere in the poem. In each case the person or persons denoted by *alius* is linked to, but contrasted with, a group previously mentioned. So in 2.465–67 the Trojans push a tower over upon Greek soldiers, crushing them; *ast alii subeunt.* In 4.487–88 the Massylian witch claims power to set free from the pangs of love "mentes / quas uelit, ast aliis duras immittere curas." Charon in 6.315–16 admits now this group and now that to his boat; *ast alios longe summotos arcet harena.* When the Trojans are driven back into their camp, Pandarus closes the gate, leaving many of his own people outside; *ast alios secum includit,* among them the enemy Turnus (9.727).

On the basis of these parallels it seems likely that in 7.392–96 one term of the contrast implied by *ast aliae* is missing. *Omnis* will not stand in opposition to *ast aliae.* The pattern desiderated is (1) *omnis*; (2) *x*; (3) *ast aliae.* What is *x*, the missing second term?

The answer is suggested by one of the passages which were at the back of Vergil's mind: Catullus's description of the bacchantes in 64.254–64.

> quae tum alacres passim lymphata mente furebant
> euhoe bacchantes, euhoe capita inflectentes.
> harum *pars* tecta quatiebant cuspide thyrsos,
> *pars* e diuolso iactabant membra iuuenco,
> *pars* sese tortis serpentibus incingebant,
> *pars* obscura cauis celebrabant orgia cistis,
> orgia quae frustra cupiunt audire profani;
> plangebant *aliae* proceris tympana palmis
> aut tereti tenuis tinnitus aere ciebant;
> *multis* raucisonos efflabant cornua bombos
> barbaraque horribili stridebat tibia cantu.

[2]Curiously, he omits any mention of Peerlkamp on p. 82 of his *Prolegomena critica ad P. Vergili Maronis* (Leipzig, 1866), writing, "Turbatum versuum ordinem perverse insertis quae in marginem coniecta fuerant deprehendi vv. 395 sq."

Here the first two lines describe in general terms the women's frenzy. (Catullus's *euhoe bacchantes* has suggested Vergil's *euhoe Bacche fremens* in 7.389, and his *passim furebant* reappears in Vergil as *furiisque accensas pectore matres . . . omnis.*) Thereafter Catullus describes six typical manifestations of bacchic excitement, distinguishing them by *pars, pars, pars, pars, aliae, multis.*

Similarly Vergil begins by describing the bacchic frenzy in general terms (392–94). But thereafter only one single group of the bacchantes appears, introduced by a phrase, *ast aliae*, which implies that there were others.

There are a number of gaps in the texture of the *Aeneid:* places where Vergil, having worked on a passage, left it temporarily unfinished, even if its logical or imaginative sequence was incomplete. Two clear cases are 10.721–29, where one stage in the simile is lacking, and 10.328–44, which stops long before the incident comes to an end.[3] I suggest that there is a similar gap in this passage—not a lacuna in the manuscript tradition, but a lacuna in the poet's composition. Vergil intended to describe one or several groups of revelers (introducing them by *pars, pars*) before *ast aliae*. Had he lived to do so, the passage would have been complete and the logical inconsistency would have ceased to exist. Therefore an editor of the poem who takes account of such gaps (as all modern editors by their typography acknowledge the existence of unfinished lines) will print the passage thus:

> deseruere domos, uentis dant colla comasque.
>
>   *   *   *   *   *
>
> ast aliae tremulis ululatibus aethera complent . . .

[3] Discussed in G. Highet, *The Speeches in Vergil's Aeneid* (Princeton, 1972) 167–68.

A Dissertation on Roast Pig

THERE ARE gaps in the narrative of the *Aeneid*. Some of these come within episodes which Vergil had not completed when he died. Such is the combat between Aeneas, assisted by Achates, and seven brothers (10.328–44), which was surely meant to end with Aeneas killing all seven, but breaks off inconclusively, leaving Achates wounded and Aeneas confronting five surviving brothers still eager for battle. Other gaps appear at points where Vergil moves from one series of events to another, passing over intervening incidents, which are to be understood by the reader κατὰ τὸ σιωπώμενον.

One of these occurs in the lightest and brightest book of the poem, Book 8. Troubled by the outbreak of war between his people and the Italians, Aeneas sleeps (18–30). The god of Tiber river appears to him in a vision and reassures him, telling him that nearby he will find a white sow with a litter of thirty pigs—the omen guaranteeing that he has reached his home (31–65).[1]

At sunrise Aeneas wakes, prays to Tiber and the Nymphs, chooses two ships for the upriver expedition to Pallanteum which the god instructed him to make, and puts crews aboard (66–80).

Then he finds the white sow with her farrow, sets up an altar, and sacrifices them to Juno (81–85).

That whole long night (says Vergil, 86–89) the Tiber stems his current so that the Trojans can row on it as smoothly as on a lake. They row *noctemque diemque*, and sight Pallanteum at noon next day. It is an

Reprinted from CW 67 (1973) 14–15.
[1] Helenus gave him the same sign in 3.388–93.

idyllic picture, the galleys gliding upstream in darkness beneath the wondering trees.

But why did they set off at night? and what happened to the rest of the previous day? It does not take twelve hours for experienced sailors to man and launch two ships.

The latter part of the day must have been occupied by the sacrifice. About its details, Vergil preserves a dignified silence, but it was an embarrassing and unpleasant ceremony. The sow was clubbed on the head and her throat was cut (cf. *Od.* 14.425–28), and the piglets were killed, all thirty of them. Men of the heroic age were accustomed to such scenes: Homer rather enjoys describing them, Vergil does not. Meanwhile the altar was raised, the fire was kindled, and soon the smell of roast pork filled the air. Sucking-pig is delicious, and the Trojans had gone hungry (7.112–15) until they started hunting (7.477–82), so this little banquet might have been welcome enough. But, although toothsome, it lost its savor because of one fact. The meal was shared by their persistent enemy, the malevolent Juno. To her the altar was built, to her the swine were dedicated, and for her specially selected portions were burned in the sacred fire.[2] We are not told that she rejected the offering, as angry gods sometimes did. She accepted it, then, although as always with hatred for Aeneas and his men. She shared the communion meal with them. They felt her baneful presence, as menacing as Banquo's ghost at Macbeth's feast or the Stone Guest at Don Juan's final dinner. The meat would stick in their throats, lie heavy on their stomachs. After such a repast, they could not possibly lie down to sleep in peace. No: with a shout of relief Aeneas and his picked crews boarded their ships and shoved off (90).

One single line (admittedly not wholly in Vergil's style) would, if inserted between 85 and 86, sum up the situation:

ocius ad naues: fugat indigestio somnum.

After a dinner of roast pork and wine, most people would prefer not to go out rowing. For the Trojans it was a welcome escape from a painful ordeal.

[2] Aeneas followed the advice of Tiber (8.59–61) reinforcing that of Helenus (3.435–39).

Speech and Narrative
in the *Aeneid*

THIS PAPER is a study of Vergil's methods of interweaving speech and narrative.

There are different techniques of introducing speeches into a narrative poem. Homer does it regularly and formally. He employs a fairly limited range of verbs of speaking to mark the opening of a speech and its conclusion: ἀγόρευε, ἠμείβετο, προσέειπε, προσέφη, ἦ, ὧς εἰπών, ὧς φάτο.[1] Vergil is more concerned to vary the introductory and terminal verbs, and often makes them indicate the emotional state of the speaker, together with his relation to his hearers. Therefore he uses many and various verbs and verbal phrases: *canit, hisco, incipio, memorat, uox excidit ore, caelum questibus implet, haec insuper addit, maestas expromere uoces.* Furthermore, Homer almost invariably begins a speech with the first word of a line and ends it with the last word of a line, and introduces it by a sentence of one or sometimes two complete lines, standing outside the speech. He even inserts padding to fill out the lines introducing a speech, e.g. καὶ μετέειπεν (*Il.* 1.73) and πεπνυμένα μήδεα εἰδώς (*Il.* 7.278, just after πεπνυμένω ἄμφω in line 276).

The other Greek epic poets follow him faithfully. This was pointed out long ago by J. Kvíčala in a study of Vergil's practice.[2] He found one

Reprinted from *HSPh* 78 (1974) 189–229.

[1] These formulae are examined by A. Fingerle on pp. 306–448 of his dissertation "Typik der homerischen Reden" (Munich, 1939, unpublished). He shows that προσέφη is the commonest opener, occurring 205 times, and ὧς φάτο the commonest closing phrase, used 138 times.

[2] "Über den Anfang und Schluss der Reden der Aeneis," pp. 265–74 of his *Neue Beiträge zur Erklärung der Aeneis* (Prague, 1881). Kvíčala does not mention the little speech of Achilles beginning at *Il.* 23.855, which is pointed out as unique in Homer by

departure from the rule in Quintus Smyrnaeus and some in Nonnus, but dismissed them as being "not real speeches." It would have been better to admit that these late writers (who both apparently knew Ovid at least among the Roman poets) were attracted by the freer movement of Latin epic. In Quintus, 14.602–4 is a τις-speech like *Il.* 4.178–81. So, in Nonnus, are 39.143–44 and 145–48, while 27.49, 35.49–53, 45.92–93, 45.170–71, and 47.433–34 are imagined objections (ἀλλ' ἐρέεις) within speeches; 1.129 is an imagined outcry of the sea and its coasts; 15.390–91, 15.406, and 16.291 are spoken by trees; but 15.417–19 and 42.38–39 are uttered by gods. Some at least of these are real speeches and none begins at the beginning of the line. In his hexameter hymns, which are quite close to the tone of epic, Callimachus occasionally starts a speech in midline: witness the speeches of Leto in the *Hymn to Delos* 150 and 212 and the speech of Zeus in the *Hymn to Artemis* 29–39. The informal speeches in Erinna's *Distaff* (D. L. Page, *Literary Papyri* III [Cambridge, Mass., 1950] p. 486) and in the anonymous lament (Page, p. 500) need not be considered, since the poems although in hexameters are not epic. The hexameter poem on the Persian war (Page, p. 542) may have contained a *cohortatio* ending in the first foot of the line with βούλομαι; but we have only that one word, restored, and cannot be sure.

As for the ends of speeches, Homer once and once only closes a speech before the termination of the line, in *Il.* 2.70; and then it is the speech of the Dream, which Agamemnon is repeating verbatim from *Il.* 2.23–34, merely curtailing its final words. Never does Homer do this elsewhere, or Hesiod, Apollonius, and the others.[3]

The first hexameter poet in Latin, Ennius, sometimes abandons Homeric practice, at least as far as concerns the opening of speeches: e.g.

simul inter
sese sic memorant: "o Romule, Romule die!"

(*Ann.* 110–11 Vahlen)

and

infit: "o ciues. . . ."

(*Ann.* 394)[4]

J. R. Gjerløw on p. 46 of his "Bemerkungen über einige Einleitungen zur direkten Rede in Vergils Aeneis," *SO* 32 (1956) 44–68.

[3] R. Führer, *Formproblem-Untersuchungen zu den Reden in der frühgriechischen Lyrik* (Munich, 1967), shows in §6 that the lyric poets are more careful to make the end of a speech correspond with a metrical pause than the beginning: e.g. the Centaur's speech in Pindar, *Pyth.* 9.39–65 Bowra.

[4] Compare also the brief speech of Mars within Ilia's account of her dream in *Ann.* 45–46.

Lucretius (although there are few speeches in his poem) does the same at 3.900 and 3.914. Catullus, however, starts all the speeches in his "miniature epic" at the first syllable of the verse (64.132, 215, 323), doubtless because he desires to be correct and formal in this neoteric work.[5] The fragments of Ennius do not show us any speech terminating before the end of the line, nor do the six books of Lucretius, nor Catullus's Peleus and Thetis poem. Cicero's hexameter translations from Homer begin and end speeches exactly at the beginning and end of the verses (see fragments 22.23–28 and 24.1–2 Morel).[6]

Vergil, however, is very free about placing his speeches within the narrative framework. Sometimes he will begin a speech in the middle of a line and close it at the line-ending (e.g. 6.713–18), sometimes the reverse (e.g. 8.560–83); and sometimes neither the opening nor the close of a speech coincides with the opening and close of metrical lines (e.g. 9.281–92). On pp. 266–68 Kvíčala (note 2 above) gives some statistics for the speeches in the *Aeneid* which have regular and irregular beginnings and endings—if we may use the term "regular" to mean coincident with the opening or close of the metrical line. His figures and his references are not always accurate; still, they show that roughly one quarter of Vergil's speeches in the *Aeneid* have an irregular opening, and one quarter an irregular close.

Commenting on his study, Norden (note 5 above, p. 136) suggests that the Greek poets, with their finer sense of style, instinctively refrained from breaking the rhythm in the middle of a verse by changing from narrative to speech. This may be. Yet modern knowledge of the background of the Homeric poems makes it certain that the practice was established by centuries of oral composition—which makes padding such as καὶ μετέειπεν almost necessary and relatively inoffensive to the ear. It was doubtless continued because of the traditional reverence of Greek epic poets for the style of Homer. Ennius, although *alter Homerus*, departed from it because he was writing in a different tongue and without the tradition of oral composition in hexameters: this was only one of his many un-Homeric experiments in rhythm. As for Vergil, analysis of his

[5] In the appendixes of his *P. Vergilius Maro Aeneis Buch VI* (Stuttgart, 1957[4]), E. Norden signalizes some metrical observances which are unusually frequent in Catullus 64, and indicate an attempt to maintain particularly high standards of formality: avoidance of enjambment (pp. 387–88); avoidance of a pause after the fifth trochee or fifth dactyl (p. 389); neat framing of a line between adjective and noun, as in 64.54, 72, 77 (p. 391); reluctance to place an unimportant word at the end of the verse (pp. 400–401); and reluctance to juxtapose words with similar endings (p. 407).

[6] Varro of Atax has two brief interjections in the middle of a verse describing a Dionysiac revel (fr. 5 Morel).

practice explains his motives in cultivating this sort of irregularity. He aimed at communicating emotion and movement to his speeches by interweaving them with the narrative. Perhaps also he was thinking of the broken rhythms of certain exciting scenes in tragedy, such as Euripides' *IA* 1368, where an important speech starts in midline.

A more extensive treatment of certain aspects of this subject is given by W. K. Loesch in his Erlangen dissertation of 1927, "Die Einführung der direkten Rede bei den epischen Dichtern der Römer bis zur domitianischen Zeit." Writing before Milman Parry's investigations of oral poetry were published, he nevertheless emphasizes (p. 3) that the Homeric poems were meant not to be read, but to be heard. The reciter therefore had to make it perfectly clear to the audience exactly when he (or the poet) was speaking the narrative, and when one of the characters was making a speech. Furthermore, when Homer wished to communicate the emotion moving one of his personages to speak, he did so not by effects of sound and rhythm, as Vergil was to do later, but by describing a gesture ($\delta\acute{\alpha}\kappa\rho\upsilon$' $\mathring{\alpha}\nu\alpha\pi\rho\acute{\eta}\sigma\alpha\varsigma$, *Il.* 9.433), by naming the speaker's emotional reaction ($\chi\alpha\hat{\iota}\rho\epsilon$ δ' 'O$\delta\upsilon\sigma\sigma\epsilon\acute{\upsilon}\varsigma$, *Od.* 14.51), or by characterizing the speech itself ($\chi\alpha\lambda\epsilon\pi\hat{\wp}$ $\mathring{\eta}\nu\acute{\iota}\pi\alpha\pi\epsilon$ $\mu\acute{\upsilon}\theta\wp$, *Il.* 2.245). Nevertheless, as Loesch observes (pp. 9–10), many of the speeches in the *Iliad* and still more in the *Odyssey* are prefaced by colorless one-line formulaic phrases. Apollonius in his *Argonautica* drops many of the formulae and puts some individuality into nearly half of his introductions to the speeches of his characters, although he still maintains neat metrical symmetry on the Homeric model. Turning to Roman epic, Loesch points out (p. 16) that Vergil's skillful *uariatio* keeps even his simplest phrases from exact repetition: e.g. *dictisque ita fatur amicis* (*Aen.* 2.147), *ultro uerbis compellat amicis* (2.372), *dictis solatur amicis* (5.770), and *dictis adfatur amicis* (8.126).

Loesch is chiefly interested in distinguishing the methods used by Vergil and his successors to convey the emotion of their characters in speech, and he pays less attention to the formal techniques by which a speech is introduced and concluded. This has recently been touched on by J. R. Gjerløw (note 2 above). He is, however, almost exclusively concerned with the words denoting the act of speech, such as *inquit* and *ait*, and in the statistics of their use. Vergil, he says (p. 56), employs *fari* and its compounds not less than sixty-six times, as "the introductory word *par excellence*," possibly following Ennius.[7]

---

[7] Norden (note 5 above) pp. 137 and 440 (cited by Gjerløw), suggests that the tag, *atque ita fatur* (e.g. 12.295), is adapted from Ennius, since the fifth-foot elision and the use of two final disyllables are not Vergilian.

BEGINNINGS WITHIN THE LINE

Most speeches in the *Aeneid* start at the opening of a line. This gives the impression that the speaker, even if deeply moved, is in command of himself, that his thoughts are regular and that his feelings are not disorderly. However, the first words spoken (or rather thought) by Juno and the first words uttered by Aeneas do not begin with the first foot of the hexameter: for the same reason. Each is overcome with emotion. Juno is still brooding over her unhealed wound, and her resentment suddenly erupts:

> haec secum: "mene incepto desistere uictam!" (1.37)

Plunged into darkness, overwhelmed by thunder and lightning, Aeneas is paralyzed with terror and despair:

> talia uoce refert: "o terque quaterque beati. . . . !" (1.94)

This is one of Vergil's motives for beginning a speech within a verse: to show emotion breaking out of control. An even more striking example comes in Book 4. Even in the utmost stress of passion, all Dido's speeches begin and end regularly with the first and last feet of the line, until the moment when, looking from her tower, she sees the harbor empty. Then for the first time she entirely loses her self-control:

> terque quaterque manu pectus percussa decorum
> flauentesque abscissa comas, "pro Iuppiter! ibit
> hic?" ait. (4.589–91)

So also the Sibyl usually speaks in calm and measured tones (e.g. 6.37, 322, 373, 399); but when the god begins to possess her, her words are irregularly situated within the hexameter lines, to show that she is no longer in full command of herself.

> uentum erat ad limen, cum uirgo "poscere fata
> tempus," ait, "deus, ecce deus!" (6.45–46)

In the council of the gods Venus (although deeply moved) starts her speech formally and regularly:

> "o pater, o hominum rerumque aeterna potestas." (10.18)

But Juno in her reply cannot wait; instead, she turns on her opponent, beginning partway through the line:

> acta furore graui: "quid me alta silentia cogis
> rumpere?" (10.63–64)

On the night before the duel, Turnus rehearses by donning his cuirass, sword, shield, and helmet. He grows more and more excited, *his agitur furiis*. Finally he grasps his spear, brandishes it, and breaks into a shout:

> uociferans: "nunc, o numquam frustrata uocatus
> hasta meos!"   (12.95–96)

In the last scene of all Aeneas stands over his victim wondering in silence whether to spare him, *iam iamque magis cunctans*. Suddenly he sees that Turnus is wearing the baldric he took from the corpse of Pallas. Rage overpowers him:

> furiis accensus et ira
> terribilis: "tune hinc spoliis indute meorum
> eripiare mihi?"   (12.946–48)

In other speeches, however, an opening retarded beyond the beginning of the line does not indicate a violent explosion of emotion. For instance, in this same scene Turnus begs for mercy.

> ille humilis supplex oculos dextramque precantem
> protendens: "equidem merui nec deprecor," inquit.   (12.930–31)

Wounded, helpless, humbled, he speaks with great difficulty. The postponement of the opening words is apparently intended to make this clear, since it is less assured and formal than a regular symmetrical opening. In the same way, Juno is humbled by Jupiter in their interview in Book 10. Both the speeches of the sovereign deity start with the first word of the line (10.607, 622). Both Juno's responses are framed as imploring questions, and both start in midline:

> cui Iuno summissa: "quid, o pulcherrime coniunx . . . ?"   (10.611)

> et Iuno adlacrimans: "quid si, quae uoce grauaris . . . ?"   (10.628)

Indeed, Jupiter, the divinity representing order and control, is the only important personage in the poem whose speeches invariably start with the first word of the line and almost always close with the last word of the line. The two exceptions are his decisive pronouncement in the council of the gods (10.113), which moves into a thunderous oath, *totum nutu tremefecit Olympum*, and his final command to Juno to cease her persecution of the Trojans (12.806), which is succeeded by a significant pause.

The first speech of Venus, addressed to Jupiter in 1.229–53, is uttered with tears, starts with a plaintive question, and begins in midline. An actress speaking such a speech on the stage would start with a sob, and her first words would be voiced very quietly. The midline opening of Anchises' first speech (2.638), which ends so decisively, is a little difficult to account for, unless it is intended to reflect his age and weakness. Speaking in the expectation of death, an old man might well start with a few faint words and then grow stronger. So King Lear, whose speeches almost always open at the beginning of the line, at last, in utter exhaustion, begins with a half-line:

> Pray do not mock me.
> I am a very foolish fond old man.   (*King Lear* 4.7.59–60)

A speaker will sometimes pause before speaking, not through embarrassment or weakness, but in order to give greater weight to his words. Vergil makes a few such speeches start in midline, but always prefaces them by formal phrases to show that the pause is deliberate. Thus, Aeneas must wait until the Sibyl's prophetic frenzy is calmed before requesting a safe-conduct through the world of death.

> ut primum cessit furor et rabida ora quierunt,
> incipit Aeneas heros: "non ulla laborum. . . ."   (6.102–3)

The Sibyl's answer also seems to come slowly and gravely:

> sic orsa loqui uates: "sate sanguine diuum,
> Tros Anchisiade, facilis descensus Auerni."   (6.125–26)

When Aeneas answers Dido's first accusation, he has to pause and struggle for self-mastery.

> *tandem* pauca refert: "ego te. . . ."   (4.333)

Such a speech is made calm and serious by the pause before its opening words. Other speeches, however, begin irregularly, partway through the line, either because there is some urgency in the situation, or because the speaker feels himself superior to his hearer, or because he is young and careless. So Aeneas, dreaming away his destiny, building an alien city and wearing alien clothes, is shocked back to reality by the messenger of God, who addresses him abruptly:

> continuo[8] inuadit: "tu nunc Karthaginis altae
> fundamenta locas?"   (4.265–66)

---

[8]*Continuo* introduces a speech only here and in 7.68 and 7.120, on which see p. 134.

A girl alone in a forest should not accost a couple of strange men; but Venus, posing as a pretty young huntress, hails the Trojans with disarming informality:

> ac prior "heus,"[9] inquit, "iuuenes!"   (1.321)

Venus preserves this air of youthful nonchalance by beginning and ending her narrative speech with half-lines (1.335 and 370). Again, in a time of relaxation, at the games, Nisus makes an eager plea for his prize:

> hic Nisus "si tanta" inquit "sunt praemia uictis. . . ."   (5.353)

A commander giving orders to his men will sometimes begin in midline because he is assured and easy. So, to the formal address of Palinurus beginning "magnanime Aenea" (5.17), the reply comes lightly:

> tum pius Aeneas: "equidem sic poscere uentos. . . ."   (5.26)

In the underworld, too, Aeneas speaks informally to Palinurus:

> sic prior adloquitur: "quis te, Palinure . . . ?"   (6.341)

By contrast, his address to his comrade and kinsman Deiphobus begins with dignified formality:

> "Deiphobe armipotens, genus alto a sanguine Teucri."   (6.500)

During the Sicilian games, all Aeneas's formal proclamations and commands begin at the opening of the verse: "Dardanidae magni" (5.45); "accipite haec animis" (5.304); "nunc, si cui uirtus" (5.363); "sume, pater" (5.533); "uade age et Ascanio" (5.548); and so does his grave intervention to save Dares' life in the boxing-match (5.465). But when he settles the argument over the foot-race he is genial, and the rhythm of his speech is informal:

> tum pater Aeneas "uestra" inquit "munera uobis
> certa manent."   (5.348–49)

Addressing a hastily collected group of fighters during the final defense of Troy, Aeneas starts rapidly:

> incipio super his: "iuuenes. . . ."   (2.348)

But when he is at the head of a regular army, his speech is more decisive and opens with greater force and symmetry:

> "maxima res effecta, uiri."   (11.14)

---

[9]*Heus* occurs in the *Aeneid* only here and in a boyish exclamation of Iulus (7.116).

"ne qua meis esto dictis mora!"   (12.565)

A subtle contrast of rhythms appears in the conversation of the two adversaries, haughty Juno and suave Venus (4.90–128). Juno's speeches both start with clear sharp emphasis at the opening of the hexameter: "egregiam uero laudem" (4.93), "mecum erit iste labor" (4.115); the first ends with the end of the line (4.104), the second more brusquely at the caesura ("hic hymenaeus erit," 4.127). But Venus, declaring that it would be madness to refuse or resist Juno, begins her reply at an unemphatic place near the end of the line:

sic contra est ingressa Venus: "quis talia demens
abnuat?"   (4.107–8)

and closes it lightly almost at the beginning of the verse:

"perge, sequar."   (4.114)

Once Juno makes a speech where neither the opening nor the close coincides with the metrical pattern: when she is hastily dismissing Allecto (7.552–60): contrast the formality of Allecto's address to her (7.545–51). So also the last challenge of Mezentius to Aeneas begins and ends asymmetrically (10.878–82), unlike the careful regularity of his dying plea (10.900–906). A speaker who despises his hearer will sometimes begin thus irregularly. Because it is a solemn declaration, Priam's curse on Pyrrhus starts symmetrically, at the opening of the verse:

"at tibi pro scelere," exclamat.   (2.535)

But the reply is curt, contemptuous, and offhand:

cui Pyrrhus, "referes ergo haec. . . ."   (2.547)

There can scarcely be any doubt that Vergil makes these varying rhythmical effects deliberately. At one point he even pads out an introductory phrase in order to make a derisive answer to a formal speech begin in midline. Allecto has addressed Turnus seriously, *his cum uocibus:*

"Turne, tot incassum fusos patiere labores?"   (7.421)

But his response is so described:

hic iuuenis uatem inridens *sic orsa uicissim*
ore refert: "classis inuectas Thybridis undam. . . ."   (7.435–36)

At times Vergil's characters begin speeches in the middle of a line when their utterance is rapid and abrupt, prompted by an unexpected and important occurrence. Such is the call of Anchises:

prospiciens, "nate," exclamat, "fuge, nate, propinquant!"　　(2.733)

Hecuba cries out at the sight of old Priam wearing armor:

ut uidit, "quae mens tam dira. . . ?"　　(2.519)

Pallas jumps up to challenge a strange squadron of ships:

et procul e tumulo, "iuuenes, . . ."　　(8.112)

Omens are interpreted without delay:

et pater Anchises, "bellum, o terra hospita, portas."　　(3.539)

continuo uates "externum cernimus" inquit
"aduentare uirum."　　(7.68–69)

continuo "salue fatis mihi debita tellus. . . ."　　(7.120)

A danger is identified:

et pater Anchises, "nimirum hic illa Charybdis."　　(3.558)

Aeneas's enquiry about the uncanny spectacle of the souls waiting for reincarnation is quickly answered, before the formal exposition which is to follow.

tum pater Anchises: "animae, quibus altera fato
corpora debentur. . . ."　　(6.713–14)

The sudden disappearance of his father's spirit startles and distresses Aeneas:

Aeneas "quo deinde ruis? quo proripis?" inquit.　　(5.741)

Brief utterances in the heat of battle have the speed of violent combat:

increpat his uictor: "nostrasne euadere, demens,
sperasti te posse manus?"　　(9.560–61)

One of these shows Vergil padding the line, apparently in order to make the speech start more abruptly:

aduolat Aeneas uaginaque eripit ensem
et super haec: "ubi nunc Mezentius acer?"　　(10.896–97)

Brusquely the hero interrupts the plea of a man who has taunted him:

pluribus oranti Aeneas: "haud talia dudum
dicta dabas: morere."　　(10.599–600)

The most impressive of these openings within the line accompany the arrival of the chthonic powers:

aduentante dea. "procul, o procul este, profani!" (6.258)

and the miraculous appearance of Aeneas from the cloud:

cum sic reginam adloquitur cunctisque repente
improuisus ait: "coram, quem quaeritis, adsum." (1.594–95)

ENDINGS WITHIN THE LINE

At least eight speeches in the *Aeneid* were apparently left unfinished at the poet's death: for eight terminate in a line which is metrically incomplete. These are the utterances which end at 2.720 (Aeneas to his family), 4.361 (Aeneas to Dido), 5.815 (Neptune to Venus), 7.248 (Ilioneus to Latinus), 7.455 (Allecto to Turnus), 10.284 (Turnus at the beachhead), 10.876 (Aeneas to Mezentius), and 11.375 (Drances' oration). In making up his statistics Kvíčala (see above, p. 125) counts these among the speeches whose endings do not coincide with the end of a line, because "man kann sich leicht überzeugen, dass an allen diesen 8 Stellen der Schluss der Rede in natürlicher Weise erfolgt und dass man gar nichts mehr erwartet" (p. 272 note). That is, he believes that Vergil would not have filled out these incomplete lines, but would have left them as they stand in the manuscripts. This raises two different but interconnected questions.

The first is the general question of the metrically imperfect lines throughout the *Aeneid*.[10] Some scholars have suggested that Vergil did not intend to complete these lines, or at least that he would have completed only the lines in which both meter and sense are crippled, such as 3.340. There are fifty-eight incomplete lines in all.[11] Some of them are effective enough just as they stand: e.g. 4.361 (closing Aeneas's speech to Dido) and 7.455 (ending Allecto's speech to Turnus and answering his gibe in 7.444); although this is not to say that it would have been impossible for Vergil to improve them. But many of them are flat, weak, and

[10] See J. Sparrow, *Half-Lines and Repetitions in Virgil* (Oxford, 1931); A. S. Pease, *Aeneidos Liber Quartus* (Cambridge, Mass., 1935) 123–24; R. G. Austin, *Aeneidos Liber Quartus* (Oxford, 1955) 36–37; K. Büchner, "P. Vergilius Maro," *RE* 8A.1 (1955) 1021–1264 and 8A.2 (1958) 1265–1486, especially 1425–26; G. E. Duckworth, *Structural Patterns and Proportions in Vergil's Aeneid* (Ann Arbor, 1962) 77–80 and Tables X and XI.

[11] Some follow Brunck in cutting out *non uiribus aequis* from 12.218 and counting it as an incomplete line; but look at the MS authority, even to M's corruption *equis*.

jejune compared with the normal hexameters that surround them. Isolated within the rich texture of Vergil's regular lines, such phrases as *hic cursus fuit* (1.534), *stant circum* (2.767), *ergo iussa parat* (4.503), *Nisus et Euryalus primi* (5.294), *tertius Euryalus* (5.322), and *Euryali et Nisi* (9.467) look as much out of place as holes in the canvas of a Rembrandt.

Of the fifty-eight incomplete lines, twenty-five occur within passages of narrative: most of them at points where the poet seems merely to have broken off, not in order to create any special effect such as dramatic interruption or suspense, but with the idea of continuing and filling out the episode later.[12] (It should be borne in mind that there are also episodes which are manifestly incomplete, although they do not end in a metrically imperfect line. Such is 10.324–44, which was surely not intended to end with a partial defeat for the Trojan side, Achates wounded and Aeneas doing nothing, but with the killing of the seven brothers who faced Aeneas: cf. 10.350–52.) Thirty-three appear in contexts of speechmaking. Of these seven are in the introductory sentences, immediately before the speakers' first words.[13] It is well-nigh inconceivable that Vergil never intended to round these out into full lines. With the example of Homer's καί μιν φωνήσας ἔπεα πτερόεντα προσηύδα and Ennius's *respondit Iuno Saturnia, sancta dearum,* and the like before him, would he have permitted his finished epic to be marred by such inadequacies as *cui Liger* (10.580) and *Turnus ad haec* (12.631)? Two incomplete lines, equally weak, are in sentences immediately succeeding the close of speeches.[14]

Sixteen incomplete lines are found within the body of speeches.[15] Eight form the final words of more or less formal speeches.[16] It is noteworthy that no less than nine of these lines in speeches appear at points where a prophecy or a revelation or some reference to the unseen world is being made.[17] Without forcing the point, we may conjecture that Vergil found such passages as that in which Venus reveals to her son the

---

[12] The following lines come in Vergil's narrative: 1.636, 4.400, 4.503, 4.516, 5.294, 5.322, 5.574, 5.595, 7.702, 7.760, 9.167, 9.467, 9.520, 9.721, 9.761, and 10.728. Within Aeneas's narrative (excluding the reported speeches) there are these: 2.66, 2.233, 2.346, 2.468, 2.623, 2.767, 3.218, 3.470, and 3.661. (Lines 2.66 and 346 are comments addressed to Dido.)

[13] These are 3.527, 8.469, 9.295, 10.17, 10.490, 10.580, and 12.631.

[14] 1.560 and 5.653.

[15] They are 1.534, 2.614, 2.640, 2.787, 3.316, 3.340, 3.640, 4.44, 5.792, 6.94, 6.835, 7.129, 7.439, 8.41, 8.536, and 11.391.

[16] The eight are 2.720, 4.361, 5.815, 7.248, 7.455, 10.284, 10.876, and 11.375.

[17] Namely 2.614, 2.787, 5.815, 6.94, 6.835, 7.129, 7.455, 8.41, 8.536; and perhaps 7.439 might be added.

hostile gods, or that where Anchises appeals to the unborn souls of Caesar and Pompey, difficult to complete without long meditation.

Most of these incomplete lines, then, look as though they were provisional and Vergil had intended to complete them. Anyone who believes he did not must meet several powerful arguments. The first is that the *Aeneid*, while complete in outline, contains many imperfections, inconsistencies, doublets, and unfinished scenes, that Vergil intended to spend three more years revising it, and that an incomplete verse would surely recommend itself for completion as well as an incomplete episode. The second is that we are explicitly informed how Vergil composed lines which were temporary expedients, intending to improve on them later; and that, when incomplete lines were being read, he improvised phrases to complete them on the spur of the moment.[18] He worked by sketching, and later filling in and altering. The third argument is that no hexameter poet in Greek or Latin ever left a hexameter line incomplete. Vergil's models did not. Vergil's imitators did not.[19] Therefore Vergil did not intend to do so in his finished poem. Modern sculptors (e.g. Maillol) will carve a torso without head or arms; Japanese artists will leave stretches of bare paper, only here and there touched with ink, around a detailed drawing; but the Greeks and Romans did not hold that formal imperfection is aesthetically or emotionally suggestive—particularly in such a majestic work as the epic poem.

Analyzing the *Aeneid* according to the proportions of the Golden Section, Duckworth (see note 10 above) calculates that in forty-one passages containing incomplete lines, these proportions will be preserved more perfectly if the incomplete lines are considered to be intentional and permanent, than if it is assumed they were meant to become full hexameters and should be counted as such. This may conceivably be true. But is it safe to assume that Vergil, when revising, would have done nothing to these passages except fill out one hemistich or a couple of words into one hexameter? Many of them would be improved or clarified by the addition of more than half a line, and one or two of them at least demand it: for instance, 6.835, where *ille* in 836 is unintelligible without a passage of transition from Caesar and Pompey to Mummius (836–37) and other earlier heroes. Therefore, when finishing his poem Vergil may well have intended to add something more than a few words to such

---

[18] *Vita Donati* (ed. Hardie) § 34.

[19] Pease (note 10 above) mentions some cases in the Vergilian centos, but a cento is bound by definition to use only the materials provided by its model, and for the *Aeneid* that includes the incomplete lines. He also cites Claudian, *Carm. Min.* 53.128, i.e. the *Gigantomachia*, which is clearly an unfinished fragment.

passages. And further, if he did wish (as Duckworth argues) to preserve the Golden Section ratios in adjoining groups of lines, then surely he could do so by adding other material elsewhere—as a painter balances a freshly added touch of color on one part of his canvas by a darker patch in another area. To compare the two versions of Palinurus's death (5.835–61 and 6.347–62) is to realize how broadly Vergil remodeled parts of his work with which, on reflection, he became dissatisfied. Some readers, impressed by the calculation which gives less than two lines a day as his total output while he composed the *Georgics*, have concluded that he was a slow worker. On the contrary, it appears that he composed rapidly and freely, but spent the greater part of his effort on revising and improving his early drafts, stage by slow stage. He even made jokes about his method, jokes which implied that the early drafts were not to be compared to the final version: they were amorphous embryos which had to be licked into shape as a bear forms her cubs, and they were scaffolding, cheap timber props put up to be torn down after the marble columns and the panelled roof had been set in place.[20] Therefore it would be erroneous to believe that, when Vergil left an incomplete line in his poem, he intended ultimately to do no more with it than, by adding a few words, to convert it into one single hexameter. This was not his view of poetic composition. He might well reduce a draft of fifty lines to twelve; he could equally well knock down a scaffolding of one and a half lines and replace it by an elaborate structure occupying ten or twenty or more.

The second question suggested by Kvíčala's analysis of the eight speeches which end in an incomplete line (see p. 135 above) is smaller and easier to solve. Kvíčala asserts that each of the speeches is finished as it stands, "und dass man gar nichts mehr erwartet." This implies that Vergil did not intend to write any more words for the speaker in each case, but meant either to leave the last line of the speech incomplete, or to add some words of *narrative* to fill it out. Against the former supposition some arguments have been given above (pp. 136–37). Against the latter, it is notable that in every one of these speeches the incomplete last line is followed by a complete line of narrative which sums up the effect of the speech, and which begins at the first word of the line: *haec fatus* (2.721), *talia dicentem* (4.362), *his . . . dictis* (5.816), *talibus . . . dictis* (7.249 and 11.376), *sic effata* (7.456), *haec ait* (10.285), and *tantum effatus* (10.877). These resumptive formulae are like Homer's ὣς ἄρα φωνήσασα and ἡ μὲν ἄρ' ὣς εἰποῦσα and nearly all appear elsewhere in Vergil: *haec fatus* (5.421), *his . . . dictis* (1.579), *talibus . . . dictis*

[20]*Vita Donati* (ed. Hardie) §§22–24.

(6.98), *sic effata* (4.30), *haec ait* (1.297), *tantum effatus* (6.547). Apparently, therefore, Vergil would have completed the last part of the speech in each of these cases, and then resumed the narrative.

Not many of the complete speeches in the poem come to an abrupt end before the finish of the metrical line. Vergil knows the value of closing an important utterance with a powerful expression of feeling (4.387, 4.628–29, 10.94–95, 11.180–81) or a memorable *epiphonema* (11.293).

When a speech does break off within the verse, it sometimes means that the speaker is overcome by emotion and can say no more. After a magnificent exposition of eschatology and prophecy, Anchises bursts into tears at the sight of the doomed Marcellus, and his speech trails off into silence like the incomplete life of a hero dying young:

> date . . .
> his saltem accumulem donis et fungar inani
> munere.   (6.883–86)

In the same falling rhythm (ending with a dactylic word in the first foot) Evander says farewell to his son, and then swoons:

> nunc, nunc o liceat crudelem abrumpere uitam, . . .
> grauior neu nuntius auris
> uulneret.   (8.579 + 582–83)

The plea of Latinus to Turnus closes with a reference to Turnus's aged father, and similarly ends with a dying fall, a one-word initial dactyl—here followed by a molossus as hard as Turnus's will.

> "miserere parentis
> longaeui, quem nunc maestum patria Ardea longe
> diuidit." *haudquaquam* dictis uiolentia Turni
> flectitur.   (12.43–46)

Camilla's last words are an urgent strategic message, and a farewell interrupted by death.

> "succedat pugnae Troianosque arceat urbe.
> iamque uale." simul his dictis linquebat habenas.   (11.826–27)

Latinus, having lost authority over his people, has no strength to finish his speech with a complete verse.

> "funere felici spolior." nec plura locutus. . . .   (7.599)

The long and carefully ordered address of Venus to Jove at the council ends unexpectedly within the line. It is natural to suppose that—unless she is interrupted by Juno, who begins her rebuttal within the verse (p. 129 above)—she breaks down into tears, real or feigned, at the ghastly idea of repeating the Trojan war.

> "iterumque reuoluere casus
> da, pater, Iliacos Teucris."   (10.61–62)

More poignantly, Andromache, after gazing at the Trojan warrior who looks like a ghost returned from the tomb, asks why it is not her lost husband, and bursts into frantic sobs.

> "Hector ubi est?" dixit, lacrimasque effudit.   (3.312)

Some serious speeches end in midline to show that they are followed by a meaningful pause. The unexpected but impressive close of the Sibyl's instructions to Aeneas reflects both her authority and her reticence.

> "sic demum lucos Stygis et regna inuia uiuis
> aspicies." dixit, pressoque obmutuit ore.   (6.154–55)

The same solemn emphasis appears in Aeneas's request.

> "ipsa canas oro." finem dedit ore loquendi.   (6.76)

This is succeeded by a long interval without speech, during which the Sibyl struggles with the god. The most impressive of such rhythmical effects are the two commands uttered by the supreme deity, one ending at the strong caesura in the third foot and followed by a solemn oath ("fata uiam inuenient," 10.113), the other concluding in the fourth foot with a powerful verb ("ulterius temptare ueto," 12.806) and followed by Juno's submissive silence.

Such speeches seldom have replies.[21] Others, which also end within the verse, do so because they are interrupted. Most dramatic of all are the epiphanies of Mercury to Aeneas. His first closes in an emphatic molossus, followed *medio sermone* by a rapid disappearance.

---

[21] Small speeches which end within the verse and are followed by a pause or silence are: a false oracle (2.119), a command which is not obeyed (5.164), a plea which is not granted (5.385), and an unanswered challenge (9.377).

"spes heredis Iuli
respice, cui regnum Italiae Romanaque tellus
debetur." tali Cyllenius ore locutus. . . .   (4.274–76)

The second, more urgent, ends with a dactylic word and an instantaneous vanishing.

"uarium et mutabile semper
femina." sic fatus nocti se immiscuit atrae.[22]   (4.569–70)

The first speech of Aeneas to his mother is rather too full of self-pity: he describes himself both as *notus* and as *ignotus*. She cuts him off briskly partway through the hexameter.

"Europa atque Asia pulsus." nec plura querentem
passa Venus medio sic interfata dolore est.   (1.385–86)

Most of the speeches ending before the close of the metrical line pass straight into action. This is one of Vergil's innovations, in which he went far beyond his Homeric model. Even in the utmost excitement Homer never interweaves words and actions as Vergil does. In *Iliad* 12 the Trojans are attacking the wall of the Greek camp. The battle is evenly divided. Hector cries, "Once more unto the breach," and, while his men climb the wall, bursts the gate open with a huge stone. Yet even in such a crisis, his speech embraces four evenly constructed lines, one introductory and one describing its effect, with the traditional expansiveness of oral poetry: ἱππόδαμοι Τρῶες, θεσπιδαὲς πῦρ, and οὔασι πάντες ἄκουον (*Il.* 12.439–42). Even in the most furious melee Homeric speeches are formal, leisurely, and complete in shape: e.g. *Il.* 16.462–632 and 21.34–199, *Od.* 22.241–325. But Vergil writes more like a dramatist. At the end of Shakespeare's tragedy, Othello makes a calm speech directing the envoys of the Venetian republic how to describe his untimely end. Once, he adds, when he saw a Turk assaulting a Venetian,

I took by the throat the circumcised dog
And smote him thus. . . .   (*Othello* 5.2.354–55)

The remainder of the line is not spoken, but is occupied by the gesture as Othello stabs himself. So in the *Aeneid* many a half-line of speech is succeeded by a half-line beginning a description of rapid action.

---

[22] The elision of a monosyllabic pronoun, *se*, is unusual, and images the disappearance of the god. Vergil could have written a line which avoided this effect: *sic fatus se nocti immiscuit atrae*.

One of the most remarkable is Aeneas's speedy departure from Carthage, when he cuts the cable.

> "adsis o placidusque iuues et sidera caelo
> dextra feras." dixit, uaginaque eripit ensem
> fulmineum strictoque ferit retinacula ferro.[23]   (4.578–80)

When the Trojan women set fire to the ships, Ascanius gallops down to stop them. Because they would not recognize him in the masking "Corinthian" helmet, he pulls it off and names himself. The line is hurried, asyndetic, broken in the second foot.

> "en, ego uester
> Ascanius!" galeam ante pedes proiecit inanem.[24]   (5.672–73)

Seizing the tactical initiative at the news of Aeneas's advance, Turnus leaves the council.

> "illi armis in regna ruunt." nec plura locutus
> corripuit sese et tectis citus extulit altis.   (11.461–62)

Aeneas orders a beaten boxer to stop fighting at once.

> "cede deo." dixitque et proelia uoce diremit.[25]   (5.467)

Challenges of rival fighters, shouts of victory, military commands—these are often broken off within the first part of the line. Thus, the attack is mounted on the Trojan camp.

> "hostis adest, heia!"[26] ingenti clamore per omnis
> condunt se Teucri portas.   (9.38–39)

A moment later Turnus passes almost instantaneously from speech to action.

---

[23] Other such rapidly concluded orders appear in 3.266 (Anchises casting off from the Strophades), 5.14 (Palinurus furling sail), and 5.197 (Mnestheus to his crew).

[24] The unusual ending with two disyllables and a jolting rhythm, *én égo uéster*, is exceptionally emphatic.

[25] In classical Latin it is unusual to couple *-que* and *et*. The tight linkage suggests that Aeneas's order and his movement of intervention were almost simultaneous. Horace has *teque et tua solus amares* (Ars P. 444). A. Szantyr, *Lateinische Grammatik* (Munich, 1965) § 283b, calls this an archaism, suited only for the grand style; but at least in these two cases it sounds light and speedy rather than archaic and dignified.

[26] Because Caicus's warning call is immediately answered by his comrades' shouts, the second syllable of *heia* is elided and "drowned" by the first syllable of *ingenti*: so closely does speech merge into narrative. Partly similar is the effect in 3.523, where the last syllable of *Italiam* in Aeneas's narrative is drowned by the shout of Achates.

"ecquis erit mecum, iuuenes, qui primus in hostem—?
en!" ait et iaculum attorquens emittit in auras.   (9.51–52)

It is with two words cut off at the beginning of the hexameter that Mezentius rises to face Aeneas (10.856) and hurls a sharp gift at him (10.882). With two initial words Pallas challenges Turnus, "tolle minas!" (10.451). The same abrupt phrasing shows how Pyrrhus seizes Priam for slaughter, "nunc morere" (2.550), Mezentius pulls his lance out of a victim's body (10.744) and hurls a spear (10.776).[27]

The same rapid transition from speech to narrative can also describe a surge of affection. So Vulcan, warmed by Venus's caress, grants her request and turns to embrace her.

"absiste precando
uiribus indubitare tuis." ea uerba locutus
optatos dedit amplexus.   (8.403–5)

But next morning he sets the Cyclopes to work:

"praecipitate moras!" nec plura effatus. . . .   (8.443)

So Hecuba to her old husband:

"aut moriere simul." sic ore effata recepit.   (2.524)

Anna to Dido's attendants:

"extremus si quis super halitus errat,
ore legam." sic fata gradus euaserat altos.   (4.684–85)

Aeneas to Lausus:

"Aeneae magni dextra cadis." increpat ultro
cunctantes socios et terra subleuat ipsum.   (10.830–31)

Similarly Apollo breaks his speeches praising Ascanius in order to glide down from heaven (9.644) and to return (9.656); Aeneas turns away from the corpse of Pallas (11.98–99); after a divine visitation, Aeneas halts (6.197) and Turnus prays (9.22).

METRICAL PATTERNS AND THEIR SIGNIFICANCE

Vergil's sense of the power of verse-rhythm to convey physical and psychical movement was so subtle that he differentiated the metrical pat-

---

[27] Other truncated pugnacious phrases appear in 9.221, 9.423, 10.298, 10.335, 10.495, 10.583. Book 10, full of fighting, has many such effects.

terns of brief phrases spoken at the openings and endings of lines. When a speech closes at the penthemimeral caesura, it is usually firm and decisive: "aut moriere simul" (2.524), "hic hymenaeus erit" (4.127), "praecipitate moras!" (8.443), "aeternumque uale" (11.98).[28] A speech which begins at this caesura is often resolute, while less formal and more apparently spontaneous than a speech commencing at the regular place, the beginning of the hexameter. The first speeches of Evander to Aeneas start in this way.

> tum sic pauca refert: "ut te, fortissime Teucrum,
> accipio agnoscoque libens!"   (8.154-55)

> rex Euandrus ait: "non haec sollemnia nobis. . . ."   (8.185)

In five balanced lines the Sibyl rebukes Aeneas for tarrying. Deiphobus (whom she ignores) interposes:

> Deiphobus contra "ne saeui, magna sacerdos."   (6.544)[29]

Many speeches beginning later in the line, at the hephthemimeral caesura, are unexpected outcries or intrusions: Dido's outburst (4.590), the alert given by the sea-nymph (10.228), the intervention of Juturna (12.625). It is not easy, however, to find a single description of the speeches which *close* at the hephthemimeral caesura. Some certainly move directly into action: 1.610, 5.14, 5.400, 10.298, and Turnus's exit speech in 11.461. Others, again, are thoughtful utterances apparently succeeded by a pause for reflection: e.g. the Sibyl's in 6.53 and the soothsayer's in 8.503.

Most speeches starting in the second foot of the line, at the trihemimeral caesura, are excited: Juno's vengeful meditation (1.37), Hecuba's plea (2.519), Aeneas's greeting to his father (6.695) and his recognition of the omen of the tables (7.120), Mnestheus's rallying cry (9.781), the defiance of Mezentius (10.878), the adulation of Drances, "o fama ingens," (11.124), and the last shout of Aeneas, *ira / terribilis* (12.947).[30]

A speech which ends within the second foot of the line is usually abrupt, eager, or disturbed: for example, Andromache's cry "Hector ubi est?" (3.312), the rebuke of Mercury (4.276), Aeneas's order to stop the

---

[28] Such are the exhortation of Coroebus (2.391), the claim of Dares (5.385), the promises of Ascanius (9.280) and the plea of Euryalus (9.292), Aeneas's fierce order (10.335), Opis's vow of venegeance (11.849), and Juno's instructions to Juturna (12.159).

[29] So also 1.595, 5.189, 9.234, 10.739.

[30] Similarly 2.733, 8.532, 9.737, 12.95. In 8.293 the Salii pass from reported speech to direct invocation of the god; the heightened exaltation of their tone may be reflected in the fact that the song is first directly heard in the second foot of the line.

fistfight (5.467), the shout of Ascanius (5.673), the Sibyl's display of the golden bough to Charon (6.407), Juno's dismissal of Allecto (7.560), and the bellicose prayer of Mezentius (10.776).[31] It is not difficult to distinguish the tempo of a speech which ends on the *first* syllable of the second foot ("diua parens," 6.197, followed by an anxious pause) from that of a speech ending on the *second* syllable of the same foot with a trochaic fall ("acceleremus!" 9.221, followed by *uigiles simul excitat*). Still more abrupt utterances run into the second foot of the line in such a way that their final syllables are elided into the first word of the narrative, giving an impression of impetuous haste.

"nunc morere." hoc dicens. . . .   (2.550)

"haud illi stabunt Aeneia paruo
hospitia." et laeuo pressit pede talia fatus. . . .   (10.494–95)

One excited speech starts partway through the first foot of the line: Amata, waving a blazing torch, *clamat* "io matres" (7.400). And in several striking speeches the last word coincides with the dactylic first foot of the verse: Mercury vanishes (4.570), Anchises mourns (6.886), Evander faints (8.583), Mezentius kills an enemy (10.744), and Latinus begs Turnus to pity his old father (12.45). Two speeches actually end on the first syllable of the first foot: Turnus's war-cry, "en!" (9.52), and Aeneas's command at the games, "dic" (5.551). The brusqueness of this latter is doubtless intended to resemble the firm authority of a Roman paterfamilias: perhaps also to contrast with the garrulity of a Homeric father on a similar occasion (Nestor to Antilochus, *Il.* 23.306–48).

The fifth and sixth feet of the hexameter line are very emphatic. The first words of two peremptory utterances by superhuman beings at critical moments occupy that position at 4.702 (Iris) and 6.45 (the Sibyl).

The pause after a dactylic fourth foot, the "bucolic diaeresis," is avoided in Latin heroic poetry, apparently because its associations are either playful or affectionate.[32] Only a few speeches in the *Aeneid* break off here: for instance, Iulus's joke, "we are eating our tables" (7.116), two kindly speeches by Aeneas to young Lausus (10.812 and 10.830), an offhand jest (10.594), and the summons of Cybele to the ships as they are transformed into nymphs (9.117):

---

[31] But the Sibyl's speech about the ritual of entrance into the other world, although it ends in the second foot ("aspicies," 6.155), is not hasty: it is followed by a somber silence. So too the wounded Mezentius's words in 10.856.

[32] There is a good discussion by R. Lucot, "Ponctuation bucolique, accent et émotion dans l' *Énéide*," *REL* 43 (1965) 261–74.

> uos ite solutae,
> ite deae pelagi: genetrix iubet.

Here, not too distantly, we can hear an echo of the last line of Vergil's last bucolic poem. As the mother Cybele speaks to her flock, so speaks the poet-herdsman:

> ite domum saturae, uenit Hesperus, ite capellae.

Even within these patterns there are further subtleties. Two speeches may both open at exactly the same spot in the line, and yet have different initial emphasis. In 4.333 Aeneas addresses Dido, beginning at the penthemimeral caesura, and in 6.341 he addresses Palinurus, beginning at the same place. In both speeches the second word is *te*. Yet the slow gravity of the question to Palinurus, "quīs tē," makes a marked contrast with the rhythm of his exordium to Dido, "ĕgŏ tē." The latter is lighter and quicker, and seems to convey something of his embarrassment—the same feeling which is expressed in the quick pace and double elisions of his later phrase (4.337):

> pro re pauca loquar. nĕqu' ĕg' hanc abscondere furto. . . .

Aeneas addresses Palinurus only twice, starting both times at the same place in the line; but the latter address, in the underworld (6.341), has the slow pace of "quīs tē," while the former (5.26) is carefree and informal, "ĕquĭdēm sīc."[33] Of Juno's two submissive speeches to Jupiter, both begin in midline with "quid?" Yet the first (10.611) is light:

> cui Iuno summissa "quĭd, ō . . . ?"[34]

The second (10.628), opening one syllable earlier in the line, is slow and plaintive:

> et Iuno adlacrimans "quĭd sī . . . ?"

NARRATIVE WORDS WITHIN SPEECHES

Hitherto we have been discussing Vergil's techniques of knitting speech and narrative together by moving from one to the other within a

---

[33] *Equidem* begins an informal reply once again, in 9.207, and it opens Turnus's humble plea in 12.931.

[34] Notice in the following line (10.612) the light rhythm and the alliteration on T, evoking timidity.

line: something eschewed by the Greek epic poets. He goes further than this. He interweaves speech and narrative by inserting narrative words within his speeches. Certain aspects of this device have been examined by J. R. Gjerløw in the article cited in note 2 above, to which many of the following remarks are indebted. He gives figures for the relative frequencies of *ait, inquit,* and *fatur: quae in uulgus edita eius uerbis inuertere supersedeo.*

Again it apparently was Ennius who introduced the device, although we have only one small fragment to guarantee this (*Ann.* 360–61):

> "malo cruce," fatur, "uti des,
> Iuppiter!"

Lucretius once inserts *aiunt* into a speech (3.898), but Catullus never permits a verb of speaking to intrude within a speech in his hexameter poems.[35] Vergil, however, is flexible and free.

His simplest method is to introduce a word of speaking such as *ait* or *inquit* between words of a continuous speech. The verb alone may be inserted:

> "cur" inquit "diuersus abis?" (11.855)

The speaker's name may be added to the verb:

> "non lacrimis hoc tempus," ait Saturnia Iuno,
> "accelera!" (12.156–57)

The verb and the name or description may be separated so as to enclose some spoken words:

> et Mnestheus "quo deinde fugam, quo tenditis?" inquit. (9.781)[36]

Or, to add emphasis, Vergil sometimes uses two verbs of speaking:

> lacrimis ita fatur obortis:
> "tene," inquit, "miserande puer. . . ." (11.41–42)[37]

A description of the speaker's manner, combined with a verb of speaking to enclose words of speech, makes a lively effect:

> constitit et lacrimans, "quis iam locus," inquit, "Achate . . . ?" (1.459)

> "immo," ait, "o ciues," arrepto tempore Turnus. . . . (11.459)[38]

[35] But note in his galliambics "agedum," *inquit,* "age ferox i" (63.78).
[36] So also 5.353, 5.741, 6.45–46, 7.68, 12.776–77.
[37] Again in 5.547–51.
[38] Cf. 2.386–87, 5.473–74, 6.317–18, 8.112–13, 10.490–91, 12.258–59, 12.930–31.

Occasionally a new verb of speaking may be added, when the speaker passes from one theme to another.[39]

> sic incipiens hortatur ouantis:
> "maxima res effecta, uiri. . . .
> ite," ait, "egregias animas . . . / decorate supremis
> muneribus."   (11.13–14 + 24–26)

Words more emphatic than *ait* or *inquit* are sometimes thus inserted: *exclamat* (2.535 and 733), *conclamat* (6.259, 12.426).

Now and then Vergil starts a speech by naming or describing the speaker, but omits the verb of speaking: this produces the effect of spontaneous candor or rapid reply.

> tum Venus "haud equidem tali me dignor honore."   (1.335)[40]

Or again, he will give the speaker's name and simply add a participle describing his demeanor:

> olli subridens sedato pectore Turnus. . . .   (9.740)[41]

In one or two passages a speech begins thus abruptly, but is announced by a word of preparation. Aeneas's supplication to Apollo in 3.85 is prefaced by the word *uenerabar*, which, although not a verb of speaking, implies a spoken prayer; and his epitaph on Palinurus (5.870) is a little apostrophe which he utters *multa gemens*.

Sometimes, again, a speech opens without a word to distinguish it from the narrative, but is set off at its close by a verb of speaking. Creusa's desperate gesture passes straight into her plea (2.674–765):

> paruumque patri tendebat Iulum.
> "si periturus abis, et nos rape in omnia tecum!"

But at the end we hear her screaming, *talia uociferans*. Dido's message sent to Aeneas through Anna has no word of introduction, but is closed by *talibus orabat* (4.437). Three of Aeneas's own speeches in his account of the fall of Troy begin abruptly because of his excitement, but close with words such as *fatus eram* (2.323, 2.588, 2.721). Three speeches by his enemies follow the same pattern: Turnus (10.279[42] and 12.676) and Camilla (11.715).

---

[39] So Gjerløw (note 2 above) p. 50, citing and correcting Loesch (see p. 128) p. 17f. Cf. 3.480 and 5.551. Gjerløw points out that *ait* is often the word that accompanies an imperative in the *Aeneid*, and proposes that *ait* in 5.551 (which is pleonastic) may have been suggested by the imperative *dic*.

[40] So 1.730, 2.41–42, 2.547, 2.674, 6.695, 9.234, 9.246, 10.896–97, 10.898, 12.631.

[41] Cf. 1.370–71, 10.611, 10.628, 10.742.

[42] Omitting 10.278, inserted from 9.127 by someone who felt the speech started too abruptly.

In a few passages of strong emotion Vergil moves from narrative to speech without any words whatever to show that a speech has begun or ended. Describing a crisis in his escape from Troy, Aeneas passes from his story to an evocation of his thoughts, and then to his actual words, which stand alone just as he recalled them years afterwards.

> rursus in arma feror mortemque miserrimus opto:
> nam quod consilium aut quae iam fortuna dabatur?
> "mene efferre pedem, genitor, te posse relicto
> sperasti?" (2.655–58)

So also when he is terrified by the noise of hell (6.560–61), when he hears of the strange system of reincarnation (6.719–21), and when his heart is moved by the love of father and son (10.825–30). In these passages his voice bursts right out of the narrative. One other character exclaims with the same urgency: Nisus, realizing that he has lost his friend (9.390–91).

The most sophisticated of all Vergil's techniques of interconnecting speech and narrative is to insert parenthetical "stage-directions." The term comes from H. C. Lipscomb, *Aspects of the Speech in the Later Roman Epic* (Baltimore, 1909), who shows on pp. 32–36 that the device was enthusiastically taken over by some of Vergil's successors—most notably the master of parenthesis, Ovid, and also Statius, Valerius Flaccus, and Silius Italicus. Lucan and Claudian, however, virtually eschewed it. Such is the dramatic gesture of the Sibyl confronting Charon:

> "at ramum hunc" (aperit ramum qui ueste latebat)
> "agnoscas." (6.406–7)

The emotional address of Aletes to Nisus and Euryalus is broken in the middle, after his thanksgiving to the gods, by a description of his embrace and of his tears of gratitude (9.250–51). It is this device which interrupts Dido's last speech, and makes it more dramatic, more human than a formal oration of farewell (4.659–60).[43]

PHRASES DESCRIBING EMOTION

An epic poet sometimes explains to his hearers or readers the emotions which move his characters to speech. In a long scene, some speeches

---

[43] Other examples in 5.162–68 and 12.206.

may be given without any marked emotional emphasis, while others may be strongly passionate; and the changing moods of one or more persons can be indicated by alterations in the phrases introducing the words they say.

Homer prefaces most speeches quite simply, by a formula which names the speaker but carries no emotional charge: τὸν δ' ἀπαμειβόμενος προσέφη πόδας ὠκὺς 'Αχιλλεύς or προσέφη πολύμητις 'Οδυσσεύς. But some speeches he introduces with a line or a few lines describing a significant mood:

"Ηρη δ' οὐκ ἔχαδε στῆθος χόλον, ἀλλὰ προσηύδα   (Il. 4.24)

or the actual force of the utterance:

Τρώεσσιν ἐκέκλετο μακρὸν ἀύσας.   (Il. 17.183)

The expression of the speaker's face is important: ὑπόδρα ἰδών, μείδησεν, δάκρυα θερμὰ χέων. So is the motive which leads him to address his companion: ἐνένιπεν, νείκεσέ τ' ἄντην, μειλιχίοις ἐπέεσσιν ἐρήτυον. A gesture often carries much force. Achilles meeting Hector at last,

ὡς εἶδ', ὡς ἀνεπᾶλτο—

and then, εὐχόμενος, speaks (Il. 20.424).

By observing these introductory phrases, a reader may feel the ebb and flow of emotion in Homer. The debate in *Iliad* 1 illustrates this. Achilles opens it by making a calm proposal, introduced with no sign of excitement (1.58). Calchas accepts the proposal, σφιν εὐφρονέων, but asks that his safety be guaranteed (1.73). Achilles, still calm, does so (1.84f.). Calchas "takes heart" (1.92) and proposes the return of Chryseis to her father. Now Agamemnon rises: he is "vexed," and his anger is described in detail before he speaks (1.103–5). Although the following exchange between Achilles and Agamemnon contains some harsh words (1.122, 1.139), the introductory phrases depict no emotion. But then Achilles at last loses his temper: ὑπόδρα ἰδών (1.148), he belabors Agamemnon with hard epithets. When Agamemnon replies, Achilles is so furious that he lays his hand on his sword. Even after Athena persuades him not to draw it, he is still in a rage, addresses his opponent ἀταρτηροῖς ἐπέεσσιν (1.223), and ends by hurling the speakers' scepter to the ground (1.245).

To introduce and occasionally to terminate the speeches of his characters, Vergil uses a very wide variety of phrases describing emotion. Such introductory phrases in Homer, Apollonius, Vergil, and others have

been studied by Loesch (cited above on p. 128), who analyzes the different types of emotion expressed—e.g. hostility (*inimico pectore fatur*, 10.556
and 11.685), entreaty (*supplex*, 1.64, 4.205, 9.624, 10.523, 12.930),
amazement (*obstipuit*, 1.613, 8.121, 9.197), or terror (*amens formidine*,
12.776). This, however, is rather a mechanical classification: readers will
learn more by examining the varying emotions of individual characters.

When Aeneas and the Trojan refugees come upon Hector's widow,
Andromache, in her distant exile, how does she behave?

At first sight of them she goes almost mad with shock. She collapses.
She can scarcely speak, and then, after the pathetic plea, "Hector ubi
est?," breaks into hysterical weeping:

> lacrimasque effudit et omnem
> impleuit clamore locum.   (3.306–13)

Later, when Aeneas asks about her life as the concubine of Pyrrhus, she
grows calmer:

> deiecit uultum et demissa uoce[44] locuta est.   (3.320)

She then makes a long speech (3.321–43) marked both by tearful emotion (321–24) and by careful detail (333–36). Finally, when the Trojans
are departing, she shows herself still sad (3.482) but now capable of
speaking with composure (*talia fatur*, 3.485) as she gives Ascanius farewell gifts. So, too, her husband Helenus weeps at the first meeting (3.348)
but is more controlled thereafter. His prophecy is prefaced by *canit* (3.373),
and in saying good-bye he addresses Anchises *multo honore* (3.474 + 480)
in terms of calm confidence.

The Sibyl is a strange being, unlike any other in the poem. Super-
naturally old and wise, she speaks with curt authority, *breuiter*,[45] or else
without a hint of feeling: *fatur* (6.36, cf. 6.666), *coepit* (6.372), *ait* (6.630).
The emphatic and unusual phrase *orsa loqui* is applied to her twice: once
at 6.125, when she begins to describe the ritual for entry into the other
world, and once at 6.562, introducing her portentous description of hell.[46]
Emotional changes appear in her, as indicated by the phrases introducing
her words, only when she becomes a vehicle for the god (6.46–51 + 77–

---

[44]*Demissa uoce* does not occur elsewhere in the *Aeneid*. *Deiecit uultum* resembles
Dido's diffidence before the Trojan envoys (*uultum demissa*, 1.561), the melancholy of
young Marcellus (*deiecto uultu*, 6.862), and the depression of Lavinia (*oculos deiecta*, 11.480)
and of Turnus (*demisso lumine*, 12.220).

[45]*Breuiter* is used thrice of the Sibyl (6.321, 398, 538); twice of Dido (1.561, 4.632);
once each of Nisus (9.353), Aeneas (10.251), and Jupiter (10.621).

[46]*Orsa* with *loqui* only of the Sibyl; *orsus* alone, of Aeneas (1.325 and 2.2), Apollo
(9.656), and Jupiter (12.806). *Orsa refert* of Turnus (7.435–36) and Drances (11.124).

80 + 98–101) and when she plunges *furens* into the caverns of Avernus (6.259, 262).

Nisus and Euryalus are sometimes conceived as impetuous young-sters who rashly undertake a mission far beyond their powers. Vergil does not convey this impression by his method of describing their talk. Al-though Nisus is called *ardens* (9.198)[47] and although he speaks quickly, almost all his speeches are prefaced by neutral phrases free from excite-ment, such as *ait* (9.184), *ad haec* (9.207), *tum sic* (9.234), *sic ore locutus* (9.319), and *breuiter* . . . *ait* (9.353–55).[48] Excitement is first shown in him by the sudden cry of 9.390–91; at the end he breaks when, *exterritus amens* (9.424), he sees his friend facing the fierce slayer. At this point he suffers anguish comparable to that of the deserted Dido. She says "hunc ego si potui tantum sperare dolorem" (4.419), and Vergil says of Nisus *nec* . . . *tantum potuit perferre dolorem* (9.425–26).

The narrative of Sinon is skillfully punctuated by phrases which re-veal it (as recounted by Aeneas) to be a lie. He first speaks *turbatus* (2.67) with a groan of apparently real and certainly effective despair (2.73). A little later his fear is described as a sham: *pauitans* . . . *ficto pectore fatur* (2.107), although he pretends to weep (2.145 + 196).[49] After his chains are removed he is all fraud, *dolis instructus et arte Pelasga* (2.152).

Camilla's two boasts in battle are accompanied by warlike gestures (11.684–85, 11.718–20). Between her other two speeches there is a touching parallel. Riding up to the gate of the Latin city to meet Turnus (11.498–501), she dismounts:

> desiluit, quam tota cohors imitata relictis
> ad terram defluxit equis: tum talia fatur.

Later, struck down by Arruns, she utters her last words, *haec ita fatur* (11.822) and falls from her horse, *ad terram non sponte fluens*. The words *fluo* and *defluo* are not typical formulae for the act of dismounting from horseback: they are rare, and in the *Aeneid* occur only in these two places.[50]

Mezentius is a hard man. His first utterance (10.737) is accompa-

---

[47] *Ardens* is also applied to Iulus (9.652) and Aeneas (10.514) among others.

[48] Likewise Euryalus, after his first excitement (9.197), speaks briefly and calmly: *ait* (9.221), *talia fatur* (9.280).

[49] Line 2.76 must be excised: Vergil would not write *deposita formidine* and follow it by *pauitans*. It is in its right place at 3.612, where it is a desirable relief to Achaemenides' terror in 3.599 + 607–8.

[50] *Defluo* of dying horsemen in Furius Bibaculus fr. 8 Morel, Livy 2.20.3, and Ov. *Met.* 6.229 (there are also postclassical occurrences); *fluo* only in postclassical imitators of Vergil.

nied by no word of emotion, not even a verb of speech, but a warlike act. He follows it with another such act, *subridens mixta ira* (10.742–44). Facing Aeneas, he is *imperterritus* (10.770).[51] For a time his son's death throws him into passionate grief (10.844–45, cf. 870–71); but he addresses Aeneas without apparent excitement (*dixit*, 10.882) and in face of death speaks calmly, *haec loquitur* (10.907).[52]

Pyrrhus son of Achilles rages during the fighting within Troy (*exsultat*, 2.470; *furentem*, 2.499). Yet after Priam has thrown a spear at him and insulted him, he addresses the old king with no trace of vengeful fury, but in words curt and cold: *cui Pyrrhus* (2.547).

The two old Italian kings are not dissimilar in manner. Latinus is tranquil as he receives the Trojan envoys, *placido ore* (7.194).[53] Evander speaks much in Book 8, but without any phrase depicting strong emotion: *pauca refert*[54] (8.154), *ait* (8.185), *tum rex* (8.313), *inquit* (8.351, 362), *rex prior haec* (8.469). Both monarchs, however, listen to the Trojans with wonder and something like awe. Evander

> os oculosque loquentis
> iamdudum et totum lustrabat lumine corpus.   (8.152–53)

Latinus remains long silent (7.249–58) before, *laetus*, he speaks. Only when saying farewell to his son (8.558–59 + 583–84) and again when receiving the corpse (11.148–51) does Evander give way to deep feeling. Latinus never speaks with such passionate emotion. He "invokes the gods and empty air" before secluding himself in his palace (7.593–600). Later he reappears at the council-meeting, gloomy (11.238) but calm enough to pray for guidance and to speak coherently (11.301–35). Even confronting the choleric Turnus, he answers *sedato corde* (12.18) and remains regal and self-controlled during the oath-taking (12.161–64 + 195–96). His final collapse (12.609–11) is wordless.

Certain secondary characters who appear only twice or thrice undergo extremes of emotion. Anna's first advice to Dido is given with the colorless word *refert* (4.31): evidently she is calm, and sure that her suggestions are prudent. Later, however, she is *miserrima* (4.437) and *maesta* (4.476). She speaks only once again, and then it is in grief and remorse, *unguibus*

[51]*Imperterritus* was invented by Vergil: "quis ante hunc?" asks Servius auctus.

[52]Contrast Turnus in the same situation, *supplex* (12.930).

[53]*Placido ore* of Diomede in 11.251, *placido pectore* of Ilioneus in 1.521, in both cases during a diplomatic conference.

[54]It is curious that Vergil should use the phrase *pauca refert* here to introduce Evander's reply to Aeneas (8.154–74), since it is rather a long speech containing some superfluous detail. However, his next speech (8.185–275) is one of the longest in the poem. Donatus comments *pauca debemus accipere, hoc est pauciora quam dici potuerunt*.

ora . . . foedans et pectora pugnis [55] (4.672–74 + 685–87). The fate of
Creusa is the reverse of this. She too speaks only twice. First, wailing
and screaming, she clutches Aeneas's feet and holds his son up before
him (2.673–74 + 679). But later, a serene spirit, she addresses him with
words of love and consolation. The phrase which precedes her address
(2.775) is tranquil:

tum sic adfari et curas his demere dictis. [56]

Amata, who speaks thrice, first sheds tears (7.358), then screams fiercely
(7.399–400), and at last weeps in suicidal despair, *moritura* (12.54–55).
Housman thought this a grotesque exaggeration, saying *"moritura . . .*
makes me blush for [Vergil] whenever I think of it." [57] But it is true to
fact: she was determined to commit suicide if Aeneas won (12.61–63)
and did so.

    Anchises, although initially shown as feeble in body, is strong in
mind. At his earliest appearance (2.634–50) he makes a firm and dignified speech, introduced by *ait* with no emotional concomitant, and ter-
minated by

talia perstabat memorans fixusque manebat.

At the omen of Iulus's flaming head he speaks with pious joy (*laetus,*
2.687). Throughout Book 3 his speeches are introduced by no phrase
hinting at excitement or feebleness: *ait, sic fatus* (3.103, 118), *memorat,
sic ait* (3.182, 189), *ait* (3.539 + 543). His prayers are tranquil (3.264,
525–27). Even when he hears the roar of the whirlpool he identifies it
with no trace of emotion (3.558). As a ghost visiting the earth to counsel
his son, he speaks with his wonted serenity (5.722–23 + *dixerat*, 740).
Even in Elysium his description of the process of transmigration and of
the future grandeur of Rome is not accompanied by phrases indicating
emotional tension: *tum pater Anchises* (6.713), *suscipit Anchises* (6.723),
dixerat Anchises (6.752), *sic pater Anchises atque haec mirantibus addit*
(6.854). This is not to say that the great speech itself is passionless. It
contains exclamations, "qui iuuenes!" (6.771), eager imperatives, "as-
pice" (6.771 and 855), apostrophes, "quo fessum rapitis, Fabii?" (6.845),
interjections, "en" (6.781) and "heu" (6.828), and a constant variety of
sentence-structure and metrical arrangement which indicates a lively rise

---

[55] The same gesture is recorded of Acoetes bewailing Pallas (11.86) and Juturna her
brother Turnus (12.871).

[56] This phrase also introduces the prophetic counsel given to Aeneas by the moonlit
effigies of the Trojan divinities (3.153) and by the Tiber (8.35).

[57] *Letters*, ed. H. Maas (London, 1971) 423.

and fall of excitement. But Vergil, through introducing it by simple verbs of speech without emotional modifiers, seems to intend to show that Anchises, now immortal, has the calm intellectual control of a great mind describing a mighty vision. Twice only in Book 6 does Vergil make Anchises speak with external indications of deep feeling. When he sees his son coming to find him in Elysium he stretches out his arms,

> effusaeque genis lacrimae et uox excidit ore.[58]   (6.686)

And when Aeneas asks him about the young soul accompanying the glorious Marcellus,

> tum pater Anchises lacrimis ingressus obortis. . . .   (6.867)

But after his mournful tribute, he once again becomes the serene and fatherly teacher: *exim bella uiro memorat quae deinde gerenda* (6.890).

The gods differ widely in demeanor. Apollo's few speeches are characterized by no strong feeling; Diana in her narrative only by *tristis* (11.534). Neptune appears twice. Observing the storm raised by Aeolus, he is *grauiter commotus*, although he raises from the water a *placidum caput* (1.126–27). His rebuke to the winds is introduced by nothing more drastic than *talia fatur* and closed by *sic ait* (1.131 and 142); yet it contains angry reproaches, a threat, several commands, and the violent aposiopesis "quos ego—!" Vergil therefore presents Neptune as a monarch who controls his anger and wields his vast authority with dignity. His speech to Venus (5.800–815) is marked by regal condescension and introduced by the lofty phrase

> tum Saturnius haec domitor maris edidit alti.[59]

Jupiter is always calm. His words may be blunt; but they are accompanied by no display of disquiet or anger, whether he is despatching Mercury to rebuke Aeneas (*sic adloquitur*, 4.222), opening and closing the debate of the gods (*incipit*, 10.5; *infit*, 10.101), or rejecting an impossible request from his own mother (*filius huic contra*, 9.93). The fact that he seeks out Juno and addresses her *ultro* (10.606) implies a reproof, and the curt style of his second speech (*breuiter fatur*, 10.621) reduces her to tears. Both then, however, and in his final interview with her

---

[58] The phrase *excidit ore* appears only once more in the *Aeneid*—again of Anchises, although in a very different context (2.658). The voice of Cybele from heaven is said *excidere* (9.113).

[59] Elsewhere in the poem *edere* in this sense is used only of Aeneas's earnest prayer to Jupiter (5.693) and Latinus's address to the Trojans (7.194).

(*adloquitur*, 12.792; *sic orsus*, 12.806) he is still tranquil, though firm. His final concession to Juno is made with a smile, which intentionally recalls the reassuring warmth of his first address to Venus (*olli subridens*, 1.254 and 12.829).

The soft heart of Venus is easily moved by grief for her son's afflictions. In tears she addresses Jupiter (1.228), with much anxiety begs Neptune for a safe passage (5.779–80), and is moved by real fear, *exterrita*, to ask Vulcan for the divine weapons (8.370–73)—although she does not forget to woo him (8.387–88 + 393). Yet she speaks to Aeneas himself with no outward show of emotion: *inquit* (1.321), *tum Venus* (1.335), *talibus adfata est dictis* (8.611). With maternal authority she represses his emotional outbreaks in Africa—*nec plura querentem / passa Venus medio sic interfata dolore est* (1.385–86)—and in burning Troy—*dextraque prehensum / continuit* (2.592–93). In her brief interview with Juno she is diplomatically discreet, *sic contra est ingressa* (4.107), *non aduersata . . . adnuit* (4.127–28). Her tactful speech ends with the brief phrase "perge, sequar" (4.114), which is curiously echoed much later by Juno herself addressing Juturna, "perge, decet"[60] (12.153). Her important oration at the Olympian council is highly emotional in tone. The sentence introducing it (10.16–17) breaks off in an incomplete line. Vergil might have completed it with a description of her imploring eyes and gestures, comparable with her earlier address to Jupiter in 1.228. The two speeches begin in almost exactly the same way.

Like Homer's Hera, who laughed with her lips while her forehead above her dark brows was troubled (*Il.* 15.101–3), Juno is adaptable, not to say hypocritical. Alone, brooding on the unhealed wound to her pride, she burns with fury (1.36–37 + 50) and is struck by a fierce pang (7.291)— the same raging wrath which prompts her speech in rebuttal to Venus (10.63). She starts her second monologue shaking her head in incredulous anger, like Poseidon at the sight of Odysseus (*Od.* 5.285 and *Aen.* 7.292). Yet she deigns to coax Aeolus (*supplex*, 1.64), spur on Allecto (*his acuit uerbis*, 7.330), and encourage Juturna (*exhortata*, 12.159). In her negotiations with Venus she contrives to conceal her disdain and hostility, at least in manner. *Talibus adgreditur dictis* (4.92) is a neutral phrase, which Vergil employs of Aeneas addressing Helenus in 3.358 and Dido making a request of Anna in 4.476; and so is *sic excepit* (4.114, used of Ascanius in a friendly colloquy, 9.258). With Jupiter, however, she is *summissa* and then *adlacrimans* (10.611, 628), while her final

---

[60] "Perge modo" says Venus twice to Aeneas (1.389 and 401). These, with the above, are the only occurrences of the imperative in the poem.

claim of victory is disguised as a surrender and delivered *summisso uultu* (12.807).

The painful changes in Dido's personality are strongly marked in the phrases that introduce the words she speaks. At first, in spite of her in-born pride, she feels a little inferior to the Trojan prince and his follow-ers. After listening to Ilioneus's speech,

> tum breuiter Dido uultum demissa profatur,   (1.561)

and her speech contains an implicit apology together with a defense of her people against the charge of being remote and uncivilized (1.563–68, cf. 1.539–41). The sudden appearance of Aeneas startles her (1.613), and at the feast she questions him eagerly (1.748–56).

A few hours afterward, *male sana*, she speaks urgently to Anna and ends in a flood of tears (4.8 and 30). On learning of Aeneas's proposed departure, she raves like a maniac (*furenti, saeuit inops animi, incensa bacchatur*, 4.298 + 300–301). It is in this mood that she seeks him out to address her first reproaches to him *ultro* (4.304). His speech of defense kindles her to a furious retort in which she curses him, *accensa* (4.364), before rushing away and collapsing in a swoon (4.388–92). She will never speak with him again. Her departure is strangely like the vanishing of his dead wife Creusa, who gave him her last message and then

> lacrimantem et multa uolentem
> dicere deseruit, tenuisque recessit in auras.   (2.790–91)

So here Dido disappears from the eyes of her lover

> linquens multa metu cunctantem et multa parantem
> dicere.   (4.390–91)

Yet she weeps bitterly as she sends Anna to him pleading for delay (*gemitus*, 4.409; *lacrimas*, 4.413; *fletus*, 4.437).

The next stage begins when she determines to commit suicide, for she conceals her true emotions while addressing her sister (4.474–77) although the effort and her suffering make her turn pale (4.499). Sleepless, she is torn between the pangs of unfulfilled love and surging anger (4.529–32). Her fury masters her when she sees that Aeneas has sailed away; and now she makes her first violent gesture, striking her bosom and tearing her hair (4.589–90).[61] Yet, still a queen, she gives her orders to the old nurse briefly and clearly (4.632–41). Her last utterance begins

---

[61] The same gesture, described with only the change of one adjective, is made in 12.155 by Juturna.

with a gush of tears (4.649) and ends, after a kiss, with the thrust of Aeneas's sword (4.659–65).

Turnus, as revealed by the tone of his speeches, passes through five distinct emotional phases.

In the first he is a confident young warrior, laughing in scorn at an old priestess (7.435–36), encouraging his soldiers at a setback (9.126–27), and completely devoid of excitement in the duel with Pallas: witness *haec ait* (10.444), *ita fatur* (10.480), followed by the deceptively bland remark

> aspice num mage sit nostrum penetrabile telum,

then *inquit* (10.491) and *talia fatus* (10.495). As he listens to the threats of Pandarus and prepares to slay him, he is calm and smiling; his lofty manner is described in a slow line full of spondees (9.740):

> olli subridens sedato pectore Turnus.

Vergil uses this archaic phasing only thrice elsewhere. Once it describes the balanced calm of King Latinus talking to Turnus himself (12.18), and twice it evokes the tranquil smile of the supreme deity (1.254, 12.829). The implication here is that Turnus feels himself to be superior and unassailable.

Still, there is in him a latent instability, almost a psychosis, which at intervals dominates him very much to his detriment. It is this excitable element in his personality which is inflamed by Allecto (7.456–66). Because he yields to this frenzy, he misses two important tactical opportunities—to capture Troy (9.756–61) and to ambush Aeneas's army (11.896–905): note *furor* in 9.760 and *furens* in 11.901. In this mood the adjective *turbidus* describes him; and the passion itself is his *uiolentia*.[62] The second phase, therefore, is one of dangerous excitement, during which he runs shouting after the phantom Aeneas (10.647–52), then raves with suicidal despair (10.666–86), then blazes out again during the debate (11.376). Almost speechless with passion during his interview with Latinus (12.9–10 + 45–47), he reaches a critical summit in the night before the duel, putting on his armor and shouting a sort of prayer to his spear (12.92–102): *his agitur furiis*.

Then comes the depression which follows berserk fits. During the

---

[62]*Turbidus* is applied four times to Turnus (9.57, 10.648, 12.10, 12.671), once each to Mezentius (10.763), Tarchon (11.742), Arruns (11.814), and the troubled spirit of Anchises seen in dreams (4.353). *Violentia* of Turnus in 11.354 and 376, 12.9 and 45.

ceremony of oath-taking which is to precede his duel, Turnus is pale and silent: he does not look like the same man (12.219–21).

But a few moments later the fight breaks out. Aeneas is wounded and retires. At once Turnus *subita spe feruidus ardet* (12.325). Killing a Trojan nobleman, he taunts him coldly, *haec insuper addit* (12.358); but he does not speak again until he hears the attack on the Latin city (12.620–21). Then, although gloomy in the expectation of death, he is quite firm (12.631–49, 676–80, 693–95) and faces Aeneas courageously.

The last phase begins when his sword is broken, and he runs away like a stag pursued by hounds. For the first time he speaks *amens formidine* (12.776).[63] A little later, shaking his head sadly, he says that he is doomed (12.894); and finally he prays for mercy (12.930–31).

It is Aeneas whose speeches evince the broadest range of emotions. They are very rarely prompted by happiness: his remarks at 6.193 and 10.874 are brief. When he is, or may be assumed to be, happy, he speaks with serene tranquillity. For example, when he proclaims the commemorative festival in Sicily, "laetum cuncti celebremus honorem," his speech is preceded only by the plain words *tumulique ex aggere fatur* (5.44).

During the capture of Troy he weeps during his vision of Hector (2.279–80), then rages with fury (2.575, 588), and at his father's refusal to leave home determines to die fighting ("mortem miserrimus opto," 2.655). Then, after Anchises is convinced, Aeneas gives orders for evacuation very rapidly, without a modifying phrase or even a verb of speech (2.707).

On his journeys in Book 3 he manifests no emotion through his speeches except when consoling Andromache (*turbatus,* 3.313–14) and when parting from her and her husband (3.492). But during the storm and after the landing in Africa his sufferings are more intense. He groans with despair as he wishes he had died years ago (1.93), sighs as he tells his mother of his wanderings (1.371), and weeps when he sees the paintings of the Trojan war (1.459). Nevertheless, he addresses his men with confident words and conceals his own anxieties from them (1.197 + 208–9).

So again, when confronted by Dido, he is compelled to disguise his feelings, although with a hard effort, *obnixus,* which makes it difficult

---

[63] It is a sign of Turnus's instability that *amens* is applied to him five times: he is *amens* with warlike fervor in 7.460, with shame in 10.681, with amazement in 12.622, and with terror in 12.742 and 776. Aeneas is *amens* in Troy, with alarm and rage (2.314) and with despair at the loss of his wife (2.745); later, with horrified surprise at the epiphany of Mercury (4.279). Others so described are Panthus (2.321), Iarbas (4.203), and Nisus (9.424).

for him to speak in reply (4.331–32). He continues to make the same effort to control his emotions when Anna brings persuasive and loving messages from Dido to him (4.437–49).

There has long been a question whether, in line 449, the tears which flow uselessly are those of Aeneas or those of Dido. (The tears of Anna are unimportant, and are excluded by Dido's in 413 and 437.) The question is determined by the syntax:

> mens immota manet, lacrimae uoluuntur inanes.

It is scarcely possible for two nouns as subjects in the same line to belong to two different people, unless clearly differentiated, for instance by possessives such as *huius* and *illius*. Therefore, since the *mens immota* belongs to Aeneas, the *lacrimae inanes* belong to him also. Furthermore, after the opening sentence, Aeneas is the theme of the entire paragraph: all our attention is focused on him and his thoughts and feelings: *ille* (438), *uiri* (440), *heros* (447). It is scarcely logical to introduce a more distant subject as a reference for the final three words alone. And emotionally the picture is correct. *Mens* here signifies not the vague word "mind," which in English can include the emotions, but "will," "purpose," as in 5.812, 8.400, 10.182. This is the *mens* which Dido has urged Aeneas to abandon (4.319). But his emotions are in conflict with it, *magno persentit pectore curas*, and it is the pangs of that conflict which wring tears from him. These are the same tears that he will shed for Dido in the world of the dead: tears of love (6.455) and of pity (6.476). The image in lines 441–46 points to the same conclusion. Aeneas is the oak rooted in the rock. The persuasions and lamentations of Dido strive to move him as the storm-wind strives to uproot the oak-tree. The branches of the tree scream and its leaves fall heavily on the ground; but the trunk is steadfast: so Aeneas's heart labors with pain and his tears fall, but his resolution remains unmoved. Finally, this interpretation is supported by the Homeric parallel. A hero in love with a beautiful woman, a hero who conceals his emotions and sheds tears without altering his purpose— this is Odysseus with Penelope in *Od.* 19.203–12. First, a weather-image (19.205–9); then Homer tells us that Odysseus feels pity in his heart, but his eyes are as firm as horn or steel, ἀτρέμας ἐν βλεφάροισι: so Aeneas also *immota tenebat / lumina* (331–32). Odysseus weeps, but δόλῳ . . . δάκρυα κεῦθεν; from Aeneas (just after a significant repetition of *immota* = ἀτρέμας) *lacrimae uoluuntur inanes*.

Fear is an emotion which Vergil's Aeneas seldom feels. Homeric heroes are often frightened. Achilles himself, facing the Homeric Aeneas in *Il.* 20.259–66, is afraid ("foolishly," adds the poet); the Homeric Aeneas is still more scared when Achilles' spear nearly kills him (*Il.* 20.273–83); and Hector trembles and flees from Achilles like a dove from a falcon (*Il.* 22.136–44). In the hurricane, Vergil's Aeneas groans and suffers traumatic shock (like Odysseus seeing the great wave, *Od.* 5.406); but he speaks coherently enough (*Aen.* 1.92–101). At the first appearance of Mercury he is paralyzed with awe (4.279–80), and his voice is impeded by fear of Dido's rage in 4.390–91. With the second appearance of Mercury, he wakes *exterritus* (4.571). (The word is used of Aeneas only twice: once there, and once when he sees hell surrounded by the river of flames, 6.559.) Once and once only after leaving Africa is his resolution severely shaken: when his ships are burning in Sicily. Then he tears his festal robe and prays Jove either to save his fleet or to strike him dead (5.685–92); and even after the miraculous rainstorm he is still *casu concussus acerbo* (5.700).[64] Thereafter he never quails again. In the presence of the Sibyl possessed by Phoebus, he and his attendants tremble, but the long prayer he utters shows no trace of alarm or excitement (6.54–76). So, after the Sibyl has uttered her predictions, he remains unmoved even while asking her to guide him through the other world (6.102–3 + 124). Here there is an intentional contrast with Homer. When Circe tells Odysseus that he must go to the land of Hades, his heart is broken and he weeps and grovels: he is still crying when he sets out on the voyage (*Od.* 10.496–99 + 11.1–5). The monsters of the underworld alarm Vergil's Aeneas, as Odysseus was frightened by the thought of seeing the Gorgon, but instead of trying to escape he draws his sword to attack them (*Od.* 11.632–37, *Aen.* 6.290–94).

Aeneas rarely speaks under the pressure of the softer emotions at any time after his entry into the underworld. Twice more he weeps bitterly: once when addressing the ghost of Dido (6.455 + 476) and once when speaking of the dead Pallas (11.29 + 41, 11.59). Once, over Lausus, he groans (10.823). As he comments on the omen of the tables, he is struck by wonder (7.119), and he receives the envoys of the Latins graciously (11.106–7). But even when he embraces his son, Vergil does not signalize any emotional tone in his speech (12.433–34 + 441).

On the contrary, harsher and crueler feelings begin to dominate his words. He speaks with chilly brevity (*talia reddit*) to Magus before stabbing him in the throat (10.530–36). A little later he gibes *inimico pectore* at a headless corpse (10.556), taunts a dying man *dictis amaris* (10.591), and warns or threatens Lausus before killing him (10.810). It is in this

[64] Later Aeneas is *casu concussus* at the death of Palinurus (5.869) and at the sight of Dido's phantom (6.475). Compare, in the storm-image of 4.441–46 (p. 160 above), *concusso stipite*.

phase that the poet compares Aeneas, not to a god or a hero or a noble animal, but to the monstrous fiend Aegaeon (10.565–70). Grim battle-joy appears in his challenge to Mezentius (10.874). In the last conflict he speaks little. His command that the Latin city be stormed is prefaced by the bellicose line:

> continuo pugnae accendit maioris imago.   (12.560)

Yet although his speech made then is full of hard angry words and sounds, it is accompanied by no phrase indicating emotion: Vergil may therefore intend us to understand that it was uttered in a tone of icily controlled anger: *fatur* and *dixerat* are the words (12.564 and 574), not *conclamat* or *talia uociferans*.

Aeneas's two final speeches display him as cruel and terrible. He utters his last challenge to Turnus *saeuo pectore* (12.888). *Saeuus* is used four times of the remorseless enemy Juno (1.4, 2.612, 7.287, 7.592), twice of Achilles (1.458, 2.29) and Pallas Athena (2.226, 2.616) and Mars (7.608, 11.153) and, strikingly, of Jupiter himself in the final books (11.901, 12.849). It is never applied to Aeneas until the last books of the epic, and then five times (*saeuae irae*, 10.813; "saeuissime," 10.878; 11.910, 12.107 and 888). At the end, after recognizing Pallas's sword-belt, Aeneas condemns his victim to instant death, *furiis accensus*. This is a very strong phrase, which Vergil uses elsewhere of the raving Latin women (7.392) and, with a slight alteration in form, of Dido in her rage (4.376).[65] As Aeneas plunges the sword home, he is still ablaze with passion, *feruidus*. This word also shows the change in his temper. Of its eleven occurrences the most striking are its applications to Amata (7.397), Hercules (8.230), Turnus (9.72, 12.325), and Aeneas himself four times (10.788, 12.748, 894, and 951). It would be more humane to view Aeneas here as a judge executing a righteous sentence, *debellans superbos*. But that is not how Vergil describes him: he is killing a suppliant in a fit of passionate rage. When we first see Aeneas, in Book 1, he is deathly cold. When we last see him, he is burning.

[65] Dido is said *concipere furias* when resolving on suicide (4.474). Others moved by *furiae* are the Locrian Ajax (1.41), Orestes (3.331), Hercules (8.219), the Etruscans when enraged by Mezentius's cruelties (8.494), Cassandra as described by Juno (10.68), and Turnus (12.101 and 668). The reading in 8.205 is *furis*, not *furiis*, since the deed of Cacus is one of cunning (*scelerisue doliue*, 206) rather than of wild excitement.

The Key of the Pantry
(*Moretum* 15)

THE LITTLE epic of a peasant's life, called *Moretum*, begins with the cock crowing in the darkness before dawn (1–2). Simulus, awakened as much by hunger as by the cockcrow, gropes for the embers of his fire, and finds them when they scorch his fingers (7). Then he lights the lamp (10–12), and, guarding it carefully from being blown out, opens his pantry door, takes some grain, and starts to prepare his midday meal.

There is a textual problem in the line which describes Simulus opening the pantry where he keeps his "poor heap of grain."

> oppositaque manu lumen defendit ab aura
> et reserat clausae qua peruidet ostia claui.   15

The MSS variants are set out by A. Salvatore in his "Tradizione manoscritta e lingua del Moretum," *Studi in onore di L. Castiglioni* (2 vols., Florence, 1960) 835–37, and reprinted in his text of the *Appendix Vergiliana* (Naples, 1964); by E. J. Kenney in his text of the *Moretum* (*Appendix Vergiliana*, Oxford, 1966); and by E. Courtney in his "Notes on the *Appendix Vergiliana*," *Phoenix* 21 (1967) 44–55, esp. 55.

Many attempts have been made to do away with *clausae*, which Kenney obelizes: e.g. *casulae* (Scaliger), *cellae* (Barth), *caueae* (Heinsius). But Leo in ALLG 10 (1898) 438 interprets it as a noun, formed on the same pattern as *offensa* and *repulsa* and actually found in Titinius fr. 61. (*Close* in English and *clos* in French are nouns similarly formed from adjectives.) The word therefore designates Simulus's *cella penaria*, his pantry.

We are left with the door and the key and the verb connecting them.

Unpublished, appearing here for the first time.

Does the key look at the door? Salvatore suggests that it is imagined as a sentinel "che scruta e vigila"; but surely this is farfetched, since the key is not left in position continuously. It is the door and the lock that guard Simulus's supplies. Mr. Courtney proposes that Simulus himself looks at the pantry, *quam ⟨iam⟩ uidet* because the lamplight shows it to him. True, but rather flat; and the author of the *Moretum* was sophisticated.

Surely it is more suitable to his technique of describing all the farmer's actions stage by stage, to substitute another verb for the awkward *peruidet*. One solution might be:

> *qua perforat ostia claui.*

On keys made to penetrate the door see R. Vallois in Daremberg-Saglio (s.v. *sera*) 4. 1246–47. *Perforare* occurs (in tmesi) in Lucretius 5.1268. I cannot suggest a reason for the appearance of the corruption, unless the scribe had in his mind the line from Ovid, *Met.* 14.375, which ends *qui peruidet omnia Solem.*

Libertino Patre Natus

ALTHOUGH HORACE was born free, his father had been a slave. Horace's enemies did not forget this, nor did he. In one of his autobiographical satires he thrice calls himself *libertino patre natum* (*Serm.* 1.6.6, 45, and 46); over fifteen years later he inserts the same injurious words into the signature-poem of his first book of poetic letters (*Epist.* 1.20.20).[1] Was his father a slave imported from abroad, or a native Italian—perhaps captured and enslaved in the Social War?[2] In *Serm.* 2.1.34–39 Horace speaks as though he came of old Italian stock (*Lucanus an Apulus anceps*); and elsewhere, in a significant phrase, says that his father's ideal was *traditum ab antiquis morem seruare* (*Serm.* 1.4.117). That has the Roman ring of Ennius's *moribus antiquis res stat Romana uirisque* (*Ann.* 500 Vahlen). No Hermeros or Trimalchio could have spoken or thought like that.[3] However, the essential thing was that, although he obtained his freedom before Horace was born, he had been a slave; and no ex-slave was equal to a freeborn Roman citizen. Augustus himself drew the line sharply. He would never have a freedman at his table, doubtless because he felt that, having once led the physically and spiritually degrading life of a slave, such a man could never be wholly trustworthy.[4]

Reprinted from *AJPh* 94 (1973) 268–81.

[1] When set at the end of the hexameter the phrase sounds somewhat harsh, because it creates a clash between word accent and meter: *lí/bertí/no pátre / nátum.* I have sometimes thought that, taken out of its quantitative context, it might resemble an accentual form of the *versus quadratus* used in popular taunts: with *libertíno pátre nátum* compare *Christiános ád leónem!* (Tert. *Apol.* 40) and the retiarius's *nón te péto, píscem péto, quíd me fúgis, Gálle?* (Festus 358.8–9 Lindsay).

[2] So (following Niebuhr) E. Fraenkel in *Horace* (Oxford, 1957) 2–3.

[3] See Petron. *Sat.* 57.4 and 75.10.

[4] According to Messalla, the only exception he made was Sextus Pompey's freedman Menas, who deserted to him and was given the status of a freeborn citizen and a knight;

Horace was deeply concerned by his own status as the son of a former slave: all the more so when he came to move in lofty social and intellectual circles. Glance at *Serm.* 1.10.81–90, where he names those, *doctos et amicos*, for whom he writes—among others Messalla (consul 31), Pollio (consul 40), L. Gellius Poplicola (consul 36), and L. Calpurnius Bibulus, stepson of Brutus—and consider how often he must have felt uncomfortable about having no *maiores*. It is natural, therefore, that he wrote a good deal about slaves and slavery: the subject haunted him. But it is surprising to observe that his tone is seldom sympathetic, and often downright cruel. No doubt Seneca is philosophizing when he says: *Serui sunt. Immo homines. . . . Serui sunt. Immo humiles amici* (*Epist.* 47.1); yet Trimalchio seems to be speaking sincerely when he tells his guests, *Et serui homines sunt et aeque unum lactem biberunt* (Petron. *Sat.* 71.1); and one of his friends is not in the least embarrassed to begin a story with *Cum adhuc seruirem* (*Sat.* 61.6), while another ex-slave in a pugnacious speech praises himself for being the architect of his own freedom (*Sat.* 57.4–6). But the gnawing tooth of envious criticism had wounded Horace when he was still a young man, an officer in Brutus's army: *quod mihi pareret legio Romana tribuno* (*Serm.* 1.6.48). In an early poem he discharged some of his resentment on a victim who was in the same position as he had been, but was still more exposed to hatred. *Epod.* 4 is addressed to a man who was once a slave and is now a military officer. He began lower down than Horace: his back is scarred with the lash and his legs calloused with fetters. And he rose higher: he was very rich, and a knight; he was pushy, and showed off by sitting in the theater seats reserved for senators. The poem expresses a warrantable hatred and scorn. Yet it contains two lines which Horace might very well have heard applied to himself: the derisive *hoc, hoc tribuno militum* and the aphoristic *fortuna non mutat genus.*[5]

In Horace's first book of *Sermones* there are a few curt and rather callous allusions to slavery. A "bought slave," a *uenalis*, carries the bread for the household but gets no more to eat than the rest (*Serm.* 1.1.46–49); others bear the stingy official's chamber-pot and decanter-basket behind him en route to Tibur (*Serm.* 1.6.108–9); while only a lunatic would crucify a waiter for licking a dish (*Serm.* 1.3.80–83). It seems more than callous, however, it seems brutal for Horace to say that when

Augustus himself mentioned another exception, a man who had once served him as a spy (Suet. Aug. 74).

[5] Cf. *Serm.* 2.6.48–49: *ludos spectauerat una* (sc. *Maecenas*), / *luserat in campo:* "*fortunae filius!*" *omnes.*

you are sexually aroused it is logical to attack any slave girl or slave boy who happens to be handy, and to add that he does so himself (*Serm.* 1.2.116–19).[6]

In the journey to Brundisium, the largest episode is a battle of wit between an Oscan jester and a freed Tuscan slave, staged for the amusement of Maecenas and the other guests (*Serm.* 1.5.51–70). The jokes are not much worse than those one hears at night clubs nowadays, and much cleaner. Sarmentus, the freedman, jeers at his opponent's deformed forehead. Messius Cicirrus, the jester, gibes at Sarmentus, suggesting that he was never legally set free but ran away from this owner, and that, although now working as a government clerk, he might be hauled back into servitude at any time.[7] "That lengthy dinner-party was truly delightful," says Horace with emphasis (70). Yet he himself had been a government clerk (Suet. *Poet.* 24.7–8 Rostagni) and long afterward still kept up some connection with his former colleagues (*Serm.* 2.6.36–37);[8] while his father had been on the same social level as Sarmentus. He knew this, and others at the table knew it. When they all laughed at the two comics, perhaps Horace laughed γναθμοῖσι ἀλλοτρίοισιν.

The sixth poem in the first book of *Sermones* is wholly concerned with class distinctions. Its central problem is that Horace, although a freedman's son, is a friend of Maecenas and is therefore exposed to hostile criticism. He meets the criticism not head on but obliquely, by discussing with Maecenas the nature of their friendship. He makes two main points: that Maecenas, although himself noble, cares nothing about high birth *provided a man is free-born* (*Serm.* 1.6.1–8) but chooses his friends for their character (49–64); and that he, Horace, is not ashamed of his

---

[6] Catullus does something like this in 56, but he makes a joke of it, whereas Horace's phrasing (*impetus in quem / continuo fiat*) is cruder, and is made more unfeeling by the word *uerna*: his victim was born in his own household.

[7] According to the scholiast on Juvenal 5.3, Sarmentus had belonged to Cato's friend M. Favonius. After Philippi Favonius was executed, Maecenas had the disposal of his property, acquired Sarmentus, and freed him. At this party, therefore, he was (like Horace) one of Maecenas's suite. Horace's sneer *Sarmenti domina exstat* (55) means that Favonius's widow was still alive: so F. Münzer, "Favonius," *RE* 6.2 (1909) 2074–77, especially 2076.

[8] The question is reviewed by C. B. Randolph, "Horace and the Scriptus Quaestorius," *TAPhA* 56 (1925) 130–49. He suggests that although Suetonius, who had access to official records, told the truth in stating that Horace himself was a *scriba*, Horace disguised it by never mentioning his own situation ("poverty made me versify," *Epist.* 2.2.50–52) and by ridiculing Sarmentus the *scriba*.

father, who kept him pure and shaped his moral disposition (65–99). A third point, subordinate to these, is less clearly argued: almost as though Horace were embarrassed in discussing it. He has been tempted to enter politics, but has decided in view of his humble origins to remain a private citizen. He compares and contrasts himself with several ambitious men, two perhaps imaginary, one real or based on reality. One is a former slave, now free and pointedly called Novius, which sounds like Newman (40–41); one is, like Horace, the son of a former slave, *Syri Damae aut Dionysi filius* (38–39); the third is one Tillius, who was apparently ejected from the senate and then contrived to reenter it, rising to the rank of praetor (24–26 + 107–11). That is, the three men represent the three lowest types of political careerist: an ex-slave, a freedman's son, and a freeborn individual with a black mark against him and without background or connections, lacking parents *honestos / fascibus et sellis* (96–97).[9] Horace will not join them in competing for office, but prefers to remain a private citizen, living freely and pleasantly (100–131). There were many ambitious men in the era of the Roman Revolution. Some no doubt were freedmen or the sons of freedmen, but surely they were far outnumbered by the freeborn *arrivistes*.[10] It is because Horace is so

[9] Tillius here cannot have been (as Porphyrio says) the once banished brother of L. Tillius Cimber, one of Caesar's murderers: for he could not have returned to the senate, far less risen to the praetorship, while Caesar's heir and avenger was in power. F. Münzer's remark in "Tillius," *RE* 6A.1 (1936) 1037–40, especially 1038, that the praetorship is only a *Phantasiegemälde* is scarcely convincing, since the man was apparently well-known, and the other details appear to be carefully individualized. I cannot see why "the context requires that Tillius was the son of a freedman," as suggested by T. P. Wiseman in *New Men in the Roman Senate* (Oxford, 1971) 266. Horace is drawing a contrast between the life styles of Tillius and himself. Both travel economically, but Horace is a private individual, whereas Tillius is a senior senator and therefore can be derided as stingy. Instead of slaves carrying his household goods, he ought to have had horses and grooms and carriages: *Serm.* 1.6.100–104.

[10] During Caesar's dictatorship freedmen and freedmen's sons had been senators, but they were relatively few (so R. Syme, *Roman Revolution* [Oxford, 1939] 78 and 80). Later Octavian and Antony admitted freedmen's sons and even slaves (Dio Cass. 48.34.4), but that was during a tumultuous era when all traditions seemed to be crumbling away. But in 28 B.C., after gaining supreme power, Octavian (together with Agrippa) took on the censorship and thoroughly purged the senate. After that time—although one freedman's son is known to have been a magistrate (Gaius Thoranius, Dio Cass. 53.27.6)—it is difficult to believe that such cases were frequent. See Wiseman (note 9 above) p. 16, with the prosopographical appendix: in which some examples (e.g. P. Popillius, no. 338) far antedate the epoch of which Horace is writing. S. Treggiari, *Roman Freedmen during the Late Republic* (Oxford, 1969) 62–63, does not clearly distinguish the disorderly senate of the 'forties and 'thirties from the reformed senate of which Augustus was *princeps*.

sensitive about his personal origins that he gives these particular types so much importance.

Slavery, from several new points of view, is the theme of *Serm.* 2.7. It begins and ends with a brief dialogue between Horace and a house slave called Davus, who asks and obtains permission to address his master during the Saturnalia, when slaves could do pretty much as they liked. The core of it is a sermon preached directly to Horace, opening with criticisms of faults which he admits elsewhere and with an intimately personal reference to his tie with Maecenas (22–35). This Horace receives with anger (43–44); but Davus then continues with preachments which he says he learned from the doorkeeper of the Stoic sage Crispinus, one of Horace's *bêtes noires* (45, cf. *Serm.* 1.1.120–21 and 1.3.138–39). Their topic is that Horace, although the master of Davus and other slaves, is himself a slave to his lusts. This is illustrated with many examples of his misconduct and folly. It ends by infuriating Horace, who chases the fellow out, threatening to relegate him to hard labor on his Sabine farm.[11]

The latter part of the sermon (from the mention of Crispinus onward, 46–94) is chiefly concerned with adultery. In this there is a difficulty which it is not easy to resolve. Davus explicitly accuses his master of being a slave to lust, and in particular of enjoying affairs with married women. But elsewhere Horace himself has emphatically condemned this type of sexual adventure, declaring that it does not attract him in the least and is both unnecessary and dangerous (*Serm.* 1.2.37–134). Indeed, what Horace said there of himself, *parabilem amo uenerem facilemque . . . nec uereor ne, dum fuluo, uir rure recurrat* (119, 127), is here turned directly against him by Davus: *te coniunx aliena capit, meretricula Dauum* (*Serm.* 2.7.46). Furthermore Horace tells us that one of the precepts his father gave him when molding his character was *ne sequerer moechas, concessa cum uenere uti / possem* (*Serm.* 1.4.113–14); and he strongly implies that he followed his father's advice: *ex hoc ego sanus ab illis ⟨uitiis⟩*

---

[11]The satire is amiably misinterpreted by Treggiari (note 10 above) 12–13. Quoting lines 75–82, she declares, "Horace concludes that the *sapiens* is free (83ff.)"—whereas the argument is put in the mouth of Davus and is implicitly rejected by Horace in the comically violent final lines of the poem. "Such considerations," she remarks, "might act on a Horace or a Cicero, making them treat their slaves as human beings and think it almost a duty to reward good service with freedom." But there is no trace whatever of such kindhearted intentions in Horace; indeed, Ms. Treggiari mentions another freedman's son, Vedius Pollio, who treated his slaves with disgusting and deliberate brutality, far outdoing Horace's chilly callousness.

/ *perniciem quaecumque ferunt* (*Serm.* 1.4.129–30). Granted, there is an early poem (*Epod.* 8) where he denounces in gross terms a rich and noble matron who is too old and ugly to attract him as a lover. But thereafter, although he permits himself without protest to be charged with *mille puellarum, puerorum mille furores* (*Serm.* 2.3.325), he never speaks of wife-chasing without disapproval. Then how could he write a long carefully wrought poem in which one of his own house servants accused him of being a compulsive adulterer?

Scholars have noted this inconsistency with some embarrassment. W. Y. Sellar on p. 74 of his *Horace and the Elegiac Poets* (Oxford, 1924) offers a tactful solution. "In this analysis of the bondage to the pleasures of sense he has in view the rich, idle, and for the most part, noble classes, who formed the bulk of his readers, whose favour he enjoyed, and whom he did not care to offend. He avoids the invidiousness of appearing a censor of this class, by making himself the object of the satire." But this will scarcely convince anyone who remembers *Serm.* 1.2, where Horace takes a diametrically opposite point of view and delivers many an attack on socially eminent amorists. P. Lejay on p. 550 of his edition of the *Satires* (Paris, 1911) asserts that Davus is talking to an imaginary interlocutor, "la seconde personne didactique"; but then spoils this effect by adding "C'est Horace ou c'est un autre: qu'importe?" Yet it is very important. W. Wili on pp. 106–7 of *Horaz und die augusteische Kultur* (Basel, 1948) notes the incongruence without really explaining it, save as "farce" and as a falsification of fact created by "Sklavenperspektive." Kiessling-Heinze on line 45 observe "Davus . . . einen ungesehenen, den besseren Ständen angehörigen Dritten abkanzelt. . . . Erst mit v. 72 wendet sich der Vortrag wieder Horaz selbst zu"; and on line 72, "Diese ganze Auseinandersetzung, *trotz der Ankündigung in v. 22*," (my italics) "auf ⟨Horaz⟩ selbst gar keinen Bezug hat." Further, on 116, "In Davus' nicht aus der Kenntnis seines Herrn, sondern aus Büchern geschöpften Zerrbildern des Weiberknechts usw., hatte H. sich nicht wiedererkennen können." Davus has not been reading ethical treatises, he has been listening to Crispinus's doorman; but apart from that, why should a poet portray one of his own servants as making a single continuous speech, now describing him in his true character and now presenting him in an unrecognizable and easily repudiated and highly offensive caricature? Mr. N. Rudd on pp. 188–95 of his *Satires of Horace* (Cambridge, 1966) sees this difficulty. He implies that in lines 46–71 Davus—even when he keeps saying *tu* and *te*—is simply addressing an imaginary debauchee (Lejay's *seconde personne didactique*); and he points to the objection which Davus attributes to Horace in line 72, "non sum moechus," *ais*, as showing that Davus realizes his criticisms are at least in part off target. Horace (says Mr. Rudd) *is* subservient to a *meretrix* (89–94) but has had no illicit relationship with a married woman. In that case, why should Davus, after timidly asking permission to speak, as though he knew he might offend, deliver a long denunciation of an adulterous seducer (*corruptor*, 63) which is wholly irrelevant to Horace's real failings? It is like hearing a lifelong teetotaler reproached for habitual drunkenness, or a man who has never even smoked marijuana being pilloried as a drug fiend. The trouble is that Davus's speech is apparently continuous throughout. It is hard to believe that *o totiens seruus* (70) is addressed to one person, a wholly imaginary being, and that *tune mihi dominus?* (75) and *tu mihi qui imperitas alii seruis miser* (81) are directed to another, the real man sitting in front of his servant Davus and trying to control his indignation. Furthermore, the faults of which Horace is accused at the beginning and the end of Davus's speech are indubitably his. They worried Horace himself: restless instability (28–29 and 111–15, cf. *Epist.* 1.8.12) and hot temper (43–44, cf. 116–17 and *Epist.* 1.20.25).

There are, as far as I can see, only two possible solutions to the problem. Either Horace was, in spite of his father's advice and his own earlier pronouncements on the subject, guilty of seducing other men's wives.[12] Or else he composed a clumsy and confusing poem, in which his genuine self-criticisms (put in the mouth of a servant) are disagreeably mingled with sermonizing addressed to an imaginary third party. Such confusions appear elsewhere in his *Sermones*. He begins *Serm.* 1.1 by addressing Maecenas, and is still talking to him in line 14; but a few lines later (32–40) he remarks that the ant rests in the winter, living on her savings,

> cum *te* neque feruidus aestus
> demoueat lucro, neque hiems ignis mare ferrum,
> nil obstet *tibi* dum ne sit *te* ditior alter.

Clearly this has nothing to do with the rich and epicurean Maecenas: although we must force ourselves to remember that, when Horace cries *quid rides? mutato nomine de te / fabula narratur* (1.1.69–70).[13]

Whichever of these solutions may be acceptable, the central fact remains. Horace was keenly sensitive to the problem of slavery, enough to show himself in *Serm.* 2.7 as being denounced by a slave for behaving

---

[12] So G. Highet, "Masks and Faces in Satire," *Hermes* 102 (1974) 321–27.

[13] Similar imaginary interlocutors appear in *Serm.* 1.4.86–100 (where note the insulting *ut tuus est mos*), in *Serm.* 1.10.52, and elsewhere.

like a slave, and as responding to the denunciation like an ill-tempered and tyrannical master.

In his next long poem dealing with servitude (*Epist.* 1.14) he is almost equally hardhearted.[14] It is directed to the foreman of his Sabine farm, himself a slave, whom Horace does not condescend to address by name.[15] As often elsewhere, he compares city life and country life, to the disadvantage of the city; but instead of expounding the delights of the calm and beautiful countryside as in *Epod.* 2, he gives a Hogarthian character sketch of the city-loving foreman, stressing his vulgar tastes, worthy only of the rabble that enjoys whorehouses and greasy taverns.[16] Once the man was a *mediastinus*, a low drudge in Horace's city house. Then he longed to be out in the country; but now, promoted to *uilicus*, he hates his situation.[17] Horace has no intention of summoning him back to Rome. This sounds deliberately unkind. Horace makes it worse by pointing out that the farm gives the foreman a good deal of hard work, and does not even allow him to grow his own grapes, or boast of a little inn near by. Naturally Horace's own tastes were once much more urbane and elegant: fine clothes, gleaming hair, love-making with Cinara, and drinking good Falernian as early as midday (32–34). But now no more: he loves rest and tranquil nature; he is happy. He tells the slave that he too ought to be content, and ends with singularly unconvincing aphorism, perhaps drawn from a fable: "the slow ox longs for the saddle, the horse longs to plough"—that is, "you are a farm foreman: don't try to go beyond yourself, give up any dreams of betterment, stay in the lonely countryside." Apparently Horace's active mind was never visited by the idea that the foreman was (except for one legal disability) very like the impoverished farmer Ofellus, whose character he admired (*Serm.* 2.2.112–36), or even like his own father, who had been *macro pauper agello* (*Serm.* 1.6.71).

[14] There is a thoughtful analysis of the letter by O. Hiltbrunner, "Der Gutsverwalter des Horaz (epist. 1.14)," *Gymnasium* 74 (1967) 297–314.

[15] Contrast the tone of Cicero to his freedman in *Fam.* 16: *mi Tiro* and *Tiro noster; cura, cura te, mi Tiro.*

[16] See lines 21–22. It is difficult to interpret Horace's attitude to the foreman as "fast freundschaftlich" (C. Becker, *Das Spätwerk des Horaz* [Göttingen, 1963] 21) or to believe that in such contemptuous phrases as *cum seruis urbana diaria rodere mauis* (40) he is speaking "gently" and "sympathetically" (Fraenkel, note 2 above, 312).

[17] Columella warns landowners not to appoint a foreman who is city-bred and therefore accustomed to luxury: *Rust.* 1.8.1–2, noted by P. Guthrie, "A Note on Horace *Epistle* 1.14," *CPh* 46 (1951) 116–17.

In two late poems Horace compares one of his own books, and himself, to slaves.

In *Epist.* 1.20 he addresses his newly completed volume of poetic letters. His terms will suit either a fresh clean papyrus book waiting to be bought and read and passed on from hand to hand until at last it is sold secondhand in the provinces, or a handsome young slave boy tired of being admired only by his master's friends (line 4), and eager to escape into the world and find lovers, with the prospect at last of being deserted and forgotten. This is an unpleasant idea, for several reasons. One is that it assumes a handsome slave boy's career will be that of a catamite—as though he could do nothing better with his life. Another is that it equates publication with prostitution. Horace's prospective readers are told that they will degrade his book by enjoying it and passing it from hand to hand (11–12) and that Horace has warned it of its future humiliation but will merely laugh when his forecasts come true (14–16). But this is consistent with Horace's ideas about publicity. Again and again he has expressed his scorn for the general reader, for the ordinary man: *nulla taberna meos habeat neque pila libellos* (*Serm.* 1.4.71, and see 72–74); *contentus paucis lectoribus* (*Serm.* 1.10.74); *odi profanum uulgus et arceo* (*Carm.* 3.1.1); *non ego uentosae plebis suffragia uenor* (*Epist.* 1.19.37). Now he goes even further. He publishes his collection of poetic letters with something very like contemptuous distaste, and shows no affection for those who will now read it. Those who really matter to Horace have read it before publication. His book is a *uerna*, a homebred slave: it should stay in the household where it was born (and where its master might caress it from time to time, *Serm.* 1.2.117–18) rather than venture out to be fumbled by the sweaty hands of the populace (*Serm.* 1.4.72). The poem concludes with a short autobiography (19–28), in which Horace describes himself, his origins, and his career—not mentioning his poetry (as in *Serm.* 1.10, *Carm.* 3.30, and *Epist.* 1.19) but concentrating on what he prized most, his remarkable achievement: *me libertino natum patre et in tenui re . . . me primis Vrbis belli placuisse domique.*

He begins the second poem in his second book of verse letters by comparing himself to a slave (*Epist.* 2.2.1–22). Explaining to Julius Florus, friend and companion of Tiberius, that he is too old and too tired and too harassed by city life to write poetry, he says, "It is like a man buying a slave with a fault about which the seller warns him. I told you when you left that I was lazy and a poor correspondent: why complain now?" It is a curious piece of imagery for a poet and a man sensitive to fine social distinctions, particularly when addressed to someone younger than himself. Furthermore, it is very peculiar indeed that the slave to whom he compares himself should be, not a foreigner, *Syrus Dama aut Dionysus*, but a native Italian like Horace, born at Gabii or Tibur— Tibur, with which he often explicitly associates himself.[18]

Horace, then, was always painfully aware of the fact that his father had been a slave—which meant that he might have been a slave himself. This had queer effects on his poetry, and on his character as therein depicted. It made him sometimes associate himself indirectly with slaves, in a way that other poets never did; but it deprived him of sympathy for them, making him speak of them and to them coldly, sometimes brutally. His work contains nothing comparable to Juvenal's kindly feeling for the slaves shivering in winter's cold (*Sat.* 1.93, 9.63–69), for the victims of the sadistic matron (6.219–23, 475–95), and for the homesick country slave boys (11.145–60).

When he entered Maecenas's coterie, his life became far more comfortable than it must have been while he was a government official: both materially, through the *dolce far niente* which he could now enjoy (*Serm.* 1.6.110–31), and spiritually, through his friendship with brilliant men who cared nothing about his origins. And yet some of his early malaise still persisted: for now—although he never uses the word *cliens* of himself—he was one of the great man's dependents;[19] and while he could not be given orders or punished for disobedience like a servant, he had obligations which must be fulfilled and which he tells us were far from easy to discharge.

Was he formally a client of Maecenas? I do not know of any solid evidence to determine the point.[20] He habitually calls their relation friendship (*Epod.* 1.2; *Serm.* 1.6.50, 53, 62; *Carm.* 2.18.12; *Epist.* 1.7.12). No doubt it was.[21] Yet once, in an important letter explaining that he must have independence even at the risk of poverty, he tells a story intended to illustrate the situation, in which the two men involved are expressly named client and patron.[22] In the same poem he says he

[18]*Carm.* 2.6.5–6, 3.4.23, 4.2.30–32, 4.3.10; *Epist.* 1.7.45, 1.8.12.

[19]*Rerum tutela mearum*, . . . *de te pendentis, te respicientis amici* (*Epist.* 1.1.103, 105).

[20]K. J. Reckford, "Horace and Maecenas," *TAPhA* 90 (1959) 200, assumes the fact though citing only *Epist.* 1.7.37 to prove it.

[21]Suetonius speaks only of affection, using *diligere* to describe the feelings of Maecenas, *amicitia* for both Maecenas and Augustus (*Poet.* 24.9–47 Rostagni). Juvenal uses *amicus* for both patron and client (*Sat.* 5.32, 108, 113, 146; cf. *amicitia magna* in 5.14).

[22]*Epist.* 1.7.46–95: note lines 75 and 92. K. Büchner on pp. 139–57 of his *Horaz* (Wiesbaden, 1962) analyzes the letter carefully, but goes too far in saying the client was a

often calls Maecenas *rexque paterque* (37–38);[23] and *rex* at a later date was certainly the client's word for a rich patron.[24]

In two letters carefully placed together in Book 1 (17 and 18) Horace talks to young friends about the problems they face in associating with rich and powerful men.

The addressee of the former, one Scaeva, is poor, and wants a patron simply for material gain. Horace's examples concern food (*Epist.* 1.17.12, 13–15), clothes (25–32), and gifts (43–51). Scaeva is told how to make sure of getting these perquisites, but is warned that "to use the great" is an arduous career requiring energy and courage (lines 2, 6–10, 36–42; cf. *Serm.* 1.9.54–55).[25]

Lollius of *Epist.* 1.18 appears to have been already accepted by his wealthy friend, but wishes to maintain the feeling of independence: he does not want to be a *scurra* like Sarmentus in *Serm.* 1.5.[26] Horace warns him chiefly about his manners and his conversation, saying that he should not display his sense of freedom by talking too boldly and preferring his own pursuits to those of the millionaire.

Horace does not use quite the same terminology in the two letters. In *Epist.* 1.17, the rich and noble are *maiores*, *principes uiri*, and (collectively) *rex* (lines 2, 35, 43); while in 1.18 the phrases are *diues amicus*, *potens amicus*, and *uenerandus amicus* (24, 44, 73), which imply a closer attachment. Each of the young men is called a *comes* (17, 52; 18, 30). Only Lollius is referred to as an *amicus* of the great man (18, 2). Neither the word *cliens* nor the word *patronus* appears.

If these young fellows are clients, they stand on different levels. Scaeva is the ancestor of Juvenal's Trebius, whose career is *aliena uiuere quadra* and who never exchanges a sentence with his patron (*Sat.* 5.2 and 125–31). But Lollius is neither undistinguished nor financially insecure: his father has an estate with a lake on it, and he is a popular athlete (*Epist.* 1.18.52–64). We cannot imagine him, like Scaeva, complaining that his

coactor like Horace's father (he was a *praeco*—which Horace might have become, *Serm.* 1.6.86) and that he got the Sabine farm "als Geschenk": the patron gave him half the price and lent him the rest (*Epist.* 1.7.80–81).

[23] Fulsome: Jupiter himself is *pater et rex* in *Serm.* 2.1.42.

[24] Juv. *Sat.* 5.14.130, 137, 161; 7.45; and 10.161 with a double meaning.

[25] Scaeva is younger than Horace (16) and is really poor (43–51). Evidently he has no career in view except that of being a client. Thus he cannot be the hard-working and well-rewarded senator P. Paquius Scaeva, as suggested by T. P. Wiseman on p. 180 of his book cited in note 9 above.

[26] He is often identified with Lollius Maximus of *Epist.* 1.2; but it seems unlikely that Horace would address two different protreptic letters to the same young man in the same book of poems.

bag was opened and his travel money stolen (17, 54). Horace's advice to him is on a higher plane: don't admire a pretty slave belonging to your rich friend, and be careful whom you propose as a new member of the group (18.72–77).

In his relationship to Maecenas, Horace has something of both men. He uses almost the same phrasing of Scaeva and of himself: *principibus placuisse uiris non ultima laus est* (*Epist.* 1.17.35), *me primis Vrbis belli placuisse domique* (*Epist.* 1.20.23). He loved Maecenas's good dinners, says Davus (*Serm.* 2.7.32–35). Maecenas made him rich (*Epist.* 1.7.15). He was a *comes* of Maecenas on journeys (*Serm.* 1.5, 2.6.42–43) and chatted with him on trifling subjects (*Serm.* 2.6.43–46, cf. *Epist.* 1.18.19–20). But his most serious allusions to Maecenas are those where his home appears as a sanctuary of disinterested friendship (*Serm.* 1.6.1–8 and 62–64, 1.9.48–52) and he himself as the central inspiration of Horace's poetry (*Serm.* 1.1, *Carm.* 1.1, *Epist.* 1.1).

For the first years at least, Horace was a client, or something closely equivalent to a client. But he always longed for complete freedom. In *Serm.* 1.6 and 2.6, in *Epist.* 1.7 and 1.14, he writes chiefly, not about passing delightful hours with Maecenas and his friends, but about getting away from them and staying away. He never once describes the conversations at Maecenas's table, although we should dearly love to know what Vergil and Varius and the others talked about: anything better than the miserable gibes of Cicirrus and Sarmentus. He refuses to mention such intimacies. When he cries O *noctes cenaeque deum!* (*Serm.* 2.6.65), he means the dinners in his own home in the country. Evidently he felt that his position was halfway to slavery. Among the retinue of such magnates there were not only starveling citizens like the *scurrae* (*Serm.* 2.8.21–22, cf. *Epist.* 1.17.13–22 and 1.18.1–4) with whom it would scarcely be pleasant to associate, but also the master's freed slaves, the *liberti*; and the freeborn clients were bound to be brought into contact with them. (Juvenal, 5.26–29, says the two groups sometimes came to blows.) Once Augustus himself pointedly referred to Horace's position as a dependent, in a letter asking Maecenas to release him so that he might become Augustus's secretary: *ueniet ergo ab ista parasitica mensa ad hanc regiam* (Suet. *Poet.* 24.22–23 Rostagni). But Horace would not accept even that honor. His father had spent some of his life in slavery, and he himself in something uncomfortably close to it. He was determined to be free.

Consonant Clashes in Latin Poetry

ALLITERATION WAS an important element in Latin poetry from very early times.[1] The language contained a large number of alliterative phrases, such as *forte fortuna, donum do dedico, felix faustum fortunatumque*, and speakers of Latin evidently felt a natural affinity for the device.[2] Only in Rome would the Commissioners of the Mint be called *IIIuiri AAAFF*.

Much has been written by students of Latin literature about the alliterative effects produced by the repetition of initial consonants and vowels, as in Vergil's "saepe leui somnum suadebit inire susurro" (*Buc.* 1.55). The Latin poets used this device so often and so skillfully that much remains to be written. But they also practiced another type of alliteration, which has been very little studied. They employed the same consonant to end one word and to begin the next. This may be called collisive alliteration.

Obviously a sound which is repeated, not after an interval occupied by other sounds (as in initial alliteration), but immediately, after a minimal pause between two words, will be striking in its effect. Thus we actually seem to hear the hiss of the serpents in "tot Erinys sibilat hydris" (Verg. *Aen.* 7.447). Very frequently the particular sound of the two colliding letters is heard elsewhere within the line or near it, and is thus strengthened still further, as here in "hydris."

Reprinted from *CPh* 69 (1974) 178–85.

[1] Thus Naevius writes, "scopas atque uerbenas sagmina sumpserunt" (*Bellum Punicum* 31 Morel); "magnum domum decoremque ditem uexerant" (*BP* 51); "magnae metus tumultus pectora possidet" (*BP* 53); "prius pariet lucusta Lucam bouem" (*BP* 63); "libera lingua loquemur ludis Liberalibus" (fr. inc. 5 Ribbeck).

[2] See J. B. Hofmann and A. Szantyr, *Lateinische Syntax und Stilistik* (Munich, 1965) 700–704, and J. Marouzeau, *Traité de stylistique latine*[4] (Paris, 1962) 45–50.

Collisive alliteration is most effectively used in onomatopoeia, to echo sound or to image movement, for example:
a runner slipping and stumbling:

haud tenuit titubata solo   [Verg. Aen. 5.332]

the noise of moving water:

inque sinus scindit sese unda reductos   [Aen. 1.161]

fit sonitus spumante salo   [Aen. 2.209]

septem surgens sedatis amnibus altus   [Aen. 9.30]

winds roaring within a mountain prison:

magno cum murmure montis
circum claustra fremunt   [Aen. 1.55–56]

the harsh feel of a sick horse's dry skin:

ad tactum tractanti dura resistit   [G. 3.502]

waves raving and foaming:

indignatum magnis stridoribus aequor   [G. 2.162]

the growl of an angry man:

nec uereor ne dum futuo uir rure recurrat
[Hor. Serm. 1.2.127]

the hiss of flames in grain stalks:

interdum segetes stipulamque uidemus
accidere ex una scintilla incendia passim   [Lucr. 5.608–9][3]

bees buzzing within their nest:

uoluitur ater odor tectis, tum murmure caeco
intus saxa sonant   [Verg. Aen. 12.591–92]

a ship grinding to a halt on a reef:

infelix saxis in procurrentibus haesit   [Aen. 5.204]

Does this evoke the noise of breaking bones as a body is dragged over rough ground?

huic ceruixque comaeque trahuntur   [Aen. 1.477]

[3] Vergil adapted this passage twice: once to depict fire in stubble—"in stipulis magnus sine uiribus ignis" (G. 3.99)—and once to imitate the scratch of steel on flint—"silici scintillam excudit Achates" (Aen. 1.174).

And this the delicate touch of a skillful weaver?

> fecerat *et t*enui telas discreuerat auro   [*Aen.* 4.264]

There are many instances of collisive alliteration in the poets where no echoic sound effect is intended. It is often used only to intensify the emotion. Since the repetition of a single sound was felt by the Romans to be impressive, repetition strengthened by close juxtaposition was even more telling. Furthermore, when one word ends with a given consonant and the next begins with the same consonant, any careful speaker must pause slightly between the two, must pause a little longer than he would normally pause between words which could be allowed to slide into each other. Therefore the line containing such a clash will be more slowly and weightily spoken.

A solemn thought will become more solemn:

> mortalem uita*m m*ors cum immortalis ademit   [Lucr. 3.869]

The same device can bring out scornful reproach:

> et uigilan*s s*tertis nec somnia cernere cessas   [Lucr. 3.1048]

> quidnam torpente*s s*ubito obstipuistis, Achivi?[4]
> [Cic. fr. 22.23 Morel]

or indignation:

> ne*c c*um capta capi ne*c c*um combusta cremari
> [Enn. *Ann.* 359 Vahlen]

> barbarus ha*s s*egetes   [Verg. *Buc.* 1.71]

> scilicet i*s s*uperis labor est   [*Aen.* 4.379]

or hate:

> quin idem Veneri partu*s s*uus et Paris alter   [*Aen.* 7.321]

or scorn for a soft, effeminate enemy:

> Maeonia mentu*m m*itra crinemque madentem   [*Aen.* 4.216]

Of course I do not wish to imply that such emotional effects are produced by these consonant clashes alone: rather the clashes greatly enhance the surrounding alliteration. Thus, Juno's angry prediction cited in part above (*Aen.* 7.320–21) contains eleven sibilants in two lines.

In such passages collisive alliteration is used to strengthen the emo-

---

[4] Cicero has used alliteration to strengthen Homer's τίπτ᾽ ἄνεῳ ἐγένεσθε (*Il.* 2.323).

tion evoked by the particular consonant in a particular context of meaning. But consider this famous line: "si canimus siluas, siluae sint consule dignae" (Verg. *Buc.* 4.3). Why does Vergil use seven sibilants, emphasized by two clashes or coincidences, at key points of the line? N. I. Herescu, who had thought much about these matters, asked, "Ne veut-il pas évoquer le bruissement de la forêt?"[5] But the line is not part of a description: it is the climax of an invocation to the Muses, and its content is discursive or justificatory rather than picturesque. L. P. Wilkinson saw this, and expressed doubt about Herescu's suggestion; yet he himself, beyond saying that Vergil "had clearly no intention of being cacophonous," offered no explanation of this very marked sound effect.[6]

The fact is that classical Latin poets often used alliteration, strengthened by a collision, sometimes even two collisions, of identical sounds, in order to give rhetorical emphasis to an important statement. Instances are easy to find.

In the same poem we have a mystical prophecy, thus emphasized:

> alter erit tum Tiphys et altera quae uehat Argo   [*Buc.* 4.34]

Elsewhere, an earnest adjuration:

> te nec sperant Tartara regem,
> nec tibi regnandi ueniat tam dira cupido   [G. 1.36–37]

an elaborate compliment:

> tua, Maecenas, haud mollia iussa:
> te sine nil altum mens incohat   [G. 3.41–42]

and a serious warning:

> concussaque famem in siluis solabere quercu   [G. 1.159]

Lucretius has many:

> incassum magnos cecidisse labores   [2.1165]

and sometimes two together:

> quin etiam multis solis redeuntibus annis   [1.311]

> naturam mores uictum motusque parentum   [1.598]

> percussit thyrso laudis spes magna meum cor   [1.923]

> caligare oculos, sonere auris, succidere artus   [3.156]

[5]*La poésie latine: étude des structures phoniques* (Paris, 1960) 38.
[6]*Golden Latin Artistry* (Cambridge, 1963) 14 with note.

Catullus employs it in a refrain:

currite, ducentes subtegmina, currite fusi   [64.327]

and Cicero in a piece of self-glorification:

o fortunatam natam me consule Romam!   [fr. 17]

as well as in a religious prescription:

sancta Iouis species claros spectaret in ortus   [fr. 11.56]

Horace has it in a moral denunciation:

nil obstet tibi dum ne sit te ditior alter   [*Serm.* 1.1.40]

Readers of Vergil who know his exquisite ear for rhythm and melody might assume (like Herescu) that he uses alliteration solely to echo natural sounds or to evoke emotions. But in fact he also uses alliteration, and particularly collisive alliteration, for rhetorical emphasis more often than any other Latin hexameter poet. On the first page of the *Bucolics* he employs it to stress the mighty name of Rome: "urbem quam dicunt Romam, Meliboee, putaui" (*Buc.* 1.19). By juxtaposing the final and the initial *m* (though the final *m* was at least partly nasalized), and by inserting the vocative, he makes the speaker pause a little, as in wonder. A little later there is a reflective line with two such pauses: "respexit tamen et longo post tempore uenit" (*Buc.* 1.29). Being didactic, the *Georgics* have many lines in which this strong type of alliteration is introduced to give weight to statements or exhortations or forecasts, as in the opening words, "quid faciat laetas segetes" (not "quid laetas faciat segetes"). Thus:

anne nouum tardis sidus te mensibus addas   [G. 1.32]

nec fuit indignum superis bis sanguine nostro   [1.491]

arma ferunt: saeuit toto Mars impius orbe   [1.511]

in medio mihi Caesar erit templumque tenebit   [3.16][7]

glacies ne frigida laedat
molle pecus scabiemque ferat turpisque podagras   [3.298–99]

principio sedes apibus statioque petenda   [4.8]

in medium, seu stabit iners seu profluet umor
transuersas salices et grandia conice saxa   [4.25–26]

exportant tectis et tristia funera ducunt   [4.256]

[7] This passage has many such effects, e.g. 3.21, 34, 38, 40.

In the *Aeneid* Vergil's art is approaching full development: "lugende, heu, uates, si qua fata aspera rumpas!" He uses this device constantly and yet often almost imperceptibly. There is an instance on the opening page of the poem, where a consonant clash slows up the rhythm of the line and stresses the difficulty of the hero's task: "multum ille *et t*erris iactatus et alto" (1.3). Other instances occur throughout:

> sin aliquam expertu*s s*umptis spem ponis in armis   [2.676]

> cum fatalis equu*s s*altu super ardua uenit / Pergama   [6.515–16]

> Iuppiter, *et T*urnum *et t*erras inuita reliqui   [12.809]

Collisive alliteration has another function in Latin poetry. Vergil and other poets introduce consonant clashes to mark punctuation pauses, for example:

to set off a parenthetical remark:

> urbs antiqua fui*t* (*T*yrii tenuere coloni)   [1.12]

to separate two sentences in a speech:

> en Priamu*s. s*unt hic etiam sua praemia laudi   [1.461]

to separate two sentences in the narrative:

> sic prior Aenea*s. s*equitur sic deinde Latinus   [12.195]

and to distinguish speech from narrative:

> "ulterius ne tende odii*s." s*tetit acer in armis / Aeneas   [12.938–39]

The delicacy of these effects reminds us that Latin poetry was meant to be spoken rather than read with the eye alone:

> impuleri*t. t*antaene animis caelestibus irae?   [1.11]

Ovid's rhythm in the *Metamorphoses* is much evener than Vergil's, and he takes fewer pains to make the sound and rhythm of his verses mirror the meaning. Nevertheless, he occasionally brings in collisive alliteration for earnest emphasis:

> di, precor, et pieta*s s*acrataque iura parentum
> hoc prohibete nefa*s s*celerique resistite nostro   [10.321–22]

and for punctuation:

> Iuppiter alter auu*s: s*ocero quoque glorior illo   [6.176]

> hoc quoque quis dubite*t? t*utam me copia fecit   [6.194]

sed tamen et gaudet: tanta est discordia mentis   [10.445]

Statius too employs the device for these two purposes. He is particularly fond of interrupting the flow of a sentence to insert a parenthetical
comment or explanation, and of disjoining a long paragraph into brief
clauses. Such breaks are sometimes marked by consonant clashes. From
two books of the *Thebaid* taken at random, these examples of punctuation
pauses:

exclamat (tremuere rogi et uox terruit ignem)   [4.472]

tandem inter siluas (sic Euhius ipse pararat)   [4.740][8]

ita est. ueniunt. tanta autem audacia Thebis?   [7.125].[9]

From the same two books, instances of consonant clash to mark heavy
emphasis:

uersat onus: squalet triplici ramosa corona   [4.168]

post exsultantes spolia armentalia portant
seminecesque lupos scissasque Mimallones ursas   [4.659–60][10]

uincimur: immitis scis nulla reuoluere Parcas / stamina
                                                       [7.774–75][11]

But furthermore, there are many clashes of consonants in Latin poetry which, compared with the above, are unobtrusive, and which appear
to have relatively little significance. By far the largest number of them
occur at the caesurae. Thus, when they have no other discernible function, they at least assist in marking the rhythm. A few instances will make
this clear.

quid tum si carpunt | tacita quem mente requirunt? [Catull. 62.37]

siue Aquilo radit | terras | seu bruma niualem [Hor. *Serm*. 2.6.25]

montibus et siluis | studio iactabat inani   [Verg. *Buc.* 2.5]

nec calamis | solum aequiparas | sed uoce magistrum   [*Buc.* 5.48]

umbrae ibant | tenues | simulacraque luce carentum   [G. 4.472]

---

[8] Cf. also 4.85, 102, 521, 735, 777.
[9] So also 7.175, 218, 237, 485, 560.
[10] Cf. also 4.15, 68, 214 (heavy with c's), 374, 517, 552–53, 639, and 741.
[11] So also 7.146, 264, 437, and 482.

deficeret | tantis nauis | surgentibus undis   [*Aen.* 6.354]

moenia lata uidet | triplici circumdata muro
quae rapidus flammis ambit | torrentibus amnis   [*Aen.* 6.549–60]

sic ait adductisque amens | subsistit habenis   [*Aen.* 12.622]

Yet Vergil (at least in the *Aeneid*) rarely uses collisive alliteration unless it serves more than one purpose. For example, the last quotation, *Aeneid* 12.622, is preceded by several lines marked with the penthemimeral caesura: 616, 617, 618, 620, 621. The reader will unconsciously expect this rhythm to continue. But line 622 moves on past the place for that pause, into the fourth foot, and then stops abruptly. Both the rhythm and the collision of final and initial *s* image the arrested drive of the chariot.

The device of collisive alliteration is not (to my knowledge) common among poets writing in modern languages, although many readers have been struck, perhaps without knowing exactly why, by the slow expansive movement of Shakespeare's "This my hand will rather / The multitudinous seas incarnadine" (*Macbeth* 2.2.60–61). Pope employs it thrice in one line in order to make the rhythm slow and heavy: "When Ajax strives, some rock's vast weight to throw" (*Essay on Criticism* 370). Tennyson, always in love with alliteration, uses this special type in the refrain of an early poem, *Claribel*: "Where Claribel low-lieth." Jules Marouzeau, usually so sensitive, quotes on page 42 of his *Traité* (note 2 above) a line from Verlaine ("ton cher corps rare, harmonieux") in a discussion of cacophony, implying that it is an unintentional (*rapprochement fortuit*) error of taste; but surely it is meant to evoke a sensuous purr of delight.[12] Twice in one line Mallarmé introduces such a clash, in his *Tombeau* written in memory of Verlaine. Normally a Frenchman would write *le roc noir*, but Mallarmé has "Le noir roc courroucé que la bise le roule" (Pléiade edition, p. 71).

We have now discussed five effects produced by collisive alliteration: onomatopoeia, emotional emphasis, rhetorical emphasis, punctuation, and the strengthening of verse rhythm. For the benefit of any who may wish to examine the device in more detail, I append lists of its occurrence in a few notable books of Latin poetry. They were not easy to compile,

---

[12]Verlaine was highly sensitive to sound effects: witness the last line of his sonnet *Parsifal* (Pléiade edition, p. 427): "Et, ô ces voix d'enfants chantant dans la coupole!" While still a schoolboy he translated part of Cicero's *Marius* (fr. 7 Morel) and introduced several striking alliterations suggested by the Latin original: "Un serpent, s'élançant du tronc creux d'un vieux chêne, / Darde son noir vénin sur l'aigle ami des dieux. / Le noble oiseau s'abaisse . . ." (Pléiade edition, p. 13).

and they may not be quite complete; but I hope that the ratios are roughly correct. The most noticeable point is that while clashes are common at the caesurae they are much less frequent elsewhere in the hexameter line. There is one exception to this: they appear often between the fourth and fifth feet:

> libratum tereti uersabat turbine fusum   [Catull. 64.314]
>
> corque meum penitus turgescit tristibus iris   [Cic. Fr. 27.1]
>
> hic erus "Albanum, Maecenas, siue Falernum"
>
> [Hor. *Serm.* 2.8.16]
>
> multaque praeterea uariarum monstra ferarum
>
> [Verg. *Aen.* 6.285]
>
> non tamen aut patrio respersus sanguine Pentheus
>
> [Stat. *Theb.* 7.211]

Clashes within the first foot are relatively rare, except in Lucretius, who begins many lines with *nec* and produces some awkward effects: "nec calidos aestus tuimur nec frigora quimus" (1.300). Since Ovid's ear was less sensitive than his Augustan predecessors', he also allows lines like these: "ad delubra deae, quorum fastigia turpi" (*Met.* 1.373); "quod de Dardanio solum mihi restat Iulo" (*Met.* 15.767). Only Horace in his satirical poems is free with clashes inside the fifth and sixth feet: other poets avoid them, except for unusual effects such as Vergil's "rapidus Sol" (*G.* 2.321). Finally, it is observable that a clash at the trihemimeral caesura is usually less telling and less weighty than clashes at the other two caesural pauses in the hexameter verse.

The following lists contain some lines in which final *m* and initial *m* come together, as in "o miseras hominum mentis" (Lucr. 2.14). Final *m* usually signified only a nasalization of the preceding vowel, which was then elided in poetry, as in "mult(um) ille et terris." But it is not quite clear whether final *m* before an initial *m* may not have been pronounced bilabially, on the model of such words as *commodus* and *communis*. W. S. Allen, in *Vox Latina* (Cambridge, 1965), page 31, says, "Where a final *m* was followed by a closely connected word beginning with a stop (plosive or nasal) consonant, it seems to have been treated rather as in the interior of a word, being assimilated to the following consonant," and cites Cicero's statement that *cum nobis* would be pronounced *cun nobis*; but he does not say whether assimilation would cause final *m* to be pronounced bilabially in a phrase such as *cum mater* or *hominum mentis*. Nor does M. Leumann, *Lateinische Laut- und Formenlehre* (Munich, 1963), pages 174–75, who however writes, "Diese reduzierte Aussprache führte dann im Satzzusammenhang vor Konsonant in der Schriftsprache zu neuerlicher Befestigung des -m." I have therefore preferred to include the lines which contain juxtapositions of final m and initial m, while noting that the question of their actual pronunciation is not settled.

CONSONANT CLASHES IN LUCRETIUS 1 AND 2

Within the first foot: 1.300, 447, 476, 534, 537, 588, 769, 787, 1023, 1050, 1070, 1077, 1079; 2.34, 52, 53, 141, 142, 191, 248, 331, 585, 592, 791, 852, 868, 898, 936, 941.

Between the first and second feet: 2.274, 902.

At the trihemimeral caesura: 1.251, 304, 311, 598, 610, 659, 730, 806, 817, 871, 920, 923, 1088; 2.35, 88, 103, 113, 181, 385, 391, 477, 592, 625, 637, 659, 766, 898, 911, 914, 977, 1106, 1109, 1156.

Between the second and third feet: 1.104, 130, 168; 2.1067, 1088.

At the penthemimeral caesura: 1.95, 168, 186, 190, 274, 311, 346, 350, 353, 388, 463, 497, 718, 820, 866, 876, 972, 991, 1029, 1033, 1081, 1082, 1092; 2.14, 68, 87, 99, 111, 123, 142, 219, 244, 268, 269, 307, 316, 326, 327, 355, 393, 410, 429, 463, 485, 520, 554, 598, 624, 638, 735, 738, 842, 887, 891, 917, 970, 978, 988, 1015, 1029, 1070, 1140, 1153, 1158, 1165.

Between the third and fourth feet: 1.761, 1053; 2.194.

At the hephthemimeral caesura: 1.30, 78, 92, 133, 193, 340, 462, 534, 598, 619, 701, 720, 763, 807, 845, 858, 886, 893, 923, 924, 1031, 1039, 1091; 2.2, 7, 22, 143, 261, 283, 326, 342, 556, 648, 785, 836, 862, 903, 910, 915, 932, 1028, 1033, 1038, 1085, 1098, 1164.

Between the fourth and fifth feet: 1.913, 1065, 1102; 2.192, 265, 294, 325, 527, 564, 582, 714, 755, 888, 889, 913, 991, 1068, 1123, 1144.

Within the sixth foot: 1.697; 2.526, 720.

CONSONANT CLASHES IN CATULLUS 62, 64, 66, 67, AND 68

Within the first foot: 62.41; 64.258, 262; 66.5, 21, 45; 68.51.

Between the first and second feet: 64.294; 66.7, 29.

At the trihemimeral caesura: 64.23, 23b, 51, 68, 86, 147, 175, 202, 223, 230, 311, 328, 336, 370, 389; 66.69; 67.33; 68.43, 63, 71, 129.

Between the second and third feet: 62.61.

At *the penthemimeral caesura*: 62.17, 37, 39, 57; 64.102, 167, 178, 192, 258, 323, 327 (repeated later), 331, 397; 66.29, 31, 75; 68.137.
Between the third and fourth feet: 66.9; 68.155.
At *the hephthemimeral caesura*: 62.50; 64.67, 173, 247, 269, 279, 404; 66.45.
Between the fourth and fifth feet: 62.37, 47; 64.93, 165, 210, 212, 223, 230, 249, 264, 289, 300, 314; 66.75; 68.137.
Within the fifth foot: 64.252; 66.25 *(ex coni.)*; 68.155.
Within the sixth foot: 66.63, 91.

CONSONANT CLASHES IN HORACE'S *SERMONES*

Within the first foot: Book One, 2.105; 4.19, 28; 6.100; 8.17; Book Two, 1.76; 3.188; 4.84; 6.42; 7.13, 76; 8.2.
Between the first and second feet: Book One, 3.100; 6.10; Book Two, 1.72; 2.35; 3.273, 283, 305; 6.53; 7.66, 88, 90.
At *the trihemimeral caesura*: Book One, 1.29, 38, 40, 46, 93; 2.14, 21, 56, 58, 129; 3.133; 4.142; 5.1, 53; 6.54, 87; 7.20; 8.50; 9.8, 11, 57; Book Two, 1.34, 81, 86; 2.39, 42; 3.6, 71, 84, 102, 129, 194, 200, 204, 212, 245, 322; 4.49, 73, 86; 5.21, 40, 52, 68, 72, 79, 84, 97; 6.2, 12, 57, 93; 7.33, 35; 8.87, 92.
At *the penthemimeral caesura*: Book One, 1.68, 80, 106; 2.78, 82, 97, 109, 111; 3.4, 14, 33, 117, 124, 133; 4.29, 35, 123, 135; 5.6, 21, 29, 40, 64, 85; 6.129; 7.26, 28; 8.2; 9.14, 32, 41, 68, 78; 10.12, 35; Book Two, 1.2, 38, 49, 74; 2.3 (reading *abnormis*), 20, 34, 51, 84, 85, 86 (an unusual sequence); 3.28, 30, 54, 64, 67, 87, 116, 121, 140, 240, 296, 304, 313; 4.6, 17, 19, 27, 44, 79; 5.9, 19, 28, 44, 60, 66, 68, 77, 82, 97; 6.25, 31, 44, 47, 69, 78, 80; 7.11, 24, 39, 49, 70, 77; 8.16, 18, 24, 58, 60, 77.
Between the third and fourth feet: Book One, 1.71; 4.51; Book Two, 2.118; 3.1, 32, 167; 4.5; 7.13.
At *the hephthemimeral caesura*: Book One, 1.40, 64, 89; 2.15, 28, 58, 116; 3.28, 51, 63, 65, 103, 120, 132; 4.55, 64, 116, 134, 135, 142, 143; 5.52; 6.44, 69, 72, 97; 7.3; 9.16; 10.76; Book Two, 1.29, 51, 72; 2.82, 115, 134; 3.17, 70, 97, 218, 262, 283, 317; 4.44, 50, 52; 5.5, 47, 51, 59, 66, 91; 6.25, 79, 80; 7.83; 8.1, 19, 90, 93.
Between the fourth and fifth feet: Book One, 2.17, 33, 120, 127; 3.136; 4.16, 20, 37; 5.13; 6.39; 8.41; 10.36; Book Two, 2.67; 3.23, 37, 39, 127, 262, 272, 325; 6.38; 8.16, 48.
Within the fifth foot: Book One, 3.27, 48; 4.22, 95, 138; 6.60; 9.26, 53; Book Two, 1.6; 2.64; 3.318; 6.82; 8.15.
Within the sixth foot: Book One, 1.62, 82; 2.77; 4.57, 103, 112; 6.114; 9.16; Book Two, 3.260, 322; 5.108; 6.53; 8.61.

CONSONANT CLASHES IN VERGIL'S *BUCOLICS*

Within the first foot: 1.22, 43, 65; 3.22, 104, 106 (cf. 104), 108; 4.18; 5.42, 88; 8.35, 44; 9.31; 10.30.

Between the first and second feet: 6.73; 9.22, 26.

At the trihemimeral caesura: 1.29, 52, 68, 71; 3.61, 80; 4.3, 34, 47; 5.28, 48, 50, 58, 61, 73; 6.46, 81; 7.42, 49; 8.1, 37; 9.29, 33, 37, 38, 67; 10.8, 67, 75.

Between the second and third feet: 3.10.

At the penthemimeral caesura: 1.16, 22; 2.5, 23, 26, 36; 3.60, 71; 4.3, 30, 33; 5.6, 7, 8 (an unusual sequence), 12, 39, 42, 45, 56; 6.10, 22, 43, 53, 61, 85; 7.32, 52; 8.9, 66, 68 (repeated refrain), 105; 9.34, 46, 52; 10.4, 9, 32.

Between the third and fourth feet: 1.31; 2.2, 19; 6.7; 8.39; 9.41; 10.33.

At the hephthemimeral caesura: 1.2, 19, 22, 35, 42; 2.44, 54, 68; 3.90; 4.54; 5.48, 89; 6.18, 41, 57, 82; 7.17, 40, 57, 68; 8.8, 9, 21 (refrain); 9.50, 55; 10.21, 22, 24, 37, 49, 66, 68, 73, 74.

Between the fourth and fifth feet: 1.29, 32, 58, 67 (cf. 1.29); 2.49; 5.12, 82; 6.22, 61; 7.2, 70; 8.16, 38, 55; 10.62.

Within the fifth foot: 2.53

Within the sixth foot: 5.83; 7.35.

CONSONANT CLASHES IN VERGIL'S *GEORGICS* 1 AND 4

Within the first foot: Book One, 5, 20, 82, 161, 386, 449, 506; Book Four, 30, 327, 344, 473, 549.

Between the first and second feet: Book One, 176, 348; Book Four, 422.

At the trihemimeral caesura: Book One, 13, 118, 173, 190, 202, 215, 243, 379, 448, 493, 507; Book Four, 19, 26, 117, 137, 143, 182, 187, 196, 239, 252, 256, 267, 294, 352, 363, 395, 472, 520, 524, 531, 534, 546.

Between the second and third feet: Book One, 24; Book Four, 356.

At the penthemimeral caesura: Book One, 1, 21, 30, 32, 65, 67, 115, 129, 144, 193, 195, 198, 225, 230, 242, 289, 323, 331, 355, 356, 413, 441, 442, 480, 511, 512; Book Four, 2, 6, 72, 79, 93, 138, 189, 247, 264, 281, 292, 334, 349, 405, 417, 420, 425, 452, 472, 480, 499, 563.

Between the third and fourth feet: Book One, 341; Book Four, 100, 207, 256.

At the hephthemimeral caesura: Book One, 8, 20, 26, 37, 41, 44, 45, 46 (an uncommon sequence), 57, 76, 124, 152, 159, 190, 210, 229, 287, 327, 341, 406, 431, 449, 456, 494; Book Four, 8, 15, 25, 46, 53, 69, 86, 111, 142, 187, 245, 323, 328, 411, 447, 458, 494.

Between the fourth and fifth feet: Book One, 36, 43, 56, 66, 223, 386, 491; Book Four, 65, 129, 198, 332, 425, 560.

CONSONANT CLASHES IN VERGIL'S *AENEID* 1, 2, 6, AND 12

Within the first foot: Book One, 17, 154, 179, 298, 343, 383, 527, 534, 656, 742, 751, 752; Book Two, 31, 38, 190, 535, 589, 629; Book Six, 24, 87, 134, 309, 311, 335, 367, 442, 520, 534, 536, 602, 608, 652, 694, 706, 754, 816, 885; Book Twelve, 22, 158, 179, 187, 218, 239, 342, 362, 468, 480, 572, 918.
Between the first and second feet: Book Two, 162, 180, 322, 370; Book Six, 115; Book Twelve, 143, 592, 629, 815, 818, 846, 858, 860.
At the trihemimeral caesura: Book One, 11, 20, 37, 71, 74, 76, 104, 127, 134, 147, 180, 201, 290, 295, 322, 342, 343, 346, 352, 393, 406, 461, 506, 537, 644, 665, 674, 702, 707; Book Two, 29, 32, 46, 49, 71, 125, 126, 128, 144, 159, 164, 174, 193, 209, 221, 222, 231, 261, 306, 308, 333, 359, 377, 418, 434, 470, 478, 492, 544, 555, 566, 568, 620, 631, 682, 771, 772, 801; Book Six, 13, 39, 44, 47, 69, 83, 87, 107, 186, 291, 296, 332, 354, 370, 380, 438, 477, 497, 505, 534, 562, 595, 597, 675, 716, 770, 791, 830, 858, 869, 871, 884; Book Twelve, 6, 36, 113, 134, 160, 243, 267, 278, 338, 360, 421, 439, 454, 459, 498, 503, 530, 536, 539, 595, 604, 615, 621, 642, 645, 649, 689, 776, 787, 809, 813, 825, 836, 864, 892, 930.
Between the second and third feet: Book Two, 633; Book Six, 220; Book Twelve, 163.
At the penthemimeral caesura: Book One, 3, 12, 27, 60, 63, 69, 74, 144, 145, 161, 164, 190, 253, 271, 329, 390, 422, 448, 473, 477, 547, 569, 578, 610, 619, 628, 637, 640, 658, 696, 724; Book Two, 35, 41, 60, 62, 70, 80, 105, 122, 124, 125 (part of an impressive sequence), 163, 166, 172, 179, 210, 232, 245, 248, 364, 370, 395, 442, 543, 582, 603, 611, 636, 669, 671, 676, 715, 758, 786, 791; Book Six, 7, 72, 101, 154, 241, 253, 286, 312, 349, 369, 370, 380, 391, 405, 425, 439, 479, 515, 546, 548, 549, 552, 556, 559, 610, 620, 626, 646, 666, 675, 680, 726, 736, 750, 812, 855, 857, 866, 872, 896; Book Twelve, 8, 25, 113, 173, 175, 195, 239, 307, 325, 339, 375, 382, 390, 393, 422, 438, 452, 467, 506, 515, 616, 684, 686, 687, 730, 762, 801, 803, 809, 830, 867, 870, 896, 907, 931, 935.
Between the third and fourth feet: Book One, 83, 119, 481, 555, 566; Book Two, 85, 111, 283, 446, 450; Book Six, 204, 731, 759, 789; Book Twelve, 12, 178, 231, 409, 899.
At the hephthemimeral caesura: Book One, 35, 36, 75, 190, 203, 207, 217, 225, 228, 267, 268, 304, 356, 446, 462, 467, 501, 627, 630, 710; Book Two, 2, 36, 38, 160, 167, 171, 173, 202, 226, 274, 307, 359, 371, 451, 538, 583, 587, 612, 621, 642, 645, 676, 715, 721, 742, 757, 771, 780, 797, 798; Book Six, 5, 15,

28, 37, 38, 40, 115, 125, 138, 240, 292, 317, 323, 351, 354, 364, 370, 412, 432, 507, 514, 518, 520, 550, 567, 651, 683, 741, 787, 800, 819, 840, 841, 856, 863, 872, 899; Book Twelve, 26, 38, 53, 96, 133, 148, 190, 197, 243, 252, 307, 341, 385, 417, 418, 441, 442, 449, 456, 457, 564, 622, 635, 654, 707, 718, 761, 769, 777, 778, 784, 831, 834, 850, 851, 860, 874, 882, 903, 914, 925, 938.

Between the fourth and fifth feet: Book One, 55, 57, 146, 164, 245, 437, 442, 499, 601, 635, 741, 752; Book Two, 57, 94, 140, 277, 293, 477, 491, 576, 667, 786; Book Six, 6, 22, 53, 192, 223, 285, 365, 409, 463, 467, 605; Book Twelve, 11, 50, 79, 107, 164, 173, 256, 294, 463, 514, 704, 793.

Within the fifth foot: Book One, 290; Book Twelve, 317, 933.

CONSONANT CLASHES IN OVID'S *METAMORPHOSES* 1 AND 15

Within the first foot: Book One, 1, 8, 12, 197, 246, 251, 274, 343, 356, 373, 375, 408, 480, 553, 658, 756, 760; Book Fifteen, 34, 43, 69, 188, 237, 242, 340, 379, 431, 463, 508, 536, 713, 767, 769.

Between the first and second feet: Book Fifteen, 751.

At the trihemimeral caesura: Book One, 5, 6, 15, 68, 151, 157, 161, 176, 291, 293, 302, 305, 309, 383, 400, 492, 493, 499, 516, 521, 563, 569, 600, 645, 686, 701, 741, 746, 763; Book Fifteen, 2, 15, 71, 124, 148, 160, 176, 193, 195, 202, 231, 252, 294, 302, 308, 333, 336, 376, 398, 401, 407, 422, 451, 509, 568, 633, 714, 839.

Between the second and third feet: Book Fifteen, 589.

At the penthemimeral caesura: Book One, 20, 57, 71, 77, 79, 80, 83, 133, 151, 153, 167, 189, 199, 203, 206, 237, 247, 250, 253, 264, 315, 317, 318, 324, 341, 370, 383, 389, 397, 399, 436, 565, 586, 620, 650, 653, 655, 661, 684, 697, 774; Book Fifteen, 67, 78, 82, 128, 142, 169, 173, 177, 180, 199, 211, 286, 330, 338, 360, 378, 384, 387, 412, 423, 466, 485, 500, 510, 514, 554, 576, 577, 578, 616, 649, 700, 708, 712, 737, 755, 785, 791, 824, 849, 853, 855.

Between the third and fourth feet: Book One, 22, 200; Book Fifteen, 39, 281, 295, 320.

At the hephthemimeral caesura: Book One, 54, 108, 180, 185, 191, 200, 227, 380, 398, 422, 463, 465, 506, 541, 556, 591, 604, 615, 667, 689, 763; Book Fifteen, 29, 244, 254, 291, 410, 440, 477, 513, 621, 628, 632, 714, 715, 727, 767, 874.

Between the fourth and fifth feet: Book One, 116, 179, 394, 505, 664, 682, 751, 776; Book Fifteen, 119, 122, 141, 170, 230, 377, 536, 595, 746, 790, 796.

Petronius the Moralist

PETRONIUS IS usually thought to be the wickedest of ancient authors. The Milesian tales and the shameful books of Elephantis have, fortunately, perished; Martial and Strato are dirty rather than evil; and Apulcius's hero leaves his bestial life behind, to end as Isis's bedesman in the odor of sanctity. But the *Satirica*[1] have always been the abomination of moralists and the admiration of the carnally-minded. Many a historian has condemned them as vicious, or wondered at their Dionysian freedom from moral standards.[2] For Sienkiewicz, Petronius typified the Cyrenaic aristocracy of the decaying pagan world. For Nietzsche, he was "one of the few really healthy men." He is a difficult man to estimate; but he is not considered a moralist.

Then again, it is not clear what form his book really had. Heinze[3] proposed that it was a parody of Greek love-romance; and Klebs[4] that it was a parody of an epic of wandering like the *Odyssey* and the *Aeneid*. These explanations may well be partially true, but they are inadequate: for a parody on the scale of the *Satirica* would be intolerably tedious, and there are numerous large episodes in it which cannot be interpreted as parodies or part of a parodic scheme. At most, it may have had a mock-heroic skeleton and occasional mock-heroic incidents, like *Tom*

Reprinted from *TAPhA* 72 (1941) 176–94.
[1] The title in the best MSS is *Satiricon* or the like—evidently the genitive plural of the Greco-Latin word *Satirica* or *Satyrica* (a hybrid like the heroes themselves). It is surely impossible to treat this as a neuter singular, and to speak of "the *Satircŏn*."

[2] "It would be as ridiculous to apply moral standards to this [Petronius's sexual] impulse as to a storm or a cyclone" (O. Kiefer, *Sexual Life in Ancient Rome* [London, 1935] 249).

[3] R. Heinze, "Petron und der Griechische Roman," *Hermes* 34 (1899) 494–519.

[4] E. Klebs, "Zur Composition von Petronius Satirae," *Philologus* 47 (1889) 623–35.

Jones; but it was evidently something much bigger than parody. Bürger[5] suggested that it was one of the Milesian tales at which the Parthian general Surena pretended to be so shocked; and Perry[6] that it was a comic or picaresque romance like the Lucianic *Onos*. But who ever heard of Milesian tales or comic romances full of literary criticism and serious heroic poetry?[7] Rohde,[8] Lommatzsch,[9] Collignon,[10] and others held that this strange mixture of prose and verse, narrative and disquisition, had at least the form appropriate to a Menippean satire. But it cannot be a satire, if Petronius is not a moralist.

Conversely, if Petronius *is* a moralist, his work is a satire. It is not always recognized that in ancient literature the genres were very rigidly defined, and that within each genre the style, the type of subject, the models to be imitated, even the vocabulary were prescribed by tradition. The genre which an author chose depended on his intention. *A priori*, it is excessively improbable that Petronius invented a brand-new genre or created a perfectly unique blend out of two or three existing types. What he really did cannot be estimated until we recover much more of his work. But there are enough fragments to allow us to define his intention in writing the book. If their purpose can be shown to be identical with that of other satirists, then we may define the *Satirica* as satire. It is his reputation for wickedness which has made so many readers reluctant to admit that the book really is a satire.[11]

I

The purpose of satire, as conceived by the Romans, was to correct or chastise social, aesthetic, and moral anomalies by ridicule and reproof.

[5] K. Bürger, "Der antike Roman vor Petronius," *Hermes* 27 (1892) 345–58.

[6] B. E. Perry, "Petronius and the Comic Romance," *CPh* 20 (1925) 31–49.

[7] W. Kroll, *Studien zum Verständnis der römischen Literatur* (Stuttgart, 1924) 224, says that it is based on a very old form of narrative which varied between prose and verse; he is following O. Immisch, "Über eine volkstümliche Dartellungsform in der antiken Literatur," *NJA* 47 (1921) 409–21. Yet most of the verse in our fragments is not narrative but parodic or critical.

[8] E. Rhode, *Der Griechische Roman* (Leipzig, 1914²) 267.

[9] E. Lommatzsch, "Bericht über die Literatur der römischen Satiriker (ausser Horaz) von 1892–1907," *JAW* 139 (1909) 211–33, especially 217–25.

[10] A. Collignon, *Etude sur Pétrone* (Paris, 1892) 20.

[11] "Die Mischung von Poesie und Prosa . . . erinnert uns an die menippische Satire Varros, auf die noch andere Züge hinweisen. Nur von *moralischer Tendenz*, die das oberste

(Those satirists who discuss their function seldom say it includes aesthetic criticism, but they acknowledge it in practice: cf. Horace, *Sermones* 1.4 and 1.10, Persius, *Satires* 1.) This being so, how far is Petronius a true satirist?

That part of his book which is extant is largely concerned with *social criticism.* The dinner of Trimalchio is a monumental exposé of the revolting and ludicrous aspects of bad manners. It is a development of Horace's satire on the parvenu host (*Sermones* 2.8),[12] which treats vulgarity as "a monster of such hideous mien, as, to be hated, needs but to be seen." The narrator scarcely ever says that Trimalchio behaved atrociously, and only now and then mentions his own disgust. But everything that Trimalchio does is meant to be wrong, and to horrify people of taste. Some of the grossest blunders in history and criticism have been made by simple souls who believed that Trimalchio was a typical well-to-do Roman at home. In Becker's *Gallus*, for example, the entire banquet-scene is modeled on Trimalchio's, even to the boar gutted at table, and gushing forth strings of sausage-intestines: which is as if some future antiquarian were to base his description of upper-class American home-life upon the habits of Diamond Jim Brady.[13] Mr. Jérôme Carcopino's recent book (translated under the title *Daily Life in Ancient Rome*) often cites the glaring vulgarities of Trimalchio as instances of typical, though possibly excessive, Roman luxury.[14] Such are the dangers incurred by the

---

Ziel der menippischen Satire ist, kann keine Rede sein," says Mr. Hosius, and goes on, following Rosenblüth, to compare it to the mimes (M. Schanz and C. Hosius, *Geschichte der römischen Litteratur* [Munich, 1892] § 395). "La morale ou plutôt l'immoralité de Pétrone," says Collignon (note 10 above) 61.

[12] This is amply proved by J. Révay in his excellent paper, "Horaz und Petron," *CPh* 17 (1922) 202–12, and L. R. Shero in "The Cena in Roman Satire," *CPh* 18 (1923) 126–43, especially 134ff. W. Kroll's hasty and wholly arbitrary remark in "Petronius," *RE* 19.1 (1937) 1201–14, especially 1204, that Trimalchio's dinner is, "trotz Shero, nicht von Horaz' cenae beeinflusst," carries no conviction and is demonstrably false.

[13] Brady was accustomed to start dinner with three dozen oysters and a quart of orange-juice; he gave his mistress a gold-plated bicycle whose wheels were adorned with diamonds and rubies; he himself had a dozen or so bicycles with gold-plated frames and silver-plated spokes, and a different set of gigantic jeweled studs, tie-pin, cuff-links, etc., for every day in the month. See Parker Morell, *Diamond Jim* (New York, 1934).

[14] The most typical pages are 34, 68, 69, and 272 of the English translation (by E. O. Lorimer, ed. H. T. Rowell, New Haven, 1940). On p. 147, Mr. Carcopino says (apparently referring to the time of Trajan!) "Petronius' romance . . . represents Trimalchio as 'a highly fashionable person' (*lautissimus homo*)"—a distorted allusion to the *slave's* remark in 26.9. On p. 69 he says: "One gathers that there were at least four hundred of Trimalchio's slaves"—although one day's gazette of Trimalchio's estate recorded the birth of seventy slave-children (53.2). The same savant informs us (p. 271) that belching at table was

author who satirizes through direct description, without drawing the moral and underlining the lesson at the end of every paragraph. From Trimalchio's first appearance, playing handball with a constant supply of fresh balls, and treating the masseurs to champagne,[15] to his final display of bad taste, reading his own will to his guests and staging his own funeral at a dinner party, everything he does is not simply eccentric or extravagant, but wildly and appallingly wrong. Even the few details whose wrongness we cannot quite see (such as the colors of the costumes, 27.1, 28.8, etc.) are, we may be perfectly sure, wrong too.[16] Petronius describes wrong conduct without comment, assuming that his readers will apprehend it, laugh at it, and despise it. The care and detail with which he does so implies that he and his readers possessed very elaborate standards of conversation and behavior, and that Trimalchio is being devastatingly criticized for transgressing or ignoring them.[17] Criticism of this sort is unquestionably satire. It is none the less satire because Petronius leaves his readers to draw their own conclusions.[18]

There is one passage of social criticism where the moral is actually drawn. Our fragments begin with a very sensible attack on the excesses of contemporary rhetorical education, which says all that Seneca senior had said, and all that Tacitus was to say, but with more force and wit than either. This tirade (1–5) is spoken partly by the disreputable narrator Encolpius, and partly by Agamemnon, a ridiculous old pedant. Similarly, one of the most pointed sermons in Horace (*Sermones* 2.7) is delivered by his slave, much to the poet's discomfort and exasperation, and another (*Sermones* 2.3) is repeated by an ardent but silly convert to Stoicism. Plato chose to relate the ecstatic speeches of the *Symposium* through

good manners in Rome. He supports this remarkable assertion by quoting Cic. *Fam.* 9.22.5, Juv. 3.107, and Pliny, *Pan.* 49, which prove the exact opposite.

    [15] Petronius (28.3) says: *tres interim iatraliptae in conspectu eius Falernum potabant, et cum plurimum rixantes effunderent, Trimalchio hoc suum propinasse dicebat.* Mr. Carcopino (262) interprets this as "three masseurs . . . quarreling for the honor of grooming him" (s'étant disputé l'honneur de son pansage).

    [16] One point not noticed by Révay is the quarrel at table (*Sat.* 57–58). Such quarrels are merely comical in Horace (*Serm.* 1.5.51–70) and detestable in Juvenal 5.26–29. Petronius expands his quarrel to enormous length, with long and ridiculous streams of abuse from the freedman, met with contemptuous silence and laughter from the *scholastici*.

    [17] "Petron in der Figur des Trimalchio *die moralische Tendenz* der Diatribe zur Geltung gebracht hat," says Révay (note 12 above) 206.

    [18] Occasional remarks like *putidissimam eius iactationem* (73.2), the laughter of the narrator and his friends, and the ultimate flight of the three *tam plane quam ex incendio* (78.8, cf. Hor. *Serm.* 2.8.93f.) are enough to make the satiric purpose of the episode clear, without interfering with the general technique, which is narrative and descriptive rather than openly critical.

Socrates' most eccentric pupil, the "crazy" Apollodorus. It is scarcely possible to doubt that the speeches of Agamemnon and Encolpius have a serious protreptic purpose. Petronius gives them to funny characters because satire is σπουδογέλοιον, and its essence is *ridentem dicere uerum*, "telling the truth in a joke." Here also, then, Petronius is writing satire; and he even alludes to the traditional founder of the genus by inserting what Agamemnon calls a *schedium Lucilianae humilitatis* (4.5).[19]

Education, however, takes up less space in the book than *aesthetics*. Few authors in the whole history of literature have used language as sensitively as Petronius. The subtle and Joycean accuracy with which he recorded the speech of everyday life is all the more amazing in the Greco-Roman world, where literature usually strove to be aristocratic, and dignified, and (particularly in his era) loftier than reality. The same clever mind which remembered and reproduced the vulgarians' *fericulus* and *exopinissent* and *burdubasta*, and which could exactly imitate the sentence-structure of the Greekling and the Levantine,[20] was offended by the bad taste of the young poets of the day, and undertook to correct them. In the very same period, Persius (*Satires* 1.93f.) was using parody to criticize the silky and affected epics of his contemporaries, and Seneca was parodying himself in the *Apocolocyntosis*. Petronius, working on a bigger scale, went further, and offered a deliberate challenge to contemporary epic poets. It is not a parody, but a serious demonstration of the way to produce good poetry within the limits of the epic genre. Many of the criticisms in the prefatory speech are quite general (as Collignon has shown) but the subject of the poem and the special emphasis laid on the introduction of the gods into historical epic are both aimed at Lucan, the wonder boy of Nero's court.[21] I will not say that all Petronius's talent

[19] On the phrase and the poem, see Collignon (note 10 above) 228f.

[20] See, for instance, M. Hadas, "Oriental Elements in Petronius," *AJPh* 50 (1929) 378–85; A. Marbach, *Wortbildung, Wortwahl, und Wortbedeutung als Mittel der Charakterzeichnung bei Petron* (Giessen, 1931); and A. Salonius, *Die Griechen und das Griechische in Petrons Cena Trimalchionis* (Helsinki, 1927).

[21] See Collignon (note 10 above) 149f. "Ecce *belli ciuilis* ingens opus quisquis attigerit, nisi plenus litteris, sub onere labetur. *non* enim res gestae uersibus comprehendendae sunt, quod longe melius historici faciunt, sed *per ambages deorumque ministeria* et fabulosum sententiarum tormentum praecipitandus est liber spiritus": so says Eumolpus (118.6f.); and even *nisi plenus litteris* may well be a criticism of the hurried and often superficial poetry of Lucan, who thought he had rivaled the rich and thoughtful plenty of Vergil. Even that short speech by Eumolpus contains two phrases of incomparable taste and elegance: he calls Vergil *Romanus Vergilius* (which Tennyson borrowed for the first words of his commemorative ode) and he speaks of Horace's *curiosa felicitas*—a paradox which we might apply to Petronius himself. Oddly enough, the witch's boast in *Sat.* 134.12 looks like rivalry or parody of Lucan's famous description of Thessalian witchcraft in 6.461f.

went into writing the poem, or that it is wholly successful; but it is serious
and competent—although once again it is put into the mouth of a ridiculous character. It is declaimed by Eumolpus, who had previously been
stoned for his bad verses (90.1). To attack false taste, and to produce
either a parody of it, or work of a quality calculated to correct it, is the
mark of a serious critic. To do so through Eumolpus is to be a satirist.[22]

Manners, education, aesthetics: in these three fields Petronius has a
serious intention to correct or to chastise, although there is always something comic about the way he does it. But, in addition, there is at least
one *moral* theme which he handles in the tradition of satire.

Toward the end of the extant fragments, Encolpius and his companions are staying in Croton, which, they are told (116.6), has only one
interest. It is a Magic Mountain full of legacy-hunters and rich "pros-
pects": "aut captantur aut captant . . . tamquam in pestilentia campos,
in quibus nihil aliud est nisi cadauera quae lacerantur, aut corui qui
lacerant." The abject morality of the legacy-hunters is demonstrated by
two incidents. Eumolpus poses as an heirless millionaire, and a woman
legacy-hunter attempts to extract an inheritance from him by handing
over her pretty daughter and her son to his guardianship. She knows
perfectly well what will happen to them, for when she was young she
had exchanged her own youth and beauty for legacies: *multas saepe her-
editates officio aetatis extorserat* (140). Eumolpus treats the girl in a particularly disgusting and slavish way, although his acts are described as if
they were uproariously funny, *ingenti risu*.

And then Eumolpus induces a group of resident legacy-sharks to
believe he is leaving them all his vast wealth. But the inheritance has
one condition: they must cut up and publicly eat the body of the de-
ceased.[23] If we could only recover a fragment telling us how they solved
this problem, and how Eumolpus's party escaped! As it is, the legatees
are left in the agonizing but ludicrous dilemma, and every reader knows
that, rather than relinquish the cash, they will eat the corpse: "operi
modo oculos, et finge te non humana uiscera sed centies sestertium co-
messe," says one of them to the other.

Now, both of these episodes are shocking,[24] and both are treated as

[22] Note that Eumolpus introduces himself with a tirade (83–84) on the enmity of the
rich toward culture, and an argument (88) on the decadence of art caused by wealth: both
were favorite topics of Juvenal.

[23] For once, someone out-hyperbolizes Juvenal: see *Sat*. 12.98f. But Juvenal takes up
the theme in *Sat*. 15: Petron. 141.9f. = Juv. 15.87f. Note especially *exemplis* = *exemplum*;
carnes = *carne*; *Saguntini* = *Zacynthos*; *Numantia* = *Vascones*.

[24] It is significant that today we are more shocked by fornication than by cannibalism.

humorous; but still, they are both satiric. As the dinner of Trimalchio is to Horace, *Sermones* 2.8, so is this account of life and death among the legacy-hunters to Horace, *Sermones* 2.5. In each case, Petronius takes over the themes from Horace, and exaggerates them to the point of Rabelaisian farce. For instance, the tapestry falls onto the dining-table in Horace 2.8.54, and an acrobat falls onto the host in Petronius 54; the legatee has to carry the oil-smeared corpse of an old lady in Horace 2.5.84, and the legatees have to eat the corpse of an old man in Petronius 141. Horace's Tiresias advises Ulysses to hand over his wife to the old gentleman for whose inheritance he hopes:

> scortator erit: caue te roget: ultro
> Penelopam facilis potiori trade;

and says that she will be very glad to cooperate. In Petronius, a mother hands over her children, and they cooperate too. In both Horace and Petronius, these notions are meant to be ridiculous and shocking; but they are moral criticism, and they prove that Petronius was a satirist.

II

What has kept many readers from acknowledging that fact is, mainly, the conduct of the narrator and his friends: their sexual license, and their apparent lack of any moral scruples whatever. The author never says that they are wicked men, and they seldom if ever behave as if they felt they were wicked. The *Satirica* have therefore been called "a realistic novel of manners" which describes without passing judgment; or a romance of roguery, where we are only meant to admire the tricks and rascalities of the chief characters; or a Menippean satire with the spirit of the mime— that is, concentrated on humor and obscenity rather than morality. But before any of these descriptions can be accepted, it must be proved that this work, with the shape of a Menippean satire[25] and so much of the critical purpose of satire, lacks the all-pervading moral purpose of satire.

---

[25] Eg.: fantastic autobiographical narrative of adventure, Varro's *Eumenides*, *Sesculixes*, *Sexagessis*, and Περίπλους, to say nothing of Lucian's *Icaromenippus*; verse in narrative sections, Varro passim; verse parodying serious poetry, Seneca, *Apocol.* 2, 7, 12; serious verse-interludes, Seneca, *Apocol.* 4; intermixture of colloquial speeches, Seneca, *Apocol.* 6 and 8, Varro, *Modius*, and cf. Collignon (note 10 above) 309f.; etc. I have said little of the common theory that the book is a novel of erotic adventure. This seems to me partly

In the first place, the book is certainly a tale of roguery, so far as its plot is important. But we are not intended to admire the rogues. We are rarely told of their successes. We are constantly told of their failures and their dangers and their fears. Encolpius is not simply a wandering Don Juan with a list like that which Leporello recites to Donna Elvira. He and his companions are worse—as their very names (compared with the aristocratic Don Juan and the deliberately neutral Lucius and Gil Blas and Tom Jones) demonstrate. They are outlaws, and unhappy outlaws at that: "Dii deaeque, quam male est extra legem uiuentibus! quidquid meruerunt, semper exspectant!" cries the narrator once (125). And his crimes have been remarkably atrocious and varied: theft (12), sacrilege (114.5), adultery (106.2), and murder (81.3). He has been a gladiator, which was the lowest pit of degradation (Juvenal 8.199f.; 11.1–20) and escaped by a trick (9.8, 81.3). He often complains how miserable he and his friends are, and their life is a perpetual escape. Of course it is interesting and amusing to read, but it is at the same time vile and shocking. And it was intended to be both. No audience, *ancient or modern*, could approve of theft, murder, and outlawry; no audience could do anything but disapprove of them, unless they were presented as attractive, successful, and rewarding ways of life. To show their repulsiveness, to describe their constant danger and guilt, without ceasing to be interesting, is to be a moralist and a satirist.[26]

The erotic adventures of the three chief rascals are extremely complicated, and are narrated with great detail and gusto. No one who has read Horace, *Serm.* 1.2 will expect a Roman satirist to advocate or represent a high standard of sexual morality; but Petronius seems to go much further than Horace or similar writers. And yet, what we chiefly notice about all the liaisons in the *Satirica* is that they are painful or ridiculous. Few better ways of condemning lewdness could be devised than to show

exaggerated and probably false. (1) There is apparently no single motive ruling the whole plot, and certainly the wrath of Priapus does not govern even those episodes which we have. See E. Thomas, *Pétrone*[3] (Paris, 1912) 65–66, note. The leading motive is the excitement of fear and disgust, not that of lust. (2) The girlish morality and silly melodrama of Heliodorus and the other novelists are leagues removed from even the mildest passions and tempests of Petronius. (3) The thematic resemblances to love-romance, which are undeniable, are far less important than the passages of satire. (4) In general, I find it easier to believe that the plot of the *Satirica* was inspired by the real adventures of Nero and his court (as the *Apocolocyntosis* and the μώρων ἐπανάστασις were inspired by Claudius's own character and destiny) than that it was based on the vapid or vulgar tales of the novelists.

[26] There are numerous good modern examples: Defoe's *Moll Flanders*, his *Roxana*, and Fielding's *Jonathan Wild the Great*.

the miserable collapse of physical love. Ovid (*Amores* 3.7) had treated impotence with the polish and subjectivity characteristic of elegy. Petronius takes the same theme and (very much as he does with Horatian themes elsewhere) makes it extravagant and farcical: the lovers are surrounded by flowers like Zeus and Hera (*Iliad* 14.347f. = *Satirica* 127.9), but they cannot achieve their purpose, and the affair degenerates into a record of repulsive superstitions and abject thrashings. It is perfectly obvious that the spells and propitiations to which Encolpius is subjected in 134–38 are described in such a way as to make him ridiculous, as ridiculous as Trimalchio was with his astrology (30.4, 35, 39, 76.10f.) and his belief in witchcraft (61f.). The same applies to the adventure with Quartilla, herself a monster, presiding over monstrous practices; and even to the long liaison with Giton, full of random jealousies and futile passions.

This attitude can best be illustrated by a parallel. There is a long passage in Lucretius,[27] where the poet advises his reader not to give way to love, because it causes trouble, and therefore, from the Epicurean point of view, is wrong. He enumerates, first, the worry and extravagance to which even the successful lover is subject, and then the tortures of unsuccessful love. In a remarkable tirade which is so accurate in observation, so ironic in humor, and so colloquial and particular in language, that it is much closer to satire than to any graver form of didactic poetry, he lists the pet names by which lovers excuse and embellish their sweethearts' defects, and points out that even the most charming girl can be ridiculous or repulsive at times. The moral of it all is that it is unsafe to fall in love, and that love brings much more pain than pleasure. That is genuine Epicurean doctrine, to which Lucretius has added Roman concreteness, and, I believe, a good deal of personal feeling. The relevant Epicurean passage is Diogenes Laertius, *Vita Epicuri* 118: ἐρασθήσε-σθαι τὸν σοφὸν οὐ δοκεῖ αὐτοῖς. . . . συνουσίη δέ, φασίν, ὤνησε μὲν οὐδέποτε, ἀγαπητὸν δὲ εἰ μὴ καὶ ἔβλαψε (cf. Epicurus, fragment 51, Bailey). This is the point of view from which Petronius shows the lewdness of his heroes to be preposterous and painful. It is worse than a crime: it is a blunder.

On this assumption, the purpose of the entire work is satiric. It is an Epicurean satire. Epicurean philosophy preaches tranquillity, freedom from desire and disturbance, physical and spiritual repose, and retirement. These wandering, passionate, terror-stricken, lust-ridden, ridiculous outlaws are examples of what to avoid.[28] Petronius does not and

[27] Lucr. 4.1058–1191.

[28] Epicurus is twice quoted, distortedly by Eumolpus (104.3), and in terms of great respect, apparently by Encolpius (132.15). Note also that the fragmentary poems attributed

to Petronius in the *Anthologia Latina* betray a very close acquaintance with Epicurean doctrine:

(*a*) Primus in orbe deos fecit timor. . . .
profecit uitium, iamque error iussit inanis
agricolas primos Cereri dare messis honores,
palmitibus plenis Bacchum uincire . . .
               natat obrutus omnis
Neptunus demersus aqua.

                 (*Anth. Lat.* 466, fr. 27 Buecheler)

hic si quis mare Neptunum Cereremque uocare
constituet fruges, et Bacchi nomine abuti
mauolt quam laticis proprium proferre uocamen,
concedamus ut hic terrarum dictitet orbem
esse deum matrem, dum re uera tamen ipse
religione animum turpi contingere parcat.

                 (Lucr. 2.655f.)

(*b*) turris prope quae quadrata surgit
detritis procul angulis rotatur.

                 (*Anth. Lat.* 650, fr. 29 Buecheler)

quadratasque procul turris cum cernimus urbis
propterea fit uti uideantur saepe rotundae
angulus obtusus quia longe cernitur omnis . . .
fit quasi ut ad tornum saxorum structa terantur
non tamen ut coram quae sunt uereque rotunda.

                 (Lucr. 4.353f.)

(*c*) somnia quae mentes ludunt uolitantibus umbris
non delubra deum nec ab aethere numina mittunt,
sed sibi quisque facit. nam cum prostrata sopore
urguet membra quies et mens sine pondere ludit,
quidquid luce fuit, tenebris agit. oppida bello
qui quatit et flammis miserandas eruit urbes,

tela uidet uersasque acies et funera regum
atque exundantes profuso sanguine campos.
qui causas orare solent, legesque forumque
et pauidi cernunt inclusum chorte tribunal. . . .
                eripit undis
aut premit euersam periturus nauita puppem.
            (*Anth. Lat.* 651, fr. 30 Buecheler; cf. *Sat.* 128.6)

et quo quisque fere studio deuinctus adhaeret˙ . . .
in somnis eadem plerumque uidemur obire:
causidici causas agere et componere leges,
induperatores pugnare ac proelia obire,
nautae contractum cum uentis degere duellum. . . .

could not say that the wages of sin is death. What he does say throughout is that the wages of folly is contempt and ridicule and discomfort. That is the attitude which best suits the character of Petronius himself, in whom ἀταραξία (coldly described by Tacitus as *ignauia*) dominated, but who was not unconscious of duty nor incapable of action when it was truly necessary: *proconsul tamen Bithyniae et mox consul uigentem se ac parem negotiis ostendit*, adds Tacitus with obvious respect.[29] Such a man was not an immoral man: his morality was Epicurean, and his book is a moral work.

III

The main objection to this thesis is that the book contains no open moralizing on these topics. As Mr. Perry says,[30] "Petronius shows no evidence of moral seriousness. Everything is presented from a purely objective point of view, . . . without any trace of the author's approval or disapproval." That is true, although only to a limited extent, for an author who writes of a murderer in flight is certainly not full of admiration for him. But it is possible to prove that this attitude does contain moral seriousness, by pointing to other instances of the same method in the work of acknowledged satirists, by explaining it further from the *Satirica*, and finally by exemplifying it from Petronius's own life.

In one of Juvenal's most disgusting and most moral poems (*Satire* 9) he addresses a professional pervert. He asks, with a semblance of contemptuous sympathy, why Naevolus looks so miserable. Naevolus replies that his occupation's gone. He lists his complaints against his former patron, groans with dismay over his uncertain future, and pathetically

> reges expugnant, capiuntur, proelia miscent,
> tollunt clamorem, quasi si iugulentur, ibidem.
>
> (Lucr. 4.962f.)

The general Epicurean principles applicable to the *Satirica* can be found in Epicurus, *Ad Menoec.* 132: Οὐ γὰρ πότοι καὶ κῶμοι συνείροντες, οὐδ' ἀπολαύσεις παίδων καὶ γυναικῶν, οὐδ' ἰχθύων καὶ τῶν ἄλλων ὅσα φέρει πολυτελὴς τράπεζα, τὸν ἡδὺν γεννᾷ βίον. And see also *Sent.* 144.17: ὁ δίκαιος ἀταρακτότατος, ὁ δ' ἄδικος πλείστης ταραχῆς γέμων, κτλ.

[29] *Ann.* 16.18.3.
[30] (Note 6 above) 34f.

expounds the miseries of his vocation. Juvenal reassures him with blasting irony:

> Ne trepida, numquam pathicus tibi derit amicus
> stantibus et saluis his collibus!

But throughout the entire poem, Juvenal never once condemns him, or draws the moral which every reader feels to be implied. He makes him condemn himself, simply and solely by exposing his own viciousness and his own despicable state.

Similarly, the fragment of Ennius's satires quoted by Donatus on Terence's *Phormio* 339 comes from a boastful speech by another disreputable character: a parasite, who explains the glories of his own profession in such a way as to convict himself of greed, vulgarity, and ingratitude. Both these poems are of course witty and amusing—otherwise they would have been unreadable; but their entire effect is produced by suppressing the author's moral approval or disapproval and making the guilty person expose himself.

Again, it is obvious that Petronius follows this plan throughout the dinner-scene. The author and his narrator rarely express open disapproval of Trimalchio's atrocious manners. At most, a phrase like *hominem tam putidum* (54.1) slips out here and there, and is more than balanced by the ironical respect with which Trimalchio is usually described: *laudatus propter elegantias* (34.5), *gratias agimus liberalitati indulgentiaeque eius* (47.7), *tam elegantes strophas* (60.1) are phrases especially piquant coming from the *elegantiae arbiter*. Meanwhile, Trimalchio convicts himself by every action, by every word.

Another parallel comes from Petronius's own life. When he was falsely accused by Tigellinus, he killed himself with an Epicurean leisureliness and nonchalance, *ut quamquam coacta mors fortuitae similis esset*.[31] Tacitus goes on to say that he did not follow the usual practice of men dying by imperial decree, and insert flattery of Nero and Tigellinus in his will. Instead of that, he wrote out a detailed description of the emperor's vices, giving the names of his accomplices, male and female,[32] and detailing each novel kind of perversion. He sent this to Nero, under seal. When Nero got it, he was furious, and exiled a lady called Silia for betraying his evil secrets. Now, it has actually been proposed that what Petronius wrote in his last hours and sent to Nero was the *Satirica*, and that Trimalchio is Nero. That is so ridiculous that it needs no refutation;

---

[31] Tac. *Ann.* 16.19.4.

[32] *sub nominibus exoletorum feminarumque* means "classifying his several vicious acts under the names of his accomplices": see Furneaux *ad loc.*

and yet it is a distorted image of the truth. Petronius's method in delivering this attack was exactly the same as that which he employed in
writing the *Satirica*. We are not told that he wrote a denunciation of
Nero's perversions. What he wrote was a description of them—done, we
cannot doubt, with the same amused and ironical care as he used in
describing the social and grammatical blunders of the freedmen and the
disreputable adventures of the Graeculi. That was for Petronius the
equivalent of a denunciation as bitter as Savonarola's addresses to Florence, and Isaiah's to the kings of Judah. And it was taken by Nero to be
a condemnation. Tigellinus, even if ordered to kill himself, would have
been perfectly incapable of writing such a letter. He was a bad man. But
Petronius—although, as a true Epicurean, he identified morality with
ease of life and good taste—was a moralist.

IV

    Yet why should an Epicurean trouble himself so far as to write a
gigantic Menippean satire, full of moving accidents by flood and field, of
hairbreadth escapes and distressful intrigues, of elaborate chastisements
of errors in taste, subtle imitations of vulgar speech, and detailed descriptions of atrocious debaucheries? Surely it would be more natural and
philosophical for him to plunge into deep leisure, passively experiencing
(like Des Esseintes in Huysmans's *A Rebours*) rather than actively observing, recording, and creating? Can he have had a serious purpose which
prompted him to write the *Satirica*, and to make them more than mere
diversions, more than a series of funny and exciting adventures?
    The answer to this fundamental problem lies in the definition of
satire. It is $\sigma\pi\text{ουδογέλοιον}$, joking in earnest. If satire were merely
laughter for laughter's sake, it would be mime or epigram. If it were
merely serious truth-telling, it would be didactic poetry, and would then
belong to a nobler and less populous genus. Its charm is that it joins the
remotest poles, and unites the forces of wisdom on the one hand and
laughter on the other.[33] The proportion of these two motives need not
be constant, throughout the genus or even in any one author. For instance, in the work of Horace there are several satires which are almost

[33] "False be every truth which hath not had laughter along with it"—Nietzsche, *Also
sprach Zarathustra* 3.56.23.

pure sermonizing, with little that is funny in them apart from the comical examples, the light play of wit, and the oddity of the speaker.[34] There are others which turn almost entirely on their humor, and contain hardly any serious criticism or observation.[35] Most of the *Apocolocyntosis*, which is not far from contemporary with the *Satirica*, is farcical exaggeration: themes are brought in for a moment's amusement, and discarded at once;[36] the conclusion is such a ridiculous gag that it has often misled editors into expecting a different one or supposing a lacuna; while the only two serious passages[37] are easily overlooked in the torrent of epigrams and parodies which surrounds them. Nevertheless, the satire is built upon two foundations, not one: serious criticism and wild farce.

These, in combination, are the motives of satire, and both of them dominate the *Satirica*. What proportion they bore to each other in the entire work we cannot tell. Meanwhile, nearly half of what we have is not farcical and mime-like adventure, nor romantic intrigue, but satirical observation and criticism; and it is merely begging the question to say with Mr. Perry that the Cena is an "elaborate side-show."[38] Therefore, it ought to be possible to account for the presence of both motives in the book and in its author, if we are to understand them properly.

V

There was a fashion in Nero's court of going slumming in disguise.[39] Nero, dressed as a slave, visited brothels, saloons, and mean streets. His companions robbed shops and insulted passers-by, until the young emperor himself got into a fight and was thrashed. After that, the fun was out of these escapades, for he had to take a bodyguard with him. The caliphs of the Arabian empire did the same—the name of Haroun-

---

[34] Hor. *Serm.* 1.1, 2.3, 2.7.

[35] Hor. *Serm.* 1.7, 1.8, and especially 1.5, which is actually less satiric than the journeyings of Encolpius.

[36] E.g. the authority of Livius Geminius quoted in 1–2, dropped in 9.2; Augurinus and Baba (3.4), not mentioned again, even in 13; etc.

[37] These are the eulogy of Nero, 4.1–2, and the condemnation of Claudius, 10.1–11.5.

[38] (Note 6 above) 31.

[39] Tacitus, *Ann.* 13.25, says it began in 56, when Nero was nineteen; cf. also Suet. *Ner.* 26, Dio Cass. 61.8.1.

ar-Raschid has become proverbial for such adventures[40]—and later monarchs have had similar affectations. The interest that Nero and his courtiers derived from these excursions was obviously that of seeing how the canaille lived, and of subjecting themselves to their excitements, without having to bear their exigencies—poverty, prison, infamy, and the like. Petronius, who slept all day and devoted the night to business and pleasure,[41] was certainly a leader in these slumming trips; and the Satirica are, in part, a gigantic imaginative record and expansion of them. It is scarcely necessary to say that Eumolpus is not Nero and Encolpius is not Petronius, any more than Tannhäuser is Ludwig II of Bavaria.[42] But the life of the Satirica is exactly the kind of life into which Nero and Petronius plunged, to see for themselves how the other half of the world lived.

Indeed, the narrative portions of the Satirica have a much closer correspondence with Nero's adventures than with any hitherto-discovered novel or romance of ancient times. Tacitus begins by saying: itinera urbis et lupanaria et deuerticula . . . pererrabat. The Satirica are full of wandering: nec uiam diligenter tenebam nec quod stabulum esset sciebam. itaque quocumque ieram, eodem reuertebar, donec et cursu fatigatus et sudore madens accedo aniculam quandam . . . et "rogo," inquam, "mater, numquid scis ubi ego habitem?" (6.3). So also 79.1. As for the lupanaria, when Encolpius asked the old woman to direct him to his inn, she took him into a dark alley, et "hic," inquit, "debes habitare" . . . tarde, immo iam sero intellexi me in fornicem esse deductum. Then there is an elaborate scene in one of the deuerticula (which Suetonius more bluntly calls popinae) in 92–99, full of detail, even down to the bedbugs.

---

[40] My colleague Professor Hadas was good enough to remind me of Haroun, and to add a reference to the Memoirs of the twelfth-century Arab writer Usamah ibn Munquidh (tr. P. Hitti, New York, 1927). Such also were the young nobles who haunted the London streets in disguise, behaving like thieves and savages—the Mohocks, the Tityre Tus, and so forth; see Milton, Paradise Lost 1.497f.; compare of course Juvenal 3 ad fin.

[41] Tac. Ann. 16.18.1.

[42] If we are to find any real people in the Satirica at all, perhaps Petronius's enemy Tigellinus has something in common with Trimalchio. See his life in schol. Juv. 1.155, and compare it with Trimalchio's autobiography in Sat. 75f. (1) Tigellinus was the favorite of two of Caligula's kinsmen and intrigued with their wives too = "ad delicias ipsimi annos XIV fui . . . et ipsimae satis faciebam." (2) He came back to Rome when he inherited a large legacy = "accepi patrimonium laticlauium." (3) He bought ranches in Apulia and Calabria: cf. "quod si contigerit fundos Apuliae iungere, satis uiuus peruenero." (4) He bred horses for the circus = "uenalicia coemo iumenta." Of course the Asiatic millionaire is not a direct portrait of the vicious Agrigentine, but it is possible that Petronius would insert just enough allusions to Tigellinus's own nature and history to amuse other members of the court. When Juvenal speaks of the dangers of writing satire, he chooses as his example the danger of satirizing Tigellinus, 1.155.

An odd coincidence is that Juvenal describes an important nobleman of Nero's court as slumming in the saloons of Ostia (8.171f.):

> mitte Ostia, Caesar,
> mitte, sed in magna legatum quaere popina:
> inuenies aliquo cum percussore iacentem,
> permixtum nautis et furibus et fugitiuis,
> inter carnifices et fabros sandapilarum
> et resupinati cessantia tympana galli;
> aequa ibi libertas, communia pocula, lectus
> non alius cuiquam, nec mensa remotior ulli.

Tacitus then proceeds: *ueste seruili in dissimulationem sui compositus.* The Encolpius gang disguise themselves on board ship in the same way, or even worse (103.3): *capita cum superciliis denudanda tonsori praebuimus. impleuit Eumolpus frontes utriusque ingentibus litteris, et notum fugitiuorum epigramma per totam faciem liberali manu duxit.* Next, Tacitus says, Nero's companions used to rob shops, and Suetonius adds that the stolen goods were auctioned off in the palace. This is reminiscent of the stolen cloak, which Encolpius & Co. try to sell in the half-darkness toward evening, and which they exchange for a shirt lined with gold pieces (12.1f.). Finally, even the details of the fights mentioned by Suetonius and Tacitus reappear in Petronius. Suetonius says: "saepe in eiusmodi rixis *oculorum et uitae* periculum adiit" (*Nero* 26.2). Compare *Satirica* 95.8: "interim coctores insulariique mulcant exclusum, et alius uero extis stridentibus plenum *in oculos* eius intentat"; and the half-serious battle on the ship (108): "illis pro ultione, nobis *pro uita* pugnantibus." Our fragments contain nothing like the scandalous attacks Nero made on ladies and gentlemen going home late; but we can be pretty sure that the lost portions of the *Satirica* did. Encolpius had even committed murder. Note that no ordinary decent people appear. Nero and his friends were not interested in respectable characters unless as butts. The decent middle class, and the virtuous provincials who entered the senate thirteen years later with the Flavian régime,[43] did not come within their purview. That is not to say that they sought out only monsters of vice. Trimalchio's dinner is primarily amusing, not because of the immorality of the host and guests, but because of their bad manners and false culture. But in one way or another, everyone Nero and his friends met was the opposite of their own elegant, safe, and sheltered life, and of the ideals to which they paid at least lip-service.

    Much of the *Satirica*, then, is an exciting and comical evocation of

---

[43] Tac. *Ann.* 3.55.

the kind of slumming-trip that Nero and his court loved. The frame into which these adventures were fitted has been broken, and we can scarcely guess what it may have been: only that it was a tale of wandering through the Greek cities of the western Mediterranean. Certainly the existing fragments seem to be deliberately casual, and (like the adventures of Apuleius's hero) to be governed more by fear than by lust, by fortune than by Priapus.[44] However, it is the author's motive with which we are concerned. The adventures were evidently written to be amusing, as Nero's nocturnal excursions had been. That alone is a sufficient reason for Petronius to have composed the enormous book—which was no doubt read (like the *Apocolocyntosis*) to the gayest and most select circle of his friends at "Nero's midnights." His aim was not realism, and he was not a photographer. One of his motives was laughter and excitement. But he had another.

VI

The *Satirica*, as we have seen above, is much more than mere fun. It contains social, aesthetic, and moral criticism, and it is satire. One motive of satire is laughter, and the other is truth-telling. Not truth-telling without a moral purpose, like Eugène Atget's documentary photographs of Paris or a meteorological report; but truth which teaches, the satiric truth which Horace[45] says he learnt from his father:

> ut fugerem exemplis uitiorum quaeque notando.

All these contemptible characters—from the narrator, with his revolting name, dangerous past, and dubious future, to the Levantine ex-slave and the perverted lady of pleasure—are not merely photographed. As we read their words and watch their actions, we are conscious that they are governed by a careful choice, a selective principle which is in itself an implied criticism of them. They nearly all suffer—not tragically but ludicrously. They all expose themselves to contempt or ridicule. We are not meant to sympathize with them, nor to regard them dispassionately. We

---

[44] E. Thomas (note 25 above) 65–66, note, says, "D'ailleurs, la tentative même de ramener le roman à une action une et suivie partout est pour moi malheureuse et contraire à l'allure et à l'esprit du Satiricon."

[45] *Serm.* 1.4.105.

are meant to laugh at them and criticize them. They are in trouble, but it is their own fault.

And that is why an Epicurean would take the trouble to write about them. They are lessons in the foolish activity which is opposite to the wise man's ἀταραξία and is therefore wrong. Diogenes Laertius, in the summary of Epicurus's moral principles which is part of his biography of the master,[46] says that one of them is this: "the wise man will enjoy someone else's troubles for the sake of moral correction" (ἐπιχαρήσεσθαί τινι ἐπὶ τῷ διορθώματι). And Lucretius, in the most important place in his poem next to the prelude to the whole work,[47] states the same maxim in deathless poetry:

> Suaue, mari magno turbantibus aequore uentis,
> e terra magnum alterius spectare laborem:
> non quia uexari quemquamst iucunda uoluptas,
> sed quibus ipse malis careas quia cernere suaue est.
> suaue etiam belli certamina magna tueri
> per campos instructa, tua sine parte pericli.
> sed nil dulcius est bene quam munita tenere
> edita doctrina sapientum templa serena,
> *despicere unde queas alios, passimque uidere*
> *errare atque uiam palantis quaerere uitae.* . . .
> o miseras hominum mentes, o pectora caeca!

For the Epicurean, it is valuable to record the follies of one's fellow men in order to feel superior to them, and perhaps to correct them. There could be no more precise statement of the principle which we recognize as underlying the amused superiority of Petronius to all his characters, the contemptuous exactness with which he not only records the blunders and perversions of Encolpius's acquaintances, but makes Encolpius narrate his own follies, his own agonies, and his own frustrations. It is all done in the same spirit as that with which the Epicurean poet lists the nicknames of lovers for their unworthy darlings, and describes the servants giggling at the stenches surrounding their mistress while the lover pines and sighs outside. Petronius was quite evidently a thorough Epicurean—although he also had much of the Roman gentleman's devotion to duty, as far as it was possible under the Empire. That is why, when writing the *Satirica*, he included so little express moralizing and criticism, and so much derisive description of human folly. I have already

---

[46] Diog. Laert. 10.1.121.
[47] Lucr. 2.1f. Cf. Nietzsche's fine description of Petronius: "Wohlwollender Hohn, echter Epikureismus" (*Werke* 14.176).

pointed out that this coheres with the last action of his life—sending Nero a description of his vices, without comment. It also, and even more convincingly, coheres with his characteristic wit, as described (not without a grudging respect) by Tacitus.[48] *Dicta factaque eius*, he says, *quanto solutiora et quandam sui neglegentiam praeferentia, tanto gratius in speciem simplicitatis accipiebantur.* His jokes and his escapades were assumed to be ingenuous betrayal of his own feelings, whereas really they were a calculated and stylized affectation of Epicurean laisser-faire.

And his suicide was as carefully arranged as that of any Stoic: its very nonchalance was meant to be significant. He did not emit any memorable last words, or listen to readings from great philosophers. He made his secretaries read him light poems and cheerful verses, and he talked to his friends on subjects which were not serious—not designed to win him a reputation for Stoic endurance and single-mindedness.[49] And yet, his suicide was planned with the same artful carelessness as his character. His life, his death, and his book were masterpieces of that Epicurean superiority and pride in which something of the old Roman courage still survived.

[48] Tac. *Ann.* 16.18.2.

[49] Tac. *Ann.* 16.19. Notice the significant difference between Petronius's suicide and the pompous Stoic suicides of Cato, Seneca (*Ann.* 15.63), and Thrasea (*Ann.* 16.35): *porrectis utriusque bracchii uenis, postquam cruorem effudit, humum super spargens . . .* "Libamus" *inquit* "Ioui Liberatori! specta, iuuenis!" Cf. Epicurus, *Ad Menoec.* 126: ὁ δὲ σοφὸς οὔτε παραιτεῖται τὸ ζῆν οὔτε φοβεῖται τὸ μὴ ζῆν. . . . ὥσπερ δὲ σιτίον οὐ τὸ πλεῖον πάντως ἀλλὰ τὸ ἥδιστον αἱρεῖται, οὕτω καὶ χρόνον οὐ τὸν μήκιστον ἀλλὰ τὸν ἥδιστον καρπίζεται. And so Lucr. 3.935f.:

> nam si grata fuit tibi uita anteacta priorque . . .
> cur non ut plenus uitae conuiua recedis,
> aequo animoque capis securam, stulte, quietem?

The Mediocrity of Celsus

IN THE last few paragraphs of his book (12.11.21–24) Quintilian encourages his readers to devote their minds to study and to aim high. He gives some examples of men who were all-but-universal geniuses: Homer; Hippias of Elis; Gorgias; Plato and Aristotle; and then from Rome Cato the elder—who even learnt ⟨Greek⟩ literature when he was getting old; Varro; Cicero; and Cornelius Celsus, *mediocri uir ingenio*, who not only wrote books about all the subjects Quintilian has mentioned but produced manuals of strategy and agriculture and medicine, so that you may well believe he knew everything.

How can Celsus be described—especially at the end of a climactic development—as *mediocri uir ingenio?* In "The Mediocrity of Celsus," *CJ* 70.1 (1974) 41–42 D. Daube proposes that *mediocre ingenium* should be taken to signify "comprehensive mind" or "versatile capacity." However, *mediocris* in an intellectual context means neither "comprehensive" nor "versatile."

The solution is simple. Before *mediocri* we must insert *non*. A much more important word, *Graecas*, has apparently fallen out before *litteras* in the same chapter (12.23.15 Winterbottom). No doubt this *non* was omitted by a scribe who saw the second *non* in the same line (*non solum de his omnibus . . . artibus*) and wanted to make sure the syntax was correct. *Non mediocris* is one of the commonest phrases involving litotes: e.g. Quintilian 9.1.10.

Reprinted from *CJ* 70.4 (1975) 57.

Notes on Juvenal

(1) 9.76

NAEVOLUS, THE piratical man of all work, is explaining how he saved his patron Virro's marriage from breaking up on the wedding-night:

> fugientem saepe puellam
> amplexu rapui; tabulas quoque ruperat et iam
> signabat: tota uix hoc ego nocte redemi.

Something must be wrong with *signabat*. If the bride had already torn up the marriage contract, she could not be signing it a little later (*iam*). And *tabulas ruperat et signabat* cannot mean "she had destroyed one document and was now signing another document." It is wildly improbable on the face of it that the disappointed woman, after tearing up her marriage-lines on her wedding-night, would be negotiating a marriage with somebody else while still in her bridegroom's house; and the Latin makes it quite impossible.

Weidner proposed that *signabat* meant "she was signing a declaration of divorce"—but the essential noun is lacking. The scholiast conjectured she was making a new will—which is the invention of desperation.

Let us read *migrabat*. She was leaving the house of her impotent bridegroom for good—one of the decisive steps in a divorce. The act is also known as *discedere* and *deserere* (E. Levy, *Der Hergang der römischen Ehescheidung* [Weimar, 1925] 5–8); Juvenal himself calls it *exire* in 6.146–47, *regna relinquere* in 6.224, and *migrare* again in 6.171.

It might be objected that *migrabat* merely repeats *fugientem*, but that would be a misunderstanding. In the earlier stages the bride was

Reprinted from CR 2 (1952) 70–71.

merely rushing out in a huff and a dressing-gown, to spend the night at a hotel. But *quoque* shows that her later decision was more serious: "furthermore" she was going to leave Virro for good, tearing up the marriage-lines and returning bag and baggage to her own home.

The cause of the corruption was either the misreading of *r*, making *mignabat*, which was then falsely corrected into *signabat*; or else a deliberate alteration by an editor who misunderstood the point. (*Signarat*, a further distortion, appears in one manuscript.)

There are two different scholia on the passage. The second has been mentioned above: "signabat tabulas, siue alio ut nubat siue alium uolens facere heredem"—which is an attempt to explain the corruption. But the first looks as though it had been written before the corruption appeared:

> dotales tabulas frangentem (= ruperat)
> et repudium uolentem tibi dare (= migrabat) saepius reuocaui.

Here as elsewhere the scholia show us glimpses of the very earliest stage in the history of Juvenal's text.

(2) 12.31

Juvenal's friend the merchant Catullus was caught in a storm. The ship filled and began to roll dangerously, so much so that the experienced pilot could not save it from the risk of foundering. Catullus had to order his valuable cargo to be jettisoned.

> cum plenus fluctu medius foret alueus et iam
> alternum puppis latus euertentibus undis
> arboris incertae nullam prudentia cani
> rectoris cum ferret opem, decidere iactu
> coepit cum uentis . . .
>
> *incertae* P al.: *incerta* F: *incerto* P²Ω: *incerti* A al.

The difficulty is that both *puppis* and *arboris* seem to be genitives attached to *latus*. The scholiast does not help. Editors have tried various solutions, emending to *arbori incertae* (which sounds hideous), calling *arboris* a genitive of definition, and so on.

Let us take *puppis* to be an interlinear gloss on the difficult expression *arboris*, and excise it. What should go into its place? Clearly an adjective agreeing with *undis*. We might try *saeuis*—used of hail in 5.78 and of the Alps in 10.166, and actually coupled with *undis* by Lucr. 5.222.

alternum saeuis latus euertentibus undis
                    puppis
arboris incertae, nullam prudentia cani

What the original adjective was, no one now can tell, except that it
began with a consonant and ended in -*is*. But now the sentence reads
and construes smoothly, and the corruption is explained.

After working this out, I discovered that Ruperti in 1803 had proposed a similar solution, though without much conviction ("nisi malis
pro *puppis* reponere *in puppi*, vel *tumidis*, vel *curuis*") and without suggesting the cause of the corruption. No notice seems to have been taken
of his conjecture, and it is a pleasure to help in bringing it to light.

A Fight in the Desert:
Juvenal XV and a Modern Parallel

IN HIS fifteenth satire, Juvenal describes a savage fight between the inhabitants of two neighboring Egyptian towns. It was the result of an old feud, stimulated partly by religious conflicts—for one of the towns worshiped Set the crocodile-god, while the citizens of the other, who adored the mild goddess Hathor, enjoyed hunting and killing crocodiles; and partly also by the normal hatred felt by close neighbors for each other's differences. Both towns have been identified. The crocodile-worshipers lived in Ombi, and the Hathor-worshipers in Tentyra.[1]

Which began the fight we are not told, but it was a carefully planned operation. One of the two towns was having a festival, with what Juvenal contemptuously describes as half-civilized orgies that sometimes lasted for a week on end. If he did not detest all the Egyptians so bitterly, he might give us further details; but (like some moderns who have lived for a time in the Middle East) he wishes to imply that all these wogs are the same to him, and that it does not really matter which group was the aggressor. Yet it is possible to conjecture that it was more probably the cruel crocodile-worshipers who attacked to avenge the slaughter of their deity, and the luxurious Tentyrites who were holding holiday.

The battle began with insults, then went on to fistfighting, then to stone-throwing. One side next brought up reinforcements armed with

Reprinted from *CJ* 45 (1949) 94–96.

[1] These towns were originally thought to be many miles apart, but the true site of Ombi has now been found, near the ruins of Tentyra; a wall runs between them, evidently dating back to the feud. See P. H. Boussac, "L'exil de Juvénal et l'Ombos de la XVe satire" (*RPh* 41 [1917] 169–84), and G. Highet, "The Life of Juvenal" (*TAPhA* 68 [1937] 487). Aelian, *De natura animalium* 10.21, gives further details on the crocodile-cult of the Ombites, and records reasons for the loathing of crocodiles felt by their neighbors.

swords and arrows. At this, the Tentyrites ran away: so it is obvious that the weapons were produced by the men of Ombi, and more probable still that they had prepared the whole attack.

During the rout, one of the Tentyrites fell down and was captured. He was torn to pieces by the victors, and eaten. Characteristically, Juvenal adds that they could not wait to cook him, and that they enjoyed the cannibal meal so much that the last-comers picked the blood from the ground and licked it off their fingers. No doubt they felt they were true sons of the crocodile.

Juvenal himself felt that this might be incredible, and mentioned other cases of cannibalism. These, however, had been induced by extreme starvation—which was a well-known theme for the declamations of rhetoricians.[2] Yet during Juvenal's own lifetime there were several much closer parallels in the history of Egypt and North Africa: Plutarch, *De Iside et Osiride* 72, describes a similar religious feud, and Dio Cassius (68.32 and 71.4) relates even worse atrocities which occurred during rebellions. Odd that Juvenal does not cite them.

There is also a striking parallel from modern history, which as far as we know lacks only the final outrage. In Tunisia, Norman Douglas met an engineer, who told him the following story about a fight at the phosphate mines of Metlaoui.[3] Note how closely its various stages correspond to those of Juvenal's narrative.

> Those barren slopes where the mines lie, and where the different races now work together in apparent amity, were once the scene of a sanguinary primitive battle. There is a steep gully at one point, a dry torrent; the Khabyles lived on one side of it, the Tripolitans on the other, and between these two races there occurred, on a starlit night in May, 1905, an affray of unearthly ferocity.

> inter finitimos uetus atque antiqua simultas   (Juv. 15.33)

> The Khabyles, prudent folk, many of whom had served in the French Army, had long been laying in a store of warlike provisions; their secret was well kept, although it was observed that piles of stones were being collected round their huts, and that a goodly quantity of dynamite and petroleum was missing from the stores; some of them possessed guns and revolvers, the rest were armed with knives, daggers, and savage mining gear.

---

[2] See the 12th of the *Magnae declamationes* attributed to Quintilian. However, this is all about a city stricken by famine, which is not the same as Juvenal's atrocity: J. de Decker therefore exaggerates in saying "N'oublions pas que le sujet même de la XVe satire (l'anthropophagie) est du domaine de la rhétorique pure" (*Juvenalis declamans*, Recueil de travaux publiés par la Faculté de Philosophie et Lettres 41 [Ghent, 1913] 53).

[3] Norman Douglas, *Fountains in the Sand* (London, 1912).

pars altera promere ferrum
audet et infestis pugnam instaurare sagittis   (Juv. 15.73–74)

They chose a Sunday for the attack, well knowing that the Tripolitans, who are good-natured simpletons, would be least prepared to resist them on that day, and half of them in a state of jollification.

sed tempore festo
alterius populi rapienda occasio cunctis
uisa inimicorum primoribus ac ducibus, ne
laetum hilaremque diem, ne magnae gaudia cenae
sentirent . . .
adde quod et facilis uictoria de madidis et
blaesis atque mero titubantibus   (Juv. 15.38–42, 47–48)

And they were so sagacious, that they actually induced a few drunken Tripolitans to insult them, before beginning the conflict. This, they knew, would be counted in their favour afterwards.

iurgia prima sonare
incipiunt animis ardentibus, haec tuba rixae.   (Juv. 15.51–52)

Hardly was the night come before they advanced in battle array—the fighting contingent in front; behind them the boys and older men, who kept them supplied with stones and weapons. A well-nourished volley of missiles greeted the Tripolitans, some of whom rushed to the fray, while others took refuge in their huts or with the Moroccans who lived in their own village near at hand. It was now quite dark, but at close quarters the stones began to take effect. . . .

saxa inclinatis per humum quaesita lacertis
incipiunt torquere, domestica seditioni
tela   (Juv. 15.63–65)

. . . and hardly was a man down, before five or six Khabyles ran out of the ranks, to finish him off with their knives; others, meanwhile, went to the locked huts and fired them, or burst them open with dynamite.

The explosions and lights began to attract attention in Metlaoui; the whole sky was aflame; there were mysterious bursts of sound, too, and a chorus of wild howls. Something was evidently wrong, up there.

A party of Europeans, accompanied by a small force of local police, went up to the mines to investigate. They found themselves powerless; "keep yourselves out of danger," they were told, "and let us settle our own affairs." The carnage was in full swing; it was hell let loose. Not content with killing, they mutilated each other's corpses, bit off noses, gouged out eyes, and thrust stones in the mouths of the dead . . .

paucae sine uolnere malae,
uix cuiquam aut nulli toto certamine nasus
integer. aspiceres iam cuncta per agmina uoltus
dimidios, alias facies et hiantia ruptis
ossa genis, plenos oculorum sanguine pugnos   (Juv. 15.54–58)

. . . burnt and hacked and slashed each other till sunrise; no element of bestiality was lacking. The wounded crawled away to caves, or were carried to nomad camps. The number of the dead was never ascertained; Dufresnoy says "about a hundred," which is probably below the mark, as an eye-witness saw three railway trucks loaded with the slain. To this day they find mouldering human remains, relics of that battle, hidden away in crevices of the rocks.

Although, once roused, the Tripolitans fought like demons, they were worsted; the others were too numerous. They had a brief moment of revenge, however; for during their retreat, on Monday morning, they encountered two young Khabyle boys who had been on absence and were now returning to work at the mines, blissfully ignorant of what was going on. These unfortunate lads were torn to shreds.

praecipitans capiturque. ast illum in plurima sectum
frusta et particulas . . .   (Juv. 15.78–79)

The parallelism of this story to Juvenal 15 is so close that, when we read that "it was not reported in the local newspapers," we might be inclined to think that either Douglas or his informant had made it up as an elaborate hoax. It would be quite a typical French *mystification* to relate, as a true contemporary incident, something which had happened 1800 years before. But the same riot is mentioned in a description of the region by a serious ethnologist, Pierre Bodereau, who writes:

A la suite de rixes sanglantes et mortelles qui eurent lieu à Metlaoui, entre les ouvriers de la compagnie des phosphates, en 1907, le gouvernement tunisien songea à rétablir une garnison à Gafsa.[4]

The facts as narrated by Juvenal have therefore additional probability, because they apparently spring from the folkways of North Africa, which are slow to change and which have altered little since his time. It is a pity that he should for so long have been suspected both of ignorance and of rhetorical exaggeration in telling this story about the country he detested, whereas he was evidently both moderate and accurate.

[4] P. Bodereau, *La Capsa ancienne: la Gafsa moderne* (Paris, 1907) 220 n. 3. The incident is not mentioned in C. A. Julien's *Histoire de l'Afrique du Nord* (Paris, 1931). The slight discrepancy in dates between Douglas and Bodereau is scarcely important.

Sound-Effects
in Juvenal's Poetry

MANY OF Juvenal's critics call him a declaimer and deny him the name of poet. His predecessor Horace, it is true, denied that verse satire could be called poetry and said it was closer to prose conversation.[1] But Juvenal had a higher view of its powers, comparing it with tragedy and even with epic.[2] He wrote verse which was much more ambitious than Horace's chatty hexameters; and although there are grave defects in his work, patches of flatness and vulgarity and repetition, there are some splendid passages of sustained invective and many lines which have the originality of expression and vividness of perception that mark true poetry.

Not all poets try to make the sound of their verses echo the sense. Lucan, for instance, hardly ever thinks of such an effect. But those who do, like Vergil, find it a powerful part of their technique. It enables them to do much more than merely make statements. It enhances the charm or the vigor of the words. It introduces a new level of communication, where we do not merely understand the meaning of the poem, but feel it as we feel rhythm or hear melody. When Vergil says of the Cyclopes at the forge

illi intér sesé multá ui brácchia tóllunt[3]

Reprinted from *SPh* 48 (1951) 697–706.

[1] Hor. *Serm.* 1.4.39–42.

[2] Juv. 6.634–61, an important passage; 1.51–57.

[3] Verg. *Aen.* 8.452. The very marked clashes between ictus and accent in the second, third, and fourth feet here form what E. H. Sturtevant calls "a striking feature of the verse" ("Accent and Ictus in the Latin Hexameter," *TAPhA* 54 [1923] 61). The spondaic rhythm of the first four feet makes the clashes stronger.

the slow spondees, and the accents first inverted and then crashing down together with the ictus of the final words, make us sense the effort of raising the heavy hammers and then hear the resounding blows.

All the Roman verse-satirists used onomatopoeia and other sound-effects. Horace perhaps more subtly than the others, and Juvenal more powerfully. One of Horace's cleverest effects is the line which, in its abrupt change of rhythm, reflects a hurrying step changing to a dead stop:

> ire modo ocius, interdum consistere.[4]

Many other more tenuous effects in his verses have recently been pointed out by Mr. J. Marouzeau, in an article which is a model for critics of verse-technique.[5] In Persius there are some very amusing echoes, one on the first page to show the titillating effect of a fashionable reciter:

> tunc neque more probo uideas nec uoce serena
> ingentis trepidare Titos, cum carmina lumbum
> intrant et tremulo scalpuntur ubi intima ucrsu.[6]

And there is a beauty in his third satire (3.34), echoing the bubbles of a lost soul sunk deep beneath the water of oblivion:

> demersus summa rursus non bullit in unda.

In Juvenal the commonest method of onomatopoeia is repetition of the same or similar letters. He uses *alliteration of consonants* chiefly for comic effects:

—to mimic the giggling Greeks

> rides, maiore cachinno
> concutitur   (3.100–101)

—to reflect the timidity of the poor pedagogue employed as a poison-taster

> mordeat ante aliquis quidquid porrexerit illa
> quae peperit, timidus praegustet pocula pappas   (6.632–33)

—to equal the incessant chatter of a "cultured" woman:

---

[4] Hor. *Serm.* 1.9.9.

[5] J. Marouzeau, "Quelques éléments de poétique: l'art horatien," in *Quelques aspects de la formation du latin littéraire* (Paris, 1949) 193–222.

[6] Pers. 1.19–21.

uerborum *tanta* cadi*t* uis,
*tot pariter p*elues ac *tintinn*abula dicas
*p*ulsari   (6.440–42)

—to image the nervouseness of a lawyer and the stupidity of a jury:

dicturus *d*u*b*ia pro li*b*ertate *b*u*b*ulco
iudice   (7.116–17)

—to show a neurasthenic spitting out his wine:

sed uina misellus
expuit, Albani ueteris pretiosa senectus
displicet: ostendas melius, densissima ruga
cogitur in frontem   (13.213–16)

—or to call up the greed of a mob of cannibals:

*t*otum cor*r*osis ossibus edi*t*
uic*t*rix *t*urba, nec ardenti decoxit aeno
aut ueribus, longum usque adeo tardumque putauit
exspectare focos, contenta cadauere crudo   (15.80–83)

Alliteration of vowels is more difficult to bring off. Juvenal uses this to imitate the jabbering of girls talking in a foreign language:

ite quibus g*r*a*t*a est pic*t*a lup*a* b*a*rb*a*r*a* mit*r*a   (3.66)

—the belching of an overfed courtier:

pu*r*pu*r*eus magni *r*uc*t*a*r*it scu*rr*a Pal*a*ti   (4.31)

—the drooling of an old man:

long*a* m*a*n*a*ntia l*a*b*r*a s*a*liua   (6.623)

—the wailing of Xerxes' defeated army:

sed qualis rediit? nempe un*a* n*a*ue cruentis
fluctibus ac *t*ard*a* per dens*a* c*a*d*a*uer*a* pro*r*a   (10.185–86)

—and the chatter of sailors escaped from danger (a play on *a* and *u*, with excited *r*'s to add to the effect):

ga*rr*ula secu*r*i n*a*r*r*are pericul*a* n*a*u*t*ae   (12.82)

Perhaps also the repeated *a* is meant to image the brilliance of the flaming torches in

multum praetere*a* fl*a*mm*a*rum et *a*ene*a* l*a*mp*a*s   (3.285)

The Latin hexameter was capable of some very fine *rhythmical variations*: Juvenal had learnt from Vergil and Ovid how to produce them and match them to his meaning.[7] A number of his effects are imitations, or more likely parodies, of epic meter. For instance, *a final monosyllable* shows a heavy fall:

et ruit ante aram summi Iouis ut uetulus *bos*   (10.268)

—indicates an important personage:

dominus tamen et domini *rex*   (5.137, cf. 2.129)

—or an important thing:

Iudaicum ediscunt et seruant ac metuunt *ius*   (14.101)

—and adds weight and dignity to a statement:

templorum quoque maiestas praesentior et *uox*
nocte fere media mediamque audita per urbem
litore ab Oceani Gallis uenientibus et *dis*
officium uatis peragentibus   (11.111–14)

But very often Juvenal uses the final monosyllable for the opposite effect, to break up the usual rhythm of the hexameter, to make it sound more like conversational prose and to run one line into the next:

aut positis nemorosa inter iuga Volsiniis *aut*
simplicibus Gabiis aut proni Tiburis arce   (3.191–92)

illud enim uestris datur alueolis *quod*
canna Micipsarum prora subuexit acuta   (5.88–89)[8]

The epic, elegiac, and didactic poets seldom end a hexameter line with *an Ionic quadrisyllable* (⌣ ⌣ - -). Juvenal likes to do this. Usually, he uses this means of emphasizing the foreignness and oddity of something or someone he is satirizing:

aut Diomedeas aut mugitum *labyrinthi*   (1.53)

hic Andro, ille Samo, hic Trallibus aut *Alabandis*   (3.70)

ante pedes Domiti longum tu pone Thyestae
syrma uel Antigones seu personam *Melanippes*   (8.228–29)[9]

[7] For his knowledge of Vergil and Ovid see G. Highet, "Juvenal's Bookcase," *AJPh* 72 (1951) 369–94. Juvenal also learnt a good deal from Horace's comic rhythms like *ridiculus mus* (Ars P. 139).

[8] Other examples of this conversational line-ending are 2.83, 3.90, 3.273, 3.302, 5.1, 5.15, 5.20, 5.22, 5.33, 5.86, 6.35, 6.36, 6.395, 6.405–6, 11.110, 11.114, 14.114.

[9] Similar effects are found in 1.130, 3.144, 3.217, 5.59, 5.115, 6.110, 6.156, 6.581, 6.655, 7.6, 8.108, 9.22, 9.64, 10.150, 12.101, 12.102, 13.122, 13.197, 14.20, 14.252, 15.125, and perhaps 2.1. In particular, the rhythm ´- ´ // ⌣ - ´ - parodies epic. See E. Plew,

Sometimes, however, like the final monosyllable, it is meant simply to be nonheroic, informal, and colloquial, especially with the clumsy names which a more formal poet would have to avoid:

> eloquium ac formam Demosthenis aut *Ciceronis*　　　(10.114)

> non erit hac facie miserabilior *Crepereius*
> Pollio　　　(9.6–7)[10]

Five-syllabled final words are even more rare in exalted poetry. Juvenal uses them chiefly to indicate size, importance real or bogus, and slow process:

> quandoquidem inter nos sanctissima *diuitiarum*
> maiestas　　　(1.112–13)[11]

Sometimes he uses such a word to parody the tones of epic dignity:

> Romanus Graiusque et barbarus *induperator*　　　(10.138)

> nulla super nubes conuiuia *caelicolarum*　　　(13.42)[12]

And occasionally he uses it to mock a grotesque foreigner:

> et uenere et cenis et pluma *Sardanapalli*　　　(10.362)[13]

The *spondaic end* for the hexameter, so much beloved by the Alexandrianizers of the late Republic, was employed by Juvenal for several different purposes.[14] Sometimes, like his final monosyllables, it makes his lines less formal, less neat, more like prose:

> cum quo de pluuiis aut aestibus *aut nimboso*
> uere locuturi fatum pendebat amici　　　(4.87–88)

It was handy in this connection for putting in awkward names:

> et Capitolinis generosior *et Marcellis*　　　(2.145)[15]

Sometimes it added weight to an idea, gross or shocking or important:

"Über ∪ ∪ – – als versschluss lateinischer hexameter," *JKPh* 12 (1866) 631–42, esp. 632–33 and 641.

[10] So also 1.46, 1.80, 3.133, 7.90, 7.94, 8.38, 10.229, 14.41.

[11] So also 3.131, 3.182, 5.13, 6.338, 7.50, 7.98, 7.113, 7.123, 7.148, 7.186, 7.195, 8.175, 8.190, 9.120, 14.229 (?), 15.49, 15.64, 16.17.

[12] And so 10.182, 10.325.

[13] Similarly 3.229, 6.373, 9.109, 15.4.

[14] B. Lupus, *Vindiciae Iuuenalianae* (Bonn, 1864) 6, gives an inaccurate list: see also Eskuche in Friedländer's edition 70–71.

[15] Compare 4.53, 6.71, 6.620.

uel pueris et frontibus *ancillarum*
imponet uittas   (12.117–18)

laudo meum ciuem nec comparo *testamento*
mille rates   (12.121–22)[16]

And often it mocked foreigners and affectations:

Protogenes aliquis uel Diphilus aut *Hermarchus*   (3.120)

endromidas Tyrias et femineum *ceroma*   (6.246)[17]

One device Juvenal used to add emphasis to his thought was to take an emphatic word which could be scanned as a *spondee* and place it *at the beginning of the line*, thus slowing up the rhythm and enforcing a brief pause after the key-word:

ipsos Troiugenas, nam uexant limen et ipsi
nobiscum   (1.100–101)

totos pande sinus!   (1.150)

qualis cena tamen!   (5.24)

fortem posce animum mortis terrore carentem   (10.357)

nullum numen habes si sit prudentia   (10.365)

uiuat Pacuuius quaeso uel Nestora totum   (12.128)[18]

But a sudden break after *a dactylic word at the beginning* also gives dramatic emphasis, with a touch of contempt, as in

Cannarum uindex et tanti sanguinis ultor
anulus   (10.165–66)

Once Juvenal uses this trick twice with verbs to mimic the act (and the sound) of spitting:

sed uina misellus
expuit: Albani ueteris pretiosa senectus
displicet   (13.213–15)

Since we are discussing Juvenal's rhythm, it may be interesting to point out another of his favorite devices, although it is not strictly a sound-

---

[16] So 6.429, 9.111, 10.151, 10.304, 10.332, 14.165, 14.326, 14.329; perhaps 3.17, or is that meant to sound awkward and affected?

[17] Similarly 1.52, 5.38, 6.80, 6.156 if we read *Bernices*, 6.296, 6.462, 8.218, 11.138, 14.329.

[18] So also 1.110, 2.1, 2.8, 2.14, 2.58, 7.98, 8.83, 13.20, 13.26, and many others.

effect. He loves to put an apophthegm into *the first four feet* of a hexameter line. Because his audience does not expect the rhythm to pause
after the fourth foot, the remark has the savor of the unexpected. For
instance:

> magna inter molles concordia   (2.47)

> nemo repente fuit turpissimus   (2.83)

Or he will embark on a longer sentence, and then finish it with an epigram occupying the same four feet and stopping as unexpectedly:

> nil habet infelix paupertas durius in se
> quam quod ridiculos homines facit.   (3.152–53)

> continuo sic collige, quod uindicta
> nemo magis gaudet quam femina   (13.191–92)[19]

Then, *hiatus.* There are a number of lists and discussions of the
cases of hiatus in Juvenal, but their authors do not seem to ask why
Juvenal should permit himself this "license."[20] Sometimes he does so as
a strong mark of punctuation, to compel the reader to pause:

> si fur displiceat Verri, // homicida Miloni   (2.26)[21]

Sometimes it is used to suggest clumsiness, as of the two country boys
waiting at table:

> pastoris duri // hic filius, ille bubulci   (11.151)

or of the lumbering war elephant:

> partem aliquam belli // et euntem in proelia turrem   (12.110)

There is one peculiar case, in a list of the Greek immigrants:

> hic Andro, ille Samo, // hic Trallibus aut Alabandis   (3.70)

Here, no doubt, the hiatus is meant to add to the exotic and imitative
sound of the line, but it is also a reminiscence of the hiatus in Vergil
(*Aen.* 1.16):

[19] So 9.130–31, 11.14–15, 13.109–10, 13.186–87, 13.187–89, 15.30–31, and many
more.

[20] See E. Bickel, "Iuvenaliana," *RhM* 67 (1912) 145–46; W. Bogen, *De locis aliquot
Juvenalis explicandis scholiorum ratione saepe habita* (Bonn, 1849) 7–9; G. Eskuche's inadequate treatment in Friedländer's edition (Leipzig, 1895) 60–61—on which see Lucian
Müller's thorough and relentless review in *BPhW* 16 (1896) 1270–73; Lupus (note 14 above)
6–7; and R. Weise, *Vindicae Juvenalianae* (Halle, 1884) 62–63. There is an interesting
analysis of the meter of *Sat.* 1, concentrating chiefly on the caesurae, by H. Bornecque in
"La métrique de Juvénal dans la Satire I," *REA* 3 (1901) 200–204.

[21] So also 1.151, 6.468, perhaps 8.105, 12.36, 13.65, 15.126.

posthabita coluisse Samo. // hic illius arma . . .

Four times the hiatus mimics the sense perfectly. Once it shows the gape of unsatisfied greed:

<blockquote>

mimus
quis melior plorante gula? // ergo omnia fiunt . . .   (5.157–58)
</blockquote>

Once it echoes a breath drawn just before weeping:

<blockquote>
uberibus semper lacrimis semperque paratis
in statione sua // atque exspectantibus illam   (6.273–74)
</blockquote>

Once it sounds like the death-sigh:

<blockquote>
si circumducto captiuorum agmine et omni
bellorum pompa // animam exhalasset opimam   (10.280–81)
</blockquote>

And once it sounds a warning stop:

<blockquote>
sed peccaturo // obstet tibi filius infans   (14.49)
</blockquote>

Elision was used so expressively by Vergil that his successors could not equal him. Juvenal seldom seems to employ it to echo the sense, but there are a few remarkable lines.[22] For instance, here is one in which he puts an elision between the fifth and sixth feet, to show the vulgar eagerness of the Oriental shoving his way ahead:

<blockquote>
prior, inquit, ego͜adsum   (1.102)
</blockquote>

And once he uses the same trick to show how disgusting certain merchandise can be:

<blockquote>
nec te fastidia mercis
ullius subeant ablegandae Tiberim͜ultra   (14.201–2)
</blockquote>

Several times he places an elision where the reader expects the caesura. His critics say this is an ugly effect, as though he had not intended it to be ugly. Of course he did, and meant it to show gross appetite:

<blockquote>
optima siluarum͜interea pelagique uorabit   (1.135)

tunc prurigo morae͜inpatiens   (6.327)

pallida labra cibum͜accipiunt digitis alienis   (10.229)
</blockquote>

[22] Lists of his elisions are given in R. Weise (note 20 above) 64–65. In their standard article, "Elision and Hiatus in Latin Prose and Verse" (*TAPhA* 46 [1915] 147–54), E. H. Sturtevant and R. G. Kent suggest, on the basis of *Sat.* 1–3, that Juvenal elided roughly 33 times in 100 lines, a frequency "midway between the usage of Horace's *Satires* and that of the [other poems of the] Augustan Age."

nec ardenti decoxit aeno
nec ueribus, longum usque adeo tardumque putauit (15.81–82)[23]

A double elision is used in 9.79 to reflect the instability of a marriage
that is falling to pieces:

> instabile ac dirimi coeptum et iam solutum
> coniugium.

Juvenal likes also to use *odd juxtapositions of sounds* to reflect odd
persons or ideas: such as the barbarians:

> in summa non Maurus erat neque *Sarmata nec Thrax*   (3.79)[24]

But this is approaching the point at which we may begin to see more in
Juvenal's verse than he knew he was putting in. For instance, are we
right in hearing a horrid clash of consonants (*rj*, *scr*, *sq*, *spr*) and a mixture of cruel *u* and gaping *a* in these lines?—

> uol*tur iu*mento et *ca*nibus *cru*cibus*que* relictis
> ad fe*tus pr*oper*at* p*ar*temque *ca*d*au*eris *a*dfert   (14.77–78)

Certainly we cannot but admire the skill with which he has conveyed the
staggering of drunkards in the hesitant rhythms of

> adde quod et facilis uictoria *de madidis et*
> blaesis atque mero *titubantibus*. inde uirorum
> saltatus nigro *tibicine, qualiacumque*
> unguenta. . . .   (15.47–50)

and the mixture of *p* alliteration with slow slimy spondees to image thick
ointments in

> *p*ane tumet facies aut *p*inguia *Poppaeana*
> s*p*irat   (6.462–63)

Surely it is intentional when he uses long ponderous words to image a
stately procession:

> illinc cornicines, hinc praecedentia longi
> agminis officia. . . .   (10.44–45)

But does he really mean to hiss with rage in

> tune duos una, sae*ui*ssima *uip*era, cena?   (6.641)

---

[23] So also Horace, *Serm.* 1.4.26, 1.6.129.
[24] This was observed by J. Marouzeau, *Traité de stylistique latine* (Paris, 1935) 21.

And does he deliberately echo the snick of the sword severing the neck-bones in

> praebenda est gladio pulchra haec et candida ceruix?   (10.345)

Perhaps he himself could scarcely have told. Perhaps such effects came to him unsought. But, since one mark of a poet is that his thoughts are clothed in the right sounds, the care which Juvenal demonstrably shows in matching sound to sense elsewhere will justify us in admiring such smaller effects as the product, conscious or unconscious, of a carefully practiced and loftily conceived art.

The Philosophy of Juvenal

As SOON as we ask "What was Juvenal's philosophy?" we begin to wonder if the question is not useless. Why should a satiric poet have any philosophy at all? Surely he can attack the fools and scoundrels whom he sees around him without having any positive creed of his own? A swindler is a swindler, whether it is a Stoic or an Epicurean who watches him rolling past in his big car; an adulterer is still an adulterer, and a murderess a murderess. Juvenal himself says (1.79) that the force which makes his poetry is indignation.

Yet, although he was primarily an observer and a critic, he was also a thinking man. And every thoughtful man has a structure of moral and metaphysical and religious ideas on which the rest of his judgments are built. He may have taken this structure over as a whole from some philosophical school or teacher. That was how Persius got his Stoicism, from his friend Cornutus. He may build it up himself by reading and self-examination, changing it as his mind develops, through a period of many years. That was how Horace formed his own eclectic philosophy. Or he may acquire it far less systematically, by listening to the propagandists of various sects, assimilating the ideas that harmonize best with his own experience, perhaps never making a sustained effort to think them out, to remove contradictions in them, or to solidify them into a permanent system. In politics, how many of us adhere firmly to one particular creed which we use as a solution for all social and international questions, how many call ourselves "interested in politics" to the point of reading discussions of governmental problems and trying to work out our own answers, and how many simply accept general slogans often repeated, so that,

Reprinted from *TAPhA* 80 (1949) 254–70.

without professing to be politically informed in any way, we still base our talk and actions upon certain clearly definable political ideas?

And Juvenal was not merely a negative critic. He was a teacher. The difference between satire and lampoon is that the writer of personal invective has no reason for his hatred, and needs none, except a private feud; while the satirist must be able (at least by implication) to transcend the particular and forget his individual feelings. If questioned, the satirist should be able to say "This is wrong *because*—" or "That is stupid *because*—"; and then to generalize. He need not always generalize. Usually he should not. He should merely point the accusing finger, raise the whip. But sometimes Juvenal, in his later satires, permits himself to utter positive judgments. He will declare firmly

nobilitas sola est atque unica uirtus   (8.20)

or speak of tears shed for the sufferings of others as

nostri pars optima sensus   (15.133)

or say, in words (14.47) which no father or teacher, no man or woman, should ever forget,

maxima debetur puero reuerentia.

These generalizations as well as the negative judgments which fill his work evidently flow from some group of living philosophical beliefs. In earlier times, perhaps, we should not need to look for any philosophy in a satirist's mind. I doubt whether Lucilius had any ideas that could be called a philosophical creed. But although Juvenal is often said to be a voice of the old Roman traditional morality, that had never been a doctrine systematic enough to provide consistent and comprehensive guidance for life in difficult spiritual crises, while by the end of the first century A.D. it was losing its coherence, its authority, and its once formidable sanctions. And yet most of Juvenal's readers have felt that the moral verdicts of his satires show so much depth, sincerity, and consistency that they must come from a strong character with well-matured convictions.[1]

---

[1] Recently Mr. E. V. Marmorale, *Giovenale* (Naples, 1938), has suggested that Juvenal cannot properly be called a moralist because (1) he had no training in moral philosophy, (2) he thought philosophy useless anyhow, (3) Greco-Roman religion had no moral content, (4) he thought religion useless anyhow, (5) he lacked good sense, (6) such moral opinions as he does utter are all taken from the public domain or from his own ill-assimilated life-experience, and (7) he is really rationalizing his own resentments. Of the above reasons 2 and 3 are false and 4 is oversimplified (see Juv. 13.19–20, 199–207, 15.140–42),

Juvenal must, therefore, have had some philosophical creed. Let us try to discover what it was.

He himself says that he has never been trained in the study of philosophy. Once, while writing a poem of consolation, he explains that it will not be a philosophical treatise (nothing like those of Seneca, for instance) but something simpler and more realistic, offered by one like himself

> qui nec Cynicos nec Stoica dogmata legit
> a Cynicis tunica distantia, non Epicurum
> suspicit.[2]

From the last phrase it might be argued that he had in fact read the Epicureans and disliked their teaching. However, I do not think he usually draws such fine distinctions: probably he is only trying to vary his turn of phrase, and means that he is not a student of any of the three great schools.

Now, the fact that Juvenal had not read the technical books of the three schools would not be enough to keep him from having a set of philosophical beliefs, although they might not be very deep or consistent. Just as nowadays millions of people use ideas drawn from the theories of evolution and relativity without ever having studied Darwin and Einstein, so in antiquity the doctrines of the big schools were so widely disseminated and so energetically propagandized that it was virtually impossible for an educated man living in a large city to be ignorant of their main outlines. Juvenal's statement not only sounds credible, but also coheres with what we know of his life and his poetry.

He never claims to have had what we should call a college education. In his introductory address to the public (1.15–17) he declares that he has as good a chance of writing poetry as anyone else, because he has been to elementary school, and then to high school:

---

5 needs proving, 1 and 6 are irrelevant, since few poets deeply concerned with morality have built up ethical systems of their own; while 7 is true of all satirists, whose success depends on the completeness with which they generalize and impersonalize their rancor. What Mr. Marmorale does not explain, or even consider, is the deep impression that Juvenal has made on many generations of intelligent readers, as different as Byron and Ariosto, Gibbon and Hugo.

[2] Juv. 13.121–23. The assertion of R. Schuetze, *Juvenalis ethicus* (Greifswald, 1905) 5, that Juvenal here does not mean himself but someone quite different ("fingit enim amico a tali homine solatium afferri") is improbable, since J. goes on to give a long consolation in a tone of voice and thought unmistakably his own; nor does Mr. Schuetze support his suggestion by any argument.

et nos ergo manum ferulae subduximus; et nos
consilium dedimus Sullae priuatus ut altum
dormiret.

The first of these two stages is the education of the grammaticus, the
second the education of the rhetor. But apparently Juvenal did not, like
Horace, go on to a university, or, like Persius, study advanced philosophy
with a tutor. This harmonizes with at least one reconstruction of his life-
history, according to which after leaving school he entered the army and
tried to make his way up in the equestrian career. It was only after failing
in that ambition that he turned to satire, and by then he was too old and
too resentful to attend philosophical lectures.[3]

The statement is also borne out by his own references to philosophers and philosophy. They are shallow, occasionally mistaken or meaningless. Let us look at them. Here are the eminent thinkers whom he
mentions:

Aristotle 2.6

Chrysippus 2.5, 13.184

Cleanthes 2.7

Democritus 10.28–53

Diogenes (in periphrasis) 14.309–
13

Epicurus 13.122–23, 14.319

Heraclitus (in periphrasis) 10.30–
32

Pittacus 2.6

Pythagoras 15.171–74

Socrates (in periphrasis) 13.185–
87, 14.320

Thales 13.184

Zeno 15.107

Seneca—who appears in 5.109, 8.212, and 10.16—is treated not as a
thinker, but merely as the wealthy tutor and victim of Nero. Besides
these, there arc two or three near-contemporaries like Barea (3.116 and
7.91) and Secundus Carrinas (7.204–6). The sects which are named are:

Cynics 13.121–22

Pythagoreans 3.229

Socratics 2.10

Stoics 2.64–65, 3.116, 13.121–
22, 15.106–9

with the Stoics occupying the place of dishonor at the opening of Satire
2.

[3] The statement in some of the Lives, *ad mediam fere aetatem declamauit*, may be
true or (if constructed from 1.15–17 plus 1.25) imaginary; but it proves nothing either way:
since we do not know who wrote the Lives and on what authority, and since one could
"declaim," just as one could write poetry, without having studied philosophy. For a reconstruction of Juvenal's career along the above lines see G. Highet, "The Life of Juvenal,"
TAPhA 68 (1937) 480–506.

As we look over these names and the passages in which they occur, we see clearly that Juvenal knows scarcely anything about them. Aristotle, Chrysippus, and Cleanthes appear only as busts in the homes of poseurs; and so does the remote Pittacus, who is so far from being a real philosopher that Juvenal evidently took him, as he took Thales, from a list of the seven sages. Plato is not mentioned. Nearly all the others appear merely as clichés learnt in school from handbooks like that of Valerius Maximus to which Juvenal owes so much. Just in the same way as Xerxes = overweening pride and Alexander = inordinate ambition, so Epicurus = frugality, Pythagoras = vegetarianism, and Democritus and Heraclitus = laughter and tears at human folly.

Only one philosopher is actually quoted, and he is quoted wrongly. After describing a riot which ended in lynching and cannibalism, Juvenal goes on (15.93f.) to speak of the siege of Calahorra in which the living ate the dead. Then he adds (15.106–9):

> melius nos
> Zenonis praecepta monent, nec enim omnia †quidam†
> pro uita facienda putant: sed Cantaber unde
> Stoicus, antiqui praesertim aetate Metelli?

Although the antithesis is labored, it is in Juvenal's manner; but the contrast is quite false. The Stoics did not forbid cannibalism. On the contrary, they held that it was οὐκ ἄτοπον and therefore permissible and even recommendable—always, not only in times of famine. Chrysippus is reported to have taught that we should eat the bodies of our parents after their death, provided the meat were still good.[4]

The conclusion is clear. The leading Greek philosophers Juvenal seems to know only as shallow stereotypes. They are not for him the creators of so many vast systems of thought; they are quaint and eccentric personages who lived in tubs or ate vegetables: sometimes not even that, but merely plaster busts on a shelf. In this his poems are a striking contrast to the satires and letters of Horace and Persius, both of whom knew a good deal of philosophy and had vital and original ideas about the subject.

Nevertheless, Juvenal knows something of philosophy, though he stands outside it. He calls it *sapientia*, and it is one of the few things in life he is found to praise (13.187–89):

> plurima felix
> paulatim uitia atque errores exuit omnes,
> prima docet rectum sapientia.

[4] Sext. Emp. *Pyr.* 3.207, 247–48; Diog. Laert. 7.188.

And once (14.321) he says its teachings coincide with those of nature:

> numquam aliud natura, aliud sapientia dicit—

a phrase familiar to both Stoics and Epicureans.[5] However, his most important utterance about it treats it as somehow opposed to the experience of life possessed by himself and others who have suffered much. It is in the consolation address to his friend Calvinus robbed of several hundred dollars by a false confidant. Juvenal points out (13.19–22) that experience should teach him not to be surprised:

> magna quidem, sacris quae dat praecepta libellis,
> uictrix fortunae *sapientia*: ducimus autem
> hos quoque felices qui ferre incommoda uitae
> nec iactare iugum *uita* didicere magistra.

And off he goes into a disquisition on the evil of the world, taken from experience and history, not from philosophy. It is in this same satire that Juvenal says (13.121–23) he has read no Stoic or Cynic works and does not admire Epicurus. If he had (he implies) he would be able to offer consolation for ills more serious, but even without that he can help his friend in present trouble.

He knows something about philosophy, then, and he respects it. And, as we have seen, he must have been equipped with some set of philosophical ideas on which to base his ethical judgments—ideas which he apparently acquired by osmosis, through hearing speeches and debates and street-corner sermons and recitations of poems in which they were embodied. What were those ideas? were they Cynic, or Stoic, or Epicurean? They are scarcely likely to have been drawn from any of the more obscure schools of philosophy. Or were they, perhaps, a blend of several different doctrines?

Most of those who have studied Juvenal conclude that he was a Stoic. Friedländer, who knew him well, assembled a number of quotations pointing toward Stoicism.[6] Certainly Juvenal is familiar with some important Stoic maxims, and places them at key points in some of his most ambitious poems:

> permittes ipsis expendere numinibus quid
> conueniat nobis rebusque sit utile nostris,
> nam pro iucundis aptissima quaeque dabunt di   (10.347–49)

---

[5] Marc. Aurel. 5.9; Diog. Laert. 7.88; Epicurus fr. XXI Bailey, and cf. fr. 45 Bailey.
[6] L. Friedländer, *Juvenal* (Leipzig, 1895) introd. 36–42.

nullum numen habes si sit prudentia: nos te,
nos facimus, Fortuna, deam caeloque locamus

(10.365–66; cf. Sen. *Ep.* 118.4)

Yet even in these he is sometimes inconsistent, for (as Friedländer points out) he also says that fortune has a random and senseless power over the lives of men, which no Stoic would believe: he says with a sneer (7.197):

si Fortuna uolet, fies de rhetore consul,

and he declares that careerists are men such as

extollit quotiens uoluit Fortuna iocari   (3.40)

The most impressive of his Stoical utterances is the fine passage in Satire 15 where he says that kindness is the essence of humanity and comes from God the Creator (15.143–49):

uenerabile soli
sortiti ingenium diuinorumque capaces . . .
sensum a caelesti demissum traximus arce,
cuius egent prona et terram spectantia. mundi
principio indulsit communis conditor illis
tantum animas, nobis animum quoque.

Also, Juvenal knows at least one of the Stoic saints, for he says (10.360–62) that the ideal mind will prefer the labors of Hercules to the pleasures of Sardanapallus, and elsewhere (2.19–20) speaks of false Stoics as using Hercules' words. And there is a grim austerity about his manner, a refusal to compromise, a proud scorn of timeservers and cheats, that looks like the spirit of the rigid Cato and his fellow Stoics.

Yet his knowledge of Stoicism is limited, as his mistake about cannibalism shows. And when we look at his use of Stoic doctrines we find that he seldom or never adopts them wholeheartedly and usually alters them freely. For example, he seems to have read Seneca fairly carefully: although Seneca quotes the Epicureans and admires some Cynics and deprecates the extremes of Stoicism, he is on the whole a Stoic teacher, combining enthusiasm and tact, high principles and easy progressive adaptability. Even after Dr. Carl Schneider's valuable dissertation *Juvenal und Seneca* (Würzburg, 1930), much still remains to be discovered about the relation between the two writers. While Dr. Schneider has been very diligent in collecting parallel utterances by both authors on certain large themes such as Superstition and Women, he has not pointed out those differences between them which become clear as soon as one reads Seneca continuously with Juvenal in mind. But the differences are as important as the resemblances.

For example, Seneca writes that one serious cause of anger is the spectacle of prosperous vice and successful crime which can be seen in the streets of Rome (*De ira* 2.7–9). So does Juvenal (1.22–80). But Juvenal draws one conclusion, that he must write angry satire; while Seneca draws the other and opposite conclusion, that the wise man must restrain his anger at this sight. Again, Juvenal often complains bitterly of insults offered to him and other poor men by the rich and their proud servants. Seneca explicitly denounces such protests, *quae quid uocem nisi querelas nauseantis animi?* (*Constant.* 10.2); and later he says it is actually funny to watch people like Juvenal being indignant at *ostiarii difficultatem, nomenclatoris superbiam, cubicularii supercilium* (*Constant.* 14.1). Juvenal, like Seneca, declares that noble birth is nothing and virtue is everything; and the beginning of his eighth satire looks like a close quotation of Seneca (*Ben.* 3.28.2 and *Ep.* 5.44.5). Yet Juvenal ends by exploding the myth of nobility on the ground that the "first families" of Rome were either herdsmen or outlaws (8.272–75), while Seneca says the opposite: *quidquid in medio sordidi iacet transilite; exspectat uos in summo magna nobilitas* (sc. *origo diuina*) (*Ben.* 3.28.3). Again and again Juvenal rages where Seneca advises calmness. And there are important differences in the illustrations which they choose. Seneca thinks of brave nobles resisting bad emperors, Juvenal of weak courtiers surrendering to bad emperors; Seneca worries about illness but says he can easily ignore poverty, Juvenal pays little heed to illness but thinks constantly of the pains and humiliations of poverty; Seneca thinks adversity is exercise, Juvenal thinks it is torture. It looks as though Juvenal had read Seneca with a keen eye for vivid phrases, but without the intellectual training to enable him to follow and retain an argument, and with no sympathy for the Stoical lessons that Seneca was trying, with all his tact and all his eloquence and all his sometimes tiresome wit and all his hard-breathing insistence, to instil.

What is more important, Juvenal's enthusiasm for Stoicism is very limited. He speaks of Hercules twice. But he never mentions the other Stoic hero, Ulysses, as a Stoic hero—only as a slightly ridiculous figure from the Trojan saga (9.65, 11.31, 15.14). And he pointedly refrains from praising the Stoic martyrs who died in opposition to absolutism. The bravest thing the Stoics did in Juvenal's own time, and under the early empire generally, was to oppose the growing power of the emperors. Juvenal scarcely mentions this opposition. Even in Martial (1.13) there is a laudatory reference to the famous republican Arria, who stabbed herself and handed the dagger to her husband with the Stoical remark "Paete, non dolet." Even in Tacitus there is a good deal of respect for Helvidius Priscus and others like him; and Seneca's prose works are full of trumpet-tongued eulogies of the younger Cato. In Juvenal Cato appears only once (2.40) in a comparison with his hypocritical followers; Helvidius Priscus and Thrasea Paetus are touched once with a smile (5.36); the heroic Arria is not mentioned; the other Stoics of the aristocratic republican opposition are ignored, or derided as *ficti Scauri* (2.34–35) and *libertatis magistri* (2.77) making moral speeches in immoral costume.

He denounces the Stoics far more than he praises them. In the first book, immediately after the announcement of his program in 1, he begins an attack on male perverts with a violent denunciation of those who masquerade as Stoics (2.1–65). It is full of biting antitheses evidently produced by the most profound disgust, and dictated more by personal observation than by literary convention: *Socraticos cinaedos* (2.10), *de uirtute locuti clunem agitant* (2.20–21). This same passage contains a bitter parody of a famous phrase, which shows us that Juvenal could never take Stoicism seriously. The shaggy legs and bristled arms of these pretenders, he says (2.12),

> promittunt atrocem animum,

but in fact they are habitual perverts. The epigram is a sneering allusion to Horace's ennobling words (*Carm.* 2.1.23–24):

> cuncta terrarum subacta
> praeter atrocem animum Catonis.

Instead of mentioning the valor of the Stoic opposition, he uses one of its tragedies, the accusation of Barea Soranus, as another proof of the hypocrisy of Stoics and the treachery of Greeks (3.116–18): for it was Barea's own client, the philosopher P. Egnatius Celer, who stood witness against him, and *auctoritatem Stoicae sectae praeferebat* (Tac. *Ann.* 16.32, cf. *Hist.* 4.10). No aristocratic opposition to the principate, Stoic or other, has ever achieved anything at all: so Juvenal says in 4.96–103 and 4.151–54, and implies it elsewhere. We cannot therefore put him down as an admirer of Stoicism, even though he quotes Stoic precepts. Probably he did not begin by studying Stoicism and then decide that the Roman gentlemen who claimed to be followers of Zeno were unworthy of their profession; he began by watching the Roman gentlemen, decided that they were corrupt and hypocritical, and then concluded that their creed was worthless. He worked, as he himself says, from the experience of life itself.[7]

---

[7] Juv. 13.21–22. Surely it is misunderstanding Juvenal's attitude to the Roman nobles and millionaires, those weak and selfish monsters, as he saw them, to say as Friedländer

But his character was not really sympathetic to Stoicism either. He is too passionate. He protests too much, far too much. He is too anxious. He is too angry, too scornful. He hopes too much, and therefore despairs too much. In fact, he is too unhappy; and the perfect or progressing Stoic was not unhappy. He has little or none of the Stoic sense of duty, and never conceives that he has any obligation to serve the human community.[8] Secretly he is too ambitious; or else he was too ambitious, long ago. In his early poems he says that vice and crime will not let him sleep, that he cannot control himself, that his guts are parched with burning anger, his disgust and fury make him want to escape to the North Pole. Only in his later satires does he speak more calmly; and then he does not speak with the rigid determination of the Stoic, but with a more emotional, more tragic, less lofty, perhaps more human resignation.

If Juvenal is not a Stoic, is he perhaps a Cynic? No, obviously not. He was poor for a long time, but he never became the carefree scornful barefoot boy of the streets, the classless self-outcast, the hermit of the sidewalks, the moral anarchist who demanded the abolition of all accepted standards, who flouted all the social conventions and the timid people who kept them, the exploder of society. Juvenal thought that Roman metropolitan society in his time was bad, but he did not think that all society was bad. (Little towns in the countryside, even a quiet house in Rome away from the crowds and the noise, these were desirable.) Nor did he preach the worthlessness of all existing ethical and social standards, as a Cynic would do. Most of the moral actions of his time were bad, he said and proved; some few were good; and the standards remained though few adhered to them; at least they remained in memory (13.53f.):

> improbitas illo fuit admirabilis aeuo
> credebant quo grande nefas et morte piandum
> si iuuenis uetulo non adsurrexerat . . .

but they were not, as the Cynics taught, worthless and meaningless.

Nevertheless, Juvenal uses a number of the propaganda points worked out by the Cynics—or else by the popular Stoic preachers who (he says in 13.122) differed from them only by a shirt. It is this that has made a number of his critics say he employs the clichés of "popular philosophy."

does (note 6 above) introd. 39, "dass so viele hervorragende Männer sich zu ihr (= der stoischer Philosophie) bekannt hatten, muss ihr in den Augen eines Laien wie er, ganz besonders zur Empfehlung gereicht haben."

[8] Cf. Marc. Aurel. 9.23; E. Zeller, *Die Philosophie der Griechen in ihrer geschichtlichen Entwicklung* (Leipzig, 1923) 3.1⁵.293–95.

Yet that is a dangerously vague phrase. It might mean either "a single philosophical system popularized by propaganda" or "a set of floating general ideas shared by the majority of the public—the Lowest Common Denominator of philosophy." Sometimes Juvenal's critics speak as though he were an adherent of "popular philosophy" in the first sense, because he had assimilated a number of Cynic or Stoic principles through propaganda; and sometimes they seem to imply that he was merely a loudspeaker catching and mouthing the notions which wandered through the collective mind.[9]

It was, however, chiefly the Cynics who worked out the most effective lines of social criticism, and Juvenal like other publicists borrowed them freely. Yet his results are not so completely negative as those of the Cynic diatribes. When he attacks the corrupt and cruel city, he does not suggest that it should be destroyed and that honest men should live like animals or vagrants, abandon family ties, and give up the apparatus of civilized existence; but that they should live in small towns, with modest homes of their own, and eat from pottery instead of gold and silver plate bought with borrowed money (3.164–81, 223–31). When he inveighs against greed, he ends with the Cynic argument that the millionaire is made wretched by the worry of his millions, while Diogenes takes his ease in his fireproof tub; but then he goes on to give a positive ideal— not Cynic poverty, but Epicurean and "Socratic" economy, the little which is sufficient (14.303–21):

> in quantum sitis atque fames et frigora poscunt,
> quantum, Epicure, tibi paruis suffecit in hortis,
> quantum Socratici ceperunt ante penates.

So then Juvenal is not a Stoic, nor a Cynic. What is his attitude to the Epicureans?

The first thing we notice is that he treats them with respect. Convinced opponents of Epicureanism were always very savage in their attacks on its followers, calling them voluptuaries who rationalized their debaucheries as the pursuit of a philosophical ideal. Cicero, usually so suave in philosophical discussions, grows very bitter when he speaks of

---

[9] C. Schneider, *Juvenal und Seneca* (Würzburg, 1930) 11–12, speaks of Juvenal's "popular philosophy" as a blend of Cynicism and Stoicism. R. Schuetze (note 2 above) 6–9, states firmly that he was neither a Stoic nor a Cynic nor an Epicurean, but liked discussions of morals in the manner of the Cynics and Stoics. He then goes on to show that Juvenal picked up topics treated by all kinds of philosophers from Theophrastus to Plutarch—a thesis so vague as to be virtually useless, apart from Mr. Schuetze's valuable collection of parallel passages.

them; and Horace characteristically turns a similar attack into a joke by calling himself (*Epist.* 1.4.16)

> Epicuri de grege porcum.

In Juvenal there is no such criticism. He heaps scorn upon the sham Stoics. He never mentions any bogus Epicureans, he has no sneering names for their sect comparable to his *Stoicidae* (2.65), and—although he does not "look up" to the Founder—he never speaks of Epicurus personally without sincere respect.

Then we find, as we reread the satires, that he does know something of Epicurean dogma. Not, of course, the atomic hypothesis: he is quite ignorant of all such theoretical matters. But he can quote hedonistic moral precepts of Epicurus, and he has heard something of Epicurean social teaching. In 11 he invites an old friend to take the day off and sunbathe and dine with him, when all the rest of Rome will be at the races. It is delightful; but, he adds, not a thing to be done often:

> uoluptates commendat rarior usus.

This is the Epicurean doctrine of distributing pleasures so as to make their enjoyment keener.[10] In a later satire he produces an equally orthodox Epicurean argument to console his defrauded friend: that the embezzler can be left to the tortures inflicted on him by his conscience, not the sense of guilt alone, but the fear of discovery which Epicurus himself called the one sure safeguard against crime: the *perpetua anxietas* that will not allow him to eat or drink or even sleep at ease.[11] In the poem which opens with the attack on false Stoics he denies the existence of ghosts and the underworld, in terms evidently suggested by Epicurean arguments.[12] And once, in a page where he does not hate but admires the human race, a rare page written not in his usual burning lava but in living water breaking through the rock, he paraphrases an Epicurean description of the beginnings of society and the natural growth of sympathy.[13]

Yet, as we look into his mind, what strikes us most is not his occasional quotations of Epicurean formulae, but his adoption of certain basic Epicurean principles. Take one of his most famous satires, the tenth. It is often called *The Vanity of Human Wishes*, but it would be better

---

[10] Juv. 11.206–8. Epicurus, *Ad Menoec.* 131 Bailey.

[11] Juv. 13.211–22. Epicurus, K.Δ. 17, 34–35 Bailey; fr. 82 Bailey; Lucr. 3.1011–23; Seneca quoting Epicurus, *Ep.* 16.97.13–15.

[12] Juv. 2.149–52. Compare Seneca's quotation of the *Epicurea cantilena* in *Ep.* 3.24.18.

[13] Juv. 15.147–58. Lucr. 5.1011–27; see esp. 1019–24.

described as *The Dangers of Ambition*. The prayers which Juvenal explodes are all for extremes of power or eminence or happiness: to be as powerful as Sejanus, as famous as Cicero, as glorious in conquest as Hannibal and Alexander, even to live to 100 and have children of godlike beauty. He begins by asking if all such desires are not "superfluous"—an Epicurean term for desires neither natural nor necessary, such as the desire for wealth (10.12–27) and for "crowns and statues" (10.56–113).[14] And the final argument he levels against all these is not that the objects of such wishes are indifferent, or injurious to the pursuit of virtue. It is that, when attained, they do not bring happiness. They bring danger and suffering. That is the only reason why we should avoid them. The ambitions themselves are neither morally good nor morally bad. They are simply unremunerative in pleasure. Even the writing of Cicero's *Philippics*—which a Stoic would think an act of virtue because it served the commonwealth—is condemned by Juvenal's hedonistic calculus because it resulted in Cicero's decapitation (10.124–25):

> ridenda poemata malo
> quam te, conspicuae diuina Philippica famae.

Toward the end of the poem, the best hopes of man are defined in the famous line,

> orandum est ut sit mens sana in corpore sano,

which is a broader and less technical version of Epicurus's definition of happiness.[15] Juvenal follows this with an unmistakable reference to Epicurean "robustness" and freedom from the fear of death:

> fortem posce animum mortis terrore carentem.[16]

Elsewhere too, in the same vein, Juvenal says it is better to live away from the world, because ambition and the struggle to shine or even to live in Rome cause constant heartbreaks. Better to live in a small town, to avoid the crowded circus, to dine soberly and frugally with one friend, than to inhabit the great city, to be the presiding magistrate at the games, to have a sumptuous banquet; better, not because it is possible to live

---

[14] See Epicurus, K.Δ. 29 Bailey; C. Bailey, *The Greek Atomists and Epicurus* (Oxford, 1928) 493–96 and 500–501.

[15] Juv. 10.356. So Seneca, *Ep.* 7.66.45: *apud Epicurum duo bona sunt ex quibus summum illud beatumque componitur, ut corpus sine dolore sit, animus sine perturbatione.*

[16] Juv. 10.357. Cf. Diog. Laert. 10.83, and Cicero's statement of the same theme in *Fin.* 1.15.49.

more virtuously by the former alternative, but because it means living
more pleasantly, more happily.[17]

In his early poems Juvenal appears to know few of the pleasures of
friendship. He walks alone through the streets with his notebook, *inquie-
tus* as Martial imagined him (1.63–64; Mart. 12.18.1–2); he says good-
bye to the aging Umbricius, leaving Rome in defeat and despair (3); when
he advises Trebius and Postumus to shun clienthood and marriage, he
sounds rather as though he were talking to himself (5 and 6). In 7 he is
still alone, looking gloomily around at the starving intellectuals of his
youth; in 8 he addresses a young nobleman in terms which are earnest
but far from warm; in 9 his interlocutor is a professional pervert whom
he despises; in 10 he fixes his eye on the whole world and speaks to no
individual.

But in 11, for the first time, his voice is heard talking to a friend as
a friend. With genuine though hitherto unprecedented warmth, he invites an elderly friend to dine with him—forgetting all the troubles of
every day, money and marriage, and household cares, and *above all* un-
grateful friends. This is a high tribute to friendship, all the more marked
because the eleventh satire is the first extant poem which Juvenal devotes
to praise rather than criticism. The twelfth, which follows, is even warmer.
It is an account of the storm in which another of Juvenal's friends, Catullus, was almost shipwrecked—an account set within a description of a
thanksgiving service. Juvenal tells us that it is quite disinterested, since
Catullus has children who will inherit his money; but his cynical warning
is quite unnecessary, for there is an unmistakable gusto about his description of the white lambs and the fighting bull-calf led to the green altar,
the garlanded household-gods and the branch-wreathed door set with re-
joicing lights. The thirteenth satire too, although less warm, is dictated
by the same emotion: for it is a consolation addressed to an aged companion, and though pessimistic in its view of human honesty, it is still
sincerely friendly. Somehow it complements the other satires by creating
a little world of old friends outside which all is false and hostile. Of all
the three main sects, it was only Epicureanism which paid so much
attention to friendship, only Epicureanism which taught that friendship

---

[17] Juv. 3.164–231, 11 *passim*, 10.36–50. Epicurus fr. 86 Bailey; fr. LVIII Bailey; and
see Bailey's discussion in *Greek Atomists* (note 14 above) 515–17. Juvenal's view that it is
silly, uncomfortable, and dangerous to devote one's life to serving the state and gaining
political power (10.56–132) corresponds closely with that of the Epicureans as reported by
Cicero, *Rep.* 1.4–6: they called Cato a "madman" for entering politics (*Rep.* 1.1) as Juvenal
calls Hannibal crazy for invading Italy (10.166).

was one of the surest sources of happiness, only Epicureanism that ranked friendship, as Juvenal does, above the ties of the family.[18]

In his sixth satire Juvenal considers marriage, and gives almost every possible reason against it. It was an old philosophical question whether the wise man should marry or not, and he appears to be drawing on several earlier discussions and shifting the point of view from the "wise man" to Everyman.[19] The first reason he examines and demolishes is that marriage is a duty to society; but he spends only a few lines on this, which was the chief Stoic justification for the practice; and then for 600 lines he gives what is in fact the Epicurean argument that marriage is inadmissible "because of its many unpleasantnesses."[20]

Even in his attitude toward one of the central problems of life, the relation of man to society, is Juvenal not an Epicurean? The Cynic thought the wise man would ignore and deride the artificial structure of the state. The Stoic held the wise man would help his fellow men from a sense of duty, if not in a corrupt contemporary state, at least in the cosmic community.[21] Juvenal, like the Epicureans, never mentions duty as a motive (officium in his poems means nothing more than "social obligation"[22]) and the way of life to which (after what struggles and anguishes?) he was drawn or driven was summed up in the Epicurean dogma: λάθε βιώσας, "live in hiding."

Still, anything we say about the philosophy of Juvenal must be carefully limited and qualified. As he says himself, he had no training in the subject; and at the beginning of his career as a poet he had no philosophy. His early satires are violent. They are sometimes disorderly. They are concentrated on the particular, and scarcely admit general ideas. They are unbalanced. They are extreme. They contain no rules for life, and very little hope that life can be made worth living. To the intolerable situations he describes, Juvenal offers no reasoned and philosophical alternatives: only escape to the frozen deserts (2.1–2) or to a deserted village (3.2–3), beggary (5.8–11) or suicide (6.30–32). The sole trace of interest

[18] So Epicurus, K.Δ. 27 Bailey; Bailey, Greek Atomists (note 14 above) 517–20.

[19] See, for instance, E. Bickel, Diatribe in Senecae philosophi fragmenta 1 (Leipzig, 1915); F. Bock, Aristoteles Theophrastus Seneca de matrimonio (Leipziger Studien 19, 1899); J. van Wageningen, "Seneca et Iuuenalis," Mnemosyne 45 (1917) 417–29.

[20] For the Stoic view see R. D. Hicks, Stoic and Epicurean (New York, 1910) 137–40; Zeller (note 8 above) 3.1⁵.301–2. For the Epicurean, Bailey, Greek Atomists (note 14 above) 520–21.

[21] Zeller (note 8 above) 293f. and 302f.

[22] Officium occurs in 2.132, 2.134, 3.126, 3.239, 5.13, 6.203, 7.107, 10.45 (where by extension officia means the clients themselves), and 11.114 (= "role").

in philosophy is Juvenal's express hatred for the perverts who call themselves Stoics.

It is in his second and third books that he first begins (in satires 6 and 8) to use philosophical material. But it is not until his fourth book that he starts to talk like a philosophical teacher and to approve a way of life modeled on that of one of the philosophical sects. And then it is toward Epicureanism that he turns—although even then he does not adopt all its tenets and share all its comforts. This conversion was part of a much wider development in his life, which manifested itself in an important change of his poetic method and aim, and which can be best understood through a survey of his entire career as a satiric poet; but for that we have no space here. It is often said that Epicurus's teachings originally appealed to the Greeks at a time when they were trying to find some means of making a good life for individual men within political conflicts and social pressures too violent and irrational for them to join or control or conquer. Perhaps then Juvenal was pushed toward adopting Epicureanism more or less unconsciously, not as a solution for the corruption and crimes which he had once tried to combat, but as a retreat from them. If so, his conversion meant that he abandoned his first vocation as a satirist of contemporary life, but became, at last, a happier man.

Juvenal's Bookcase

It is always interesting to try to discover what books an eminent writer liked best. In fact, without knowing them, it is impossible to understand him fully; for they were part of his experience, they molded his mind, they gave him subjects to ponder over, forms to adapt, thoughts to assimilate, and suggestions to reject with a violence which was itself a stimulus. This is particularly true of the Roman poets, who preferred tradition to revolution, and who often thought more of literature than they did of life, its raw material.

This essay will attempt to set out the favorite reading of the satirist Juvenal. Is it a pointless task? At first sight we might think so. Juvenal professes to hold that most books are silly or useless, that they are unreal and irrelevant, and that even when they are being most boldly imaginative they are still feeble in comparison with the horrible truths of daily life.[1] Yet, as we read him, we realize that he was not attacking literature as a whole, but declaring that in his own time it ought to concern itself more closely with life and have a social purpose. The great writers of the past he admired. But he felt that what was needed in his generation was satire.[2]

Also, his poetic technique is undoubtedly very skillful. Rhythms varying all the way from disjointed conversation to nobly sustained rhetoric, bold and subtle sound-effects, brilliant epigrams, unforgettable images, light jokes and formidable denunciations, a voice that can speak in nearly all tones, even those of pity—such an art does not grow sponta-

Reprinted from *AJPh* 72 (1951) 369–94.
[1] See Juv. 1.1–14, 52–57, 162–64; 6.634–61; 15.13–32.
[2] *hoc potius* . . . *campo* 1.19; 1.51–54; 6.634–40.

neously but is nourished by years of meditation on literature, and refined by emulation of the best and cleverest authors. Then, a good deal of his thought is drawn from books. He takes many illustrations from myth and history. He builds many arguments on philosophical themes, and has some acquaintance with Stoic, Cynic, and Epicurean doctrine. Further, he is a successful parodist, and no one can write parody without a fairly intimate sense of literary craftsmanship. And finally, a careful study of his work reveals a surprising number of deliberate imitations—reminiscences of many different authors, as well as multitudinous echoes, often subconscious, coming from many recesses of a complex and richly stored memory. If, therefore, we can reconstruct Juvenal's bookcase, we shall have penetrated a little further into his curious and powerful mind.

First, his subject-matter. How much did he take from his own observation, and how much did he owe to books? Surely much of his work is original? His fourth and fifteenth satires are about events of his own lifetime. The ugly second and ninth are on subjects apparently new to satire; we hear of nothing like the huge attack on marriage, the sixth, before his day in poetry; and others, such as the third and twelfth and sixteenth, would be hard to parallel, at least on the scale to which he develops them. Also, he alludes in passing to many topical events which he saw himself and did not copy from others: Crispinus, waving his sweaty fingers with their light summer-weight ring, and Eppia adoring her blear-eyed gladiator.[3]

Yet he owes more to earlier satirists than he might care to acknowledge. Persius he never names; but Persius's second satire is one of the main models for his tenth.[4] Horace as a satirist is mentioned only once; but the frugal dinner in Juvenal 11, the attack on avarice in 14, and other disquisitions on morals owe much to Horace's thought. As for Lucilius, whom he claims as his model, the fragments of Lucilius's satires are usually too scanty to show whether Juvenal copies many themes from him or not.[5]

His friend Martial gave him more subjects than any other extant poet. Again and again, if we study the two poets together, we can see how a neat little epigram by Martial has been taken over, expanded, deepened, often cleaned up and given a moral purpose, and at last de-

---

[3] 1.26–29; 6.82–110.

[4] See pp. 263–64.

[5] But note Lucilius, fragments 676–87, on the troubles of marriage: although no close resemblances are visible, the themes and the attitudes of the two poets are similar.

veloped into one of Juvenal's most striking descriptions, sometimes into a whole satire.[6] Thus, Satire 3, with its main theme:

quid Romae faciam? mentiri nescio,

is essentially an elaboration of Martial's general complaints against the huge cruel city, of several of Martial's epigrams such as 3.38, 4.5, 10.96, and perhaps of Martial's own departure for the remote and quiet Bilbilis. The fifth satire, basically a variation on the traditional satiric topic of the horrible meal, is inspired by several poems of Martial, who had himself suffered in the same way; while the pleasanter dinner described in Juvenal 11 is also based on Martial.[7] Some of the women in Juvenal come from Martial's *chronique scandaleuse*, as well as a certain number (though fewer than we might at first think) of his objectionable men.[8] One of Juvenal's most interesting achievements was to make serious and positive poetry out of Martial's little intimations of immorality.

Of history, Juvenal had a picturesque but superficial knowledge. He seems to have read the historians not with the aim of understanding the deeper causes of past events, but in order to find illustrations which would be dramatic, or laughable, or odd. Many of his references to historical figures clearly come from handbooks used in the rhetorical schools, such as Hyginus, Valerius Maximus, and Cornelius Nepos.[9] But he also read more serious historians. Gercke thought Juvenal got a good deal from the elder Pliny's *History*; but it is absolutely lost, and philosophers tell us that an unverifiable statement is meaningless.[10] Gercke also suggested that he

---

[6] This subject, discussed in essays by H. Nettleship ("Life and Poems of Juvenal," *Lectures & Essays* [2nd series, Oxford, 1895]) and H. L. Wilson ("The Literary Influence of Martial upon Juvenal," *AJPh* 19 [1898] 193–209), has now been fully explored by Dr. R. E. Colton in a Columbia University dissertation, *Juvenal and Martial* (New York, 1951), to which I am indebted for quotations and parallels. See also G. Boissier, "Relations de Juvénal et de Martial," *Revue des Cours et Conférences* 7.2 (1899) 443–51.

[7] See L. R. Shero, "The Cena in Roman Satire," *CPh* 18 (1923) 126–43; Martial 3.60, 3.82, 9.2; Martial 5.78, 10.48.

[8] Fabulla (Juv. 2.68, Mart. 4.81); Glaphyrus (Juv. 6.77, Mart. 4.5); Hamillus (Juv. 10.224, Mart. 7.62); Matho (Juv. 1.32, 7.129, 11.34; Mart. 7.10, 10.46); Naevolus (Juv. 9; Mart. 3.71, 3.95); Saufeia (Juv. 6.320, 9.117; Mart. 3.72).

[9] The Nepos suggestion comes from W. Christ, "Beiträge zur Erklärung und Kritik Juvenals," *Sitzungsberichte der Bayerischen Akademie der Wissenschaften* (Munich, 1897) 131, note 1. It was O. Ribbeck who first developed the Valerius Maximus parallels in *Der echte und der unechte Juvenal* (Berlin, 1865): see pp. 22–23. On Val. Maximus and Hyginus see also K. Alewell, *Über das rhetorische Paradeigma* (Leipzig, 1913) 115–17, and F. Gauger, *Zeitschilderung und Topik bei Juvenal* (Bottrop, 1936) 47–48, 63, 71–72.

[10] A. Gercke, *Seneca-Studien* (Leipzig, 1895) 186f.

used Suetonius.[11] This is more difficult to believe: Suetonius is full of wonderfully vivid details, often driven home with a barbed and poisoned malice, which Juvenal would have loved to use if he had seen them. But so few of them appear in the satires, and the divergence between Juvenal's and Suetonius's views of emperors such as Tiberius and Caligula is so great that we may conclude that Juvenal made little, if any, use of the *Caesars*.

But what about Tacitus? Juvenal and Tacitus were contemporaries. Under Domitian they had both endured the torture of silence and the threat of death. They both loathed the imperial system and the corruption which it enforced on all but the best of citizens. Both, as Norden said, worked in the "grand manner," and both were retrospective satirists, showing the vileness of the present by exposing the vices and sins of the past.[12] They had much in common, from their fundamental pessimism to the proud and sombre dignity of their style.[13] Yet Juvenal never mentions Tacitus by name, and sneers at one of his greatest public achievements.[14] In his survey of contemporary literature he passes slightingly over history.[15] And once at least he appears to mock Tacitus's work as a historian. In a particularly savage account of a group of male homosexuals he describes a pervert using a mirror which once belonged to the emperor Otho and has apparently been handed down in that society; and then he gives ten lines of contempt and hatred to Otho himself, filling them with the ludicrous antitheses that characterize a homosexual's life (*occidere Galbam / et curare cutem*) and closing with a comparison of Otho to two other warlike queens, Semiramis and Cleopatra.[16] This paradox, he says, the paradox that a hand-mirror was part of Otho's equipment in a civil war, ought to be brought out in the new *Annals* and the

---

[11] Gercke (note 10 above) points to the story about Caligula in 1.44, which he says is so obscure that it is more likely to have come out of a book (Suet. *Calig.* 20, cf. Dio Cass. 59.22.1) than to have lived on in popular memory. But A. Hartmann, *De inventione Juvenalis* (Basel, 1908) 17–18, note 1, remarks that many of the details Gercke believed must come from history-books can be more easily traced to commonplaces of the rhetorical schools: e.g. *nigros maritos* in 1.72 and "Quintilian," *Decl. mai.* 15.4.10.

[12] E. Norden, in *Vom Altertum zur Gegenwart* (Leipzig, 1921²) 42.

[13] See Pliny, *Ep.* 2.11.17, on the lofty style of Tacitus.

[14] In 1.49–50 Juvenal says that the impeachment of Marius Priscus by Pliny and Tacitus—which Pliny describes in *Ep.* 2.11–12 with an eager sense of its importance—was quite useless.

[15] 7.98–104.

[16] 2.99–109. On the passage see J. Dürr, *Die zeitgeschichtlichen Beziehungen in den Satiren Juvenals* (Cannstatt, 1902) 9, note 24.

recently published *History, novis annalibus atque recenti / historia*. Evidently he means that Tacitus's characterization of Otho was too kind, made Otho too noble, concealed his basic corruption. The report that Galba was killed by Otho's soldiers Juvenal corrects, putting the responsibility on Otho himself.[17] He mocks the will power and determination of which Otho boasted, and the titles he took.[18] Perhaps he thinks that Tacitus, himself an aristocrat, has a blind eye for the weaknesses of another aristocrat—since Juvenal is never tired of repeating that the Roman nobles, once strong and proud, are now grown weak and nasty. Certainly the passage is a sneer at Tacitus, a pointed and bitter sneer.

But in later satires Juvenal introduces a number of impressive scenes and characters from periods in the earlier Empire which were described by Tacitus: Nero, Sejanus, Messalina, Lateranus.[19] It seems likely that he was (however unwillingly) impressed by the vividness and vigor of Tacitus's *Annals*, which directed his mind, as with age it turned away from the present, more and more toward the monstrous history of the Julio-Claudian house. Yet it is difficult to point to any one large description in Juvenal and say that it came from Tacitus—whether because the parallel parts of the *Annals* are lost, or because Juvenal deliberately chose scenes which Tacitus had omitted. The latter is probable, but while Tacitus's books are incomplete it cannot be proved.[20]

In philosophy, Juvenal said he had read no books.[21] But this is an exaggeration. He began, apparently, with a very thin and sketchy knowledge of philosophical systems, but learnt a number of Stoic doctrines, and toward the end of his life became more and more firmly converted to Epicureanism.[22] It was the Epicurean mode of life which he came to follow, and his attitude to pleasure and pain and ambition was fundamentally Epicurean. Much of his philosophical material came from sources now impossible to trace—popular lectures, the poems of his contemporaries, lost handbooks. But the extant author whom he surely read

---

[17] Juv. 2.104: *summi ducis est occidere Galbam*; contrast Tac. *Hist.* 1.41.

[18] Contrast *constantia* in Juv. 2.105 with Tac. *Hist.* 2.47: *nec diu moremur, ego incolumitatem uestram, uos constantiam meam; summus dux, summus ciuis* in Juv. 2.104–5 with Tac. *Hist.* 2.47: *alii diutius imperium tenuerint, nemo tam fortiter reliquerit*.

[19] Nero, 8.211–30; Sejanus, 10.56–107; Messalina, 6.115–32; Lateranus, 8.146–82.

[20] For further discussion of Juvenal's debt to Tacitus see Dürr (note 16 above); Gercke (note 10 above); and F. Wolffgramm, *Rubellius Plautus und seine Beurtheilung bei Tacitus und Juvenal* (Prenzlau, 1871). Gercke thought Juvenal got the mirror from Pliny's history *A fine Aufidii Bassi*; the scholiast mentions Cornelius (Tacitus) and Pompeius Planta.

[21] 13.120–23.

[22] Details of this argument in G. Highet, "The Philosophy of Juvenal," *TAPhA* 80 (1949) 254–70.

was Seneca: not to study him and follow or refute his arguments, but (as with Tacitus) to extract striking ideas and vivid phrases. Again and again we find that Juvenal will adapt a sentence or two from Seneca, and then break away from Seneca's argument to draw a different conclusion.[23] Still, there are a number of striking resemblances which prove either that Juvenal read Seneca with an alert but skipping eye, or that he was familiar with the philosophical commonplaces which Seneca put so crisply. Here are two from a long list:

> hic ultra uires habitus nitor, hic aliquid plus
> quam satis est interdum aliena sumitur arca.
> commune id uitium est, hic uiuimus ambitiosa
> paupertate omnes. quid te moror? omnia Romae
> cum pretio.   Juv. 3.180–84

nos sine duce erramus et dicimus, "non ego ambitiosus sum, sed nemo aliter Romae potest uiuere. non ego sumptuosus sum, sed urbs ipsa magnas impensas exigit."   Sen. Ep. 50.3

cantabit uacuus coram latrone uiator.   Juv. 10.22

nudum latro transmittit: etiam in obsessa uia pauperi pax est.   Sen. Ep. 14.9

Besides these, there is reason to believe that some of the arguments and several vivid illustrations of the sixth satire, against women, come from a lost work by Seneca On Marriage.[24]

Turn now to style. Here Juvenal uses the work of his predecessors in four different ways.

The first of these is *parody*. He is a skilled and dangerous parodist. Since he thinks that satire is real and natural, he takes most pleasure in parodying the grand style and mocking famous passages from epic poetry. The poor man whose apartment-house is burning beneath him is compared to Aeneas caught in the conflagration of Troy—by one word only, the name of Aeneas's neighbor. Vergil (Aen. 2.311–12) says:

> iam proximus ardet
> Vcalegon

and Juvenal (3.198–99) makes it:

[23] Contrast Juv. 1.22–80 and De Ira 2.7–9; Juv. 10.28–53 and De Ira 2.10.5; Juv. 10.188–288 and Ep. 96.2–3, 99.10–11, 107.6–7; Juv. 1.135–41 and Ep. 94.69–70; Juv. 1.87–88 and 147–49 and Ep. 97.1.

[24] For further discussions of Juvenal and Seneca, see F. Bock, Aristoteles Theophrastus Seneca de matrimonio (Leipziger Studien 19 [1899] 46f.); F. Gauger (note 9 above); C. Schneider, Juvenal und Seneca (Würzburg, 1930); R. Schuetze, Juvenalis ethicus (Greifswald, 1905).

iam poscit aquam, iam friuola transfert
Vcalegon.

The nervous lawyer appearing in one of the lowest types of case, a slave's claim to citizenship, is likened to Ajax claiming the arms of Achilles. Ovid begins Book 13 of the *Metamorphoses* with his speech:

consedere duces, et uolgi stante corona
surgit ad hos clipei dominus septemplicis Aiax

Juvenal compresses it into one line, followed by a delightful onomatopoeia (7.115–17):

consedere duces, surgis tu pallidus Aiax,
dicturus dubia pro libertate bubulco
iudice.

Cicero in one of his greatest speeches defied Antony in a nobly cadenced sentence: *contempsí Catilínaé gladiós, non pértiméscám tuós* (*Phil.* 2.118). After quoting one of the worst lines of Cicero's poetry, Juvenal adds (10.123–24):

Antoni gladios potuit contemnere, si sic
omnia dixisset.

He has many more parodies, equally amusing. Perhaps the main body of his fourth satire comes under this head. It tells, in language and rhythms which are often mock-heroic,[25] of a council called by Domitian to discuss the best way to cook a giant turbot; it lists and describes the eleven councilors as they arrive. The Renaissance editor Valla, who had access to a set of scholia now lost, here quotes four lines from "a poem by Statius on the German war conducted by Domitian":

lumina; Nestorei mitis prudentia Crispi,
et Fabius Veiento (potentem signat utrumque
purpura, ter memores implerunt nomina fastos),
et prope Caesareae confinis Acilius aulae.

Crispus, Fabius Veiento, and Acilius are three of the ministers in Juvenal's satire, and they are described in terms closely similar:

uenit et Crispi iucunda senectus . . .
proximus eiusdem properabat Acilius aeui . . .
et cum mortifero prudens Veiento Catullo . . .

---

[25] E.g. 4.34–36, 45–46, 60–61, 65, 130–35. On the subject of serious and parodic grandeur in Juvenal there is a valuable treatise by I. G. Scott, *The Grand Style in the Satires of Juvenal* (Northampton, 1927), to which I am much indebted.

Perhaps the blind Catullus was described by Statius in the clause ending with *lumina*. We know nothing more of the piece, but this resemblance is close enough to make it probable that Juvenal's entire satire was a mock-heroic gibe at an epyllion in which Statius glorified the emperor and flattered his chief satellites.[26]

Sometimes Juvenal uses the thoughts and phrasing of his predecessors with no intention of mockery, but merely to recall an idea or a description which had already been so well put that it could scarcely be bettered. Usually he quotes a few words, but rewrites the passage so that it blends with his own style and is not set off, as it were, by quotation marks. For instance, in the eighth satire, on true and false nobility, he is contrasting the noble scoundrel Catiline with the patriotic Cicero. What, he asks (8.231f.), could be loftier than the descent of you, Catiline, and your accomplice Cethegus?

> *arma* tamen uos
> *nocturna* et *flammas* domibus templisque paratis . . .
> sed *uigilat* consul uexillaque uestra coercet.

This is an allusion to Cicero's first denunciation of Catiline, in which (1.8–9) he shouts "Recognosce tamen *noctem* illam superiorem; iam intelleges multo me *uigilare* acrius . . . ; discripsisti urbis partis ad *incendia*. . . . " This type of allusion could be called *reminiscence*.

Again, when saying good-bye to his friend Umbricius, Juvenal turns with him into the grove of Egeria, which like Rome itself has been spoilt by artificial luxury (3.17–20):

> in *uallem* Egeriae descendimus et *speculuncas*
> dissimiles ueris. quanto praesentius esset
> numen aquis, uiridi si *margine* cluderet *undas*
> herba, nec *ingenuum* uiolarent marmora *tofum*!

Here he is recalling Ovid's graceful description of the woodland spring of Gargaphie, which Diana and her nymphs loved, as Egeria once loved

---

[26] Surely *dux magnus* in 145 is a scornful allusion to the title of Domitian, *magnus dux*, used by Stat. *Silu.* 3.1.62. Elsewhere in Juvenal the most notable parodies are these: 1.25 and 10.226~Verg. *Buc.* 1.28; 1.43~Hom. *Il.* 3.33–35 and Verg. *Aen.* 2.379–80; 1.81–84~Ov. *Met.* 1.260–61, 381, 400–402; 2.12~Hor. *Carm.* 2.1.23–24; 2.77~Catull. 103.2 and Lucan 1.146; 2.99–100~Verg. *Aen.* 3.286 and 12.94; 2.149–51~Prop. 4.7.1 and Verg. *Aen.* 6.296, 302–3; 3.250 and 7.213~Verg. *Buc.* 2.65; 5.137–39~Verg. *Aen.* 4.328–30; 5.142–43~Verg. *Aen.* 12.475; 6.8~Catull. 3.18; 6.43~Verg. *G.* 3.188; 6.177~Verg. *Aen.* 8.42–48; 6.238~Lucan 6.424; 6.559~Lucan 9.190; 9.37~Hom. *Od.* 16.294; 9.69~Verg. *Aen.* 1.207; 9.102~Verg. *Buc.* 2.69; 10.178~Ov. *Met.* 1.264; 10.230–32~Hom. *Il.* 9.323–24; 12.110~Verg. *Aen.* 10.427 and 737; 14.213–14~Ov. *Met.* 15.855–56.

this spot now ruined by extravagance and avarice; and, by recalling it, he emphasizes the contrast (Ov. *Met.* 3.155–62):

> *uallis* erat piceis et acuta densa cupressu . . .
> cuius in extremo est *antrum* nemorale recessu,
> arte laboratum nulla: simulauerat artem
> ingenio natura suo. nam pumice uiuo
> et leuibus *tofis natiuum* duxerat arcum.
> fons sonat a dextra, tenui perlucidus *unda*,
> *margine gramineo* patulos incinctus hiatus.

In such passages Juvenal probably expects some at least of his readers to pick up the reminiscence and to hear not only his own voice but the voice of the master whom he has recalled. But there is a third type of borrowing, which is less easy to detect. Sometimes one poet expresses a certain thought so gracefully or so pungently that a successor is haunted by the cadence, and finally copies the words and the rhythms in a slightly different context. The Greek and Roman poets evidently did not think this was plagiarism, provided the copyist did not borrow extensively and did not use his borrowings in exactly the same kind of poem. Sometimes, as when Vergil quoted Lucretius and Varius and Gallus, and Vergil's admirers quoted him, it was intended as a compliment. Sometimes, as when we use phrases from famous writers in daily speech (e.g. Shakespeare's "foregone conclusion" and Churchill's "iron curtain"), it is a tribute to the power of the phrase, which has detached itself from its author and become public property. Sometimes it is the inevitable result of close study, as when Strauss and Schönberg in their early works use Wagner's chords, rhythms, and orchestration. This could be called, with no injurious overtones, *imitation*.

For instance, Lucan in a famous passage describes the prodigies that preceded Caesar's advance. There were omens and prophecies (1.566–67):

> crinemque rotantes
> sanguineum populis ulularunt tristia Galli.

Four of these words appear in Juvenal (6.315–17):

> cornu pariter uinoque feruntur
> attonitae crinemque rotant ululantque Priapi
> maenades.

The context of course is different—and yet is it so different? Lucan is evoking the antics of a group of frenzied oriental dervishes, Juvenal the madness of a group of drunken Roman women worshiping the Good

Goddess: in both there is the same atmosphere of frenzy, of sexual perversion, yes, and of the impending doom of Rome.

Again, Juvenal makes at least one quotation from Lucilius which fits fairly neatly into his verse, and which we should never have recognized if the scholiast had not told us. The tyrant is dead, he cries (10.65–66):

> pone domi laurus, duc in Capitolia magnum
> cretatumque bouem. Seianus ducitur unco.

At most, we might have remarked the repetition *duc . . . ducitur*; but it is the scholiast who says "ut Lucilius,

> cretatumque bouem due[it] ad Capitolia magnum."[27]

This is fragment 1145 in Marx's collection, but its context in Lucilius is lost, so that we cannot tell how Juvenal has altered the line apart from rearranging it metrically. The history of Roman satire would be a great deal clearer if we had even one book of Lucilius.

One further example. Here the resemblance is so tenuous that it may scarcely have been felt by Juvenal himself. Horace criticizes Lucilius for carelessness. Might it not, he says in *Serm.* 1.10.56–59, have been Lucilius's own character and the character of his subject that kept him from writing smoothly?

> quid uetat et nosmet, Lucili scripta legentes,
> quaerere num illius, num rerum dura *negarit*
> *uersiculos natura* magis factos et euntes
> mollius?

Juvenal sets out to tell us why he follows Lucilius. Rome, he cries, is so full of horrible and unnatural sights that he must write satire, he has no choice, he cannot sleep for thinking of them; and then, in an imitation emphasized by the context, he says (1.79):

> si *natura negat*, facit indignatio *uersum*.

Sometimes these resemblances are made more cogent by strong similarity of thought, together with one or two memorable words, as when Lucan (7.404–5) speaks of the degenerate metropolis

> nulloque frequentem
> ciue suo Roman sed mundi *faece* repletam,

and Juvenal protests (3.60–61):

---

[27] *duc* for *ducit* Müller; *magnum* for *magna* Wessner.

non possum ferre, Quirites,
Graecam urbem—quamuis quota portio *faecis* Achaei?

Sometimes we are helped in interpreting a difficult passage when we see that the author was not being intentionally obscure, but was merely adapting a phrase he took from a favorite writer. How many modern printers have tried to correct the last word in a sentence like "the best of all these proposals are only such stuff as dreams are made on," without knowing that it closed a concealed quotation from *The Tempest?* There are several passages like this in Juvenal. For instance, he warns the poor client Trebius that the only way to become a real friend of his patron .is to be childless, so that the patron can expect to be remembered in his will. Then (a little inconsistently) he goes on to say (5.141) "but since you are poor now, it doesn't matter if you have triplets . . ."

sed tua nunc Mycale pariat licet . . .

The commentators have wondered why the wife should be called by this odd name Mycale. The scholiast read Migale, and says *nomen mulieris: ex ipsa coitione etymologia*, which means that he did not know, . and guessed at a rather improbable derivation from μίγνυμι.

Ruperti was led by this guess to think that Mycale must be the name of a mistress, so that the children were illegitimate and could not affect the patron's chances in the will. Weidner said Mycale was a comic name for a wife, and meant *Schnäuzchen*, Nosy, presumably deriving it from μύξα, a farfetched idea. Friedländer followed Bücheler and Lenel (apparently a legal expert), who followed Ruperti. Duff in one of his usual sensible notes disproved Ruperti's suggestion, but still could not explain the fertile lady's name, except by saying that she might be a freedwoman. R. L. Dunbabin ("Notes on Latin Authors," *CR* 39 [1925] 111–13, esp. 112) suggested that she might be a Jewess, and implied that her name was a variation of that borne by Saul's daughter, Michal.

However, Juvenal was not so subtle as some of these interpretations make him, and in particular he was not very subtle at names. Many of the names Horace uses in his satiric writings have ironic or wounding meanings: few of Juvenal's names have any concealed meaning at all. Mycale is (as Duff saw) the client's wife. He is poor and ignoble, so she does not bear an aristocratic name like Cornelia. But why should she be called Mycale? Because she is fertile, and because Juvenal (perhaps unconsciously) is recalling one of his favorite passages in Ovid, the fight of the Centaurs and Lapithae (*Met.* 12.210f., cf. Juvenal 1.11), and from it the phrase (12.263) mater erat Mycale.

Mycale here is only one of several women whom Juvenal has named after figures from his best-liked poem: Cyane (8.162 ~ Ov. *Met.* 5.409), Psecas (6.491 ~ Ov. *Met.* 3.172), and Phiale (10.238 ~ Ov. *Met.* 3.172).

Now and then these imitations are not taken from one single passage, but blended from two or more. To mock the ambition of Alexander, Juvenal says (10.168–69):

> unus *Pellaeo* iuueni *non sufficit orbis,*
> *aestuat angusta* rabies ciuilis harena,

which is a composite of Lucan on Caesar (10.456, cf. 5.356):

> hic cui Romani spatium *non sufficit orbis,*

and Lucan on the civil war (6.63):

> *aestuat angusta* rabies ciuilis harena.

with a hint from Lucan on Alexander (3.233–34):

> hic ubi *Pellaeus* post Tethyos aequora ductor
> constitit, et magno uinci se fassus ab *orbe* est.

Similarly, to describe the Egyptians sailing in their clay boats (15.127–28),

> paruula fictilibus solitum *dare uela phaselis*
> et breuibus pictae remis incumbere testae,

Juvenal combines Vergil's (G. 4.289)

> et circum *pictis* uehitur sua rura *phaselis*

and Ovid's (*Met.* 3.639)

> meque iubent *pictae dare uela* carinae.

Often we come upon a passage in which Juvenal has used only two or three words which coincide with a phrase in one of his favorite authors. Although these may be interesting and distinctive, they are scarcely enough as they stand to convince us that they are a deliberate quotation. The two poets might have written the same phrase by sheer coincidence—although, if one lived two generations after the other and knew his predecessor's work well, the chance of sheer coincidence is much reduced. Or Juvenal may have had them floating vaguely in his mind, as we all have fragments of music and wandering phrases, and so he may have used them with no clear consciousness of their source. But then we find that, in another poem, Juvenal has introduced another phrase from the same passage of the same author. For example, Horace says to Maecenas, in his whimsical first letter (*Epist.* 1.1.101–4),

> insanire putas sollemnia me neque rides,
> nec medici credis nec *curatoris egere*
> a praetore dati, *rerum tutela mearum*
> cum sis.

In his fourteenth satire (112) Juvenal says that a greedy miser is praised

> tamquam parcus homo et *rerum tutela suarum*.

A coincidence? Possibly, but look on to line 288 of the same satire, where Juvenal says that a greedy miser is crazy:

> *curatoris eget* qui nauem mercibus implet.

We can scarcely believe that a poet would twice in one poem accidentally hit on phrases used in one single sentence by one of his most distinguished predecessors: the chances are enormously against it. If we agree that he knew and remembered the poem we shall be prepared to admit other fainter echoes of the same poem as imitations, such as (5.1)

> si te propositi nondum pudet atque *eadem est mens*,

from Hor. *Epist.* 1.1.4:

> non *eadem est* aetas, non *mens*. [28]

Here, for convenience, is a list of the most striking such verbal imitations in Juvenal. (Many of the references come from the parallels given in Friedländer's edition, but they have been revised to suit the definition set out on p. 252 above, uncertain and improbable parallels cut out, and others added.)

Juvenal 1 :	46–47	~Sen. *Ben.* 4.27.5
	73	~Sen. *Oed.* 879
	79	~Hor. *Serm.* 1.10.57–58
	143	~Hor. *Epist.* 1.6.61 and Pers. 3.98
	168	~Ter. *An.* 126 and Lucan 1.173
Juvenal 2 :	25	~Lucr. 3.842
	37	~(?) Cic. *Phil.* 5.8
	51–52	~Hor. *Serm.* 1.9.39

[28] Another of these double coincidences is Lucan 8.542–44 with *hos animos* in Juv. 1.89 and *barbara turba* in Juv. 15.46.

	72–74	~Ov. *Fast.* 1.207
	125	~Mart. 6.21.9
	155	~Lucan 2.46
Juvenal 3:	30	~Ov. *Met.* 11.314–15
	35	~Mart. 3.95.7
	41	~Mart. 3.38.13
	72	~Lucan 7.579
	91	~Mart. 13.64.1
	100–101	~Lucr. 1.919 and 2.976
	121–22	~Lucan 1.290–91
	130	~Hor. *Serm.* 2.6.24
	190–92	~(?) Hor. *Carm.* 3.4.22–23
	196	~Lucan 1.494–95
	254–56	~Sen. *Ep.* 90.9
	279–80	~(?) Sen. *Tranq.* 2.12
	290	~Mart. 1.53.12
Juvenal 4:	74–75	~Ov. *Met.* 2.775
	93	~Lucan 10.55
	117	~Mart. 2.19.3
Juvenal 5:	10	~Ov. *Met.* 8.791
	12	~Verg. *Aen.* 1.708
	57	~Hor. *Carm.* 4.7.15
	94–96	~Sen. *Ep.* 89.22
	107	~Hor. *Serm.* 1.1.22
	113	~Mart. 9.2.1
	147	~Mart. 1.20.4
	162	~Mart. 1.92.9
Juvenal 6:	11	~Lucr. 5.907
	12	~Verg. *Aen.* 8.315
	146	~(?) Petron. 81.1
	207–8	~(?) Hor. *Carm.* 2.5.1
	272–75	~Ov. *Ars Am.* 3.291–92 and 677
	306	~Ov. *Ars Am.* 2.222
	406	~Ov. *Am.* 2.8.28
	556	~Hor. *Carm.* 3.29.29–30
	634–36	~Verg. *Buc.* 8.10, together with imitations of Seneca, *De matrimonio*
Juvenal 7:	8	~Mart. 2.44.9 and 9.84.3
	20–21	~Stat. *Silu.* 5.2.125
	27	~Mart. 9.73.9
	130	~Mart. 2.40.7
	145	~Petron. 83.10
	190–91	~Hor. *Serm.* 1.3.124–25

Juvenal 8:	1–9	~Sen. *Ep.* 44.5
	145	~Mart. 14.128.1
	161	~Mart. 10.10.5
	218	~Lucan 3.135–36
	235	~Mart. 10.25.5
	270	~Verg. *Aen.* 3.234 and 8.535
Juvenal 9:	32	~Manilius 4.14
	89	~Lucilius, fr. 1337
Juvenal 10:	50	~Hor. *Epist.* 2.1.244
	188	~Verg. *Aen.* 3.85
	196–97	~Ov. *Am.* 2.10.7
	202	~Mart. 13.17.1
	268	~Verg. *Aen.* 5.481
	297–98	~Ov. *Her.* 15.290
	299	~Ov. *Am.* 2.4.15
Juvenal 11:	38	~Hor. *Epist.* 1.4.11
	82	~Ov. *Met.* 8.648
	116	~Lucan 9.519
	121–22	~Cic. *Acad.* fr. 11 Müller
	203	~Mart. 10.12.7
Juvenal 12:	83	~Ov. *Met.* 15.677
	110	~Verg. *Aen.* 10.427 and 737
	125	~Hor. *Epod.* 15.17–18
	130	~Cic. *Amic.* 52
Juvenal 13:	193	~Lucr. 3.1018–19 and Verg. *Aen.* 1.604 and Ov. *Met.* 8.531
	239	~Hor. *Epist.* 1.10.24
Juvenal 14:	25	~Hor. *Epist.* 1.2.42
	45	~Ov. *Met.* 15.587
	69	~Ov. *Tr.* 2.110
	111–12	~Hor. *Serm.* 1.3.49
	112 & 288	~Hor. *Epist.* 1.1.102–3
	133	~Mart. 13.18.1
	139	~(?) Ov. *Fast.* 1.211
	188	~Verg. *Aen.* 5.83
	214	~Ov. *Met.* 15.856
	215	~Verg. *G.* 2.363
	218	~Ov. *Am.* 1.10.37
	250	~Ov. *Met.* 8.71
Juvenal 15:	34	~Ov. *Rem. Am.* 101
	46	~Lucan 8.542–44
	86	~Ov. *Met.* 10.305–7
	146–47	~Ov. *Met.* 1.84–86
Juvenal 16:	54–56	~Hor. *Serm.* 2.5.57f.

We have looked at three different ways in which Juvenal uses the work of writers whom he admires: parody, reminiscence, and imitation. But there can scarcely be sharp distinctions between these methods of borrowing, and the last of the three shades off into something approaching unconscious recall, or chance parallelism. Most often, when we find that Juvenal uses a few words which appear in an earlier poet, we see that there is no cogent resemblance in the contexts, and that the words form a neat metrical unit which, divorced from meaning, might well have occurred to several authors independently. And often we find that such a metrical unit—one foot, *si uacat*; a foot and a half, *inque uicem*; or a hexameter ending, *pectora palmis*—has been used by several different authors in different contexts. There is an admirable essay on this by C. Hosius, *De imitatione scriptorum Romanorum imprimis Lucani* (Greifswald, 1907), who points out that it is natural (for example) that *Bootes* should appear at the end of a hexameter line, and equally natural that it should then be preceded by a third-declension ablative singular (*axe Bootes*, Val. Fl. 7.457) or a neuter plural (*plaustra Bootae*, Lucan 2.722; *serraca Bootae*, Juv. 5.23). Or again, if a poet mentions a spider, *aranea*, her name is bound to suggest *tela* as a following spondee (Catull. 68.49; Ov. *Met.* 6.145; Mart. 8.33.15; Juv. 14.61). Just now and then we can trace how an interesting phrase has been apparently coined by one poet, improved by another, parodied by a third, and revitalized by a fourth: for instance—

ueteris uestigia poenae	(Catull. 64.295)
ueteris uestigia flammae	(Verg. *Aen.* 4.23)
ueteris uestigia pugnae	(Ov. *Am.* 3.8.19)
Pudicitiae ueteris uestigia	(Juv. 6.14)

But clichés like *proelia miscent* and *quid referam?* became part of the general rolling stock of poetry, so that it would be pointless to trace them from one author to another.

There are dozens of these parallelisms in Juvenal's satires. They are scarcely more than *echoes*. Some are quite faint: for instance, *nouissimus exit* applied to the morning star in Ov. *Met.* 2.115 and 11.296 and to the bankrupt knight's gold ring in Juv. 11.42. Others are strong and surprising, like *manantia fletu* in Catullus 101.9 and Juvenal 15.136. Others again are very doubtful, like *deuia rura* in Juvenal 14.75 and Prop. 2.19.2 and Ov. *Met.* 1.676 and Ov. *Fast.* 2.369. At this point, the search for sources becomes meaningless—or indeed before it, in the work of a boldly original poet like Juvenal. Since so many of his finest lines are all his own, we need not look too far for the origins of his more ordinary remarks. Deliberate borrowing, as in his parodies, his reminiscences, and his imitations, is part of his poetic purpose, and is therefore important in assessing his competence as a writer; but the echoes in his work are simply chords of the rich resonance of Roman poetry.

Now we are in a better position to name Juvenal's favorite authors. First comes his friend, the master of miniature, the versatile little Spaniard Martial. Apparently Martial did not think of Juvenal as a productive author, only as someone "interested in literature";[29] and certainly he had come to the end of his career in Rome and gone back to Spain before Juvenal published any of his extant poems—although some of the satires were based on much earlier experiences. But the two men knew some of the same people, they had lived the same kind of life, they both enjoyed sharp-edged and keen-pointed witticisms, they had a similar taste for slang and conversational jokes (though Juvenal avoided most of the dirty words that Martial enjoyed), and both were fundamentally pessimistic about the standards and the future of Rome. Juvenal knew Martial's works book by book, and studied them with care.[30] From Martial he took jokes, such as Claudius's mushroom;[31] neat metrical patterns such as *moueat fastidia*;[32] odd words, like *uardaicus* and *umbella*;[33] personalities, or at least names, such as Chione and Matho;[34] many subjects of complaint and derision; the observant eye and the open notebook, which he used in the earlier satires, but which gradually closed as he grew older; a feeling of empathy with the rich busy corrupt fascinating metropolis; and the art of cutting epigrams as sharp, as bright, and as hard as diamonds. The arts of satire and epigram are clearly akin. They differ chiefly in length and in purpose. Just as Martial marks the culmination of the Roman epigram, so Juvenal marks the culmination of Roman satire; and some at least of Juvenal's best work would have been impossible without Martial.

Next comes Ovid, of whose poems there are at least fifty adaptations in Juvenal, and probably ten or twenty more. About half of these come

---

[29] *Facunde . . . Iuuenalis*, Mart. 7.91.1.

[30] It is inexplicable that L. Friedländer, who knew both poets so well, should have written, "Ihre Übereinstimmung in Worten und Wendungen ist grösstenteils zufällig und natürlich: eine absichtliche Beziehung möchte ich nur bei Iuvenal 5.147 auf Martial 1.20.4 annehmen" ("Jahresbericht über die Litteratur des Iuvenal in der Zeit von 1886–1891," *JAW* 72 [1892] 189–217, especially 191.

[31] Juv. 5.147–48 ~ Mart. 1.20.4.

[32] Juv. 10.202 and Mart. 13.17.1.

[33] Juv. 16.13 and Mart. 4.4.5; Juv. 9.50 and Mart. 11.73.6.

[34] Juv. 3.136 and Mart. 1.34.7, etc.; Juv. 1.32, 7.129, 11.34, and Mart. 7.10.3–4, 10.46.

from the *Metamorphoses*, and a surprisingly large number from the *Amores*. Probably Juvenal read Ovid at school. Even so, it strikes us as a little odd that Ovid, who loved women, irresponsible debauchery, and mythological learning, should have appealed to Juvenal, who hated all three. However, Ovid is such a skillful writer, so constantly interesting, witty, various, and lively, that he has charmed many men who might seem quite unsympathetic to him: Milton and Montaigne, Wordsworth and Macaulay. What Juvenal admired most in him was his craftsmanship with words. The myths Juvenal despised and parodied; the apples of love had turned sour in his mouth; but Ovid's graceful verse, as smooth as conversation and as melodious as a flute, haunted him, and partially created his poetic technique.

Third is Vergil. Practically every Roman author who lived after Vergil knew much of his poetry by heart. Seneca is full of Vergilian quotations. Ovid and Lucan had to make great efforts to rival Vergil without imitating him. His poems had much of the authority possessed in the nineteenth century by the Bible, and all the pervasive charm of Shakespeare. Juvenal recalls him in his satires at least fifty times, and must have known some of his poems very intimately indeed. For instance, in listing the different parts of the Greek world which send Rome greedy immigrants, he says (3.69–70) that one man comes from Sicyon, another from Amydon,

> hic Andro, ille Samo, hic Trallibus aut Alabandis. . . .

Notice the gap in the verse at *Samo* / / *hic*. Why does Juvenal do that? Because he has the first page of the *Aeneid* at the back of his mind. There (1.15–17) Vergil speaks of Carthage as the city

> quam Iuno fertur terris magis omnibus unam
> posthabita coluisse Samo. / / hic illius arma
> hic currus fuit. . . .

That allusion, too slight to be called parody, perhaps too tenuous to be deliberate, shows a close knowledge of the author Juvenal himself says he loved.[35]

The other school author was Horace.[36] He was also one of Juvenal's

---

[35] Juv. 11.180–82. Cf. 7.233–36 for an exaggeration which shows how eagerly and closely Vergil was studied. On this subject see also J. Gehlen, *De Iuvenale Vergilii imitatore* (Göttingen, 1886), who finds that Juvenal copies Vergil much more in his early books than toward the end of his career. Gehlen wildly exaggerates scanty resemblances such as Juv. 10.310 and Verg. *Buc.* 2.17, but he is good on the persistence of echoes such as Verg. *Aen.* 1.708 in Juv. 5.12.

[36] Juv. 7.226–27. The two are coupled again in 7.56–71.

predecessors in the field of satire. Temperamentally they were not sympathetic. Juvenal could not admire the friend of Octavian, the protégé of Maecenas.[37] He thought that folly was vice and sin was damnable, while Horace thought most vices were merely follies and most sins excusable. Juvenal hit hard, Horace teased and tickled. Lucilius (whom Horace mocked a little) was the chief model claimed by Juvenal, who speaks of Horace's satires only once, in a periphrasis.[38] And the peculiar style which Horace developed in his hexameter poems, that very light, chatty running meter with many little words and jolty rhythms and casual unpoetic verse-endings, is markedly different from the heavier, more sonorous, more energetic style of Juvenal. Still, Horace was a skillful poet. His phrases stick in the mind. Juvenal was bound to admire him as a craftsman, and quotes or echoes him at least forty times.[39]

These four were the poets he knew best. Next to them comes a small group of authors whom he apparently read less thoroughly, with an eye for bold pictures or striking phrases. Homer he says he admired.[40] In 9.37 he produced a wicked parody of him, and he has eight or ten allusions, all rather obvious, to characters and incidents in the epics. There is no clear evidence that he knew any other Greek author. If this is true, it means that the bilingualism of the Golden Age of Roman literature was disappearing by Juvenal's time. He would not (like Horace) pack Plato next to Menander for vacation reading; he would not (like Persius) study Greek philosophers, or (like Martial) borrow effects from Greek poets. In this he looks forward to Augustine[41] rather than back to Horace and Vergil. Anyhow, he loathed Greece and the Greeks.

Cicero he respected personally, as a lover of freedom, a patriot, and a middle-class man from a country town like himself, who saw through the corrupt noblemen.[42] His tribute to Cicero in 8.231–44 seems more genuine than his gibes at Cicero's poetry and ambition in 10.114–26. From the *Tusculan Disputations* and other philosophical treatises of Ci-

---

[37] On Octavian, see Juv. 5.3–4, 8.241–43; on the supine Maecenas, 1.66 and 12.39, with only one meager compliment in 7.94.

[38] 1.51.

[39] See further H. Berning, *Dissertatio de satirica poesi Q. Horatii Flacci collata cum satirica poesi D. Junii Juvenalis* (Recklingshausen, 1843); P. Schwartz, *De Juvenale Horatii imitatore* (Halle, 1882).

[40] 11.180–82.

[41] August. *Conf.* 1.13.20; 14.23.

[42] According to one theory, Juvenal himself at the outset of his career had been a *municipalis eques* like Cicero (8.238).

cero Juvenal apparently took some arguments, and he alludes six or eight times to his speeches.[43]

Although he never mentions Persius, and although his style, bold and expansive, differs widely from Persius's constricted, distorted wit, Juvenal apparently knew and occasionally imitated Persius's satires. There are of course a number of coincidences which are probably due to use of a common theme, a proverb, or a piece of slang: for instance, *rara auis* in Pers. 1.46 and Juv. 6.165, and purification in the Tiber in Pers. 2.15–16 and Juv. 6.523–24.[44]

A few close imitations, however, show that Juvenal occasionally remembered his young predecessor's work. When he writes of the poor lawyer getting his fees in kind (7.119–21):

> quod uocis pretium? siccus petasunculus et uas
> pelamydum, aut ueteres, Maurorum epimenia, bulbi,
> aut uinum Tiberi deuectum, quinque lagonae,

he is surely thinking of Persius's description of the same humiliation (3.73–76):

> nec inuideas quod multa fidelia putet
> in locuplete penu defensis pinguibus Vmbris,
> et piper ct pernae, Marsi monumenta clientis,
> maenaque quod prima nondum defecerat orca.

Persius describes a glutton seized with syncope after having a hot bath during a heavy meal, and goes on to sketch his funeral procession. Juvenal does practically the same, restating several of the most striking details, but compressing the whole picture.[45]

But Juvenal's chief dcbt to Persius is like his debt to that other miniaturist Martial—for suggestions which he expands into large, apparently independent portraits or tirades. The whole of Persius 2 deals with foolish prayers: it is 75 lines long. The whole of Juvenal 10 deals with foolish

---

[43] It is as usual difficult to determine whether these are real and conscious parallels. For instance, when Juvenal makes a hypocrite cry *ubi nunc lex Iulia?* (2.37), is he thinking of *ubi lex Caecilia et Didia?* in Cic. *Phil.* 5.8? For more on this subject see H. F. Rebert, "The Literary Influence of Cicero on Juvenal," *TAPhA* 57 (1926) 181–94, who derives part of Juvenal 10 from the *Cato maior*, and E. Strube, *De rhetorica Juvenalis disciplina* (Brandenburg, 1875) 2. On the *Tusculans* see H. C. Nutting, "Three Notes on Juvenal," *AJPh* 49 (1928) 253–66.

[44] So also Pers. 1.112–14 and Juv. 1.131. Odd little echoes in Pers. 2.7 and Juv. 6.18, Pers. 3.26 and Juv. 3.261.

[45] Pers. 3.98–106 ~ Juv. 1.142–46; compare also Pers. 1.129–30 ~ Juv. 10.100–102.

prayers: it is 366 lines long. One of the foolish prayers is for long life—Persius gives it three lines (2.41–43) and Juvenal a hundred and one (10.188–288). Another is for good looks and happiness in love—Persius gives it nine lines (2.31–40) and Juvenal fifty-six (10.289–345). Persius ends (2.71–75) by saying that what we really ought to pray for is

> compositum ius fasque animo sanctosque recessus
> mentis et incoctum generoso pectus honesto.

Virtue: yes, but Juvenal, who knew more of life, expanded this (10.354–62) into the immortal

> orandum est ut sit mens sana in corpore sano:[46]
> fortem posce animum mortis terrore carentem. . . .

Juvenal speaks with envious deference of the rich young Lucan "content with his glory."[47] Several times he pays him the compliment of parody, and copies or echoes him ten or twelve times.

He based a number of striking phrases on the prose of Seneca, although he refused to accept Seneca's conclusions—and, what is more striking, he gives no sign of knowing the most sensational stories told by Seneca about vicious millionaires and cruel emperors. Some of Seneca's worst character-sketches would make not only Juvenal but his own Naevolus turn pale. We can conclude, then, that he did not read Seneca with sustained attention but knew some of Seneca's work and could not help admiring it.

These nine authors were the chief extant sources of Juvenal's style. We cannot say what he owed to others now lost. In a jest at the practice of hunting for sources, A. E. Housman once said that some scholar would soon assure us that the satires of Juvenal were all copied from the satires of Turnus.[48] There is scarcely enough evidence for even the most imaginative *Quellenforscher* to do that, and yet, when we hear that Turnus was a freedman's son who became influential in the courts of Titus and Domitian, and when we see that his only extant lines deal with Nero and the court-poisoner Locusta—two of Juvenal's own subjects, treated in Juvenal's method of retrospective satire—we cannot help wondering how closely Juvenal followed him.[49]

---

[46] Here are other such expansions of brief passages: Pers. 1.114–23 ~ Juv. 1.150–70; Pers. 3.27–29 ~ Juv. 8.1–23; Pers. 5.132–42 ~ Juv. 14.190–209, probably; Pers. 6.75–80 ~ Juv. 14.322–31.

[47] Juv. 7.79–80.

[48] Preface to A. E. Housman's edition of Juvenal (Cambridge, 1931²) xxviii.

[49] See Schol. Vall. on 1.20 and Schol. on 1.71.

Throughout the satires there are traces of Juvenal's acquaintance with other Roman writers whose work survives. Apparently he cared very little for Republican poetry.[50] There are six or eight *known* borrowings from Lucilius;[51] possibly three from Catullus[52] and one or two from Terence.[53] From Lucretius Juvenal got four or five turns of phrase: probably he also knew Lucretius's diatribe on the passion of love, and his analysis of the growth of sympathy among mankind.[54] Odd as it seems, he knew Propertius's love-poems; he read them with Ovid's when his heart was young and soft.[55] Scholars have pointed out a few reminiscences of Livy, and there are parallels in Juvenal for the antiaristocratic bitterness of Sallust.[56] There are one or two parodies of Statius and one imitation.

Did he know Petronius? Any resemblances we might find between the rich nonchalant prosateur and the poor grim poet would surely be rather remote. And yet look at these:

Juv. 6.146 collige sarcinulas ∼ Petron. 81.1: collegi sarcinulas

rara in tenui facundia panno	(Juv. 7.145)
sola pruinosis horret facundia pannis	(Petron. 83.10)

Note also that in 1, telling of the dangers of satirizing the living, he foretells disaster for anyone who attacks Tigellinus. Now, although the *Satirica* is not a direct satire on Nero's courtiers, it is possible that the vulgar millionaire Trimalchio is an indirect caricature of Tigellinus,[57] and it was Tigellinus who was responsible for Petronius's death. It was not far behind Juvenal, all that. He had seen men who had joined in Nero's

[50] In 9.28 and 12.127, *operae pretium* is too general a phrase to prove that he knew Ennius (fr. 14 Warmington): it is not a parody like Persius 6.9.

[51] Lucilius, fr. 203–5 ∼ Juv. 14.322–29; fr. 331–32 ∼ Juv. 10.198–206; fr. 504–5 ∼ Juv. 6.461–65; fr. 1120 ∼ Juv. 3.142–43; fr. 1145 ∼ Juv. 10.65–66; fr. 1337 ∼ Juv. 9.89; possibly fr. 638 ∼ Juv. 9.18, and perhaps fr. 1378 ∼ Juv. 14.207 (see Marx *ad loc.*).

[52] Catull. 3.18 ∼ Juv. 6.7–8; also Catull. 62.2 ∼ Juv. 8.87; Catull. 101.9 ∼ Juv. 15.136; Catull. 103.2 ∼ Juv. 2.77, these last three very tenuous.

[53] Ter. *An.* 126 ∼ Juv. 1.168, and probably *Haut.* 77 ∼ Juv. 15.142; but *Haut.* 77 and Juv. 6.284, *An.* 314 and Juv. 3.209 can be neglected.

[54] Lucr. 1.919 and 2.976 ∼ Juv. 3.100–101; Lucr. 3.1018 ∼ Juv. 13.193–94; Lucr. 5.907 ∼ Juv. 6.11; Lucr. 5.1011f. ∼ Juv. 15.151–58. We can probably neglect Lucr. 3.299 and Juv. 1.166, Lucr. 3.1048 and Juv. 1.57, the contexts being so widely different.

[55] Prop. 2.32.2 ∼ Juv. 13.210 perhaps; Prop. 2.9.41 and 4.11.37 ∼ Juv. 8.146–50; Prop. 3.25.1 ∼ Juv. 15.42; Prop. 4.7.1 ∼ Juv. 2.149.

[56] Livy 1.13.2 ∼ Juv. 6.164; Livy 5.32.6 ∼ Juv. 11.111–14; Livy 25.40.2 ∼ Juv. 11.100; Sall. *Iug.* 85.23 ∼ Juv. 8.139.

[57] See G. Highet, "Petronius the Moralist," *TAPhA* 72 (1941) 176–94, especially p. 190, note 42.

revels.[58] But perhaps his pervasive grudge against the rich and noble would keep him from giving the Arbiter of Taste his due.

Other assertions about Juvenal's knowledge of literature have been made, but sometimes they are based on inadequate parallels and sometimes they suffer from the twin assumptions that he must have known *all* the books available to us and could have known *no others*. For example, his first words are a protest against the constant outpouring of meaningless literature which he hears at recitations. He exclaims

Semper ego auditor tantum?

as though he had sprung up from his seat in a recital hall and turned to face the audience. Many have suggested that the angry phrase was inspired by Horace (*Epist.* 1.19.39):

Non ego nobilium scriptorum auditor et ultor.

Yet the word *auditor* is common enough; the contexts are only remotely similar; the rhythms are quite different. Again, it is usually said that the opening of Satire 6, on the Golden Age, is taken from Hesiod's *Works and Days*; yet there are no clear verbal parallels, there is no proof that Juvenal ever thought of reading Hesiod (would anyone, with Vergil's *Georgics* available?), and he could find dozens of Roman mythological poems and manuals about the Golden Age which have now disappeared. He himself complains that there is far too much contemporary poetry for anyone to cope with.[59]

So then we have looked through Juvenal's bookcase, as far as we can still read the titles and recognize the books.[60] It tells us several things about him. As we could have guessed, he cared little for Greek literature, and would have scorned to justify himself, as Horace did, by parading a list of Greek models.[61] In Latin he knew the best available nondramatic poems and knew them very well, with the general exception that (like all Silver Age writers) he neglected the poets of the Republic. His style was really formed by Vergil, Ovid, and Martial more than by his fellow satirists. His thought came from the bitter experiences of his own career and

---

[58] Juv. 4.136–40: *tempestate mea.*

[59] Juv. 1.2–18.

[60] Besides those cited in the notes, the following are useful in discussing Juvenal's sources: J. de Decker, *Juvenalis declamans* (Ghent, 1913); C. Hosius, *Apparatus criticus ad Iuuenalem* (Bonn, 1888); R. Weise, *Vindiciae Iuuenalianae* (Halle, 1884) III. Friedländer's edition gives many parallels, which vary so much in probability that they have to be scrutinized with care before acceptance.

[61] Hor. *Serm.* 1.4.1–2, *Epist.* 1.19.23–25.

from the absurd and revolting sights he saw around him every day in every street and house.[62] It was partly the earlier satirists who helped him to give it artistic form, partly the philosophical essayists and propagandists of the Silver Age, and partly the neat, compact, vivid skill of Martial. When he himself speaks of his own work, he claims that it is in the most energetic tradition of satire, that of Lucilius, but also that it rivals epic and tragedy, either by mocking them or by outdoing them in gravity; and he says that thereby it has transcended the limits set by his predecessors.[63] Evidently he did this by combining the strong common sense of Lucilius and the moral purpose of his own philosophical models like Seneca, with Martial's acute and pitiless observation and his power to create deathlessly bitter epigrams, with the variety and verbal dexterity of Ovid, and finally with the scope, the power, and the loftiness of Vergil. It was through the multiplicity and the grandeur of his models that Juvenal raised satire to the level of great poetry.

[62] Juv. 1.63–64, *medio quadriuio*; 13.160, *una domus*.
[63] Juv. 1.19–20; 4.34–36 (jestingly, but note the mock-epic tone); 6.634–61, an important passage; 15.13–32.

Masks and Faces in Satire

WHAT RELATION does an author's individuality—his life, circumstances, and character—bear to his work? When we examine a piece of literature, ought we—as well as attending closely to the text, with everything that implies (themes, structure, language, models, imagery)—to study the biography of its writer, try to find out as much as possible about his personality, and use such information in the hope of improving our appreciation of his writings? Or again, if we know little of the author as an individual, should we endeavor to extract data about him from his work, believe statements which he makes or implies about himself, and use such material in making critical judgments about his literary worth? Or should we entirely shun such procedures, and confine ourselves to the text, studying it alone for the message it seeks to convey?

Thirty years ago these questions were answered firmly and clearly with reference to the Greek and Roman classics by H. F. Cherniss, in an admirably reasoned essay called "The Biographical Fashion in Literary Criticism."[1] Cherniss is utterly against any attempt to associate an author's work with his personal life. "Several years ago," he says, "a professor of English literature was widely acclaimed for having made an important discovery in his field of research; he had found in certain English archives the record of sale of a house belonging to John Milton. This may seem like a parody of . . . the biographical fashion in literary interpretation . . . ; but I suspect that few professors of Greek literature see anything comic in their scholarly debates concerning the number of Eu-

Reprinted from *Hermes* 102 (1974) 321–37.

[1] *University of California Publications in Classical Philology* 12 (1943). Now reprinted as "Me ex uersiculis meis parum pudicum (Catullus 16.3–4)" in *Critical Essays on Roman Literature: Elegy and Lyric*, ed. J. P. Sullivan (London, 1962) 15–30.

ripides' wives, the question of Sophocles' indictment [by] his son, Iophon, and the reasons for Aeschylus's removal from Athens. None of these questions, however, affects the works of these poets or our understanding of them. Neither has the discovery in the English archives elucidated a single word or line in the writings of John Milton. . . . It increases our knowledge not of any of the literary productions which made John Milton's name significant, but of the man himself. . . . It is because of the implied attitude toward the relationship between the author and his works that the event epitomizes the biographical interpretation of literature."[2]

There was no immediate reply to Cherniss's provocative essay, which was mainly directed against Wilamowitz's work on Plato and Sappho. However, a few years earlier two British scholars had debated the problem at greater length, taking opposite sides. The challenger was C. S. Lewis of Oxford (1898–1963); the respondent was E. M. W. Tillyard of Cambridge (1889–1962). Their debate, consisting of six essays in the form of successive attacks and rejoinders, was published in 1939 by the Oxford University Press under a rather one-sided title, *The Personal Heresy*.

"During the [first world] war," Lewis begins, "I saw an anthology which contained the work of some 'young soldier poets.' . . . The advertisement on the wrapper promised that if you bought the book these young men would tell you things about themselves which they had never told to their fathers, or their sweethearts, or their friends. The assumption was that to read poetry means to become acquainted with the poet, . . . to steep ourselves in his personality. . . . Poetry is widely believed to be the expression of personality: the end which we are supposed to pursue in reading it is a certain contact with the poet's soul; and 'Life' and 'Works' are simply two diverse expressions of this single quiddity." Lewis then goes on to impute this erroneous belief, which he christens "the personal heresy," to such eminent critics as T. S. Eliot (on Dante and Shakespeare), H. W. Garrod (on Wordsworth), H. Kingsmill (on Arnold, interpreting "Sohrab and Rustum" as an image of the relation between Arnold and his strong-willed father), and E. M. W. Tillyard, who had said of *Paradise Lost* that critics were wrong to discuss its style rather than "what the poem is really about, the true state of Milton's mind when he wrote it."

Some of the discussion which follows is rather metaphysical, and tends to substitute bold assertion for argument. For example, Lewis cat-

---

[2] For another example of this, see the article on the Belott-Mountjoy lawsuit in which Shakespeare was a witness, pp. 64–65 of the *Reader's Encyclopaedia of Shakespeare*, ed. O. J. Campbell (New York, 1966).

egorically affirms that in writing poetry "a poet . . . does not express his personality. . . . The objects which we contemplate in reading poetry are not the private furniture of the poet's mind. The mind through which we see them is not his. If you ask whose it is, I reply that we have no reason to suppose that it is anyone's. . . . The ancients called it the Muse."[3] To this Tillyard more soberly replies: "Experience shows that personality revealed through style" (and, one might add, through choice of themes) "can constitute the major appeal of poetry."[4]

This debate led to no agreement on crucial points of difference. One reason for this is that the disputants were arguing about too many different types of literature. They cited a poetic drama (Eliot's *The Rock*), a lyric by Herrick, Keats's epic fragment "Hyperion," Wordsworth's *Prelude* (that would have been a good central subject on which to concentrate the discussion), a prophecy by Isaiah, and—in spite of their manifest disparity—Tennyson's *Maud* and *In Memoriam*.

If the problem is to be illuminated, it will be necessary not to talk vaguely of "literature" or even of "poetry" as general concepts, but of the various types of literature. They differ, and it is a waste of time and energy to try to consider them together.

There are certain modes of literature in which the author deliberately excludes his own personality. There are others in which he either reveals it or else pretends to reveal it, or part of it.

In epic and didactic poetry the poet himself seldom appears. Hesiod, it is true, tells us a little about his family and home.[5] Milton, in one of his invocations to the Heavenly Muse, mentions his own blindness, and in another his loneliness in the new bad world of the Restoration.[6] Vergil in the *Georgics* speaks symbolically of his own plan to compose an epic, and "seals" the poem with name, address, date, and a quotation from his earlier work.[7] But such intrusions are rare.

The same is true, even more true, of drama and of most fictional narrative. The playwright makes a world for us to marvel at; but he himself does not inhabit it. Often the world he creates is far removed from his own time and place: Sophocles' *Oedipus Tyrannus*, Shakespeare's *Macbeth*, Goethe's *Götz von Berlichingen*. A novelist, even when he composes a narrative told in the first-person singular, is inventing a tale which does not directly involve himself, and which should, we feel, exist

---

[3] *The Personal Heresy*, pp. 26–27.
[4] *The Personal Heresy*, p. 36.
[5] *Op.* 633–40.
[6] *Paradise Lost* 3.1–55 and 7.1–39.
[7] *G.* 3.8–39 and 4.559–66.

without the interposition of his own personality. True, there are important exceptions. James Joyce made one of his heroes declare: "The artist,
like the God of the creation, remains within or behind or beyond or
above his handiwork, invisible, refined out of existence."[8] But in *Ulysses*
Stephen Dedalus resembles his creator Joyce very closely indeed: not only
in minor details of places and times and acquaintances but in major
features of character such as his attitude to his family, to his country,
and to the Christian religion. Much of the book does not read like a
fiction about an imaginary Irishman, but like a self-laudatory self-justifi-
catory biography of James Augustine Joyce.[9]

But let us exclude fiction—epic, drama, prose narrative—and didactic poetry; and let us examine those types of literature where the author
speaks, or pretends to speak, in his own identifiable person. These are:

(1) genuine *diaries* and similar books such as the so-called *Meditations* of Marcus Aurelius. (A fictional diary, such as G. and W. Gross-
mith's *Diary of a Nobody*, is a novel in an unusual form.)

(2) *autobiographies and autobiographical memoirs*: the *Confessions*
of St. Augustine and of Rousseau; Wordsworth's *Prelude*; and Caesar's
Commentarii, which (like *The Education of Henry Adams*) pretend to be
impersonal by using the third person instead of the first.

(3) genuine *personal letters* in prose or verse: some of the Epistles of
St. Paul, the letters of Cicero, and those of Horace and Pope. (Fake
letters such as the correspondence of St. Paul and Seneca should be
classed as prose fiction.)

(4) *personal lyrics*: those which say "I" and seem to mean by it the
poet himself. Within a large class, this is a small group. No one believes
that when Mörike wrote "Früh, wann die Hähne krähn, eh' die Sternlein
schwinden, muss ich am Herde stehn, muss Feuer zünden," he was
speaking in his own person rather than that of a girl seduced and forlorn.
No one thinks that Shelley claimed personally to be bringing fresh showers for the thirsting flowers: he was giving a voice to a cloud. But there
are some lyrics which carry what seems to be part of the poet's own
experience in his own words and sometimes under his own name. When
Catullus writes a brief poetic note of thanks to an eloquent advocate

[8] *A Portrait of the Artist as a Young Man*, ed. R. Ellmann (New York, 1964) 219.

[9] "With the years, the tradition of Joyce's impersonality has become harder and harder
to sustain. On the contrary, it is now clear that few writers, in Stanislaus Joyce's words,
'have ever exploited the minute, unpromising material of their experience so thoroughly',
that he was indeed the 'egoarch' that he accuses himself of being in *Finnegans Wake*. . . .
His books . . . are acts of concealment and exposure, of revenge and reconciliation, of
self-purgation and self-definition." (J. Gross, *James Joyce* [New York, 1970] 12–13.)

addressed as *Marce Tulli* and says *Gratias tibi maximas Catullus / agit pessimus omnium poeta*, it is on the whole likely that the addressee is Marcus Tullius Cicero, and that Gaius Valerius Catullus is expressing his own mind, or at least his temporary mood, and not that of some fictitious character interposed between the real poet and the real orator.[10] Therefore when he writes *Miser Catulle, desinas ineptire* or *illa Lesbia, quam Catullus unam / plus quam se atque suos amauit omnes*, it is probable that he is saying what he himself felt.[11] So in certain of his "sugared sonnets" Shakespeare introduces his own name: "Whoever hath her wish, thou hast thy Will."[12] It is conceivable that he meant a fictitious personage, or some other real man called Will; but the possibility is remote.[13]

(5) *personal elegiac poetry*. Archilochus wrote poems in the first person singular, in which the speaker, the "I," claimed to be a soldier, depending on his spear for life and livelihood, and said he had once thrown away his shield in a rout.[14] It is possible that the real Archilochus was a quiet little householder who lived on a small farm and never even saw a battle, and that these poems are pure fiction written by him and put into the mouth of a nonexistent mercenary bravo. It is also possible that when Solon composed a first-person elegy in which the speaker declared that he had given the common people their due without injuring the nobles, he was creating a fictitious Athenian political reformer, who had no essential connection with the real Solon son of Exekestides.[15] Many scholars, however, believe that in these poems Archilochus and Solon are speaking for themselves and describing their own careers, although there is no certain and feasible method of confirming this belief. In this same context the Roman elegiac poets have often been discussed, and the proportion of fact to fiction in their poems has been very variously estimated;[16] but not many critics have suggested that all the apparently autobiographical details in their poetry were pure fiction, with no relation whatever to objective reality.

[10] Catullus 49.

[11] Catullus 8 and 58.

[12] Sonnets 135, 136, 143.

[13] "Will" has another meaning, sexually obscene, but this does not cancel out the original significance. See A. L. Rowse, *William Shakespeare* (New York, 1963) 191: he adds, "The Sonnets are the most autobiographical ever written" (199).

[14] E. Diehl, *Anthologia Lyrica Graeca* (Leipzig, 1952³) fasc. 3: Archilochus, elegies 2 and 6.

[15] Diehl (note 14 above) fasc. 1: Solon, fr. 5.

[16] See, for instance, two acute studies by A. W. Allen, " 'Sincerity' and the Roman Elegists," *CPh* 45 (1950) 145–60, and "Sunt qui Propertium malint," in Sullivan's *Critical Essays* (note 1 above) 107–48.

(6) *nonnarrative satires* where the author himself appears to be speaking in the first person: for example, Persius, *Sat.* 5 (*me tibi supposui: teneros tu suscipis annos / Socratico, Cornute, sinu*: 36–37). This form does not cover satiric monologues in which someone speaks who is obviously different from the writer: for example, Browning's "Mr. Sludge, 'The Medium,' " in which a fake spiritualist exposes his own miserable character by talking continuously and trying to justify himself, for thirty-seven pages;[17] Horace, *Sermones* 2.3, a homily delivered by the Stoic Damasippus; and Juvenal 3, which (after an introduction) is a monologue put in the mouth of a certain Umbricius.

(7) *narrative satires* intended to be or to seem *autobiographical*: for instance, Horace, *Serm.* 1.5 and 1.9, which depend for much of their effect upon the mention of individual traits and personal friendships. Such works are to be distinguished from satires which are clearly fictional tales, even first-person narratives such as Horace, *Serm.* 1.8, the *Satyrica* of Petronius, and Lucian's *True History*.

The debate between Lewis and Tillyard about the "personal heresy" might have been more instructive and less inconclusive if it had concentrated on these particular types of literature. In these, the authors themselves explicitly or implicitly claim that their own personalities are somehow involved and revealed, whereas in other genres the author may remain wholly unknown or be no more than a name on the title page.

A few general truths about these forms should be noted.

None is complete or claims to be complete, not even the diaries and autobiographies. All give selective views of their writers' lives and minds. Even a huge corpus of letters such as Cicero's does not come near to representing the whole man as he was. And by their very nature, lyrics, elegiac poems, and satiric monologues are even more fragmentary than autobiographies, more emotional and less factual and more likely to be shaped by the forces of aesthetic creation.

Many, however, give the real name of their author, together with personal details of his life—details which, if false or seriously distorted, would have ruined their effect on the first public for which they were written, the author's contemporaries. They also give the names of friends and lovers and enemies, either openly or else under disguises easy to penetrate at the time of publication. We study such works generations or centuries after their authors died; but we should remember that they were first read to, and by, a public many of whom knew their writers person-

---

[17] Browning excelled in self-satirizing monologues spoken by eccentric characters: "The Bishop Orders His Tomb," "Fra Lippo Lippi," "Bishop Blougram's Apology," "Up at a Villa—Down in the City."

ally and would have detected and derided gross misrepresentations. It would have been pointless and absurd for Horace to publish a poem telling how Vergil and Varius first told Maecenas about his character and abilities, if Horace had never met Maecenas, or had not met him in that particular way.[18] Pope in his "Epistle to Dr. Arbuthnot" names its living addressee, the royal physician John Arbuthnot (133), mentions his own publisher Lintot (62), gives his own address ("Twit' nam," 21), invokes a dozen of his living or recently dead friends and enemies (135–46), ironically describes his own dwarfish stature and deformed figure (115–20), and in a preface states that the work was composed to answer two satiric poems composed by "some Persons of Rank and Fortune"—whom everyone knew to be Pope's own personal enemies Lord Hervey and Lady Mary Wortley Montagu. The conclusion which many people would draw from this is that the writers of such types of literature wish to be thought of as telling the truth, and—within certain limits variable with the person and the genre—*are* telling the truth about themselves.

Yet this has been denied, particularly with reference to monologue satire. Several scholars have asserted that the poet who composes a nonnarrative monologue satire such as the first poem in the collections of Horace and Juvenal, and (in ancient times) recites it to his friends or acquaintances, is not, and should not even be imagined to be, identical with the person who speaks the words of the monologue. When in such a poem (they declare) Horace or Pope or Juvenal or Boileau says or writes "I" he does not mean himself personally. The "I" of nonnarrative monologue satire (they say) is an imaginary figure, a mouthpiece or *persona*, which the satirical poet, like a ventriloquist with his dummy, causes to utter certain ideas formed into certain words, but not necessarily the ideas of the poet himself.

Thus, when the chief character in Tennyson's *Maud* cries

> Ah, what shall I be at fifty
> Should Nature keep me alive,
> If I find the world so bitter
> When I am but twenty-five?[19]

the speaker is not Alfred Tennyson (who was forty-six when the poem was published) but an imaginary young man impoverished and embittered. And so, when someone at the beginning of Juvenal's sixth satire says "I believe that Chastity lived on the earth in the era of the cavemen, but soon after that left the world,"[20] this should not be assumed to

---

[18] *Serm.* 1.6.54–55.
[19] *Maud* VI.
[20] Juvenal 6.1–20.

be the poet Juvenal's own personal view of sexual morality. The ideas expressed by the "I" of monologue satire are not, or are not necessarily, the ideas of the author himself. They are merely the ideas appropriate to the unreal *persona* he has created to speak the monologue. One might imagine that at least the words belong to the author. But no: they are simply the words appropriate to the *persona*. If Horace and Juvenal in such a poem use dirty locutions in a sexual context, we must by no means conclude that Horace and Juvenal personally had foul mouths: only that each of them was following satiric convention and inventing a dirty-talking *persona*.[21] For all we know, they themselves habitually talked in the purest and noblest phraseology. If they did, Horace would have been unlike his super-patron Augustus, who called him *purissimum penem*,[22] and Juvenal would have been very unlike his friend Martial. Perhaps they were; or perhaps we should not even enquire into the matter.

Thus, according to these interpreters, nonnarrative first-person monologue satire is either drama or rhetoric.

This theory has been put forward with some subtlety by one scholar interested in English literature and by another who is a classicist. Mr. A. B. Kernan is very severe on critics who confuse a satirical author with his spokesman or *persona*. This, he says, involves two errors.

The character who delivers the satiric attack is identified with the author, the biographical method; and the picture of the world given in satire is taken as an attempt to portray the "actual" world, the historical method.[23]

Even when the writer adds apparently veridical data. Mr. Kernan warns us not to take them seriously: such data are part of the satiric convention. His terminology exacts close attention: he calls the writer of a satire the "author," and the fictitious character who utters satirical observations in the first-person singular the "satirist."

The "satirist," Mr. Kernan continues, may be nameless—for instance, the narrator in "most satiric novels." Surely nearly all satiric novels told in the first-person singular have narrators with names: Encolpius (Petron. *Sat.* 20.7), Lucius (Apul. *Met.* 1.24), Lemuel Gulliver, Baron

---

[21] "Most critics have not been able to distinguish the voice of the speaker in Juvenal's *Satires* . . . from that of Juvenal himself. In some cases, the failure to draw this necessary distinction has led the critics to elaborate theories about Juvenal's . . . attitude toward sex. . . . Commentators deplore the satirist's obscenity as though it were a sign of Juvenal's poor breeding": so W. S. Anderson, "Anger in Juvenal and Seneca," *University of California Publications in Classical Philology* 19 (1964) 127–28.

[22] Suet. *Poet.* ed. A. Rostagni (Turin, 1964) 115–16. Cf. Augustus's epigram about Fulvia in *Augusti operum fragmenta*, ed. H. Malcovati (Turin, 1962) 1.

[23] See *The Cankered Muse* (New Haven, 1959) 2; also *The Plot of Satire* (New Haven, 1965).

Munchausen. But the narrator of a satiric novel told in the *third* person does not appear as a character and uses his own name only on the title-page, if there. No confusion is possible between Evelyn Waugh and Paul Pennyfeather, between Günter Grass and the stentorian dwarf of *The Tin Drum*.

Or (says Mr. Kernan) the "satirist" may bear a name different from that of the real author, for instance Colin Clout—a peasant name as unlike as possible to the aristocratic appellation Edmund Spenser. This is obvious: we naturally think of Tiresias explaining the art of legacyhunting and of Umbricius quitting Rome for ever.[24]

Or again, the "satirist" may be given the author's real name (and indeed he often bears other attributes belonging to the man who composed the satire); but he is still not to be identified with the author. Max Beerbohm has a charming story called "The Happy Hypocrite," in which a debauchee, in order to woo a pretty and innocent girl, dons the mask of a saint; but when the mask is torn off by a jealous woman, his own face has come to resemble it exactly, because his love has purified not only his inward heart but his outward semblance.[25] Now we are invited to believe the opposite of that fantasy. In the first satire of his second book, Q. Horatius Flaccus invents a "satirist" who is called Flaccus (18), who enjoys writing satiric poetry in the manner of Lucilius (28–29), and who comes from Venusia (34–39) where the real Horace was born. But—according to Mr. Kernan—this spokesman is not Horace: he does not express Horace's personal views or reflect Horace's character. The same applies to the fictitious character in the sixth satire of the first book, who was once an officer in the Roman army (48), who was brought into the circle of Maecenas by Vergil and Varius (54–55), and whose father was a freedman (6 and 45–46). This is not Horace the poet. It is a mask temporarily assumed by the real Horace. No doubt the same applies to Persius in his fifth satire, where he creates a fictional "satirist" who expressed deep personal affection for a philosophical tutor called Cornutus. The biography of Persius tells us that he was devoted to a philosopher called Annaeus Cornutus and left him a handsome legacy. But apparently, when writing poetry, he preferred to have an imaginary mouth-piece express affection for a possibly notional Cornutus, rather than do so in his own character addressing a real and beloved man.

Several scholars have accepted this theory and adapted it to their own purposes. For instance, Mr. R. Brower discusses Pope's "Epistle to

[24] Hor. *Serm.* 2.5; Juvenal 3.21–322.
[25] The inspiration of Oscar Wilde's *Picture of Dorian Gray* is clear.

Dr. Arbuthnot."[26] He styles it "a poetic biography," and explains that it is " 'the life of a poet,' not of an individual poet, but the epitome of a satirist's career as Pope saw it." Yet look at the text. In lines 380–81 we are told that "the two Curls" abuse the father and mother of the "satirist." To these lines the author appends a long footnote purporting to show that Alexander Pope's father was a gentleman and his mother a lady, and actually quoting the epitaph he placed on their grave-monument. What has this kind of thing to do with the career of a typical satirist? Dryden and Lucilius were wellborn, Boileau's father was a court clerk, Horace's father had been a slave. That particular slander and its rebuttal are not part of a typical satirist's career, but are private and special to Alexander Pope. In fact, a "typical satirist" does not exist, and we might suspect that Mr. Brower is simply trying too hard to avoid "the personal heresy."

In 1964 Mr. W. S. Anderson published an essay entitled "Anger in Juvenal and Seneca,"[27] which, after opening with a compliment to Mr. Kernan, applied his theory to Juvenal. Mr. Anderson is perfectly certain that the voice of the speaker in Juvenal's first-person monologues is not that of Juvenal himself. It is that of a fictitious "satirist," of a *persona*. If we ask him how he knows this, he replies ingeniously.

His answer is this. All satiric mouthpieces, or *personae*, are marked by tensions—which others might call inconsistencies—and Juvenal's *persona* has them all in a high degree. First, the "satirist" who speaks claims to be a plain blunt man, and yet employs the devices of rhetoric.[28] Secondly, he declares that he hates vice, and yet manifests a prurient interest in it. Thirdly, he affirms that he is only telling the plain truth, although he distorts it by omission and exaggeration. Fourthly, he poses as a lofty moralist, but takes a sadistic delight in attacking his victims. And lastly, he asserts he is speaking rationally, and still he adopts certain attitudes which are irrational.

Now, it is far from clear why these tensions, or inconsistencies, should not be inherent in the poet Juvenal himself, rather than be created by him for a fictional "satirist." All human beings are inconsistent with themselves, and more particularly so when they are sensitive enough and emotional enough to compose poetry.

> Do I contradict myself?
> Very well then I contradict myself.

[26] R. A. Brower, *Alexander Pope: The Poetry of Allusion* (Oxford, 1959) 294.

[27] Anderson (note 21 above).

[28] In fact, the "satirist" says that he has been taught rhetoric, like every other educated man (Juv. 1.15–17). For the Romans of that period, it was like going to high school.

So, with satisfaction, said Walt Whitman;[29] and before him, without satisfaction, Horace, who wrote in a poetic letter that he lived badly because

> quae nocuere sequar, fugiam quae profore credam:
> Romae Tibur amem ventosus, Tibure Romam.[30]

We cannot now know what the man Juvenal was really like. But the careers and characters of Pope and Swift and Byron and other satirical writers for whom there is rich personal documentation are full of glaring inconsistencies and painful, even ludicrous, tensions. Would it not be a waste of effort for such an author to create fictitious entities full of incongruities, designed to voice ideas not his own, and therefore two degrees removed from truth and reality? Is it logical to infer that, when a character in a quasi-autobiographical poem says "I" and manifests tensions, he must be invented rather than real?

However, Mr. Anderson goes further. He declares that the tensions in the *persona* of Juvenal's earlier satires make him (the *persona*) largely ineffective. The *persona* is a fictitious dramatic character, and an unsympathetic one—I suppose comparable to Thersites in Shakespeare's *Troilus and Cressida*. His "tensions . . . render him . . . sufficiently alien to [the] reader, so that it is *incorrect* to sympathize entirely with his passions and prejudices":[31] in fact, they "constantly oblige readers to dissociate themselves from his jaundiced assertions and to discover reality for themselves."[32] Although Mr. Anderson makes this point several times, in general terms, it seems to mean only that Mr. Anderson himself dislikes and rejects some of the moral preachments in Juvenal's earlier satiric poems. For instance, he says that the arguments of the "satirist" against marriage in Satire 6 are "utter fantasy, divorced from reality and distorted beyond measure: . . . few men would utterly spurn the fair sex, for few men can achieve a satisfactory existence without women."[33] Surely this is an illicit generalization. Apart from male homosexuals, many men have shunned, loathed, or despised "the fair sex"—there is a long history of celibate misogyny in the Christian church alone—and some of them have

Philosophy was something different (Juv. 13.120–25, to be contrasted with Hor. *Epist.* 2.2.43–45).

[29] "Song of Myself" 51.

[30] *Epist.* 1.8.11–12.

[31] Anderson (note 21 above) 134: my italics.

[32] Anderson (note 21 above) 144.

[33] Anderson (note 21 above) 144. The same line of argument would dismiss the fourth book of *Gulliver's Travels* as fantastic and ineffective, since few men would prefer horses to human beings. Swift's comment can be imagined.

written about their hatred in terms resembling those of Juvenal's sixth
satire, even (as with St. Jerome, Bernard of Cluny, and Jean de Meun)
adapted from that poem. St. Aloysius distrusted womankind so profoundly that he shunned the embrace of his own mother. At his confir-
mation James Joyce selected Aloysius for his saint's name;[34] and it is a
striking tension or incongruity in Joyce's own life that, after choosing
such an ideal, he should have delighted in the body of Nora Barnacle
and the emotions of Molly Bloom.

The theory distinguishing author from "satirist" has not yet, as far
as I know, been applied to the *Sermones* of Horace. Mr. N. Rudd observes, as though it were obvious, that in the diatribes of the first book,
Horace "spoke *in propria persona* and took direct responsibility for what
he said."[35] Similarly E. Fraenkel talks of "Horace's free self-representa-
tion in the most perfect poems of the two books of *sermones*."[36] Without
argument, Mr. G. Williams declares, "The most characteristic mode of
composition in the *Satires* is autobiographical, and . . . other modes of
composition are made to approximate as closely as possible to it."[37] In a
later work he repeats this view, speaking of "the various artistries by which
Horace expresses his concept of satire as an autobiographical form," and
declaring that *Serm.* 1.1, 1.2, and 1.3 "are generally personal because
the poet gives the appearance of talking in his own voice, and following
the wayward spontaneous turn of his own ideas."[38] To the best of my
knowledge, none of these scholars even mentions the *persona* theory in
connection with Horace's *Sermones*.

The theory is referred to now and again by Mr. C. Witke in a recent
work;[39] but he usually fails to make the clear distinction between *persona*
and poet, between "satirist" and author, which is postulated by Mr. Anderson. Thus, he writes, "Horace's great strength in the *Satires* is his uni-
fied judgment coherently presented by a stable *persona*," but by implication
he identifies this *persona* with Horace himself: "the poet exemplifies [the
moral decisions of satire] in his own life."[40] Rather equivocally he de-

[34] R. Ellmann, *James Joyce* (New York, 1959) 29–30.

[35] *The Satires of Horace* (Cambridge, 1966) 195. Mr. Rudd contrasts these poems with
monologues ascribed to speakers other than Horace, such as *Serm.* 2.2, 2.3, and 2.7: the
distinction made under rubric 6 on p. 273 above.

[36] *Horace* (Oxford, 1957) 101. So also on 145, "Unlike Horace's finest satires, [*Serm.*
2.5] is no mirror of the poet's own βίος."

[37] *Tradition and Originality in Roman Poetry* (Oxford, 1968) 456.

[38] *Horace* (Oxford, 1972) 15, notes 8 and 18.

[39] *Latin Satire: The Structure of Persuasion* (Leiden, 1970).

[40] Witke (note 39 above) 52. Similarly, Mr. Witke says that in the Misopogon of Julian
"the author's *persona* is coterminous with the outraged Autocrator, and the irony is largely

scribes the opening words of *Serm.* 2.6 as "the prayer of the poet, or of the poet's temporary *persona*," but then proceeds, "Continuing this revelation of the poet's interior monologue is the prayer to Mercury" (p. 62). In the remainder of his analysis of Horace's *Sermones* Mr. Witke abandons the *persona* theory, saying, "The poet has revealed himself as a frequenter of the old gods . . . he has further pictured himself as a man to whom the gods . . . have been disposed to listen" (p. 64); "Horace discloses his morning at home" (p. 65); "we are . . . plunged back into the poet's inner consciousness" (66). Later (90) he says that Persius begins Satire 5 "by abruptly opening his consciousness" like Horace in *Serm.* 2.6. Still later he implicitly denies that the speaker in Juvenal's first satire is a fictitious "satirist": "Juvenal offers an *apologia* for his work" (115); "the poet . . . has made a direct appeal to his audience" (117); "Juvenal here allies himself closely with Lucilius" (118). Once, indeed, he says, "Juvenal chooses to wear the *persona* of the poet striving to be *utilis urbi*" (120), but elsewhere he writes as though the voice heard in Satire 1 were the voice of Juvenal himself. And in a concluding summary he asserts unequivocally that "one of the strongest sinews running through [satire] is the concept of representation of the poet's life," and that in satire we hear "the *vates* speaking *in propria persona*" (268).[41]

Now, if the *persona* theory is valid for Juvenal, it ought to be valid for his predecessors Horace and Lucilius,[42] and for all later poets who produced the same type of monologue satire. Horace is a much better-loved poet than Juvenal. That may be why the inconsistencies in Juvenal's work are emphasized and interpreted as aesthetic and moral fakery, while the inconsistencies in Horace's *Sermones* are often explained away with such phrases as "obliqueness," "witty evasions," "ironic self-depreciation." Yet these poems are quite as full of sharp contradictions and serious inconsistencies as the early satires of Juvenal.

There is one in particular which critics have largely passed over, although it cries for notice. In *Serm.* 1.2 Horace preaches strongly against adultery—the kind of wife-chasing in which some Roman noblemen indulged, for instance Memmius and Julius Caesar. This sermon may be

interspersed with generous views of imperial anger, which surely qualify as self-revelation" (164). The mystery of the "coterminous *persona*" can easily be solved by the firm application of Ockham's razor, *numquam ponenda est pluralitas sine necessitate.*

[41] In fact, no Roman ever describes himself as a *uates* while writing satire. Persius, prol. 7 and 5.1 uses the word as Juvenal does in 1.18, to differentiate his own work from the ambitious verses written by epic and tragic poets. Horace applies it to himself in *Epod.* 16.66 (a very serious poem) "speaking as an inspired prophet" (Fraenkel [note 36 above] 48), and in *Epist.* 1.7.11 playfully as the poet of the *Carmina.*

[42] Juvenal 1.51 (*Venusina lucerna*) and 165 (*Lucilius ardens*).

only a diatribe adapted from the Greek. No: because in another poem
Horace specifically says that warnings against adultery were part of his
good father's teaching,[43] therefore this was his personal creed, sanctified
by his father's authority. And yet in a poem published some years later
(*Serm.* 2.7.45–94) Horace presents his own slave Davus as reproaching
him personally with chasing other men's wives at the risk of his reputation and his life. The explanation surely is that Horace had strong moral
principles and enunciated them eloquently, but could not always live up
to them. Inconsistency and instability were built into his character, and
he knew it: he said so in *Epist.* 1.8; and he made his slave say so in this
same poem, *Serm.* 2.7.28–29 (with the identical antithesis). *Serm.* 2.7 is
therefore a poem of self-reproach, with a house-slave who knew Horace
well acting as its mouthpiece.[44] It is not the fictitious and ineffective
"tensions" of a satirical *persona* that we see in Horace's satires, but the
ethical contradictions of a real man.

In one important area Horace deliberately falsifies his own character
and his social relationships. In *Serm.* 1.5 he describes a journey he made
from Rome to Brundisium—most of the way in company with Maecenas, L. Cocceius Nerva, and Mark Antony's friend C. Fonteius Cap-
ito.[45] Among these important and sophisticated men, Horace implies that
he himself looked like a little clown: for when they arrived his eyes were
all smeared with black ointment.[46] At the purpose of their mission he
only hints, saying that they were delegates on important affairs, and had
experience in reconciling estranged friends (28–29). Thereafter he speaks
no more about the mission, describes only trivial adventures, comical or
uncomfortable, and stops the moment Brundisium is reached without
even stating what the group did there. Inevitably this gives readers the
impression that the entire journey was pointless—or that, if it had any
purpose, Horace knew nothing of it. In fact, however, Maecenas and the
others went to Brundisium to engage in momentous negotiations between
the powerful leaders Octavian and Antony, which, if successful, would
avert another outbreak of civil war. War was avoided, or at least post-

----

[43] *Serm.* 1.4.113–15.

[44] The irascibility attributed to Horace in *Serm.* 2.7.21–22 and 43–44 and 116–18 is
admitted by himself in *Epist.* 1.20.25.

[45] Vergil, Varius, and Plotius Tucca joined the party (*Serm.* 1.5.39–42).

[46] The fact related in lines 30–31, *hic oculis ego nigra meis collyria lippus / illinere,* is
supremely unimportant. It was not worth stating at all, except to make Horace look funny
and insignificant. Yet note the skill with which the ridiculous little picture is inserted between two impressive sentences (27–29 and 31–33) and groups of potent proper names,
*Maecenas optimus atque / Cocceius . . . Maecenas aduenit atque / Cocceius, Capitoque
simul Fonteius . . . Antoni amicus.*

poned: so that the conference was of great historical importance. Yet of that we learn nothing whatever from Horace. Instead, we are given some minor inconveniences of the type familiar to travelers, and some poor jokes; and we learn that Horace had diarrhea, conjunctivitis, and an unsuccessful love-assignation, fortunately not all at the same time.

This is deliberate mystification carried out through omission and what the conjurers call "misdirection." Elsewhere Horace is more explicit. He simply lies. In *Serm.* 2.6.40–58 he declares that he has been a friend of Maecenas for more than seven years, *dumtaxat ad hoc*, only as far as sharing his carriage on a journey or going to the games with him. Maecenas never says anything to him except trivialities, "it's getting cold in the morning nowadays"; and when people ask Horace for inside information on important questions like a war in the Balkans and the allotment of land to veterans, they will not believe him when he swears he knows nothing at all about such matters.

Now, from Suetonius's life of Horace we learn that Augustus offered him the post of private secretary, urging Maecenas to transfer him to the imperial household, and that Horace declined.[47] It is impossible to believe that a man so intelligent as Horace could have shared the life of one of Octavian's chief ministers from 38 to 31 B.C., through the battle of Actium and later, without learning much about high political problems; or that Augustus himself would have offered him such an important post, had he not been certain that Horace was both wise, and knowledgeable, and discreet.

The pose of naiveté and ignorance of diplomatic affairs which Horace adopts in his *Sermones* may perhaps be called a *persona:* but not a *persona* to be separated and distinguished from Q. Horatius Flaccus. It is a pose: it is one of the faces which the real Horace wished to present to the world. By publishing *Serm.* 1.5 he was assuming, for his readers, the same attitude as he says he did verbally to his interlocutors with *nil equidem* and *at omnes di exagitent me / si quicquam* in *Serm.* 2.6.50–58. In his poetry Horace appears in many different guises—as vengeful lampoonist in the *Epodes*, in some of the *Odes* as inspired *uates* and in some as gay amorist, in the *Sermones* as critic of others and as critic of self; but each is Horace—or one part of Horace. Consider how many different Ciceros appear in the letters written by Cicero to his relatives, friends, and rivals. Yet every one is Cicero: Cicero as involved in a special social

---

[47] Suet. *Poet.* (note 22 above) 113–14; note, in an emphatic chiastic arrangement, the hortative or jussive futures *ueniet* and *adiuuabit* (J. B. Hofmann and A. Szantyr, *Lateinische Syntax und Stilistik* [Munich, 1965] 310–11). The invitation is discussed by Fraenkel (note 36 above) 17–19.

or political complex or beset by a particular mood, and Cicero as he wished to be viewed at one special time by one particular individual, be it Atticus or Brutus or Caesar or Cato or Pompey or brother Quintus.

In the ostensibly autobiographical satires of Horace the *persona* theory will not work. It is ruled out not only by Horace's practice but by his own words. He declares in praise of his great predecessor (*Serm.* 2.1.30–34) that Lucilius entrusted all his secrets to his books, so that his whole life lies there, painted as clearly and frankly and with as much desire to record the truth realistically as a votive picture. Then he adds (34) *Sequor hunc.* And although he proceeds to discuss another function of satiric poetry, censure of individual sinners and hypocrites (39–70), it is clear that he regards Lucilius's autobiographical writings as at least equally important. "Only when Horace . . . had begun to use his *satura*, not solely but largely, as an instrument of self-portraiture—only then was he capable of seeing that the work of Lucilius was primarily self-portraiture."[48]

It is almost impossible, then, to apply the *persona* theory of satire to Horace and Lucilius without distorting their work. Almost impossible also to the monologue satires of Boileau and Pope and Byron, who all in varying proportions introduce direct allusions to their own personalities, and compel any careful reader to conclude that he is hearing the voice, not of a fictitious intermediary "satirist," but of the poet himself. In *English Bards and Scotch Reviewers* Byron begins

> I too can scrawl, and once upon a time
> I poured along the town a flood of rhyme,
> A schoolboy freak, unworthy praise or blame.[49]

He is speaking of his own early collection of poems, *Hours of Idleness,* which had been mocked and castigated by *The Edinburgh Review.*[50] And after his "own review" (60) of contemporary literature and criticism, he concludes with an anticipation of his own pilgrimage:

> Yet once again, adieu! ere this the sail
> That wafts me hence is shivering in the gale;

---

[48] Fraenkel (note 36 above) 152; the whole section, 150–53, is worth reading in this connection.

[49] Lines 47–49. The model for the whole exordium is Juvenal 1.15–21 volubly expanded: thus "Should you ask me, why I venture o'er / The path which Pope and Gifford trod before" (93–94) comes from Juvenal's *cur tamen hoc potius libeat decurrere campo / per quem magnus equos Auruncae flexit alumnus* eqs.

[50] L. A. Marchand, *Byron* (New York, 1957) vol. 1, pp. 147–50.

And Afric's coast and Calpe's adverse height,
And Stamboul's minarets must greet my sight.[51]

Admittedly, his temper in this work is different from the monologue sections of a later poem:

The thorns which I have reaped are from the tree
I planted: they have torn me, and I bleed:
I should have known what fruit would spring from such a seed.[52]

But Byron himself was—as his letters and the memoirs of his friends show—a man of many moods, most of them extreme. In voicing them in the first person he is portraying, not an imaginary "satirist," but himself. Indeed, he gloried in displaying his own inconsistencies.[53] As for Pope, perhaps enough has been said above (p. 274); but it is relevant that several modern critics commenting on his work simply assume that the emotions expressed in his satires are those of Pope himself, not those of a *persona*. Thus Mr. H. M. Reichard speaks of "Pope's general outlook of gloom."[54] Boileau, a retiring man by nature, "assés foible de corps, assés doux de visage,"[55] is more reluctant to evoke his own personality in his nonnarrative monologue satires; yet they contain enough allusions to his own tastes, his friends, and his enemies to assure us that the speaker is not an imaginary "satirist," but Boileau.

The conclusion which emerges is this.

In those types of literature which are not ostensibly autobiographical (and that is far the greater part of literature) it is only a peripheral task of scholarship to discover data about the writer's personality: except in so far as they directly affect the interpretation of his work. Our understanding of Milton's *Paradise Lost* will surely be enriched by the facts—such as can be discovered—about Milton's own religious beliefs, which were far from orthodox. It is also valuable to take note of an author's references to (or silence about) his sources, models, and predecessors: e.g. Euripides' implied criticism of Aeschylus in *Electra*, Vergil's mention of Hesiod in

[51] Lines 1017–20. Byron has used Juvenal 3.316–18, making it more haughty and aristocratic and wealthy. Afric and Calpe appear later in *Childe Harold's Pilgrimage*, Canto 2.22.

[52] *Childe Harold's Pilgrimage*, Canto 4.10.

[53] See a good discussion on pp. x–xi of Marchand's preface to his *Byron* (note 50 above): "The fact may be that perfect consistency is . . . the greatest pose of all."

[54] "Pope's Social Satire," in *Essential Essays for the Study of Pope*, ed. M. Mack (Hamden, 1964) 683.

[55] Boileau, *Épîtres*, 10.90. The line is followed by a poetic autobiography (93–114) modeled on Horace, *Epist.* 1.20.20–28.

the *Georgics* and his silence about Homer in the *Aeneid*, Shakespeare's parody of Marlowe in *Hamlet*.

However, works which claim to be autobiographical—not narratives, or sermons attributed to clearly fictitious characters such as Horace's Damasippus, but works in which the author claims to give his own thoughts and feelings—we shall expect to be incomplete and partial, even distorted and inconsistent; but we shall judge them to be the utterance of the author himself, and not of a *persona* or a fictitious mouthpiece quite different from the author. Men and women are imperfect. They are often insincere, and they often exaggerate or diminish the truth. Furthermore, all autobiographical forms are incomplete. The higher they are aesthetically, the more fragmentary they tend to be. A century of sonnets, or fifty elegies, or a dozen satires do not reproduce the whole man or woman who wrote them. But, when autobiographically set out, they do represent what he or she believed were important aspects or phases of his or her true self, and not a conglomerate of words and ideas which the author would have disclaimed, put into the mouth of a phantom. Sometimes, it is true, the self thus revealed in part is difficult for readers to like or to approve. Carcopino felt the character of Cicero, as shown in his letters, so distasteful that he invented a theory that they had been collected and published on the orders of Octavian to discredit Cicero's memory and his cause. Some modern readers have found the frankness of Sappho's τεθνάκην δ' ὀλίγω 'πιδεύης / φαίνομ' ἐμ' αὔτ[αι][56] and τεθνάκην δ' ἀδόλως θέλω[57] repugnant, and have attempted to reinterpret and falsify the feeling of her words. So Mr. Anderson believes that Juvenal, in his most violently expressed and cruelly illustrated monologue satires, was creating a puppet "satirist" with intellectual and emotional defects so obvious that only a very stupid reader could attribute them to Juvenal himself.

> I would contend that Juvenal has provided ample reasons for disassociating him from the attitudes expressed by his satirist. In the first place, he depicts his satirist as torn by serious tensions that tend to disqualify the satirist's reliability as a social observer; and secondly, he assigns to the satirist moral ideas that *we* could not possibly share, not as long as *we* have our wits about us.[58]

The second of these two "ample reasons" shows how far such critics are from understanding the art of the ancient satirist, let alone of all

[56] E. Lobel and D. L. Page, *Poetarum Lesbiorum Fragmenta* (Oxford, 1955): fr. 31.15–16; c. 2.

[57] Lobel and Page (note 56 above): fr. 94.1; c. 8.

[58] Anderson (note 21 above) 148: italics mine.

satirists. The first rests on the illusion that an author's character-defects displayed in his poems are to be attributed to a puppet badly made and ineffectually manipulated by the author, and not to the man himself. Many men and women have revealed their own weaknesses in their writing; and one might well argue that an author who does so most impressively does not create a *persona* labeled with the warning that it is different from him, but brings home to his readers, vividly and directly, his own faults, tensions, prejudices, aspirations, hopes, defects, and strengths.

Housmaniana

INTEREST IN A. E. Housman's curious character and brilliant mind has increased steadily since his death in 1936, and is now very high. A collection of his letters, edited by Henry Maas, was published by Hart-Davis in London in 1971; the three volumes of his *Classical Papers*, edited by J. Diggle and F. R. D. Goodyear (Cambridge, 1972), are required reading for every classical philologist; there are some remarkable pieces outside the classical field in his *Selected Prose* (ed. J. Carter, Cambridge, 1961); and the *Times Literary Supplement* for October 26, 1973, announced the formation of a Housman Society, which intends to publish the first volume of a *Housman Society Journal* in 1974. No apology is needed, therefore, for presenting some bibliographical data which might never come to the attention of Housman enthusiasts.

First, an excerpt from the reminiscences of an English-born Californian bookdealer, *Infinite Riches* by David Magee (New York: Paul S. Eriksson, 1973), transcribed from pp. 190–92 by kind permission of author and publisher.

> In 1936 I listed two interesting A. E. Housman items. This was the year of the poet's death, and while I was in London I learned that his library had been bought by Blackwell's of Oxford. This struck me as strange since Housman was a Cambridge man. I caught the first train next day and presented myself at Blackwell's around mid-morning hoping that I was going to be the first customer to see the Housman books. . . . I finally managed to get the attention of a middle-aged man who turned out to be the manager of the rare book department. I spoke my piece and grudgingly he led me into a back room where there were about two or three hundred scruffy-looking volumes on the floor.

Reprinted from CW 67 (1974) 363–68.

"Don't expect to find any of these with Housman's name or annotations in them," the manager said. "His brother, Laurence, removed all such before we bought the library." And he left me.

I was nonplussed. Either Housman had a lousy library or a lot of people had got ahead of me and what I was gazing at were the remains of a collection. Still, I had made the journey to Oxford, and I figured I might just as well go through the lot in the hope that Laurence Housman had missed a few goodies. I am very glad I did. After an hour I had gone through all of them and had picked out five. Three were presentation copies of quite ordinary books, the other two. . . . But let me quote my catalogue:

BLUNT (WILFRID SCAWEN): The Love Sonnets of Proteus.
12mo, cloth. London, 1898. $40.00

Inscribed in pencil on the half title in Housman's hand the following quatrain:

If boots were bonnets,
These might be sonnets.
But boots are not;
So don't talk rot.

KIPLING (RUDYARD): The Seven Seas.
8vo, buckram. London, 1896. $30.00

On the last page occurs the famous line "Shall draw the Thing as he sees It for the God of Things as They Are!" under which Housman has written in pencil:
The God of Things as They Are is never the God for me,
For He is the God of Things as They Did Not Ought To Be. [1]

Mr. Magee put three worthless books on top of the group he had collected and showed the pile to the manager, who did not even examine them. " 'Ten bob a volume,' he said. It was fun outwitting that curmudgeon."

At that time I was living in Oxford. Basil (now Sir Basil) Blackwell personally gave me a few of Housman's books with Housman's own annotations. I still possess them.

One is L. Friedländer's edition of Petronius's *Cena Trimalchionis* with introduction, translation, and notes (Leipzig, 2nd ed. 1906). [2] Housman

---

[1] The style of the couplet parodies Kipling's cockney-dialect jingles, but its content recalls Housman's own *Last Poems* 9: "We for a certainty are not the first / Have sat in taverns while the tempest hurled / Their hopeful plans to emptiness, and cursed / Whatever brute and blackguard made the world."

[2] I give references not by Friedländer's book, which is now rather hard to obtain, but by K. Müller's modern edition of Petronius (Munich, 1961).

has gone through it, penciling in his comments with characteristic energy and bitterness. At 31.11 the apparatus criticus reads "tomacula Bücheler." The name is underlined, and "liar!" is written in the margin. "Fericulus jam habuit Bücheler[4]" at 39.4 elicits the correction "Gronovius and Heinsius." The pun *habere Liberum patrem* at 41.8 is declared untranslatable by Friedländer, who adds "Vgl. die Anmerkung." "Don't" writes Housman. At 50.1 Friedländer translates *plausum automatum* by "klatschte Beifall, ohne ein Signal abzuwarten." "But see note," writes the sharp-eyed Housman, and sure enough the note renders *automatum* by "Kunstleistung." On p. 180 the unfortunate editor attributes *strabus* (68.8) to Heräus. Housman remarks "you lie here or on p. 334"—where *strabus* is given to Bücheler[4]. Evidently Housman read every line of the text and commentary with suspicion verging on hostility. Page after page is left blank, and then suddenly a stinging note shows that he was perpetually vigilant. On *matella* (45.8) Friedländer gratuitously remarks "Missverstanden von Otto Spr. matula 4," to which is added "and left without explanation by Friedländer."

Once, surprisingly, both Housman and Friedländer got things wrong. In 47.12 Trimalchio summons a cook, *et clara uoce* "ex quota decuria es?" *cum ille se ex quadragesima respondisset,* "empticius an" *inquit* "domi natus?" Bücheler proposed to insert *ait* or *inquit* after *quota*. On this Heräus commented that it was not necessary: there is no verb of speaking in Phaedrus 1.29.9 (read 10) and Verg. *Aen.* 2.42. Friedländer inserts this comment at the wrong place in his note, referring it to "empticius an" *inquit*. Housman is misled, and sourly comments "it (sc. *inquit*) is in the MS" (so that, aha, Heräus was wrong).

At 57.3 something much worse. Friedländer entirely omits "larifuga nescio quis, nocturnus, qui non ualet lotium suum" from his text, but prints two explanatory comments on the sentence in the notes. Housman signalizes the lacuna with a caret mark and observes "not in your text." Clearly, as he read, he considered himself to be engaged in a constant dialogue with the author: or should we say a duel?[3] "Capite aperto ambulo," says Hermeros, proud of his independence (57.5). Friedländer declares "Öfter ein Zeichen von Schamlosigkeit." Curtly, Housman adds "but not here." "We prayed that the nighthags would stay at home," says

---

[3] As far as I know Housman published nothing, or nothing substantial, about Petronius; but some of the venom generated by his perusal of this edition of the *Cena* appears in his "Corrections and Explanations of Martial" (*Papers* [above, para. 1] 711–39), which are also corrections and excoriations of Friedländer: see in particular p. 715, where some of Friedländer's interpretations are called "not merely wrong but obviously and perversely wrong, and wrong where earlier interpreters were right."

the narrator: *ut suis se teneant* (64.1). Friedländer's comment is ". . . ist das von den Herausgebern hinter suis gesetzte sedibus zu streichen": to which the reply is "only Bücheler, you knave."

These are not all Housman's comments, by any means. Several times he inserts a marginal caret mark enclosing a word or phrase which needs explanation and does not receive it: *bono filo* (46.3), *caricae* (64.3), *semissem* adj. (64.6), *fabam uitream* (67.10). And every now and then—as when Friedländer carelessly mistranslates 72.7 or (on 27.5) misquotes Martial 14.119—the margin carries the simple mark of indignation (!).

The other two books are identical paperbacked copies of S. G. Owen's Oxford text of Juvenal with Persius (1903). On the flyleaf of each, in his firm and handsome script, is his name and address: *A. E. Housman   17 North Road   Highgate   London*. He lived there from 1886 to 1905.[4]

Housman himself produced not one, but two editions of Juvenal: one occupying pages 532–64 of the second volume of J. P. Postgate's *Corpus Poetarum Latinorum* (London, 1905), the other an independent book with a polemical title and preface, published by Grant Richards of London in the same year.[5] In the second paragraph of his preface he does not make the relation between these two editions entirely clear. The truth appears to be one which he would have been loath to admit: that his recension in the Postgate volume was based on inadequate knowledge of the MSS, and that he should not have allowed it to appear until he had done more research. He himself says that in his own independent edition he presents "to the readers and especially to the editors of Juvenal the first apparatus criticus which they have ever seen." This means not only that the apparatus in Bücheler's edition of 1893 and of course in Owen's edition of 1903 are inadequate, but that "what stands at the foot of the page" in Housman's own contribution to the Postgate *Corpus* is unworthy of the name of apparatus criticus.[6] It was because he felt this that he resolved to do the work more thoroughly, to have his edition published at his own expense, and to discharge upon his rivals and predecessors some of the rancor generated in him by his failure.

In preparing his independent edition he regularly used the Pithou MS and its congeners, a ninth-century Vienna fragment, and seven other MSS. Two of these had been collated by Hosius in 1888; two, in Oxford

---

[4] Maas, *Letters* (above, para. 1) 23.

[5] Reprinted with corrections and an additional preface by the Cambridge University Press in 1931.

[6] On p. 532 in the *Corpus* edition he introduces at least one abbreviation which he would later have rejected with scorn: "ς = librorum praeter P unus uel aliquot."

and Cambridge, he read himself. Two were in Paris. These, he says, were examined for him "by Mr Charles Samaran and afterwards in a few places by Mr Louis Brandin."[7] One, in the Vatican library, was examined for him "by Mr E. O. Winstedt and afterwards in a few places by Mr George Périnelle."[8]

The two copies of Owen's text which are being discussed are evidently the books which Housman sent to his collaborators in this enterprise, and which they returned to him, heavily annotated, to assist him in constructing his "first apparatus criticus."[9] His method was simple and sensible. He went through the text line by line and indicated questions he wished to be solved: these were the critical problems which had appeared to him as crucial. His correspondents wrote in the answers, and returned the books.

Several methods were employed. First and most important, Housman underlined every word and phrase where, in the MS under inspection, a textual variant might appear: e.g. *purpura maior* (1.106), *abrumpere* (2.116), *praesentius* (3.18), *sagina* (4.67), *artoptae* (5.72), *magnis* (6.9), *mane* (6.656), *digitos uatum* (7.89), *Antigonae personam uel Melanippae* (8.229), the Greek sentence in 9.37, *irati debet* (10.313), *quisquam erit: in magno* (11.148), *miserabile* (12.73), *minimus* (13.179), *nullis* (14.165), *praestant instantibus Ombis* (15.75), *igitur* (16.18). If the MS carried this word or phrase exactly as in Owen's printed version, Housman's collaborators wrote a single letter against it in the margin. Winstedt, collating Jahn's *h*, wrote *h*. The other two, examining Jahn's *f* and *g*, ought to have written *f* and *g*; but for some reason both put down *g*.[10] But if the MS had some other form of the underlined word or phrase, the collaborators wrote that in the margin. E.g. *purpuram actor?* (1.106), *prestantius* (3.18), *saginis   sagittis* from two different MSS (4.67), *salvisitartot opte   artecopi* (5.72), *vatum digitos   vatum digitos* (7.89), and

---

[7] 1905 preface, p. viii. Jahn had used these MSS (Parisiensis 8071 and Parisiensis 7900A), calling them *f* and *g*: Housman renamed them F and G, and so they are styled by both Knoche (1950) and Clausen (1959).

[8] 1905 preface, p. ix. This Vatican MS is Vrbinas 661, which Jahn called *h* and Housman renamed U: so also Knoche and Clausen. (Winstedt had attained a brief measure of fame in 1899 by discovering the O fragments of Satire 6.)

[9] It will strike most readers as curious that he should have used for this purpose an edition which he despised and had reviewed in terms of stinging contempt (*Papers*, above, 602–10, cf. 617–18); but his review begins by stating, accurately enough, "This edition . . . is certainly the handiest in existence. The paper and binding are good, the print is excellently clear."

[10] One used blue ink, the other red; and their scripts differ slightly. The second set of marginal *g*'s does not appear until 3.320: the F MS starts at 3.317.

so on. Occasionally they noted palaeographical details: e.g. on 7.80 *at Sarreno* ("l'e est encore visible sous la surcharge a"); and on 13.26 *numera uix sunt* ("so 2nd hand   1st as far as I could make it out -*rum uissi*").

Housman also enquired about lines and passages which might be missing. Of course in both copies he asked at the beginning of the O fragment "omissa?" and got the answers "yes," "oui," "oui." Then he asked about lines which he suspected, and which might well be expunged. Against 6.184 and 6.188 he writes "inest?" and receives affirmative replies. He was deeply concerned, too, about the order of lines in passages apparently disturbed. So in 6 he asks "inestne 615? quo ordine 614a, 614b, 615, 617a?" and at 11.165 "165 et 166 ubi sunt? post 159 an 160 an 161 an 162 an 164 an 171 an 172 an 202? num inverso ordine, 166, 165?" To this one of his informants replies "Je ne les trouve nulle part," a note which appears in his apparatus as "165 et 166 om. G."

Apparently he got Winstedt to go over *h* first, and then turned to the French MSS. This may be inferred from the fact that he interrogates his Paris collaborators on several points which he leaves without underline or query in Winstedt's copy: e.g. *uehatur* (1.158), *exigit a te* (6.35), *lecture* (6.277), *Saufeia* (6.320), *conducit* (6.353), *ferendam* (13.143).

On one textual point he did not question his correspondents. In a number of MSS Satire 16 is written before Satire 15: see Knoche's apparatus criticus at the beginning of 15.[11] Not all of these are inferior copies. One of them is Housman's own G. It is understandable that he should not have asked his assistants to check the order of the poems; but it was unfortunate that neither of those working in Paris should have drawn his attention to it. Evidently they confined themselves to answering his enquiries on single words, phrases, and lines. Later, in a hostile review of Knoche's *Überlieferung Juvenals*, he remarks rather sourly, "G has never been collated; Jahn only pretended to collate it, and I did not pretend."[12]

[11]This feature is quite frequent. I have noted it in Knoche's *Ricc 612* (Florence), in a Renaissance commentary in Milan (Ambr. A.121 inf.), in a twelfth-century copy in Vienna (Vind. 232), and in a Zurich manuscript written in humanistic minuscule (C 92 App. 24).

[12]*Papers*, above, 1106–8. Knoche must be speaking of partial collations, or be inaccurate, when he says on p.xxv of his edition (referring to G), "Kollationen bei Jahn, Beer, Leo, Housman." He says he himself collated the MS from photographs. Clausen collated it, apparently by autopsy (his preface p. xi); but he does not seem to mention the inverted order of Satires 15 and 16, doubtless because it is a medieval alteration of little importance.

These are only three books from Housman's library, but they throw a stronger light on that dark and tortuous mind. Many more of his classical texts and his instruments of scholarship are surely extant. A discreet note published in 1936 records the existence *in America* of a group of the texts which he used from his undergraduate days into his maturity, filled with handwritten comments "for the most part denunciatory and even highly insulting," and adds that his copy of J. E. B. Mayor's *Juvenal* "is particularly rich in holograph notes."[13] No doubt Housman specialists (like John Carter and John Sparrow) know where these books now are. Certainly no satisfactory biography of Housman can ever be written, unless by someone who has gone over them with professional knowledge, and with sympathetic understanding for a man who viewed not only the work of his fellow classicists but the world as a whole with "horror and scorn and hate and fear and indignation."[14]

[13] Seymour Adelman, "Dating from 1877 to 1882," in the A. E. Housman Memorial Number of the *Mark Twain Quarterly* 1 (1936) 12.

[14] *A Shropshire Lad* 48.

CLASSICAL TRADITION

Classical Echoes in *La Araucana*

ONE OF the first Spanish heroic poems which contained a substantial range of imitations of classical poetry was Alonso de Ercilla y Zuñiga's *Araucana*, the story of the resistance of the Chilean Indians to the Spanish invaders. Naturally, Ercilla was much influenced by the great Spanish poet who wrote the most original of Roman epics: Lucan of Cordova. W. Strohmeyer, in his *Studie über die Araukana* (Bonn, 1929) 26f., has pointed out some of Ercilla's imitations and adaptations of Lucan, but not by any means all.

One of these in particular is worth a brief discussion, because it is apt to escape the observation of readers unfamiliar with the classics, and has in fact been mistranslated in the recent version by C. M. Lancaster and P. T. Manchester (Vanderbilt University Press, Nashville, Tenn., 1945).

In Canto 7 Ercilla describes the sack of Concepción. He explains how the citizens fled before the advancing Indians. Doña Mencia de Nidos tried to rally them to resist, but her stirring speech of exhortation was unheeded.

> Ni á Paulo le pasó con tal presteza
> por las sienes la Jáculo serpiente
> sin perder de su vuelo ligereza,
> llevándole la vida juntamente,
> como la odiosa plática y braveza
> de la dama de Nidos por la gente;
> pues apenas entró por un oído,
> cuando ya por el otro había salido.

Reprinted from *Modern Language Notes* 62 (1947) 329–31.

The problem is the image in the first four lines. Lancaster and Manchester rashly identify Paulo with St. Paul, and translate:

> O'er the brow of Paul, the Apostle,
> Darted Jaculus, the serpent,
> Losing neither time nor movement,
> Bringing death with stinging swiftness.

Now, St. Paul did have one dangerous experience with a snake: perhaps Lancaster and Manchester were thinking of the miracle at Melita (Acts 28. 3–6). But there the Apostle was bitten on the hand, the snake was a viper, and it remained clinging instead of darting rapidly. This is a different animal, with different name and habits.

One of the great episodes in Lucan is the march of Cato and his Republican troops through the African desert, in Book 9. As well as suffering the usual hardships—heat, thirst, sandstorms—the army was attacked by a horrifying number and variety of snakes, sprung from the blood of Medusa. Lucan lists them in 9.700f., and then describes the different types of death which struck down the soldiers who were bitten. Ercilla was impressed by the picturesque names of the snakes—haemorrhois, cerastes, dipsas, etc.—and he furnished the cave of the magician Fiton with specimens of them, in Canto 23. (Some of them reappeared later in Milton's Hell: see *Paradise Lost* 10.521f.) Fiton's collection specifically included

> las dos alas del Iáculo temido.

This is the same animal, and the passage in Lucan tells us how it kills. Other snakes poison by their bite (Lucan does not mention constrictors), but the *iaculus*, whose name means "javelin," does not.

> Ecce, procul saeuos sterili se robore trunci
> torsit et immisit (iaculum uocat Africa) serpens
> perque caput Pauli transactaque tempora fugit.
> nil ibi uirus agit: rapuit cum uolnere fatum.
>
> (9.822–25)

"Look, from a barren treetrunk far off a fierce serpent, called the javelin in Africa, brandished and launched itself, and flew through the head of Paulus, piercing his temples. Poison plays no part there: death seized him at the same instant as the wound." And Lucan adds that the snake flew more swiftly than a slingstone or a Scythian arrow. By the way, he does not say that it had wings, as Ercilla does in Canto 23: he appears to have thought it projected itself like a self-propelled weapon.

This then is Paulo: not the Apostle, but a Roman soldier invented by Lucan; and the snake did not dart "o'er his brow," but through his head. The image is an attempt by Ercilla to decorate the prose into which he is constantly in danger of slipping, and which asserts itself at the end of the stanza: Doña Mencia's speech, like the snake, went in one ear and out the other.

It is worth adding that Ercilla quotes Lucan's actual words, for his

Ilevándole la vida juntamente

is nothing but a translation of Lucan's *rapuit cum uolnere fatum*. Small as this particular point is, it is another illustration of the difficulties of studying a classically educated poet without knowing the classics with which he was familiar.

The *Dunciad*

Pope's *Dunciad* is quite obviously a failure. Even in the twenties, when it was fashionable to quote and imitate the Augustans, it was rare that any passage from it was cited, except the impressive close:

> Lo! thy dread empire, Chaos! is restored;
> Light dies before thy uncreating word;
> Thy hand, great Anarch! lets the curtain fall,
> And universal darkness buries all.

These lines, and the passage which they terminate, are clearly admirable.[1] Their formality gives them strength, their cosmic quality gives them depth. They are not faultless: for it is weak and foolish to follow the powerful image of a new God uncreating the universe with the mild one of a puppeteer letting the curtain fall on his stage. As often, Pope's first version was superior to his later emendation. Nevertheless, these are rich, bold, majestic verses.

But the rest of the poem is a failure—seldom quoted and little copied.[2] It is impossible to read it without the "argument," it is impossible to remember it without special effort, and it is impossible to admire it without either an uncritical love for Pope's reputation or an unenviable pleasure in sheer spite. The reader's repugnance is increased by the os-

Reprinted from *Modern Language Review* 36 (1941) 320–43.

[1] "Mr. Langton informed me that he once related to Johnson . . . that Pope himself admired these lines so much that when he repeated them his voice faltered. 'And well it might, Sir,' said Johnson, 'for they are noble lines.' " (Boswell.)

[2] Mr. Roy Campbell's *Georgiad* and other such poems are written in heroic couplets, with much of Pope's epigrammatic vigor; but they do not imitate the central feature of the *Dunciad*, its mock-epic framework. Few of the many imitations have independent merit.

tentation of the various prefaces, notes, and advertisements, in which the author is compared with Homer, Vergil, Juvenal, Milton, Camoens, and Boileau. Much of that is pseudo-classical hyperbole, or mockery of professional scholarship; yet there is a deadly residue of serious intention. Pope and his friends did believe that the poem as a whole was uniquely valuable; they did think that it was a satire which could be justified by and compared with the *Iliad* and the *Aeneid*. The baroque age was convinced, not only that it understood the greatest Greek and Latin poetry, but that it was capable of emulating it.

Why should the *Dunciad* be such a failure? *The Rape of the Lock* glistens like a diamond. The *Essay on Criticism* glows like a planet. The *Moral Essays* stab like a bayonet. The man could write satire: why did he fail here?

I

The first and most obvious reason is the subject. The *Dunciad* is nearly all about worthless authors, journalists, and dilettanti—a worthless, ephemeral theme.[3] Pope himself (writing the *Letter to the Publisher* under Cleland's name) cites this objection in the very forefront, and answers it by a comparison between the satirist and the policeman—or perhaps between the satirist and the aristocratic disciplinarian. "Were not all assassinates, popular insurrections, the insolence of the rabble without doors, and of domestics within, most wrongfully chastised, if the meanness of offenders indemnified them from punishment?" Mr. Pope the writer, chastising his enemies, is the noble judge flogging and transporting the vulgar rioters, the hot-tempered peer cropping an insolent lackey's ears. And yet—which is he, really? Is he the judge who punishes in order to mend society, or the angry man who lays about him to salve his own dignity? *The Publisher to the Reader* will tell us: it explicitly says that the *Dunciad* "attacked no man living who had not before printed or published some scandal against this gentleman," Mr. Pope. In fact, Pope has made his enemies into criminals; and it was he who, by publishing *The Art of Sinking*, had made them into enemies in the first place.[4]

---

[3] "The subject itself had nothing generally interesting, for whom did it concern to know that one or another scribbler was a dunce?" (Johnson.)

[4] "He thought it a happiness that by the late flood of slander on himself, he had acquired such a peculiar right over their names as was necessary to his design." (Note to

In that case, the poem was doomed to failure. The classical models so often cited to justify it were irrelevant; or else actually condemned it. Latin satire and Greek satiric comedy were indeed written to improve society by pillorying knaves and fools.[5] And of course their authors disliked their victims: you cannot really love a man whom you are accusing of unmentionable vices. But few of them attacked purely personal enemies, and none of them wrote wholly, or even principally, from spite. When a classical poet wrote simply to vent his malevolence, his work was not a satire. It was a lampoon or an epigram, and as such its scope, manner, and pretensions were inferior to those of satire. Who was Aristophanes' chief enemy? Cleon? Cleon had prosecuted him, and had threatened him with further retaliation for his invectives. But Aristophanes attacked him from a different, a loftier motive—because he considered him to be a dangerous influence in a crisis of Athenian history. If Cleon had publicly retired from politics, Aristophanes would have dropped him at once, save for a retrospective sneer or two,[6] and turned to attacking his successors. Who was Horace's chief enemy? Think of the satires: you can remember no one name, except the comic tenor Hermogenes— and he is never attacked bitterly, nor at length. Horace's chief enemy was not one or two men, but human folly personified in friends and in enemies, and even in himself. Juvenal twice attacks the dead praetorian prefect Crispinus, and often the dead emperor Domitian. Some have thought that he had a grudge against Crispinus; many have held that Domitian exiled and ruined him. The second is probable, the first is doubtful. But in any case his attacks are purely impersonal in manner and theme. They are attacks on bad men, not on enemies; they are attacks on public vice, not on private opponents—for instance, they are scarcely more bitter than the posthumous denunciations of Domitian by the younger Pliny,[7] who had suffered no actual harm from him. If *The Publisher to the Reader* is true, that cannot be said of Pope's satire.

But as a matter of fact the *Dunciad* does not deal with slanderers and libelists. If it had, it might have had far more impetus and cohesion. In Book 2 there are eighty or ninety lines about journalists diving into

---

The Publisher to the Reader.) Compare the pompous image which Pope applies to himself in the *Prologue to the Satires* (219–20):

> I sought no *homage* from *the race that write;*
> I kept, *like Asian monarchs,* from their sight.

[5] Horace, *Serm.* 1.4.1–16; Juvenal 1.19–51.
[6] Cf. *Frogs* 577.
[7] E.g. *Panegyricus* 48–49.

filth; but they are political hacks, who would now be described as columnists or publicists or commentators. They are guilty of nothing more heinous than blackening the character of political opponents. In Balzac's *Le jeune poète* an intolerable deal of tears is poured out for the unhappy young author who is condemned by poverty and evil associations to write political articles for the newspapers. Pope viewed him with no such sympathy; but he dismissed him rapidly and rather leniently. Throughout the rest of the poem, he does not accuse his victims of being calumniators, but of being bores.

And in that lies the chief reason for his failure. Writing badly is one of the least offensive crimes which anyone can commit. The architect who builds a bad house, the judge who frames a bad decision, leave behind them something for succeeding generations to curse, and at last to amend. The bad writer leaves behind him nothing but shelf-papers and fire-lighters.[8] If the age admires and copies his style, if he is a temporary danger to public taste, then attack his writing impersonally and in detail, as Macaulay did with Mr. Robert Montgomery—and, after all, even that famous diatribe is rather like a steam-hammer cracking a bedbug. The attack will be most effective it if parodies his faults. Some of the most illuminating literary criticism in the world is contained and implied in Aristophanes' and Plato's brilliant parodies of other writers. Persius, usually a peevish contorted poet, suddenly breaks into a suave venomous laugh with his parody of Neronian Alexandrianism:[9]

> They fill fierce horns with Mimallonean booms,
> while Bacchant, captor of the proud steer's head,
> and Maenad, driver of lynx in ivy reins,
> ingeminate Euoe to repetitive Echo.

And indeed one of the neatest pieces of satire in the whole *Dunciad* is Pope's brief allusion to the excellent Hearne:[10]

> Right well mine eyes arede the myster wight,
> On parchment scraps y-fed, and Wormius hight.

Even better than parody is a broad general attempt to emend the taste of the age, like the *Essay on Criticism* or the first epistle in Horace's second

---

[8] Exception may be taken to this point, on the ground that modern libraries think it their duty to possess and preserve every atom of print, be it nonsense or genius: an ideal never entertained by such great librarians as the Chinese and the Alexandrians. But fortunately paper is perishable, especially in central heating.

[9] 1.92f.

[10] 3.185f.

book. But to abuse and condemn and defile the authors who write badly—
to show them chattering like monkeys and braying like asses, diving in
mud and slipping in dung—that is beneath the dignity of a satiric poet.
It arouses pity, not wise laughter: it is not *ridentem dicere uerum*.[11] It is
too harsh to be funny, and too petty to be serious.

This point can be well illustrated by a further comparison. The
Greeks did not like writing satire. Their passion for the positive and the
creative, which kept them from becoming great literary or artistic critics,
operated here too. Therefore the Romans could claim "satire is all ours,"[12]
whether on the ground of success or on that of originality. But there are
a few quasi-satiric poems in Greek, which are nearly worthy of the Romans; and the most interesting is a mock-heroic epyllion called *Squints*,[13]
by the Sceptic Timon of Phlius. Like the *Dunciad*, it was a parody of
epic. Like the *Dunciad*, it derided a large group of the author's rivals and
opponents. But there the resemblance ends. For it was a comic description, not of the power and worship of the artificial goddess Dulness, but
of the characters and conflicts of the great philosophers. The narrator, it
appears, was Timon himself. Like Odysseus in *Odyssey* 11, and Cibber
in *Dunciad* 3, he visited the underworld and saw its most interesting
inhabitants: as Odysseus met the heroes, Tiresias and Agamemnon and
Achilles, Timon met the philosophers, Heraclitus and Plato and Thales.
They and their companions were all described in amusing pseudo-Ho-
meric phrases—thus, Democritus, who taught in parables, was called
"shepherd of the fables," as Homer's Agamemnon had been called "shepherd of the peoples." Timon watched their arguments changing into a
battle royal. At last peace was imposed by Pyrrho the founder of Scepti-
cism, who addressed the combatants, destroyed their pretensions, and
made them all live at peace under his rule.

Now, although *Squints* is not satire in the true sense, it is near
enough to make a comparison with the *Dunciad* relevant. Pope's subject—the miserable obscure authors, changing their lineaments and dis-
positions between successive editions of the poem—was incapable of
powerful or even convincing treatment. Timon's subject—the greatest
philosophers of over four hundred years' great philosophy—was practically impossible to mishandle. Naturally, his treatment of the subject is
equally superior to Pope's; for it is both reasonable and witty to conceive

[11] Horace, *Serm.* 1.1.24.
[12] Quintilian 10.1.93.
[13] The curious will find a good text and prefatory essay in volume 2 of K. Wachsmuth's
Corpusculum poesis Graecae epicae ludibundae (Leipzig, 1885). Its Greek name is Σίλλοι,
and its author lived from about 310 to 225 B.C.

a Homeric war between competing thinkers, while it is labored and contemptible to present a collection of wretched hacks as competing in dirty
and improbable games in honor of the Poet Laureate. Of course they
are vulgar and low. They always were; and to insist on it is to be like the
crude wit who is mocked by Persius[14] for

> striking heroic attitudes
> in dirty clothes, and shouting Fatty at fat men.

It is worth noticing that Pope in the *Letter to the Publisher* adduces
another classical comparison. "We find," he says, "that in all ages, all
vain pretenders, were they ever so poor or ever so dull, have been constantly the topics of the most candid satirists, from the Codrus of JUVENAL
to the Damon of BOILEAU." Now, Juvenal mentions Codrus (or Cordus[15])
twice, and gives him at most eight lines. He begins Satire 1:

> Must I for ever listen? never reply,
> so often bored by bawling Codrus' epics?

And then, turning to other poets, he leaves him, bruised but not bleeding
from one of the swift topical side-blows which are characteristic of Latin
satire. Again, in 3, describing the dangers of the city, he says briefly that
a poor man like Codrus in his garret suffers far more from a fire than the
millionaire whose friends rally round him. It is foolish and wrong to
compare this rapid, elegant, glancing whiplash with Pope's systematic,
indiscriminate, boatswain-like knouting. And a still more powerful argument against the parallel is the fact that Pope, unlike Juvenal and Boileau, usually wrote of real living people by name. Satirists have never
hesitated to befool or befoul poor insignificant people if they deserved it.
But every good satirist except Pope has had enough sense to keep his real
strength for really important people. Only important people, whose distinction makes them symbolic before the poet approaches them, can be
truly satirized. Others can be lampooned or abused; but satire is far deeper
and broader than abuse. It seeks the symbol in the person, the vice hypostasized in the villain.

It might be objected that there is no other way of chastising the
insignificant but pretentious author than by making him ridiculous.
Something is wrong with Pope's method of making him ridiculous, as we

---

[14] 1.127.

[15] The MS evidence, for what it is worth on such a slender point, makes the two
littérateurs different. In the best MS the bad epic poet is Cordus, and the poor scholar
Codrus. Also, they are treated differently: the bad poet is scorned, the poor scholar is pitied.
Still Pope thought they were identical.

shall see. But I doubt whether it would ever have been worth while to do so, even if it had been done satisfactorily. He has confused an intellectual and aesthetic failure with a moral delinquency, and has tried to arouse bitter repulsion when he should have stirred ironic laughter. Don Quixote, because his delusions were far greater than those of the Dunces, was far more worth satirizing; and yet he is not thrashed with such a heavy hand. Hudibras and his rivals, the church-smashers and king-killers, deserved the poisoned fang; yet Butler made them comical and almost amiable figures. The subject of the *Dunciad*, deeply as it may have satisfied Pope, doomed his poem to artistic failure.

II. 1

Even if Pope did choose the wrong subject, he might have redeemed his poem by choosing the right method. Seneca's brilliant satire, *The Pumpkinification of Claudius*, appears to be doomed from the very outset: for it deals with the not very important ceremony of posthumous deification, and specifically with the not very offensive emperor Claudius. It would have been a gross and ugly failure if it had not been written with energy and versatility. But as it is, it is bitter, and versatile, and uproariously funny. Like Byron's *Vision of Judgment* (which closely resembles it) it is a straight narrative. It tells the story of Claudius's death, of his unsuccessful attempts to have his deification ratified by admission to heaven, and of his eventual relegation to hell or limbo. This simple narration, which sets off in the style of an official history and bursts into dozens of parodies en route, is the only possible method of satirizing a pedantic simpleton. The same applies to *The Vision of Judgment*. A more complex scheme than the tale of George's perfectly passive candidacy for sanctification would have been far too heavy artillery to level at the old idiot. Its matter-of-fact structure and diction at once mock the dead monarch and chastise the living panegyrist. Satire must be simple. It may even appear to be willful and improvisatory. The protrusion of its machinery ruins it.

But the *Dunciad* is constructed with appalling, with Byzantine, care and complexity. The preface by "Aristarchus" suggests, half in earnest, that in future it will be considered the comic relief, the satyric piece[16]

---

[16] Of course the satyr-play which completed the Attic tetralogies was not satiric, either by etymology or by definition, and satire does not derive from the tricks of satyrs.

appended to the trilogy composed of the epics of Homer, Vergil, and Milton. And it is not extravagant to suggest that, just as the baroque architect thought his Blenheim a palace worthy to compare with the houses of the Caesars, the baroque poet felt himself bound to copy, in order to equal, the achievements of the classical poets. Thus, the poem is a cento of parodies on an intricate framework of imitation. If this is to be fully appreciated, the *Dunciad* must be read in conjunction with *The Rape of the Lock*.

The plot of the *Dunciad* is as follows.

(1) The goddess Dulness elevates Cibber to the Poet Laureateship.

(2) Foolish and filthy games are held in his honor, the competitors being littérateurs of various types.

(3) In the temple of Dulness, the ghost of his predecessor Settle shows the dreaming Cibber the barbarian invasion of Europe in the Dark Ages, and the new barbarians who are to invade Europe under the rising empire of the goddess.

(4) Dulness enthroned receives the homage of her courtiers, gives them advice and encouragement, and finally yawns a supreme yawn which restores the empire of chaos and old night.

The Rape of the Lock is far simpler.

(1–2) Despite the protection of her guardian sylphs, a lock of the peerless Belinda's hair is (3) cut off by the bad Baron. She (4) reproaches, and at last (5) defeats him with a pinch of snuff and a bodkin; but the lock becomes a constellation in heaven.

Both these poems are obviously, in detail as in general scheme, parodies of classical epic and epyllion. For example, Book 2 of the *Dunciad* with its games parodies *Iliad* 23 and *Aeneid* 5; Book 3 is an imitation of the vision of future Rome shown to Aeneas in *Aeneid* 6. The cave of Spleen in Canto 4 of *The Rape of the Lock* copies the field of Hunger in Ovid's *Metamorphoses* 8 and other such classical descriptions. The Baron's fall is marked by a fine dying speech:

> Boast not my fall, (he cried) insulting foe!
> Thou by some other shalt be laid as low . . .

which is an adaptation of the apostrophes of Patroclus to Hector, Hector to Achilles, and Orodes to Mezentius.[17] The fat ghost-poet in *Dunciad* 2.39 is described as

17 *Il.* 16.844, 22.358; *Aen.* 10.739.

such a bulk as no twelve bards could raise,
Twelve starveling bards of these degenerate days . . .

the favorite motif of the *Iliad*, whose "not two men"[18] become "not twelve men" in the *Aeneid*.[19] Even that filthy image, the close-stool of Jove in *Dunciad* 2.84f., is ultimately a perversion of *Iliad* 24.527f., although Pope got it through Ozell's translation of Tassoni's *Secchia Rapita*.[20]

More immediately, of course, both Pope's poems are very powerfully influenced by Boileau's satires. Most English and American criticism of Pope is vitiated by neglect of this fact. Pope knew the classics well, but he knew Boileau intimately. Many of his finest lines and conceptions are merely adaptations from Boileau. For instance, the second line of the famous couplet:[21]

To happy convents, bosomed deep in vines,
Where slumber Abbots, purple as their wines,

is directly inspired by Boileau's *Le Lutrin* 1.19, 1.120, 2.102:

Ses chanoines *vermeils* et brillans de santé . . .
D'un *vin* pur et *vermeil* il fait remplir sa coupe . . .
L'autre broie en riant *le vermillon des moines* . . .

and 1.63:

C'est là que *le prélat*, muni d'un déjeuner,
Dormant d'un léger somme, attendait le dîner.

Similarly, the translation of Belinda's lock to the stars may seem to come from Callimachus, via Catullus 66, but there is no manner of doubt that it was suggested to Pope by Boileau's *Métamorphose de la perruque de Chapelain en comète* (which was beautifully timed to allude to the comet of 1664). Again, *The Rape of the Lock* opens with the poet's question to the muse, as do the *Iliad*, the *Aeneid*, and *Paradise Lost*, and its invocation ends with

In soft bosoms dwells such mighty rage?

which looks like a parody of *Aeneid* 1.11:

tantaene animis caelestibus irae?

[18] 5.303, 12.447, 20.286.
[19] 12.899.
[20] G. Tillotson, *On the Poetry of Pope* (Oxford, 1938) 157. Cf. Boileau, *Le Lutrin* 4.55.
[21] *Dunciad* 4.301–2.

but which is really inspired by *Le Lutrin* 1.12:

> Tant de fiel entre-t-il dans l'âme des dévots?

The exact character of Pope's dependence on Boileau has yet to be determined. These quotations are enough to show that it was very considerable. However, Pope meant it to be ignored, and his debts to the classical poets to be the more recognized.

Both *The Rape of the Lock*, then, and the *Dunciad* are essentially parodies of classical epic. The difference between them, in plan and in merit, consists in this. *The Rape* is a parody of one recognizable heroic saga. If it is applied to its model, the coincidence is almost complete. Belinda corresponds to the passionate young hero who suffers a deadly insult (Achilles, Turnus), and who, after an initial reverse, fells his opponent (Achilles, Aeneas): although—for the sake of the happy ending necessary in such a light poem—he is forestalled by a miracle (like Menelaus in *Iliad* 3). The story is plain and easy; for that reason it can without collapse bear the load of decoration which Pope imposes on it. Notice also that the few imaginative additions to the main scheme are all simple, all vivid. The game of ombre is of course a parody of the hero's aristeia—like the Prowess of Diomede in *Iliad* 5, of Patroclus in *Iliad* 16, of Camilla in *Aeneid* 11—but the parody has taken on independent life. A weaker poet would have made Belinda's attendants divine: Venus, Cupid, the Graces; Diana for her chastity, Juno for her imperiousness. With exquisite taste, Pope went outside the classical pantheon and chose far lighter and livelier ancillary deities, the Sylphs. Although he used them precisely in the heroic manner—to advise, forewarn, and protect—he made them more immediate and more credible than the guardian divinities of epic. Their charm, their inefficiency, and their volatility could not be better emphasized than by Ariel's delightful explanation [22] that he and his attendants are the spirits of departed coquettes.

But the *Dunciad*, although written in mock-heroic verse, [23] is not coincident with any classical epic pattern. [24] To begin with, it has no conflict, and no hero. Its major character is the goddess Dulness, whose

[22] 1.47.

[23] The classicist can tell by one glance at a line of Aristophanes or Juvenal when his author is parodying epic or tragedy. The metrical scheme and the vocabulary both change fundamentally: they ascend a comically precarious pedestal, on which they poise for a mock-statuesque moment before leaping down to rejoin their public. But all the *Dunciad* is an elaborate series of posturings on the pedestal.

[24] "The plan, if not wholly new, was little understood by common readers." (Johnson.)

actions (even if we exclude her glorification in 4) occupy far more lines than those of the nominal hero, Cibber. She crowns him in 1, she conducts the celebratory games for him in 2, and it is her power, not his, which is unfolded in 3. He is inactive, motionless, supine:

> Soft on her lap her laureate son reclines.[25]

Scriblerus's preface tactfully evades this point. Comparing the *Dunciad* with the *Aeneid*, he observes that the latter describes the restoration of the empire of Troy, the former that of Dulness. "A *person* must be fixed upon to support this action"—and so Cibber, or Bayes, or Theobald, or whoever he was in each edition, was discovered. But Cibber does not support the action. He neither fights, nor (after his initial prayer and sacrifice) suffers. He has no opportunity whatever to display the qualities of vanity, impudence, and debauchery which make him (according to Ricardus Aristarchus) the inevitable hero. Doubtless Pope really felt that his principal enemy *was* vain, shameless, and debauched; but he did not show him in active exercise of these qualities.

Among many parallels from parody and burlesque cited by Pope and his preliminary writers, one is omitted. For a very obvious reason, the most famous comic hero of Greek epic must not be mentioned. This is Thersites,[26] whose very name is derived from *thersos*, "impudence"; and his imitation, Irus, the shameless beggar of *Odyssey* 18. Both these men are violently active and memorable comic personalities. Making an astonishingly malicious speech against King Agamemnon, Thersites tries to rouse the whole Greek army to mutiny. He is garrulous, thin-haired, deformed, the exact converse of the tall straight blond heroes like Achilles. His speech is not applauded; he is thrashed by the wise Odysseus; he weeps with pain as no hero ever weeps; and the whole army laughs gaily over his discomfiture. But it is easy to see why he is not mentioned in the *Dunciad*. Homer describes him thus:

> Only loud-mouthed Thersites scolded away . . .
> the ugliest of all who came to Troy,
> lame of one foot, and bandy-legged; his shoulders
> were humped and arched over his chest; atop
> his head was warped, and grew a scanty down.

It would have been fatally easy for an enraged enemy to apply this to Pope himself;[27] and so Thersites, although Juvenal and Aristotle both

---

[25] 4.20.

[26] *Il.* 2.212f.

[27] "He has, in his account of the *Little Club*, compared himself to a spider, and by another is described as protuberant behind and before. His stature was so low that, to bring

use his name as the type of baseness, is entirely ignored. Yet he is a perfect type of the protagonist for a comic epic. So is his umbra, the beggar Irus, who threatens the disguised hero Odysseus, lays impudent claim to the position of official beggar in his palace, and is knocked helplessly and bloodily out by one blow from his fist. Don Quixote himself is in constant movement, and stirs others to manifold activity. Hudibras has fights and receives thwackings of positively epic dimensions. Even Margites (who is so often cited in the prolegomena to the *Dunciad*, although only two or three trifling fragments of the poem about him survive [28]) appears to have been in incessant action: he was an inverted Till Eulenspiegel, for he tried everything and made people laugh by his failures. Beside all these truly comic heroes, Cibber is intolerably weak. Even the violent vulgarity of Osborne and Curll is more probable and more laughable than Cibber's sacrifice of Gothic works upon the altar of Dulness.

The failure of the *Dunciad* is brightly illuminated by comparison with *The Rape of the Lock*. It was perfectly possible, in fact almost inevitable, for the baroque satirist to make his satire a burlesque of some serious literary type. *Absalom and Achitophel* pretends to be an epyllion on a Biblical myth, *MacFlecknoe* a heroic panegyric in the manner of Claudian, *Gulliver's Travels* a grave book of travel-experiences by a dispassionate but well-trained observer, *The Battle of the Books* a chivalrous romance, *The Beggar's Opera* a lofty operatic drama. The whole plan of the Scriblerus Club and of the Scriblerus notes and prefaces was relentlessly, even tediously, parodic. But the essence of parody is that the parody must improve on its original: it must concentrate the good qualities of its victim, and lighten his faults by humor. [29] *The Rape of the Lock* is a neat, straightforward, burlesque story of passion and conflict, told in the heroic manner. What the satirist takes from epic, he uses to decorate his poem. The beauty of *The Rape of the Lock* lies in its being a sort of concentrated *Iliad*, like Wagner's *Siegfried Idyll*, containing, or rather implying, all the major beauties of epic. The *Dunciad*, on the other hand, gains nothing and loses much by posing as a parody of epic. The only part of the pattern which is immediately familiar and comical is the Games in Book 2. The other episodes do not readily suggest their models, and form no one, consistent, recognizable epic whole. Pope has chosen,

him to a level with common tables, it was necessary to raise his seat. . . . His hair had fallen almost all away." (Johnson.)

[28] The Scriblerus notes make one of their graver errors in citing him, for Aristotle explicitly pointed out that the Margites poem was farce, not satire (*Poetics* 1448b).

[29] Thus, A. E. Housman's *Fragment of a Greek Tragedy* would have been unbearably frigid if it had been prolonged for more than one-fifth of the length of a real Greek tragedy.

not the best of epic, but the worst, to imitate. His poem contains the long pompous epic invocations and speeches and catalogues, without the large far-reaching irresistible action which should bind them together. *The Rape of the Lock* is a good epyllion. The *Dunciad* is a bad epic. Strange that the poem against dunces should itself have to incur the charge of pedantry. It reminds the dispassionate reader of nothing so much as the hideous affectations of Bloch, the learned Jew who haunts Proust like a banal alter ego throughout the social volumes of À *la recherche du temps perdu*. This, for example, is how he invites the young nobleman Saint-Loup and the narrator to dinner:[30]

> Cher maître, et vous, cavalier aimé d'Arès, de Saint-Loup-en-Bray, dompteur de chevaux, puisque je vous ai rencontrés sur le rivage d'Amphitrite, résonnant d'écume, près des tentes des Ménier aux nefs rapides, voulez-vous tous deux venir dîner un jour de la semaine chez mon illustre père, au coeur irréprochable?

These laborious mock-heroics are not far from Cibber's invocation to Dulness (with footnotes) and Settle's description of the goddess's imminent return to Britain.

II.2

A divinity cannot be the hero of an epic—far less of a comic epic—unless he is in conflict with another divinity. Without conflict, a divinity cannot act. He can merely manifest his power; and therefore he can inspire nothing but a hymn or a panegyric. Merely to describe the growing empire of Dulness as inevitably and universally established is not enough to hold the reader's attention for four books. That is one reason why the peroration of 4, which seems to relate an invasion and a triumph, is far better known than all the rest of the poem. For a moment, it has the air of real action, of a powerful conflict and a magnificent victory.

Of course, Dulness herself is a miserably thin personification, far less vivid than the classical allegories (Homer's Prayers, Vergil's Rumor, Ovid's Hunger) and infinitely meaner and poorer than the glittering sylphs of *The Rape of the Lock*. Doubtless Mr. Pope had some acquaintances who observed (with civil leer) that in order to glorify Dulness it was not nec-

---

[30] À *l'ombre des jeunes filles en fleurs* 2.202; cf. *Le côté de Guermantes* 1.195, 210.

essary to be so plaguy dull oneself.[31] Still, the basic objection to her is even deeper. It is that no one knows who she is meant to be. What sort of Dulness is Mr. Pope attacking?

In 1.65 her manifestation is incongruity—mixed metaphors,

> Figures ill-paired and similes unlike.

She is, in fact, BAD TASTE. Later in the same book[32] Cibber invokes her as STUPIDITY, and she approves this designation by appearing[33] in the avatar in which she inspires "shrieves and mayors," i.e. dull pretentious stupid officials. Another incarnation is hinted at in her evocation of her servants, who become famous[34] with

> less reading than makes felons 'scape, . . .
> Small thanks to France, and none to Rome or Greece.

There Dulness connotes IGNORANCE, for it is implied that if her ministers had read more, they would write better. The games which she institutes in 2 are obscene: her courtiers indulge in the moral equivalent of bad taste—VULGARITY—and are described[35] as

> A low-born, cell-bred, selfish, servile band.

2 closes with a competition that ends in universal sleep (an unfortunate anticipation of the peroration of 4); and there Dulness clearly means TEDIOUSNESS. In Book 3 the evocation of the medieval past presents the empire of Dulness as the tyranny of IGNORANCE.[36] But the Dark Ages give place to Grub Street's triumph, and there Dulness signifies everyone who ever offended Pope. No common quality can be discerned in the journalist Ralph, the critic Dennis, the stump-preacher Henley, and the impresario Rich. Dennis and Ralph, though spiteful, were competent. Henley was a contemptible crank. Rich was a petty Barnum. All were enemies to Pope, and very nearly strangers to one another. In Book 4[37] Dulness is IGNORANCE once more; but most of her courtiers represent the opposite of ignorance—affectation and PEDANTRY. At last, the peroration displays the goddess as TEDIOUSNESS, the spirit who nullifies all arts, all sciences, and all virtues.

[31] Probably the chief reason for the dullness of Dulness is that she is modeled on an equally dull figure, Boileau's Mollesse (*Le Lutrin* 2.69).

[32] 1.173.

[33] 1.263.

[34] 1.281.

[35] 2.356.

[36] 3.98.

[37] 4.21f.

Thus, under one vague allegorical figure, Pope has hypostasized nearly every moral and aesthetic quality of which he disapproves—as Lytton Strachey's generation did under the sinister form of the Victorian Age, as Schumann's and Goethe's did under that of the Philistines. Yet there is a compactness in the Philistine bands and the Victorian phalanxes which Dulness herself does not command. She images not one, but three enemies of the spirit. She heads the regiments of Vulgarity and Bad Taste, who write annoyingly; she captains the companies of Pedantry and Tedium, who write boringly; and she leads the hordes of Ignorance, who do not write at all. This division of interest is one of the main reasons for the failure of the *Dunciad*. Dulness is its heroine, but her character is unheroic, rather perplexing and vague. It is essential to give life and character to a personification, and that is just what Pope did not do.

Consider the three instances I have cited above. The Prayers in Homer[38] are lame, and have wrinkled faces, and follow slowly behind the bad act, always tardy. Rumor in Vergil[39] is at first a pigmy, and then swells to a giantess with her head in the clouds: she has rapid wings, and for every feather on them she has an eye, a tongue, and an ear, watching, listening, and talking for ever. Hunger in Ovid[40] has his bones showing through his flesh, and horribly swollen joints: he is scraping at the scant grass among the stones with his nails and his few teeth. For that matter, even the pantomime fairy Fame in *Hudibras*[41] and in Pope's own *Temple of Fame* has more ichor and less sawdust in her veins than his Dulness. For Dulness is not only vague but self-contradictory. She is described[42] as shining "in clouded majesty," and also[43] as "tinselled o'er in robes of varying hue." For the rest, she is veiled in fog,[44] and yet she has not even the sinister mystery of a sibyl or a witch. It is hard not to believe that Pope described her so badly because he had never seen her clearly. We cannot believe in any one goddess who is worshiped by Bentley and Burnet, Curll and Cibber. We cannot believe that a negative notion could take positive shape. We can believe only that one man could hate all these persons and their works and their ideals. It is hard not to hear, in this universal shriek of loathing and despair, the voice of

[38] *Il.* 9.502f.
[39] *Aen.* 4.173f.
[40] *Met.* 8.801f.
[41] 2.1.45f.
[42] 1.45.
[43] 1.81.
[44] 1.262.

Gulliver among the Yahoos, who was "almost stifled with the filth that fell around" him.

In fact, the influence of Swift is paramount in Book 2 of the *Dunciad*, and is, though latent, universally effective throughout the poem. In only one other passage of satiric poetry[45] does Pope dabble in dung. But his friend Swift was the greatest coprophil in English literature. The marriage of excrement to mock-heroic sentiment appears nowhere else in Pope, but it is a major theme in Swift's elegies. Surely it is to Dean Swift's invention that we owe such tidbits as Curll's slip in faeces, and the reviving effect of the ordure smeared on his face;[46] for it was Mr. Lemuel Gulliver who jumped (unnecessarily) into a gigantic patch of cow-dung and was "filthily bemired,"[47] and who apologetically but carefully explained how his own "offensive matter" was every morning "carried off in wheelbarrows, by two servants appointed for that purpose."[48] The verse-technique, of course, is Pope's throughout. Swift could never have achieved anything so admirable as 2.108:

> Nor heeds the brown dishonours of his face . . .

which has the very rhythm of *Eloisa to Abelard* 170:[49]

> And breathe a browner horror on the woods. . . .

However, the tone of furious indiscriminate hatred, the half-crazed misanthropy of the whole poem resemble Swift, who said that if there were only half a dozen Arbuthnots in the world he would burn his *Travels*, far more closely than Pope, whose own satiric poetry is a lighter, clearer, sharper, better-aimed thing than this overarching fountain of filth. Pope satirizes persons—Sporus, Atossa, Atticus. Swift satirizes classes, types, and ultimately the entire human race. Think of Alceste's bitter answer to Philinte:[50]

> PHILINTE Tous les pauvres mortels, sans nulle exception,
>   Seront enveloppés dans cette aversion?
>   Encore en est-il bien, dans le siècle où nous sommes. . . .
>   ALCESTE Non: elle est générale, et je hais tous les hommes.

The author of the *Essay on Man*, for all his hatred of individuals, could not give such an answer; but the author of *Gulliver's Travels* could, and did.

[45] *Epilogue to the Satires* 2.171f.
[46] 2.203.
[47] A *Voyage to Brobdingnag* 5 ad fin.
[48] A *Voyage to Lilliput* 2 init.
[49] Cf. *The Rape of the Lock* 4.135, 140; Tillotson (note 20 above) 154.
[50] Molière, *Le Misanthrope* 1.1.

This point is glanced at, though with insufficient emphasis, by Mr. R. K. Root,[51] who reports the significant remark in Swift's letter to the brilliant Charles Wogan: "The taste of England is infamously corrupted by shoals of wretches who write for bread; and therefore I had reason to put Mr Pope on writing the poem called the Dunciad." Swift left England in rage and despair in 1713. In 1715–25 Pope's Homer was acclaimed by the entire polite world. *Gulliver* was published in 1726. In 1726 and 1727 Swift crawled out of his cave to visit Pope. In 1728 the *Dunciad* was born. Pope was its mother, but its father was Swift. The greatest admirer of Pope cannot but feel that he suffered terribly from his association with the crueler, colder spirit: he is like Agnello dei Brunelleschi in the embrace of the snake:[52]

> Ellera abbarbicata mai non fue
>   ad arbor sì, come l' orribil fiera
>   per l' altrui membra avviticchiò le sue.
> Poi s' appiccâr come di calda cera
>   fossero stati, e mischiâr lor colore:
>   nè l' un nè l' altro già parea quel ch' era,
> come procede innanzi dall' ardore
>   per lo papiro suso un color bruno,
>   che non è nero ancora, e il bianco muore.

Seventy years later two other poets determined to chastise the Philistines, and to lash, almost indiscriminately, the world of bad critics, feeble poets, and stupid readers. Goethe and Schiller had not deliberately provoked retaliatory attack by publishing The Art of Sinking—they had been conducting an advanced but not aggressive magazine called *The Seasons, Die Horen.* Yet the enmity it evoked was so cruel and widespread that the poets resolved to answer their enemies with sharper shafts. Goethe, whose work was never distinguished for structural compactness, proposed that the answer should be in the form of disconnected two-line epigrams. Schiller agreed, and the two in concert produced the *Xenien.*[53] Schiller himself, in a letter to Körner,[54] says that "the unity of such a

---

[51] *The Dunciad Variorum*, pref. p. 6.

[52] Dante, *Inferno* 25.

[53] The usual Greek or Latin epigram, satiric or not, was four to eight lines long. Martial's are often longer, and only a few of his nastiest poems are (like the anonymous lampoons reproduced in Suetonius) single couplets. The last two books of his collected poems are couplets to be attached to such presents as A *tube of toothpaste* (14.56), A *girdle* (14.151), A *pocket edition of Vergil* (14.186). These label-tags he called "presents to guests," *xenia.* Hence the name chosen by Goethe and Schiller; cf. *Xenien* 364, "Martial."

[54] January 18, 1796.

work can consist only in a certain limitlessness, in a copiousness which transcends all measure." This is the characteristic German trick of explaining the inexplicable by the incomprehensible. As a matter of fact, the *Xenien* have not even the unity which is perceptible in a book of Martial's epigrams—Martial varies his tone and form much more, and arranges the poems in large variegated patterns which induce the reader to read further. Except in the collections of cracker-mottoes, the real *Xenia*, three poems in the same meter rarely follow one another, and ten never do. The Roman would have shrunk from the idea of making a book out of about four hundred epigrams, almost all in the same tone, all in the same meter,[55] and all of the same length. The *Xenien* close harmlessly enough in pseudoclassical meditations by Schiller; but for hundreds of lines before that the couplets have been clattering out, efficient, deadly, and graceless as machine-gun bullets. Nevertheless, the inartistic purpose of wounding the authors' enemies was admirably served by the *Xenien*—much better, in fact, than by the *Dunciad*. A real acknowledged disunity is better than a spurious unity. The scheme of the *Dunciad* was an unsuccessful attempt to impose unity on a subject which did not admit it. It was a street brawl disguised as a baroque war. The *Xenien* are, admittedly, guerrilla attacks on a disorganized enemy.

To return to Dulness, the hypostasized deity of all the barbarian hordes who criticized Mr. Pope. Even if she had been a credible and interesting figure—by the way, why is her totem the same as Athena's wise bird, the owl?—Pope gave her nothing memorable to do. She has, it appears, no opposition whatever. The "restoration of the empire of Troy"—which Scriblerus suggests as the model for the establishment of Dulness's empire—was a bitter contest between Juno and Aeneas with his mother Venus, each side assisted by dozens of other deities and heroes, major and minor. But Pope has not even given Dulness a circle of attendants comparable to Ariel's assistants in *The Rape of the Lock*—if we except such dull dogs as Chicane, and Casuistry, and the harlot form of Opera. He has given her no enemy to overcome; no despairing legions fight their last fight against the invasion of barbarism.

For that reason the poem is, as Croker observes, a series of episodes. The power of Dulness invades not only the polite world but the poem itself; for Pope shrinks from the only topic which might lead him to describe real action, real *change*. Lines 619–26 of Book 4 are an invocation to the muse to recount the steps by which Dulness took possession

[55] That is, it is intended to resemble the classical elegiac couplet; it is in fact intolerably slack and crude—"barbarous hexameter, barbarous pentameter," as Tennyson said of another Teutonic attempt.

of the realm of St. James and Whitehall. But the steps are not recounted. The invocation is followed by a line of asterisks, and the words

> In vain, in vain—the all-composing hour
> Resistless falls: the Muse obeys the power.
> She comes! she comes! [56]

Now, more skillfully handled, less melodramatically, with something of *MacFlecknoe's* frank guffawing humor, this might have been a fine comic climax. To invoke the muse, and then find that she has fallen asleep, is a brilliant conceit. It is of course not original, but adapted from Boileau's *Le Lutrin*, the second book of which closes with a sleepy speech by La Mollesse:

> "Ah! Nuit, si tant de fois, dans les bras de l'amour,
> Je t'admis aux plaisirs que je cachois au jour,
> Du moins ne permets pas . . . ." La Mollesse oppressée
> Dans sa bouche à ce mot sent sa langue glacée,
> Et, lasse de parler, succombant sous l'effort,
> Soupire, étend les bras, ferme l'œil, et s'endort.

However, Pope was quite unable to treat this large comic effect as heartily as it deserved: he felt it would be crude to explain it fully, to dwell on the joke; and so he glossed it over with the dangerously weak and pompous phrase, "the Muse obeys the power." The grand series of episodes tails off into a line of asterisks and a peroration. [57]

Pope was, as his enemies remarked, a great copyist. He copied Vergil in the *Pastorals* and the *Messiah*, Horace in the *Essays*, Ovid in *Eloisa to Abelard*, to say nothing of his direct translations and adaptations like *Sappho and Phaon*, the *Epistles*, and the *Satires*. He was in fact the ideal Augustan poet: a well-read man with a firm grasp of the heroic couplet. Therefore both his large satires are parodies: *The Rape of the Lock* is a toy *Iliad*, and the *Dunciad* is a mock *Aeneid*. But the fault of the *Dunciad* is simply that it is not parodic enough. Vast swatches of it are not amusingly incongruous description, but simple allegory. Dulness distributing her commands to her court in 4, Cibber's vision of the Dark Ages in 2, and many other large effects are not satire at all, but frank symbolism: and as such, they must fail. Nothing in *The Rape of the Lock* is allegorical—the death of the King of Clubs and the apotheosis of Belinda's curl are simply poetic fantasies, described with exquisite mock-heroic pomp. If the loss of the curl and the warnings of Ariel had con-

---

[56] I.e. Dulness comes, not the Muse.

[57] Another sign of uncertainty: it is not the empire of Dulness which is restored after all, but that of her father Chaos (1.12, 4.653).

veyed some hidden moral to mankind, the delicate structure of the poem would have crumbled to the ground beneath its weight. There is a parallel case in medieval literature. Late in the twelfth century Jean de Hauteville wrote a Latin satire more than twice as long as the *Dunciad*, called *Architrenius, The Super-sorrower*. He had a remarkable command of the language, and his parodies show that he knew quite as much classical literature as Pope. But his rich and powerful verses, like the muscular couplets of the *Dunciad*, hang dismally on one of the bony allegorical frameworks beloved of the Middle Ages. The hero Architrenius visits the Palace of Venus, the Abode of Gluttony, the Mountain of Ambition, and so forth; until finally Mother Nature marries him to the beauteous Moderation. As a whole, the poem is almost impossibly tedious: for it is, like the *Dunciad*, an exasperating blend of excellent satiric verse with a solemn inappropriate mechanical plot. Both de Hauteville and Pope might well have taken a lesson from classical satire, which is never allegorical.[58] Without his passion for allegorical instruction, without his too obvious moral-aesthetic intention, Pope could well have narrated, say, the life of Cibber, in the same mock-heroic vein which he strikes so happily for twenty or thirty lines in Book 1:

> Swearing and supperless the hero sate,
> Blasphemed his gods, the dice, and damned his fate.

John Philips had published a fine fragment of just such a comic epic, in *The Splendid Shilling*, nearly a generation before; and if Pope had written a literary *Don Quixote*, or rather a *Sanchiad*, a typical but not allegorical mock-epic life of a bad poet, it would have been as amusing and unexpected as *The Rape of the Lock*, and would have crushed Pope's enemies far more violently and finally than the anticlimax which results from the fundamental misconception of the *Dunciad*.

III

There is one more major fault in the *Dunciad*, which has often been felt, but seldom remarked. It is the fault to which all satirists are

[58] Its rare personifications, like Malaria in Seneca's *Apocolocyntosis*, or Greed and Extravagance in Persius 5, are accounted for by adherence to tradition. Malaria, for example, was a real goddess, who had shrines in most Italian cities; while Greed and Extravagance are relics of the Stoic and Cynic sermon, with its personification of conflicting vices and virtues.

naturally prone, which Persius and his imitator Donne never overcame, over which Juvenal and Byron triumphantly soared, and which Pope himself in *The Rape of the Lock* surmounted with ease. It is that the tempo of the poem is awkward. Comparatively long passages of smoothly consecutive rhythm are succeeded by abrupt jolting couplets, in which a new subject or a new point of view is suggested every four or six lines. One page can be read continuously—it carries you on through a rich full stream of rhetoric or narrative, strong but graceful, powerful but equable. The next is full of choppy little waves, in which you can neither advance nor rest.

The reason for this is not primarily the breadth of the field over which Pope's satire is ranging. In his first satire, Juvenal surveys the whole of Rome, and furiously asks if the vast sinful city, as it stands, is not an ample justification for writing satire. "Shall I not," he asks, [59]

> "shall I not gladly fill a bulging notebook
> at each street-corner?"

Nevertheless, he mentions by name or pseudonym only sixteen contemporaries in 171 lines: rather less than one every ten lines. Besides these, he has fourteen names of mythical, and eight of historical personages. Seven (nearly half) of the contemporary names in his poem occur in ten crowded lines: two gigolos are mentioned in one line, and four informers in a line and a half, to produce a sudden shocking effect of multiplicity. But that trick is not repeated elsewhere in the poem. Yet suppose that Pope had been writing the satire, and that he had (as was almost inevitable) used the technique of the *Dunciad*. He would have seized the opportunity to turn a savage and annihilating drumfire on *all* his enemies. In every three lines, another little fortification would have crumbled. The air would have been filled with the crash of masonry, the screams of the wounded, the gasps of the dying. Pope (like Asian monarchs) would have chalked up the names of his opponents, and crossed them off, one by one, as his artillery disposed of them, For the Asian monarch, it would have been exquisitely satisfactory. For the reader, it would be as painful and as tedious as other civil wars.

Now, Juvenal's field could scarcely have been broader than the whole corrupt metropolis. In Satire 10 he professes to survey mankind from China to Peru *a Gadibus usque Auroram et Gangen*, and he actually covers twelve hundred years of history, from Priam to Hadrian. Yet, even there, he mentions far fewer ancients or contemporaries than Pope, in a

[59] 1.63.

passage of comparable length in the *Dunciad*. But Juvenal's technique, and the technique of all classical satirists, is to combine bold generalizations with vivid details, and occasionally, lightly, illustratively, to throw in a topical gibe, a contemporary name.

Modern readers, with no contemporary knowledge and with inadequate help from the scholia, find these topical jokes hardest to understand, and so, very often, most memorable. They tend to believe that the brief slaps at Codrus and Cluvienus [60] were the center of Juvenal's attention when he was writing his first satire. These references are indeed very cryptic: fascinatingly dark. Many of them were intended to elicit a brief shout of laughter when the satire was recited, and their subsequent history interested the author no more. Like Aristophanic comedy, Latin satire was a blend of the topical and the eternal. Therefore the topical could not be eliminated from even the most general satire; and so we shall never know who was the Jew Apella, [61] or the huge Vulfennius, hater of philosophy, [62] or Procula, who was too big for Codrus's bed, [63] or the murderous financier Basilus. [64] But these passing taunts, interesting as they appear, are only arrows shot at a venture. They neither help nor hinder the main interest. Why does Horace suddenly drag in the Jew Apella, or Persius the huge Vulfennius? Simply in order to personify an abstract point of view. Classical satirists always strive to be vivid. They will not say "I went to school," but "I twitched my hand away from the rod." [65] Similarly, they will not say "This is silly superstition," but "Let the Jew Apella believe this." I conceive that they may have borrowed this device from the Attic comedians, to whom they owed so much. [66] In an Athenian theater it would be enormously effective. When the comic slave, trying to excuse some inexcusable absence, said "I was off on an expedition against Sparta, with Cleisthenes," he would look knowingly at the audience, and the audience would roar with laughter—because Cleisthenes, whose cowardice and debauchery they all knew, was sitting among them at that moment. Perhaps it was under the influence of the Cynic and Stoic sermon, which also liked illustrative references to notorious

[60] 1.2, 1.80.

[61] Horace, *Serm.* 1.5.100.

[62] Persius 5.190.

[63] Juvenal 3.203.

[64] Juvenal 10.222. There are many who regret with equal fervor that the scholiast to Mr. Sherlock Holmes tells us nothing about the Paradol Chamber, or Wilson, the notorious canary-trainer, or the singular affair of the aluminium crutch. (See *The Five Orange Pips, Black Peter, The Musgrave Ritual.*)

[65] Juvenal 1.15.

[66] Horace, *Serm.* 1.4.1f.

contemporaries, that Latin satire took over the trick. Horace's references, though sometimes disguised, were recognizable contemporaries, like Canidia-Gratidia.[67] But those used by Persius and Juvenal were historical w. ...orks, or nonentities, or mere fictions. Apart from Juvenal's one reference to him—or is it two?—and Martial's colorless use of the same name,[68] there is absolutely no proof that Codrus, to whom Pope attaches such ' nportance, ever existed at all. However, the scholastic attitude of the eighteenth century toward classical literature lent such references an enormously exaggerated importance: until at last Pope overweighted and spoiled his own satric poetry with an intolerable load of them, all real, all pointed, and all negligible.

This strikes the reader first in the chaotic fashion of their presentation. Horace's names (pseudonyms or not) are all recognizable Latin or Greco-Latin names. Dryden's are all Biblical and Boileau's all French or pseudo-Greek names. But the *Dunciad* is a bewildering mixture of real appellations (Withers, Ward, and Gildon[69]), English pseudonyms (Bayes, Paridel[70]), classical nicknames (Theocles, Silenus, Palinurus[71]), cryptic initials ("Great C**, H**, P**, R**, K*"[72]), and even asterisks ("Then * essayed"[73]).

Besides that confusion, the sheer number of Pope's proper names is greater than those of any other satirist. Take a specimen count.[74] In Juvenal 3, which surveys all Rome and contains 321 lines, there are forty-eight proper names, of which twenty-three denote his contemporaries. In Horace 2.3, which has a theme of comparable breadth and contains 326 lines, there are fifty-four names, thirty being contemporaries. In the first book of the *Dunciad*, with 330 lines, there are thirty-six names of contemporaries and eighty-nine names altogether.

This multitudinous variety could never be molded into a unity, unless in a scheme far larger than any satirist like Pope could possibly envisage. The catalogues in *Iliad* 2 and *Aeneid* 7 are long processions of pomp and heraldry, but they fit into the immense epic pattern. Contrast Pope's own mock-epyllion, *The Rape of the Lock*, where within the first

---

[67] Horace, *Serm.* 1.8.
[68] 3.15.84. Martial himself (1 pref., 2.23, etc.) says he uses fictitious names.
[69] 1.296.
[70] 1.108, 4.340.
[71] 4.488, 492, 612.
[72] 4.545.
[73] 2.295.
[74] Repetitions of one name within a few lines, as at *Dunciad* 1.320–24, are omitted; separate occurrences of the same name at some distance, as that of Molière in *Dunciad* 1.132 and 1.254, are separately counted.

320 lines he names only ten mythical and seven real personages: hence the exquisite Mozartian economy of the poem—a heroic operetta in one act, played by marionettes and accompanied by a muted string quartet. Nevertheless, Pope might have been more successful in marshaling his interminable procession if he had made it march in one direction and kept it together. But we have already seen that Dulness and her only-begotten Cibber do not engage in one continuous course of action: still less do their satellites. And unity was impossible without repetitions, which would have been intolerable, or action, of which Pope seems to have been incapable. The four books of the poem are all overburdened with mere catalogues of "the race that write." Like the four voyages of Gulliver—though their scope is more limited—they are four different ways of looking at human foolishness and foulness. 1.291–310, 2 entire, 3.139–332, and 4.101–564 are virtually nothing but versified reviews, where Mr. Pope's enemies appear now as contending athletes, now as courtiers, and now as prodigies of the impending future. Hence the bewilderment which overcomes the reader as he finds a constant stream of new personages passing rapidly before his eyes, never to reappear. Curll enters momentarily as a publisher in 1 and 3, at length as an athlete in 2, and nowhere else. Handel (of all people) is suddenly brought in and pushed out in 4. Henley the preacher appears for an instant in 3, preaching in implied competition with three other fanatics and three bishops (all carefully named), and then vanishes. Apart from Book 2, where the competition-scheme gives a certain appropriateness to these quick entrances and exits, the only really effective appearance is that of Bentley in 4.203. As Walker reverently takes his hat off for him, he nods bluntly to Queen Dulness, makes an admirably characteristic speech, and is suddenly offended by the sight of a too-much-traveled youth, fresh from the Grand Tour:

> "Walker! our hat—" nor more he deigned to say,
> But, stern as Ajax' spectre, strode away.

He at least remains in our mind. He has occupied it for 71 lines, 4% of the entire poem, and more than one-tenth of the fourth book. But by those numerous cursory epigrammatic mentions of others, Pope (though tactically successful) made a grave strategic error. He hurt his victims at the time. His passing blows wounded them deeply, but not to death. They remain, mutilated and suffering. By their very existence they accuse him of cruel shortsighted malice. If they were worthy objects of satire, they deserved ampler and heavier attacks. If they were not, they should have been left to oblivion, blindly scattering her poppy.

Addison, said Pope in his famous character-sketch,[75] was willing to wound and yet afraid to strike. Mr. Pope himself was seldom afraid to strike, and he was more than willing to wound. But either by his many injuries, or by his friend Swift's rancorous precepts, he was fatally misled. His blows were actually too well directed. Satire is, as we have said, a blend of the particular and topical with the general, the eternal. Pope in the *Dunciad* concentrates so carefully on the particular that he never sees the general, or sees it falsely.

After all, what is the lesson which the poem is intended to convey? It is the obvious falsehood that London, England, civilization generally were in 1720 being invaded by the irresistible forces of barbarism: that the arts were expiring, truth and philosophy disappearing, science, wit, and the muses being enchained for ever. Not only was this false in fact— at that time; but Pope himself did not believe it. He thought, like most of the Augustans, that his own age was the culmination of a long process of refinement beginning with the Renaissance, when the Goths vanished. The *Essay on Criticism* culminates with a sort of anti-Dunciad.[76] The progress of wit is traced from Aristotle through Longinus to Erasmus and the Renaissance, and thence to France, where "Boileau still in right of Horace sways." True, Pope declares that his own countrymen despised the laws of taste, "and kept unconquered and uncivilized"; but he adds that even in Britain there were some who understood taste, and "restored wit's fundamental laws." Similarly, in his imitation of the first epistle in Horace's second book, he devotes a long passage[77] to the growing delicacy of taste induced by French influence:

> Britain to soft refinement less a foe,
> Wit grew polite, and numbers learned to flow. . . .

All his work, except the *Dunciad*, is infused with a spacious baroque optimism which is directly opposed to the thesis that sin and barbarism are spreading wider and wider through the whole world. Much of it does indeed contain fierce criticism of individual barbarities or barbarians. But only in the *Dunciad* are these separate criticisms transcended by a general indictment of the human race.

There are two possible reasons for this exaggeration. One is that Pope himself was so acutely sensitive to aesthetic vulgarity that his exac-

---

[75] *Prologue to the Satires* 203.
[76] 3.643f.
[77] 263f.

erbated nerves perverted his clear mind.[78] The other is that Swift's universal hatred of mankind here infected Pope's kinder nature, and convinced him of the justice of an indictment which at all other times he knew to be, like Gulliver's *Voyage to the Country of the Houyhnhnms*, a savage hyperbole. Remembering Pope's penchant for the catalogue-poem in general, we may well conclude that both these reasons are simultaneously true. Which was the stronger? Our answer to that question must depend on our view of the characters of Swift and Pope. Johnson says of Swift that "he seems to have wasted life in discontent, by the rage of neglected pride and the languishment of unsatisfied desire"; and his last years were spent in impenetrable darkness, grief, and silence. Pope died after four days' delirium, in the intervals of which "he was always saying something kind either of his present or absent friends," so that "his humanity seemed to have survived his understanding." When Bolingbroke was told this he said, "I never in my life knew a man that had so tender a heart for his particular friends, or a more general friendship for mankind."

[78] This is the view expressed by Miss Edith Sitwell in her biography, *Alexander Pope* (London, 1930).

The Myth of Sisyphus

DURING HIS long voyage home Odysseus visited the world of the dead. Among them he talked with the seer Tiresias, and with his own mother, and with his comrade Agamemnon, who told how he had been murdered. Others among the dead he saw, but did not converse with them. He could not, partly because he was a prudent man and partly because they could not speak. They were the great sinners, condemned to eternal life in torment.

One of these was Sisyphus, who had been the cleverest man in the world. He had outwitted cunning men and powerful gods, and for a while even baffled death. But now his punishment had come, and would never end. Up a steep mountain, with heart-bursting effort, he pushed a huge rock, upward and upward toward the summit; and always, just before it reached the top, it halted and escaped him and rolled downhill faster and faster until it reached level ground; and there it lay waiting for him to make his way down again and put his shoulder and hands to it and start it up again once more, and once more, and once more. . . .

Sisyphus is the key figure in a book published by Albert Camus thirty years ago, *The Myth of Sisyphus: Essay on the Absurd*. It is still being reprinted and read; but it is far from easy reading. It throws out unfamiliar names as though we ought to know all about them: Max Scherer, a religious philosopher of the 'twenties; Kirillov, a character in Dostoevski's *Possessed*; and so on. It is couched in that peculiar style in which the French love to talk and write about abstract ideas: exquisitely cadenced, apparently quite lucid, often glittering with starry epigrams and diamond-sharp paradoxes, yet sometimes without any trace of that close

Unpublished, appearing here for the first time.

logical structure which, upon an observed fact or an admitted principle, will base a series of interconnected thoughts, clearly and firmly integrated. Both in his conversation and in his books such as *The Museum without Walls*, André Malraux is the perfect exemplar of this style. Albert Camus is less learned and less impatient than Malraux, but he still gleams with the same unstable radiance.

The Myth of Sisyphus is not about mythology. (In fact, Camus now and then gets his myths slightly wrong, poeticizing them so that they will make more easily handled symbols.) It is about human life, not in modern France, not in twentieth-century society, not in the world of history past and present, but in the universe. Man, living for fifty or sixty or seventy years. The cosmos, constantly changing and yet apparently permanent. What have these two to do with each other? Or rather, what is the meaning of man's short life within this eternal and infinite space and time?

This is not a stupid question or a superficial one. Maybe it is impossible to answer. But it has confronted everyone who has ever thought hard and steadily—I shall not say about his own destiny, but about the human race on this planet; and even more about the rest of the cosmos. The other living things, which neither know nor care about humanity— the myriad myriad insects in jungles and deserts, and the pullulating life which we can see only through microscopes; and the superhuman energies—the sun, the stars, the galaxies, all that unimaginable and incomprehensible profusion of power and vitality which astounds astronomers: what have we to do with all that? It is a mass of mighty mysteries; and within it our existence is a small mystery. Small, but to us—if we think— important.

How important?

It is, says Camus, a matter of life and death. The first words of his first chapter are "There is only one really important philosophical problem: suicide. To decide whether life is or is not worth living is to answer the fundamental question of philosophy."

This is striking. But is it true? Camus does not indulge in genuine philosophical discussion after the pattern of Aristotle or Descartes or Spinoza. Instead, he makes a bold assertion (evidently the end product of years of lonely reading and meditation) and then moves off from there into darkness shot with lightning flashes.

Is suicide the only topic which most philosophers have treated as important? Obviously not. Few philosophical thinkers have even discussed it at length. Some of them concentrate on metaphysics, analyzing such problems as the nature of time. Some think about thought itself, asking what knowledge is, and how it is conveyed or distorted by speech. Those who deal with ethics usually discuss what the good life is, and not whether life itself is good.

Or does Camus mean that the only problem of a philosophical nature which worries most ordinary nonphilosophical men and women is whether they should commit suicide or not? If so, his statement is—to use his favorite word in a crude sense—absurd. Of course there are some countries (Switzerland, for instance, and Japan) where suicide is not uncommon and many people must give it serious thought. But consider the billions and billions of human beings all struggling for life! Consider the misery in which millions of them live, and which they could escape with one blow of a knife or one leap into a river! Think of the refugees and the beggars, the cripples and the prisoners, who long to go on living in agony, when rest and peace and annihilation are within their easy grasp!

Then Camus must mean that suicide is for him, and ought to be for us if we understood our predicament, the sole important problem. Why? Because, if life is not worth living, we must kill ourselves. Yet the vast majority of the human race does believe that, even in a sodden jungle or the polar ice, even in a concentration camp or a brutal slum, life is worth living. What do they see in it which Camus does not see? and what does he see as wrong with it, which they see as right, or at least acceptable?

Here his argument becomes more eloquent and more obscure; but the essence of it is that we do not understand the world. To understand the world is to enter fully into it, to feel that all is One, of which we are a part and a necessary part. But sometimes the world seems absurd. "Get up, dress, drive to work, work, eat, work, drive home, eat, sleep, Monday Tuesday Wednesday Thursday Friday, the routine is easy to follow most of the time. Then, one day, we are faced with a WHY?" And that Why may end in suicide, says Camus. It may; but for billions of people it does not, and never will. Death too is absurd, he adds. Yes, but for all that the survivors do not kill themselves. They bury the dead and return home and go on living.

For Camus, understanding the world goes deeper than it does for most of us. His problem is that the world cannot be comprehended by the intellect. Here and there a group of phenomena may be systematized and illuminated by a special science, at least for a time. The whole cannot be explained, not even conceived as a whole from the microbe to the metagalaxy. Therefore it is absurd. Not ridiculous, not grotesque, but beyond reason.

Although striking, *absurd* is a poor word for the concept, and has led to some misunderstandings. The idea is ultimately a mathematical one. The Greek thinkers who first worked on mathematics were impressed by the fact that numbers seemed to constitute an intelligible realm of their own, full of secret and yet comprehensible properties, and containing such curious intricacies as the series of "perfect" numbers, each of which is the sum of its divisors: $6 (= 1 + 2 + 3)$, $28 (= 1 + 2 + 4 + 7 + 14)$, 496, etc. But they soon came on certain ratios which could not "make sense" in this way. Why should the diameter of a circle have such an incomprehensible relation to its circumference as 3.14159265358979384626 . . . and so on in a series as endless as the task of Sisyphus? Such a relation they called irrational, because it could not be fitted into a neat category of reason. (Modern explanations of the behavior of electrons, which are from one point of view particles and from another point of view forces or waves, are in this sense irrational.) The Romans took over the concept "irrational," but translated it rather poorly as "inharmonious," in Latin *absurdus*, and thence it came into English and other modern languages. Shakespeare got it right when it was quite new: He made King Claudius say to Hamlet that his exaggerated and prolonged mourning was "to reason most absurd" (1.2.103).

The world, then, is absurd (Camus proposes) because human reason cannot understand it. Before Camus, several philosophers had said that only God could give meaning to the world, and that if man could no longer believe in God his life became meaningless. Thus, to a God-fearing man who had lost his faith, reason would suggest suicide: indeed Jacques Maritain and his wife, when temporarily in such a situation, resolved to kill themselves. Camus mentions this point, but rather neglects it, since he seems to have been little moved by religion. Instead, as a true French intellectual, he deifies Reason. If Reason cannot solve the problems of the universe and of man's life within it, then the universe must be—now comes the catchword, ABSURD. Strange how the choice of an adjective can color one's thinking. Absurd implies *inadequate, unsatisfactory, an intellectual failure*. But surely it is the intellect that fails. Why should we expect the human mind to comprehend the universe? Can the human eye see all there is in the night sky, or even look at the sun? Can our senses receive the multitudinous messages reaching the earth from space? At the end of the Book of Job, God asks Job a number of hard questions about the cosmos. To none of them does Job attempt to reply. He bows his head, and says, "I have spoken of great things which I have not understood, things too wonderful for me to know." It is a pity that the teaching of Henri Bergson is presently neglected: for one of his central principles was that the intellect, though a useful tool for solving practical difficulties, was a poor and limited instrument for understanding such great problems.

Meanwhile, far in the background, we see Sisyphus doggedly pushing the rock up the mountain again and again, and again and again to all eternity it thunders back downward. What has Sisyphus to do with all this?

He is, for Camus, a symbol of man in an "absurd" world—or, more precisely, of an intellectual surrounded by a universe which defies his efforts to comprehend his place in it. Sisyphus cannot die, he can never stop his endless labor; and yet as long as he exists and suffers and works, he has (according to Camus) vanquished his destiny—because he despises it. Then, on the last page, comes the final paradox: "we must imagine Sisyphus as happy." To live without hope is a victory.

But this is false, both to the myth and to life. Sisyphus was in hell, damned for ever. He was worse than the captive Samson, "eyeless in Gaza, at the mill with slaves." Had he been happy even for an instant, had he been but proud and confident, the Furies would have sharpened and intensified his punishment. A greater being than he, the Titan Prometheus, was crucified on a cliff far in the frosty Caucasus because he rebelled against Zeus; and, when he was still defiant, was swallowed up within the earth, to be worse tormented there for many ages. So would it have been with Sisyphus, had he been for one moment happy in hell.

And in our world, a disillusioned intellectual may, although suicide would be logical for him, continue to live as an affirmation of pride in his selfhood. But why do most people continue to live?

Most, because they think of others: chiefly of their families. "What will happen to them if I go?" says many a despairing woman. "I can't leave her to fight it alone," says many a wretched man. Loyalty to family, to friends, to a group or institution keeps men and women alive, in two senses: it prevents them from committing suicide when they are gloomy, and it gives their lives a fuller meaning than mere individualism. (Throughout his book Camus speaks always of a man entirely alone with the universe.) In Greek legend there was one hero who survived more dangers and temptations and sorrows than all the others: he lived all through the Trojan War and helped to win it, he lost his fleet and all his men on the way back, but he reached home safely. He was close to death a hundred times, and often in mortal despair, but he never thought of killing himself. He had a home, a loyal wife, a young son, and faithful servants; and he was determined to regain that home and family. They kept him alive when he was far from them. Many a man who thinks of suicide and rejects it is an Odysseus.

There are others, both men and women, who live for themselves alone: but not for Reason, not for achievement, certainly not for their families or friends, but for pleasure. They have never known and never will know the difference between pleasure and happiness. Pleasure is brief and temporary, and must constantly be renewed or changed. Happiness, though never permanent, can be long-lasting, and grows better as it lasts. Yet the pleasures of food and sex, of drink and drugs, of possession and display, these and others close to them are the mainsprings of life for millions and millions of people. Experimenters on animals have discovered a small area in the brain which, if stimulated by an electric wire, gives intense pleasure to the animal. If they fix this wire into the brain of a rat and couple it to a switch which the rat can press, it will go on pressing it again and again till it falls exhausted. Many of us are like the rat, except that, being human and therefore more versatile, we keep experimenting on ourselves and finding new areas to stimulate. Ultimately, we fall exhausted. By will power we can control the pleasure principle, by intelligence we can divert attention and energy from flowing into it, but we can never satisfy it. When under its domination (a domination easily established by habit and surrender) we always want more and more and more . . . into an endless series, which is absurd. Yet for many people it is the sole reason for staying alive.

Just before seeing Sisyphus in the underworld, Odysseus observed another sinner: Tantalus, who had tried to cheat the gods into eating human flesh at a banquet. As a punishment he was made perpetually hungry and thirsty. He stood in water up to his neck, with sweet ripe fruit dangling above his head; but whenever he bent to drink, the water sank down, and whenever he grasped at the fruit, it sprang upward out of reach. It was impossible for him to drink the water or eat the fruit; it was impossible for him to repress his longing for them; and the longing was the essence of his immortal life, his eternal damnation. Are we to think of Tantalus as happy?

A Socrates Dialogue

AN UGLY man was questioning a quiet man. The ugly man smiled, talking fluently in a versatile voice which could convey any emotion except
anger. The quiet man looked worried and spoke slowly, but sounded
fairly sure of himself, too. He had on a gray suit, rather wrinkled. The
other, the ugly man, wore a shapeless knee-length work-shirt and was
barefooted.

The ugly man was Socrates, and he was talking to Maxwell Anderson, who had called him back from Athens to the present day.

"I used to ask playwrights why they wrote their plays," he said. "They
loved talking about show business. Sophocles would chat for hours about
the difficulties of casting and a new boy-star he had just discovered. But
they could never tell me just why they wrote their dramas. They could
never explain what they meant the plays to say. They couldn't even tell
me why they chose one story instead of another. Now, I am still anxious
to find out. I wonder if you can tell me why you chose to write a play
about anyone so insignificant as the son of Sophroniscus?"

"You mean, why I wrote a play about you, Socrates?"

"If you know, and if you care to tell me, yes."

"I wanted to write a play about the freedom of the human mind."

"Yes, I understood that. But why did you choose to write it about
me? There have been many other men who knew more than I."

"Perhaps, Socrates. But there have been very few whose minds were
as free as yours."

"Oh, surely. Let us think again. Why didn't you choose my friend
Democritus? Or my other friend Abelard?"

Reprinted from *New York Herald Tribune* (October 28, 1951) section 4, pp. 1–2.

"To tell you the truth—"

"What else is worth telling?"

"—the public knows you, and it does not know them."

Socrates laughed. "You mean that my ugly face will catch the public fancy? That is possible. One of my friends used to say that I looked like a hideous statuette with a bottle of fine perfume hidden inside."

"They know the face and the name already, Socrates. And I hope that, through my play, they will learn to love the mind concealed within."

Socrates laughed again. "Well, whether that is worth doing or not is a question which we must leave for some other time. But at least you have told me why you chose to write about this particular snub-nosed, barefooted, inquisitive Athenian. Now tell me something else. Why did you change the story?"

"In what way, Socrates?"

"My wife Xanthippe is always said to have been a terrible shrew. She beat me, they say, and neglected me. So they say. Why did you change the story so as to make her lovable and loving? What makes you think that I loved her and she loved me?"

"I think the story was wrong, Socrates. I think those who knew you were bound to love you. I believe some of your enemies, or some of those who didn't understand you."

"The only enemies we have are those who do not understand us."

"Yes, some of those, or some journalists who wanted cheap contrasts to make slashing effects, invented the tale that the wisest man in Greece had a wife who did not love him and whom he could not control."

For a moment, Socrates was silent.

"Was I right, Socrates?"

"She never left me. She gave me children. When the executioner came for me with the poison, she wept."

"And yet, Socrates—"

"Yes?"

"I wonder why you never spoke out in favor of marriage. I wonder why you suggested that the rulers of your Republic should have wives in common. I wonder why you spoke of love without mentioning the love of husband and wife."

"Perhaps you have been reading Plato, my dear sir. Remember that he was only one of my pupils, and that he had predilections of his own, which I could control, but not remove."

"You are saying, then—?"

Again the formidable smile, broad and toothy under the blunt nose and the keen eyes and the armored brow.

"I am saying nothing, my dear sir. I am enjoying the pleasure of questioning you, and of following the argument where it leads. Tell me now, why did you make me into a defender of democracy? Did you ever hear any of my young friends say I admired democracy?"

"No, Socrates. That worried me. It still worries me. Your pupil Alcibiades sold out his country. Your pupil Critias became a dictator and tried to kill you. Your pupil Plato spent his life proving that democracy was inefficient and idiotic, a government of the stupid, by the slippery for the time being. Your other pupils, as far as I can see, became scientists, or soldiers of fortune, or professional philosophers, or something equally remote. Did you really teach them to understand and enjoy democracy? Did you really show them how it was superior to the aggressive Communism of the Spartans?"

"Surely I must have done so. Your play shows that I did."

"Yes, but was I right when I showed you doing so?"

"Let us see. Did I fight for Athens against her enemies?"

"You did, Socrates, and bravely, they tell me."

"Did I always obey her laws?"

"You did. When they indicted you, it was on a trumped-up charge."

"That may be so. But did I accept the verdict of the democratic jury?"

"You did, Socrates. Even when the jailer was ready to open the door, you refused to escape. You took the poison from his unwilling hand. Even though you believed the verdict of the jury was wrong, you drank the poison."

"Of course I did. Don't you think that anyone would, if he believed as I believed?"

The playwright was silent.

"Tell me, my friend."

"Not everyone would, Socrates. Some would say that it merely proved democracy was wrong. They would say that you had spent your life trying to improve and purify your own country, and that it rewarded you by arresting and murdering you, because a democracy has no brains, only numbers."

"I believe I have heard people say that."

"Others would say something worse. They would say that you always hated the democracy of Athens. They would say you spent your life doing it outward service and undermining its foundations, teaching young men to question everything and believe nothing. And they would say you were finally exposed, and got what you had earned by forty years of anti-democratic propaganda which helped to ruin the finest democracy of your own world and time."

"I think that they might say these things. I should like to meet them, and to talk over what they say. Perhaps, with reason guiding us in our discussions, we might discover that both of these groups were wrong. Or, at least, we might find that they did not really know what they were talking about."

"Yes," said the playwright, "they would."

"But we cannot know—until we can discuss it fully and calmly. And that is what I was trying to tell the Athenians: that they should not believe anything until they had discussed it fully, and calmly, and at leisure," Socrates said.

The playwright still brooded.

"My friend, you look worried?"

"I am still wondering, Socrates, about that painful question. Why is it that, if you yourself believed in democracy, and spent your life teaching the democratic state to improve itself by free self-criticism, your pupils seem to have turned away from it?"

"My pupils?"

"Yes, your most famous pupils. In my play I show your own pupil Critias sentencing you to death because you will not be a judge on a packed court to carry out his policies. And nearly all the others seem to have gone wrong, too."

For the last time, the famous smile of Socrates, hideous and attractive. "Now I believe you are using a wrong definition. Unless I am wrong, you are taking 'the pupils of Socrates' to mean the few young men who knew me personally and talked with me—before my execution?"

"Yes, I was doing so. Was I wrong?"

"Let us think again, my friend. I do not claim to teach anybody. Yet perhaps I have helped to show the way to many men who were perplexed. And quite a number of them have thought that a man who loved Athens and gave up his life rather than desert her must be a true lover of democracy."

"If that is true, Socrates, your pupils in your lifetime and just afterward were few; and most of them were bad, or distracted. But in the last 2,000 years you have had many thousands of pupils who did not think like Plato or behave like Critias. You are still teaching."

"Do you really think so, my friend?"

"I do, Socrates."

"Then, if that is true, you must be my newest pupil; and not, I hope, my last."

A Memorandum: From Seneca to Tennessee Williams

THIS IS a fan message. You may never have heard of me: after all, I have been dead a long time. Still, I was, like you, a playwright. Like you, I loved to dominate and to horrify my audiences, and I had considerable success. My dramas have been read, off and on, for nineteen centuries. I saw them all performed during my lifetime, with an emperor as the male lead. Some of my best effects were borrowed by later dramatists, quite shamelessly. Will Shakespeare tells me he thought it was not plagiarism when he did so, but a genuine tribute to an Old Master.

You will meet us in due course, at the Dramatists' Club. We always discuss the new plays and watch the development of promising talents like yours. There are several points I want to argue with you; but meanwhile I must express my admiration for your work. Strikingly original— that is its first and perhaps its greatest merit. Even your titles: *The Glass Menagerie, A Streetcar Named Desire, The Rose Tattoo, Twenty-seven Wagons Full of Cotton, Sweet Bird of Youth.* Superb!

Equally original are your plots. Of course it is difficult to do as I did, to take a story so old that it has been used three hundred times and still to make it into an arresting piece of drama. But I think it must be even harder to invent stories which are apparently brand-new and which (although they sometimes seem crazy) still hold together and leave an indelible impression on the audience. Will used to lift all his plots straight out of history books and anthologies of short stories. He defends this by saying that no dramatist can out-invent life, which is always creating staggeringly new plot-lines. Still, I know he envies you your gift of drawing brilliant ideas out of your own strange experience and fertile invention. So do I.

Reprinted from *Horizon* 1.5 (May 1959) 54–55.

But I have a bit of advice for you about a special dramatic effect in which you have almost rivaled me: horror. Already you have made your men and women say things on the stage that paralyze your audiences with disgust and abhorrence. But why stop with words? Is it because you are still a little afraid of the public? Don't think of them as human beings. A minor member of our Dramatists' Club calls them *les cochons de payants*, which is vulgar Latin for "those swine the customers." Treat them with the contempt you feel for them. Humiliate them, as you humiliate your characters. Degrade them. You have shocked them by your words. Go further, dear boy: shock them by your actions.

Near the end of the third act of *Streetcar*, Stanley Kowalski, furious with lust, grips the perverted flower Blanche in his arms and forces her toward his bed. Then the music swells out and the curtain comes quickly down. In your next play, keep that curtain up. It will add very little to the running time of the show, and a great deal to its effectiveness. As for actors, it should be easy to find sufficiently agile performers, although for matinees you might have to get an understudy. Consult Equity.

At first a few squeamish spectators may expostulate, and there will be protests from occasional groups representing special interests; but such complaints will soon be drowned under a general wave of enthusiasm. In their own homes, your public watches romantic dramas in which, every evening, several men are struck in the face and body, tortured, and shot to death with guns or stabbed with knives; while at least once a week a girl is ravished or brutalized. I need scarcely mention the popular dramas about werewolves and nonhuman monsters. Once upon a time, perhaps, the effects I suggest might have seemed objectionable. Now they belong to the next stage of dramatic exploration. Be courageous. Innovate.

So, in the second act of *Cat on a Hot Tin Roof*, when Big Daddy realizes that he is dying, riddled with cancer, you should use the wonderful invention of light-pictures to cover the backstage wall with gigantic cancer cells, inhabiting the house that Big Daddy built, living and moving and proliferating. At the end of that same play, the curtain comes down some minutes too soon. It is absurd to have such an appetizing creature as Barbara Bel Geddes or Elizabeth Taylor beseeching a young husband to go to bed and make love to her against his will, and I have noticed some male spectators going away from the theater in fits of laughter, slapping their knees and pinching their wives and declaring, with many a bold phrase, that the climax was meant to be funny. But, my dear colleague, if you kept the curtain up for ten or fifteen minutes more, you would have a truly serious climax, combining two of your favorite themes, profound male humiliation and savage female hysterics.

You have a marvelous dramatic sense, but you are in danger of blunting it and wasting your creative energy. Let me give you an example from my own experience. In one of my own plays I brought off a powerful climax. An old father cursed his son and prayed God for the son's death. The son was thrown from a runaway chariot. His mangled remains were brought back to his home. On the stage, with infinite grief and remorse, the father picked out the fragments of flesh and bone, put the torn limbs together, and reassembled the shattered body for burial. One of my most successful scenes!

My pupil Nero, after starring in some of my plays, went me one better. He was producing a show about the aeronaut Icarus. Nero had him fall screaming out of the sky, to smash upon the stage with such an impact that his blood bespattered the audience. That is the direction in which you ought to work. You threw away a great opportunity in *Suddenly Last Summer*. I suggest that you rewrite it, using the technique of the flashback and introducing a genuine climax. Instead of merely *hearing* a bemused girl talking about the doom of her perverted cousin, let your audience *see* him on the stage being mobbed, and pulled down, and murdered, and his body being cut up and gnawed to pieces by starving, screaming, naked children.

Yet perhaps you will object that this is too difficult for your theater. I doubt it. Still, if you feel that the stage is too cramped, then use the moving illusions of the lighted screen. For instance, put *Orpheus Descending* into three dimensions. As its last act ends, its lonely hero is being burned to death by a mob leader with a blowtorch. Now, it is not enough for the audience to hear a few unconvincing off-stage squeals. On the big motion-picture screen, they could and should see this fine effect carried out to the end, enabling them to have the full dramatic experience. There are even finer possibilities in a play of yours that has not yet been produced, called (with exquisite perversity) *Not About Nightingales*. At the end of this drama, a group of convicts are roasted alive in a prison cell. Your vision of life, which can never be realized in a three-act conversation within one of your conventional theater stages, will be fulfilled on the huge screen when these images of disintegrating humanity share their agony with the spectators, screaming in their ears, scorching before their eyes, shriveling in the long agony of a climax that is both crime and punishment: a hell in which actors and audience and playwright suffer together until their mortal nature disappears into melting metal, thin ashes, searing flame, and the relief of annihilation.

Nero would have loved that.

Whose *Satyricon*
—Petronius's or Fellini's?

In his film adaptation of Petronius's *Satyricon*[1] Federico Fellini has created a memorable world of imagination. One of his reviewers compared it to an adult Land of Oz—not inappropriately, for his figures and scenery appear to exist in some other dimension, which can be entered only through the doors of hallucination. A gigantic slum tenement crumbling into earthquake-shattered fragments; a dark subterranean bath-establishment full of vaults and tunnels; a nightmare slave-ship, black and misshapen—these and a dozen other spectacles are so strange, and are presented with such clarity by the camera, that they are impossible to forget. The ordered sanity of the filmed *Julius Caesar*, the simple good-and-bad opposition of *Quo Vadis?*, have no place here. It is a real shock, right in the middle of the picture, to be shown a quiet, ordinary home inhabited by a handsome and perfectly sane lady and gentleman, with flowers and birds and running water and civilized manners. But even that home is doomed: the husband—apparently modeled on Thrasea Paetus—frees his slaves and kills himself, followed by his wife. Normal people cannot live in such a world.

Most motion pictures laid in ancient times err by making everyone too straightforward and too modern: Samson is played by Victor Mature, clean-shaven and handsome, without a hair on his chest or armpits; King Arthur, or Henry VIII, or Mark Antony, they all look and talk like Richard Burton, and they are surrounded by ordinary men and women in costume. But Fellini's *Satyricon* is full of abnormal people. A deformed

Reprinted from *Horizon* 12.4 (Autumn 1970) 42–47.
[1] I believe it ought to be *Satyrica*, like Vergil's *Georgica* and Manilius's *Astronomica*, but the other form is apparently established now.

dwarf; a hermaphrodite; an immensely fat woman, half-naked; an ancient hook-nosed crone, bewigged, lipsticked, and chalk-powdered; a maniac tied hand and foot; they bewilder and horrify the onlooker like the visions of Pieter Bruegel.

In a chapter of his book on World War II, *Kaputt*,[2] Curzio Malaparte describes how, after being released from prison in 1943, he returned to Naples at the beginning of an air raid. To escape the bombs, the populace dived into an underground city formed by grottoes and galleries excavated in the Middle Ages. They were followed by a mob of apparitions more terrifying than the bombs: the cripples, the deformed, the monsters who in normal times are kept hidden away by pity, horror, superstition, or family shame—skeletons clothed in rags, old men with dog faces, children with apelike features. They were led by a monarch too dreadful to be seen, a deity shrouded head to foot in a silken coverlet and supported by a group of hideous dwarfs. Slowly, in a sinister silence broken only by a woman's prayer or a child's scream, this procession, like an army of demons returning to hell, entered a cavern and disappeared.

To such a world belong most of the people of Fellini's *Satyricon*. Even when they are normally built, they are masked, or grotesquely painted and ornamented, or else they look ill or drunk or perverted. There is a strong, brutal sea-captain, healthy and vigorous—except that he has one dead, glaring eye. There is a Negro witch, played by Donyale Luna, who is immensely tall and immensely thin, a Masai princess. Apart from Thrasea Paetus and his wife, and their servants, the only normal-looking people I can remember are Encolpius, the strikingly handsome young hero, and Ascyltus, his jaunty young foil, part Iago, part Mephistopheles. There are one or two beautiful women, overdressed and heavily made up—although in Petronius's *Satyricon*, one of the finest episodes concerns a girl too lovely for the hero to describe, with starbright eyes and a mouth like Diana's. Most of the characters in Fellini would be at home in *The Cabinet of Dr. Caligari*.

With some reservations, I believe this is good cinema. The world of Petronius is wild. Reading the narrative, you are often stimulated but often shocked. The hero and his companions hurry from one painful adventure to another. Now they dine with a millionaire whose manners and guests are so vulgar that, first amused and then revolted, they seize the earliest chance to escape. Now they wander into a red-light district, and they are beset by whores and pederasts. Now they take ship, find that the captain is a deadly enemy, and (worst of indignities) disguise them-

[2] Translated by C. Foligno (New York, 1946).

selves as runaway slaves, shaved and branded. When Encolpius gets a pretty and loving girl on a bed of flowers, he becomes impotent. He quarrels with his companion about a young catamite, and tries to hang himself. In other parts of the satire that are now lost, the two heroes, or anti-heroes, apparently had equally agonizing trials: one or another of them appeared as a thief, as a scapegoat doomed to be cast aside after a year's high living, as a gladiator vowed to death.

Since we have only fragments of the original book, no one can reconstruct the main plot with any certainty. But it looks as though it were a parody both of the love-romances, such as Heliodorus's *Aethiopica*, and of Homer's *Odyssey*. The love is not the pure affection of a man and a woman separated by ill fortune, but the disreputable amours of homosexuals and adulterers; and the hero is not a clever prince pursued by the anger of the sea-god Poseidon, but a phenomenally endowed sexual athlete pursued by the anger of the sex-god Priapus. If this, or something like it, is true, then Petronius's *Satyricon* is a bizarre fantasy. It is at the same time more brutally realistic and more grotesquely fanciful than any classical work now extant. Its author has a marvelous ear for low conversation and a wild experience of low life. Other men must have had the second, if not the first; but only one of them has left a comparable book, the *Metamorphoses* of Apuleius, and that, although full of vile and cruel adventures, is far less realistic in style.

When the young emperor Nero was nineteen, he developed the habit of going out slumming. Disguised, he visited bars and brothels and mean streets. He and his companions robbed shops and insulted passers-by, until one night he himself got into a fight and was beaten. Once, long ago, I suggested that Petronius—who was an intimate friend of Nero, and his "arbiter of taste"—wrote the *Satyricon* partly to amuse him, and partly to educate him in the Epicurean manner by showing him how miserable, ridiculous, and dangerous such a roving life actually can be.[3] Of course it is impossible to prove this; yet the book certainly gives a powerful impression of the squalors and miseries endured by homeless wanderers without careers or trades or cash, with dirty pasts and dangerous futures. To match this, Fellini gives us a suitably phantasmagoric story line, jumping from one episode to another with little attention to logical sequence.

Mind you, speaking as a classicist, I thought most of the scenery was painfully improbable. The sinister slave-ship could not have sailed ten miles in a strong Mediterranean breeze. The gladiatorial duel did not

[3] "Petronius the Moralist," *TAPhA* 72 (1941) 176–94.

take place in a proper arena, but in a sand pit without seats or gates, which is like putting a baseball game out in the Jersey swamps. Roman baths in the period of the empire were brilliantly lit and sumptuously decorated; Fellini's baths look like the catacombs or Piranesi ruins. And so on. Yet all these scenes possess a nightmarish vividness.

So much for the characters and scenery. What has Fellini done with the story? The original *Satyricon* of Petronius got through the Dark Ages only in torn and battered copies full of gaps. Sometimes only one sentence survived out of a whole chapter. The beginning is gone. The end is gone. The continuity is lost. We do not even know how long the tale was. A note in one manuscript implies that the millionaire's banquet was Book Fifteen. Now, it runs to over fifty pages. If there were twenty such books, the whole thing would be better than a thousand of our pages, a giant half as long as Proust. (The serious Greek love-romances are pretty long, too, but do not contain so wide a variety of characters and speeches.) Fellini had the problem of making a continuous work of art out of a scarred, fragmentary torso with its head and limbs knocked off. This he has done very well. Encolpius, the anti-hero, with his vicious associates, is projected onto the screen in the first minute; their adventures link on to one another illogically but grippingly; and at the end they suddenly fade away, like modern motorcycle gypsies, into the distance.

The story, however, has been greatly changed. Fellini has introduced many new characters and incidents, has altered many episodes and borrowed some scenes from other sources. He is more than an interpreter of Petronius. He is a competitor. He is a creator. It would take considerable research to trace the sources of all Fellini's innovations, but some can be explained.

Early in the book we see Encolpius and his companions penniless, living in a slum. Petronius says little of its appearance or its inhabitants. But Fellini builds it into an enormous tenement block, populates it with a horde of loathsome men and women, and then has it tremble, sag, and collapse in an earthquake. I believe he thought of this because of the earthquake that partly destroyed Pompeii in Nero's time, and because the satirist Juvenal says:

> Our city is propped up by fragile timbers,
> or most of it. Landlords postpone collapse
> by shoring up, and plastering over the cracks—
> telling us to sleep sound in the tottering ruin.[4]

[4] Juvenal, *Satires* 3.193-96.

Later on the anti-hero, afflicted by temporary impotence, visits an old drunken witch, miserably poor, called Oenothea (Wine-goddess), and is cured. In the film, Oenothea becomes a Negro sorceress, young and handsome in a weird, exotic way. But a flashback gives us some of her history. A wizard once loved her. She humiliated him. He cast a spell that put out all the fires in the vicinity and told the neighbors they could only kindle their fires at her private parts. And so they come in, each with his bit of kindling, and Oenothea is degraded, and the fire catches, and she screams, and his revenge is complete. This is not a classical story at all: it is a medieval tale, and the obscene part of it is Oriental in origin. In the Middle Ages it was told about Vergil (then conceived of not as a poet but as a magician).[5] It is difficult to see what it is doing here, especially since it concerns a subordinate character. Except this: Fellini enjoys showing women lying down and being sexually degraded in public. Petronius does not.

Fellini invents another scene in which a writhing nymphomaniac gets temporary satisfaction from Encolpius and his friend in the presence of her husband; and still another, the most evilly fantastic, in which the hero, after fighting a gladiator dressed as the Minotaur in a labyrinth, is supposed to be Theseus, wins the princess Ariadne, and is expected to possess her before a large audience. Of course he fails, and she is furious. Fellini got this idea, I believe, from Suetonius's biography of Nero, where he says that the degenerate young emperor showed a bull mounting a wooden cow supposedly containing Queen Pasiphae (as in the Cretan legend) "so that many of the spectators believed it." But Fellini's scene is cruder and more realistic. Nor does Ariadne look like the pretty young Minoan princess who helped Theseus return from the mortal maze, but enough like a blasé Egyptian courtesan to repel even a youngster who had not just been fighting for his life.[6]

In another curiously repulsive episode Fellini shows a frail young bisexual creature, worshiped as the living god Hermaphrodite, being abducted by the anti-heroes and (like a victim of a modern kidnapping) dying of thirst and exhaustion during their escape. There is nothing like

---

[5] D. Comparetti, Virgil in the Middle Ages, trans. by E. F. M. Benecke (New York, 1908), explains that the fire part of the story is a legend told in a history of the Mongol khans of Turkestan that made its way westward through Byzantium. Richard Strauss transformed and ennobled the tale in his opera Feuersnot.

[6] The Roman official who presides over this affair tells Encolpius that the show is a festival honoring the god of Mirth. This notion comes from an isolated episode in the Metamorphoses of Apuleius (2.31 and 3.11), where the joke played on the hero is cleaner, funnier, and more imaginative.

this in Petronius. In the time of Nero I know of no such deities embodied in human form. Much later such a cult was represented by the half-Oriental god-priest Elagabal, who became emperor in A.D. 218 at the age of fourteen and was killed by the soldiers four years later; but that was in a time of social chaos, much farther down the slope than the epoch of Nero. Petronius's wandering hero did in fact commit two acts of sacrilege for which he was severely punished. He profaned the secret rites of the sex-god Priapus by witnessing them without authority, and he killed one of Priapus's sacred birds, a gander. For these offenses he had to pay humiliating penalties. Nothing of this appears in the film. Apparently Fellini sheered off from the idea that a divinity represented largely by a big male organ could be profaned and avenge itself. He chose to substitute for this a pathetic, impotent creature neither truly male nor truly female.

One further change from the original. Encolpius and his companions have an old enemy called Lichas. From certain allusions, it appears that some time ago one of them seduced his wife and insulted him. Petronius makes them board his ship, without knowing he is in command, and disguise themselves to avoid his resentment. Detected, they start a fight; but before anyone is killed, peace is made and celebrated with a drunken party. A storm follows. Captain Lichas is swept overboard and drowned. His ship is wrecked. His body is burned on the beach by the survivors, and (as they say in the Icelandic sagas) so he goes out of the story. In Petronius he is a rather simple "heavy." Fellini converts him into something more complex and sinister. In the film his ship is not a passenger vessel but a slave ship full of victims and freaks destined to amuse the emperor. He insists, after capturing Encolpius, on fighting him and humiliating him. Then he becomes a bride wearing a bridal robe and wreath, takes the dazed Encolpius as his husband, and—while the guests shout *Feliciter!* ("Good Luck!") and his own wife follows as matron of honor—proceeds simpering to a wedding chamber below decks.

In its film context this seems crazy, and very inappropriate for a tough piratic fellow such as Lichas. Apparently Fellini got the idea from the public degeneracy of the emperor Nero, who got himself married to a man called Pythagoras who had been a slave—except that Nero went further than Lichas. The historian Tacitus records it with tight-lipped disgust, saying, "The emperor was clad in a saffron bridal gown, there was a dowry and a marriage bed and bridal torches, everything was seen which even in a woman is concealed by night."[7] A generation later Ju-

[7] Tacitus, *Annales* 15.37.8–9.

venal the satirist tells a similar story about a corrupt nobleman of his own time, mentioning the shouts of *Feliciter!*[8] Yet history outdoes fiction. A little later in the film we see Lichas being seized and beheaded, his wall-eyed head floating away, gazing upward at the camera. But Tacitus, still tight-lipped, begins his next chapter with "There followed a disaster, whether due to chance or the designs of the prince . . ." and goes on to describe the great fire that destroyed much of Rome. The implication is clear.

The *Satyricon* of Petronius could be laid out as ten main blocks of action, each of them with one or more subordinate inset episodes (some mainly action sequences, others mostly speech). Fellini naturally did not try to screen two curious sections in which the disreputable old poet Eumolpus recites part of an epic on the Civil War (to cut down Petronius's contemporary Lucan) and part of a tragic description of the fall of Troy (to cut down Petronius's contemporary Seneca). Sure to stimulate discussion when read aloud at Nero's banquets, these long formal poems would be impossible in a film. Fellini also threw away most of the guests' conversation at the millionaire's banquet. In the book they chatter away, betraying their vulgarity by every sentence they utter. Most of the satirical relish is provided by their richly proliferating social, intellectual, and grammatical blunders. In the film they mainly guzzle and swill. The weight of the emphasis lies on the disgusting dishes they are offered (a whole pig, which when gutted releases not intestines but sausages, the favorite food of the lowest class of Italians) and on Trimalchio's own self-glorification.

To compensate for omitting the talk, Fellini has invented several action sequences with virtually no dialogue. A young emperor is beset and killed by soldiers, some of them wielding ten-foot-long pikes (which in fact were kept for sea battles and siege warfare, but *look* powerful). There is a glimpse of a new Caesar, stern and warlike, marching on Rome. A gigantic head of Constantine (or another very late monarch) is dragged through the streets—perhaps because Juvenal describes the head of a statue of Tiberius's fallen favorite, Sejanus, being broken up and melted down. No one who knows the history of Rome can take these little incidents seriously. The assassination of Caligula by an officer of his own guard, or Nero attempting suicide but afraid to drive the dagger home, would have been more dramatic than these sketchy scenes of immature imagination.

Knowing that both the book and the screenplay are fantasies, we do

[8] Juvenal, *Satires* 2.117–42.

not expect historical accuracy from Fellini. But we may ask for consistency and probability within the limits of the story, and we do not always get it. Many incidents seem to be either mistakes or meaningless quirks of fancy. Take the banquet. Does Fellini really think that Romans dined lying on their stomachs? They did not. It would make anyone feel sick, particularly with so much coarse food being shoved at them. Does he really believe that, just before a dinner party in Rome, all the guests bathed naked in a swimming pool lit by scores of candles? And who on earth are the poorly dressed guests dining upstairs in a gallery, some with their backs to the host? Did Fellini misunderstand the incident in which the millionaire sends the first shift of servants away to eat supper, while a second shift comes on to attend the guests? Perhaps. But this curious arrangement adds nothing to the dramatic value of the scene. Several other directors have the same passion for distorting an original story until it becomes almost meaningless. Buñuel's *Belle de Jour* tells the story of a scientist's pretty wife who feels neglected, takes to visiting a brothel, is at first revolted and then attracted and then corrupted and finally involved in violent gangland crime, through which her husband's life is ruined. When you see the film, you can scarcely make out whether all of this, or some of it, is merely her own erotic and masochistic fantasy. Only when you read the novel, by Joseph Kessel, do you realize that Buñuel has spoiled a clear and powerful story by infusing into it his own aberrant fantasies.

There are two central problems concerning Fellini's film. What is its relation to historical truth? And what is its relation to life in our own world today? Many people who go to see it will come away believing that the first-century Romans actually behaved like this. But to begin with, Petronius himself was writing an extravaganza such as *Candide*, a satiric exaggeration and distortion of life. Furthermore—a point that is seldom noticed—there are hardly any regular Romans in the book. Although they speak Latin, the three youths have Greek names; so do Lichas and his wife Tryphaena, and the poet Eumolpus, and the beautiful Circe, and the witch Oenothea. As for the millionaire, Trimalchio, he is from somewhere in the Near East, and his name is Semitic, from the root M-L-KH, "king": he and his guests speak an impure Latin and are thought of as foreign parvenus. Fellini has taken Petronius's only partly Roman fantasia and has made most of it still more curious and exotic; although he did cast, or rather miscast, a modern Roman as Trimalchio, toward the end it wanders off the Italian map altogether into North Africa and Egypt. In fact, he seems not to have made up his mind whether he was composing an authentic picture of reality—*this is how the pagan Romans lived*—or a series of surrealist visions as striking and imaginative as Goya's *Caprichos*.

He had a classicist to advise him, Luca Canali of the University of Pisa. He and his collaborator on the script, Bernardino Zapponi, visited the greatest Italian authority on Petronius, Professor Ettore Paratore, being (we are told) "a little intimidated" by his discourse. Of course they read books and visited museums. But Fellini has said several times, and I think believes, that we really *do not know* how the Romans thought and felt and lived. "It is one great nebula, full of myth . . . the atmosphere is not 'historical' but that of a dream world . . . the ancient world perhaps never existed; but we have certainly dreamed it." And yet such remarks do not explain either the energy he put into the picture, or some of his own utterances in interviews and discussions. He wants his *Satyricon* to appear as strange and forceful to us as the first Japanese film we ever saw; he even likes the assonance of *Satyricon* and *Rashomon*. In this he neglects the facts that we are closer to the ancient Romans than to the Japanese, and that the Japanese have a very keen sense for authenticity in both costume and behavior in historical dramas. But it is a misrepresentation for Fellini to suggest that the whole film is, for him, merely a psychedelic hallucination with no base in reality. He has several times remarked that the world of pagan Rome has certain analogies with our world of 1970. Therefore he must believe that we can know something about it. Rome as an ideal was (in his view) distorted by Mussolini's Fascism, which stressed its martial and organizational virtues; for these Fellini substitutes its libidinal and mystical qualities. Christianity also, he thinks, makes us misconceive paganism, for Christians see as deliberate vice what the pagans viewed as happiness and fulfillment.[9]

Thus, for Fellini, the *Satyricon* is not crude melodrama or pure fantasy, but a view of paganism as it was and as it will be. It is pre-Christian Rome. (Professor Santo Mazzarino reminded him that while Petronius was writing, St. Paul was preaching; but Fellini maintained that Christian doctrine and the Christian virtues were still known only to a very few.) And it prefigures the post-Christian world that is now lurching toward its birth. The vulgar Trimalchio is a prototype of our own rich, extravagant, selfish contemporaries (Fellini's philological adviser, Canali, is said to be a Marxist). Eumolpus is the cynical and dissolute intellectual, whose keen brain and fine taste are at war with his sensual

---

[9]One of the final scenes, in which Eumolpus's heirs sit gloomily eating his corpse in order to inherit his supposed wealth, may be a parody of the Last Supper; and surely the young hermaphroditic divinity that works miracles and is visited in its shrine by shepherds is a parody of the Christ child in the manger.

appetites. Encolpius and his two companion drifters are flower children, hippies.

Fellini admires the life-style of the hippies. He spent a whole night in a sleeping car outside Rome talking and playing with a group of them— seven girls and fifteen boys—and was delighted with the spontaneity of their emotions and thought. And the violence of the conflicts, many of them his own inventions, that punctuate the film—surely they prefigure the irrational savagery of our own era, in which kidnapping, arson, organized mob violence, and anarchic bombing threaten to supersede the orderly process of social and political life. Fellini seems to see imperial Roman society as passionate and chaotic, inhabited entirely by monsters except for two or three young, energetic, bisexual Nietzschean vagabonds. Encolpius, the best of them, is not the redeemer of this society; but, because he dodges it and uses it and derides it and evades its systematic grasp, he is its victor, not its victim.

This is a profoundly pessimistic view. The film's pessimism comes out in the overall impression it conveys. It follows something of the same emotional pattern as *La Dolce Vita*. There, Fellini began with the flight of a helicopter over Rome (flight over a handsome city is always inspiring) and soon showed us the dazzling beauty of Anita Ekberg; but he ended with a dismal, joyless orgy and a misshapen sea-monster dying on the beach. In the same way, the *Satyricon* afflicts many spectators with disgust and world-weariness. It was surprising to watch the audience emerging from the première in Venice last year: silent, sober, with none of the usual Italian vivacity; depressed and sickened. One man spoke, to an acquaintance, one phrase: "Brutto spettacolo!"

The critics in France, where both the Christian church and conventional morality are taken less seriously, were unfavorably impressed. Jean Dutourd was disappointed because the promised eroticism did not appear (or rather, appeared in sinister distortions) and said he preferred *Ben-Hur*. More thoughtful, Alberto Moravia said that in spite of all his efforts, Fellini still sees pagan Rome in the same way that an early Christian would—"natural and corrupt"; and that this is why he introduces so many sick and deformed figures and so few enjoyments devoid of sinister overtones. I believe this is true. Voltaire in writing *Candide* poured scorn on the philosophical concept that this is the best of all possible worlds, but he made no judgment on ordinary life except to say that one should cultivate one's garden. Rabelais was convinced that our world *could* be the best world possible, if only . . . But Fellini thinks it is the worst of all possible worlds, endurable only through intense irresponsible pleasure followed by interminable escape. In such a world the only real people are exiles, for whom the rest of life is a *brutto spettacolo*.

ARTICLES WRITTEN AT GLASGOW UNIVERSITY

"Innocence Abroad: More or Less (with the S.R.C. Band in Canada)," *GUM* 38.1 (October 13, 1926) 4–5.

"Twelve Little Tragedies," *GUM* 38.9 (February 23, 1927) 248.

"Three Diversions for Helen (Nocturne, Chinoiserie, Spleen)," *GUM* 38.12 (May 11, 1927) 348. See also *University Verses 1910–1927*, pp. 68–69.   *poetry*

"Rodomontades (Moods, Troy, Temptation, Lunar)," *GUM* 39.6 (December 19, 1927) 137–38.   *poetry*

"The Fleeting Hour," *GUM* 39.7 (January 25, 1928) 171–72.

"Soliloquy Beneath a Window," *GUM* 39.7 (January 25, 1928) 176.

"The Fleeting Hour," *GUM* 39.8 (February 8, 1928) 199–200.

"Piano Recital (Debussy, Chopin, Scriabin)," *GUM* 39.8 (February 8, 1928) 204.

"Rout (*Iliad* XVI: 364–393)," *GUM* 39.8 (February 8, 1928) 210.   *poetry*

"I Am Sorry," *GUM* 39.11 (April 25, 1928) 276–77.

"Two Preludes (Major, Minor)," *GUM* 39.11 (April 25, 1928) 282. See also *Farrago* 2.3 (June 1931) 161.   *poetry*

"The Fleeting Hour," *GUM* 39.12 (May 9, 1928) 297–98.

"Arcana Sidera (Doubt, Liebestod)," *GUM* 39.12 (May 9, 1928) 308. See also *SEJ* 12 (September 6, 1929) 944.   *poetry*

"The Fleeting Hour," *GUM* 40.1 (October 24, 1928) 1–3.

"From the Fence," *GUM* 40.1 (October 24, 1928) 9–10.

"The G.U.M. Staff," *GUM* 40.1 (October 24, 1928) 12–13.

"Democracy (Thucydides V.60)," *GUM* 40.1 (October 24, 1928) 17–19. *fiction*

"O Come All Ye Faithful," *GUM* 40.2 (November 7, 1928) 36–37.

"Who Is to Blame?," *GUM* 40.2 (November 7, 1928) 56.

"The Daily Excess" (with J. B. Miller), *GUM* 40.3 (November 21, 1928) 64–65.

"A Few Well-Chosen Words," *GUM* 40.3 (November 21, 1928) 68–69.

"Ode on a Distant Prospect of Profs. Rennie and Dixon," *GUM* 40.3 (November 21, 1928) 70–71.   *poetry*

"Paratragedies," *GUM* 40.4 (December 5, 1928) 87.

"Jest and Youthful Jollity," *GUM* 40.4 (December 5, 1928) 98–99.

"The Fleeting Hour," *GUM* 40.5 (December 19, 1928) 123–25.

"Charity Suffereth Long," *GUM* 40.5 (December 19, 1928) 130–31.

"Paratragedies," *GUM* 40.5 (December 19, 1928) 154.

"Odi et Amo (Catullus, in the Style of Mr. Pope)," *GUM* 40.5 (December 19, 1928) 162.   *poetry*

"Less!," *GUM* 40.6 (January 23, 1929) 187–88.

"Psychopathia Sexualis: Amorists through the Ages" (with J. N. D. Kelly), *GUM* 40.7 (February 7, 1929) 198–99.   *poetry*

"Undergraduate Apathy," *GUM* 40.7 (February 7, 1929) 200–201.

"Song," *GUM* 40.7 (February 7, 1929) 212.   *poetry*

"Correspondence," *GUM* 40.7 (February 7, 1929) 218–19.

"Flown with Insolence and Wine," *GUM* 40.8 (February 20, 1929) 238–39.

"Here Come the Soldiers," *GUM* 40.8 (February 20, 1929) 247–49. See also *Farrago* 1.1 (February 1930) 46–53.   *fiction*

"Fight the Good Fight," *GUM* 40.9 (February 27, 1929) 282–83.

"On Lord Mosenheimer's Mansion," *GUM* 40.9 (February 27, 1929) 283. See also *Farrago* 1.1 (February 1930) 56 and *Oxford Poetry* (1930) 16.   *poetry*

"The Fleeting Hour," *GUM* 40.10 (March 13, 1929) 295–96.

"Great Is Diana," *GUM* 40.10 (March 13, 1929) 304–5.

"Two Poems (Nautch, Isolation)," *GUM* 40.10 (March 13, 1929) 306 and 314. See also *Farrago* 1.1 (February 1930) 64–65.   *poetry*

"I'll Wreathe My Sword in Myrtle Bough," *GUM* 40.11 (April 30, 1929) 350–51.

"Critical Estimate," *GUM* 40.11 (April 30, 1929) 363.   *poetry*

"Alma Mater," *GUM* 40.12 (May 15, 1929) 380–81.

"She Dances," *GUM* 40.12 (May 15, 1929) 395. See also *London Aphrodite* 3 (1928) 214.   *poetry*

"You Can't Refuse," *GUM* 41.2 (November 6, 1929) 32–34. See also *This Quarter* 3.4 (April–June 1931) 669–74.   *fiction*

"The Fleeting Hour," *Ygorra* (1929) 11–14.

"The Lyre," *Ygorra* (1929) 20–21.

"Guide to Glasgow," *Ygorra* (1929) 26–29.

"Off with the Motley," *Ygorra* (1929) 49. See also *Isis* (February 5, 1930) 16.

"She Dances," *London Aphrodite* 3 (1928) 214. See also *GUM* 40.12 (May 15, 1929) 395.   *poetry*

"The Schoolmaster: Or, Ancient Methods of Education," *SEJ* 12 (January 25, 1929) 106–7.   *poetry*

"City Children," *SEJ* 12 (August 9, 1929) 876. See also *Farrago* 2.1 (December 1930) 42 and *Oxford Poetry* (1931) 18–19.   *poetry*

"Doubt," *SEJ* 12 (September 6, 1929) 944. See also *GUM* 39.12 (May 9, 1928) 308.   *poetry*

ARTICLES WRITTEN AT OXFORD UNIVERSITY

"Off with the Motley," *Isis* (February 5, 1930) 16. See also *Ygorra* (1929) 49.

"Humane Proposals. No. I (The Bottosori Method)," *Isis* (February 13, 1930) 8.

"Memorable Recital in Town Hall," *Isis* (May 7, 1930) 6.

"The Free Foozlers," *Isis* (May 14, 1930) 5–6.

"Here Are Fourteen Ladies," *Isis* (May 22, 1930) 22–23.

"Voyaging South! With Mrs. Captain da Costa!," *Isis* (May 28, 1930) 6.

"Tea with the Trojans," *Isis* (June 11, 1930) 15–16.

"Bachanalia," *Isis* (November 19, 1930) 13.

I. K. Fletcher, *Ronald Firbank: A Memoir. Isis* (November 19, 1930) 24. *review*

"The Bad Behaviourist," *Isis* (November 26, 1930) 11.

"Recessional," *Isis* (December 3, 1930) 11–12.

D. Wellesley, *A Broadcast Anthology of Modern Poetry. Isis* (December 3, 1930) 27. *review*

"Conversation with Two Crocodiles," *Isis* (January 21, 1931) 3–4.

"Fleurs du mal," *Isis* (January 28, 1931) 5–6.

"The Honeymoon Racket," *Isis* (February 4, 1931) 10.

T. McGreevy, *Thomas Stearns Eliot. Isis* (February 4, 1931) 21. *review*

"Misfortunes of Nigel," *Isis* (February 19, 1931) 15.

"Incident of the French Camp," *Isis* (February 19, 1931) 17.

"Between Dances," *Isis* (March 4, 1931) 12–13.

"The Last Insult," *Isis* (March 11, 1931) 10.

"Pastoral with Figures," *Isis* (April 29, 1931) 9–10.

"Here Come the Soldiers," *Farrago* 1.1 (February 1930) 46–53. See also *GUM* 40.8 (February 20, 1929) 247–49. *fiction*

"On Lord Mosenheimer's Mansion," *Farrago* 1.1 (February 1930) 56. See also *GUM* 40.9 (February 27, 1929) 283 and *Oxford Poetry* (1930) 16. *poetry*

"Two Poems (Nautch, Isolation)," *Farrago* 1.1 (February 1930) 64–65. See also *GUM* 40.10 (March 13, 1929) 306 and 314. *poetry*

"The Apple," *Farrago* 1.2 (June 1930) 100–106. *poetry*

"City Children," *Farrago* 2.1 (December 1930) 42. See also *SEJ* 12 (August 9, 1929) 876 and *Oxford Poetry* (1931) 18–19. *poetry*

"Acts of Faith," *Farrago* 2.2 (February 1931) 91–98. *poetry*

"Asclepiads," *Farrago* 2.3 (June 1931) 161. See also *GUM* 39.11 (April 25, 1928) 282. *poetry*

"Title to Follow," *Farrago* 2.3 (June 1931) 164–69.

"Urban Eclogue," *Farrago* 2.3 (June 1931) 188. See also *Oxford Poetry* (1931) 16–17. *poetry*

"Ninety Niggers," *This Quarter* 3.4 (April–June 1931) 669–74. See also *GUM* 41.2 (November 6, 1929) 32–34. *fiction*

"On Lord Mosenheimer's Mansion," *Oxford Poetry* (1930) 16. See also *GUM* 40.9 (February 27, 1929) 283 and *Farrago* 1.1 (February 1930) 56. *poetry*

"Urban Eclogue," *Oxford Poetry* (1931) 16–17. See also *Farrago* 2.3 (June 1931) 188. *poetry*

"City Children," *Oxford Poetry* (1931) 18–19. See also *SEJ* 12 (August 9, 1929) 876 and *Farrago* 2.1 (December 1930) 42. *poetry*

"Tennis Tournament," *Oxford Poetry* (1931) 19. *poetry*

"La Lutte au Maroc," *Oxford Outlook* 12.57 (February 1932) 25. *poetry*

"Regardait le Sillage," *Oxford Outlook* 12.57 (February 1932) 60. *poetry*

"The Revolution of the Word," *New Oxford Outlook* 1.3 (February 1934) 288–304.

Review of a collection of novels by William Faulkner. *New Oxford Outlook* 1.3
  (February 1934) 355–56.   *review*

ARTICLES ON CLASSICS AND THE CLASSICAL TRADITION

"The Life of Juvenal," *TAPhA* 68 (1937) 480–506. See also *Juvenal the Satirist*
  1–41.
Oxford Book of Greek Verse in Translation (New York, 1938).   *poetry*
  Translations of Alcaeus, Alcman, Cercidas, Herodas, Menander, Oppian,
  Semonides, Simonides, Solon, Theophilus, Timotheus, and an anonymous
  poet.
"Petronius the Moralist," *TAPhA* 72 (1941) 176–94.
"The *Dunciad*," *Modern Language Review* 36 (1941) 320–43.
"The Shipwrecked Slaver," *AJPh* 63 (1942) 462–66.
"Classical Echoes in *La Araucana*," *Modern Language Notes* 62 (1947) 329–31.
"A Fight in the Desert: Juvenal XV and a Modern Parallel," *CJ* 45 (1949) 94–
  96.
"The Philosophy of Juvenal," *TAPhA* 80 (1949) 254–70.
"Reinterpretation of the Myths," *Virginia Quarterly Review* 25 (1949) 99–115.
  See also *The Classical Tradition* 520–40.
Oxford Classical Dictionary (New York, 1949 and 1970).
  Articles on Agathias, Alcaeus (3) of Messene, Anthology, Antipater (3) of
  Sidon, Antipater (5) of Thessalonica, Antiphilus of Byzantium, Anyte, Ar-
  gentarius (1) Marcus, Argentarius (2), Asclepiades (2) of Samos, Cephalas
  (Constantinus), Dioscorides (1), Diotimus, Epigram, Erucius (1) of Cyzicus,
  Hedylus, Honestus, Juvenal, Leonidas (2) of Tarentum, Leonidas (3) of
  Alexandria, Lollius (3) Bassus, Lucillius, Meleager (2), Nicarchus, Nossis,
  Palladas, Paulus (2), Perses, Persius Flaccus, Philippus (7) of Thessalonica,
  Posidippus (2), Satura, Straton (3) of Sardis, and Zonas.
Introduction to A. Lang, W. Leaf, and E. Myers, *The Iliad of Homer* (New York,
  1950) v–xvi.
"A Socrates Dialogue," *New York Herald Tribune* (October 28, 1951) section 4,
  pp. 1–2.
"Juvenal's Bookcase," *AJPh* 72 (1951) 369–94.
"Sound-Effects in Juvenal's Poetry," *SPh* 48 (1951) 697–706.
"A Neglected Masterpiece: *Olympian Spring*," *Antioch Review* 12 (1952) 338–
  46. See also *BMCT* 62 and *Powers* 251–63.
"Notes on Juvenal," *CR* 2 (1952) 70–71.
"Books and the Crisis," *The Age of Diocletian* (New York, 1953) 49–64. Sym-
  posium published by the Metropolitan Museum of Art.
"Horace to Tibullus," *Harper's* 212 (April 1956) 48. See also *Poets in a Land-
  scape* 161.   *poetry*

Translations of Catullus, Horace, Juvenal, Ovid, Propertius, Tibullus, and Vergil in *Poets in a Landscape*.   *poetry*

Translations of Catullus, Horace, Juvenal, Lucan, Lucretius, Martial, Ovid, Plautus, Propertius, and Publilius Syrus in L. R. Lind, *Latin Poetry in Verse Translation* (Boston, 1957).   *poetry*

Introduction to Sir S. Garth, *Ovid's Metamorphoses* (New York, 1958) xiii–xxii. Printed for the members of the Limited Editions Club by Giovanni Mardersteig.

"Love among the Romans," *Horizon* 1.2 (November 1958) 108–11. See also *BMCT* 107, *Explorations* 257–64, and *Discovery of Lost Worlds* (New York, 1979) 312–15.

"A Memorandum: From Seneca to Tennessee Williams," *Horizon* 1.5 (May 1959) 54–55.

"The *Dyskolos* of Menander," *Horizon* 1.6 (July 1959) 78–89.   *poetry*
Translation of Menander's *Dyskolos*.

"Beer-Bottle on the Pediment," *Horizon* 3.3 (January 1961) 116–18. See also *Explorations* 244–56.

"The Wondrous Survival of Records," *Horizon* 5.2 (November 1962) 74–95. See also *BMCT* 36–37, *Light of the Past* (New York, 1965) 257–75, *Explorations* 341–65, and *Discovery of Lost Worlds* (New York, 1979) 290–311.

"Diogenes and Alexander: The Dog Has His Day," *Horizon* 5.4 (March 1963) 10–13.

"Lucretius," *Horizon* 6.2 (Spring 1964) 28–32.

Introduction to *The Horizon Book of Ancient Rome* (New York, 1966) 6–7.

"Greeks and Romans at Their Ease," *Horizon* 11.2 (Spring 1969) 8–11.

"Whose *Satyricon*—Petronius's or Fellini's?," *Horizon* 12.4 (Autumn 1970) 42–47.

"Libertino Patre Natus," *AJPh* 94 (1973) 268–81.

"A Dissertation on Roast Pig," *CW* 67 (1973) 14–15.

"The Huntsman and the Castaway," *GRBS* 14 (1973) 35–40.

"Consonant Clashes in Latin Poetry," *CPh* 69 (1974) 178–85.

"Housmaniana," *CW* 67 (1974) 363–68. See also *BMCT* 51.

"Juvenal," *Encyclopaedia Britannica* (1974) Vol. 10, pp. 365–66.

"Lexical Notes on Dio Chrysostom," *GRBS* 15 (1974) 247–53.

"Speech and Narrative in the *Aeneid*," *HSPh* 78 (1974) 189–229.

"Masks and Faces in Satire," *Hermes* 102 (1974) 321–37.

"Performances of Vergil's *Bucolics*," *Vergilius* 20 (1974) 24–25.

"The Mediocrity of Celsus," *CJ* 70.4 (1975) 57.

"A Lacuna in the *Aeneid*," *CPh* 71 (1976) 337–38.

"Lexical and Critical Notes on Dio Chrysostom," *GRBS* 17 (1976) 153–56.

See also entries with asterisks in the section of the bibliography on articles developed from his radio program.

REVIEWS ON CLASSICS AND THE CLASSICAL TRADITION

J. W. Duff, *Roman Satire: Its Outlook on Social Life*. CR 52 (1938) 20–21.

P. Ercole, *Studi Giovenaliani*. CR 52 (1938) 79–81.

E. V. Marmorale, *Giovenale*. CR 53 (1939) 71–72.

M. Radin, *Marcus Brutus*. New York Times (January 21, 1940) section 6, p. 12.

G. Murray, *Aeschylus: The Creator of Tragedy*. Saturday Review 22 (June 29, 1940) 19.

E. Reitzenstein, *Wirklichkeitsbild und Gefühlsentwicklung bei Properz*. CR 54 (1940) 199–200.

P. Perrochat, *Pétrone*. CW 33 (1940) 255–56.

J. Carcopino, *Daily Life in Ancient Rome*. Saturday Review 23 (January 11, 1941) 14. See also New York Times (February 23, 1941) section 6, p. 14.

T. Frank, *An Economic Survey of Ancient Rome*. Saturday Review 23 (January 18, 1941) 17–18.

J. Carcopino, *Daily Life in Ancient Rome*. New York Times (February 23, 1941) section 6, p. 14. See also Saturday Review 23 (January 11, 1941) 14.

L. Robinson, *Freedom of Speech in the Roman Republic*. AHR 47 (1941) 181.

H. D. F. Kitto, *Greek Tragedy*. CW 35 (1941–42) 284–85.

M. Rostovtzeff, *Social and Economic History of the Hellenistic World*. New York Times (January 4, 1942) section 6, pp. 3 and 16.

E. L. Highbarger, *The Gates of Dreams: An Archaeological Examination of Vergil, Aeneid VI*. AHR 47 (1942) 828–29.

A. Rostagni, *La letteratura di Roma repubblicana ed Augustea*. AJPh 63 (1942) 92–104.

F. R. B. Godolphin, *The Greek Historians*. Nation 156 (1943) 24–25.

G. Schwab, *Gods and Heroes*. New York Times (February 16, 1947) section 7, p. 22.

E. Barker, *The Politics of Aristotle*. New York Herald Tribune (April 20, 1947) section 7, p. 18.

D. Fitts, *Greek Plays in Modern Translation*. New York Times (September 7, 1947) section 7, p. 28.

R. Warner, *The Medea of Euripides* and *The Prometheus Bound of Aeschylus*; D. Fitts and R. Fitzgerald, *The Oedipus Rex of Sophocles*. New York Times (October 30, 1949) section 7, p. 29.

G. Thornley and M. Hadas, *Daphnis and Chloe*. New York Herald Tribune (December 25, 1949) section 7, p. 9.

W. H. D. Rouse, *Homer's Iliad*. New York Times (February 19, 1950) section 7, p. 21.

J. A. Notopoulos, *The Platonism of Shelley*. New York Herald Tribune (March 5, 1950) section 7, p. 8.

H. M. Poteat, *Brutus: On the Nature of the Gods, On Divination, and On Duties*. New York Times (March 12, 1950) section 7, p. 14.

I. A. Richards, *The Wrath of Achilles. New York Times* (November 19, 1950) section 7, pp. 6 and 45.

J. Marouzeau, *Quelques aspects de la formation du latin littéraire. AJPh* 72 (1951) 443–44.

G. Walter, *Caesar. New York Herald Tribune* (March 23, 1952) section 6, p. 14.

E. Freeman and D. Appel, *The Great Ideas of Plato. Philadelphia Inquirer* (April 13, 1952) 42.

R. E. Hallowell, *Ronsard and the Conventional Roman Elegy. Romanic Review* 46 (1955) 56–57.

A. L. Sells, *Animal Poetry in French and English Literature and the Greek Tradition. Romanic Review* 47 (1956) 154–55.

O. Rossettini, *Les influences anciennes et italiennes sur la satire en France au XVIe siècle. Romanic Review* 51 (1960) 60–62.

J. Marmier, *Horace en France au dix-septième siècle. Romanic Review* 54 (1963) 294–97.

H. Creekmore, *The Satires of Juvenal. CW* 57 (1964) 281.

D. S. Wiesen, *St. Jerome as a Satirist. CW* 58 (1965) 224.

O. Seel, *Weltdichtung Roms: zwischen Hellas und Gegenwart. Gnomon* 39 (1967) 42–46.

A. Mandelbaum, *The Aeneid of Virgil. Vergilius* 18 (1972) 53–55.

N. Rudd, *The Satires of Horace and Persius. CW* 68 (1975) 329–30.

T. Woodman and D. West, *Quality and Pleasure in Latin Poetry. CW* 69 (1976) 476–77.

T. P. Wiseman, *Cinna the Poet and Other Roman Essays. CW* 70 (1976) 209.

See also entries with asterisks in the section of the bibliography on reviews published by Book-of-the-Month Club.

ARTICLES OF A NONCLASSICAL AND MORE GENERAL NATURE

"The Renaissance of the Classics," *Columbia Quarterly* 31.4 (December 1939) 252–62.

"Jules Romains: Man of Good Will," *Saturday Review* 21 (April 6, 1940) 14–15 and 28–29. See also *BMCT* 57–58.

"The American Student as I See Him," *American Scholar* 10 (1941) 416–27.

"Thou Tellest Me, Comrade," *Nation* 152 (1941) 242.

"U.S.S. Jezebel," *Nation* 152 (1941) 412–13.

"J. P. Popo, Esquire," *Nation* 154 (1942) 167–68.

"Homage to Ezra Pound," *Nation* 154 (1942) 228–30.   *poetry*

"I Wuz Robbed," *Nation* 155 (1942) 581–82.

"Axis Prose," *Virginia Quarterly Review* 18 (1942) 216–25.

"Lovesome Prose," *Free America* 7 (Spring 1943) 18–19.

"How to Live with Children," *Colliers* 116 (December 29, 1945) 24 and 46–47.

"Bruegel's Rustic Wedding," *Magazine of Art* 38 (1945) 274–76. See also *Horizon* 9.2 (Spring 1967) 112–15. Converted into a lecture for CBS Television, *Camera Three*, March 24, 1968.

"Remembrance of Cheese Past," *Vogue* (April 15, 1946) 200 and 205–6.

"Subway," *Harper's* 201 (July 1950) 61.   *poetry*

"Oh, Professor!," *New York Herald Tribune* (November 26, 1950) section 8, pp. 23 and 54.

"The Art of Persuasion," *Vogue* 117 (January 1951) 142–43 and 179. See also *The Arts of Living* (New York, 1954) 180–90 and *Explorations* 123–31.

"Teaching, Not Facts, but How to Think," *New York Times* (February 25, 1951) section 6, pp. 16, 42, and 44. See also *The Immortal Profession* 117–32.

"If You're a Parent, You're a Teacher," *Reader's Digest* 59 (July 1951) 97–99. Condensed from *The Art of Teaching*.

"Another Solution," *Harper's* 203 (November 1951) 45–47. See also J. Kahn, *Chilling and Killing* (Boston, 1978) 38–42.   *fiction*

"Insomnia," *New Yorker* 28 (June 7, 1952) 85.   *poetry*

"The Old Gentleman" (New York, 1952) 31 pages. Booklet on George Washington (with illustrations) published as a Christmas keepsake by Oxford University Press. See also *People* 94–105.

"Reader's Cramp," *Wilson Library Bulletin* 28 (January 1954) 415–17.

"Her Sons—'Alert and Grateful,'" *Life* 36 (February 15, 1954) 126–31.

"Communication," *Harper's* 208 (February 1954) 94.

"Preface to *The Arts of Living*," *Vogue* 123 (June 1954) 86–87 and 115. See also *The Arts of Living* (New York, 1954) vii–xiv.

"Man's Unconquerable Mind," *Reader's Digest* 65 (August 1954) 145–54 and 100 (February 1972) 273–87. Condensed from *Man's Unconquerable Mind*.

"Renewal in Teaching," *Strengthening Education at All Levels* (Washington, D.C., 1954) 108–13. Report of the Eighteenth Educational Conference, sponsored by the Educational Records Bureau and the American Council on Education.

"It Describes the Events—and the Spirit," *Reader's Digest* 67 (September 1955) inside back cover.

"The Liberal Educator," *Association of American Colleges Bulletin* 41 (1955) 105–7.

"Sense and Nonsense," *Horizon* 1.1 (September 1958) 129–31. See also *BMCT* 140–41 and *Explorations* 274–91.

"Jimmy Wardrop," *Printing & Graphic Arts* 6 (1958) 19–22.

"The Mystery of Mad Maggie," *Horizon* 1.3 (January 1959) 44–49. See also *BMCT* 136.

"When Forgery Becomes a Fine Art," *Horizon* 1.4 (March 1959) 105–9. See also *BMCT* 99–100.

"The Great Welsh Poet: Dylan Thomas," *Vogue* 135 (March 15, 1960) 111 and 152–54. See also *Powers* 151–57.

"Their Names Are Writ in Webster," *Horizon* 2.5 (May 1960) 126–28. See also *BMCT* 171 and *Explorations* 101–7.

"An Iconography of Heavenly Beings," *Horizon* 3.2 (November 1960) 26–49.

"The Pleasures of Learning," *Vital Speeches of the Day* 26 (1960) 727–30. See also *The Immortal Profession* 1–19 and *Reader's Digest* 109 (September 1976) 95–98.

"The Art of the Hoax," *Horizon* 3.3 (January 1961) 66–72.

"Memento," *Harper's* 222 (February 1961) 62.   *poetry*

"Try 'Massachusetts' on *Your* Piano," *Horizon* 4.2 (November 1961) 118–19. See also *Explorations* 321–27.

"Red Dawn," *Vogue* 141 (April 1, 1963) 131 and 160. Written by Gilbert Gilbertovitch Highet. See also *Explorations* 204–8.

"Obit," *American Scholar* 32 (1963) 597.   *poetry*

"The Dynasty," *Vogue* 143 (February 15, 1964) 95 and 129. Written by Ghilberto degli Higheti.

"Can We Save *Cohort?*," *Horizon* 6.1 (Winter 1964) 119.

"The Class of '64," *CW* 58 (1964) 1–6. See also *The Immortal Profession* 133–44.

Introduction to *The Light of the Past* (New York, 1965) 6–7.

"Moses Hadas, 1900–1966," *Columbia Forum* 9.4 (Fall 1966) 13. See also *CW* 60 (1966) 92–93.

"Sixtieth Birthday," *Columbia Forum* 9.1 (Winter 1966) 47.   *poetry*

"Moses Hadas, 1900–1966," *CW* 60 (1966) 92–93. See also *Columbia Forum* 9.4 (Fall 1966) 13.

"Where Is the Bridegroom?," *Horizon* 9.2 (Spring 1967) 112–15. See also *Magazine of Art* 38 (1945) 274–76. Converted into a lecture for CBS Television, *Camera Three*, March 24, 1968.

"Heart Warning," *Columbia Forum* 11.3 (Fall 1968) 25.   *poetry*

"The Mad World of Hieronymous Bosch," *Horizon* 12.2 (Spring 1970) 66–81.

"Sleep after Sixty," *Columbia Forum* 13.2 (Summer 1970) 23.   *poetry*

"Venice Revisited," *Horizon* 13.1 (Winter 1971) 54–57.

"The Scholarly Life," *American Scholar* 41 (1972) 522–29. See also *The Immortal Profession* 57–74.

"What Makes It Great?" (New York, 1972) 8 pages. Commentary on Dante's *Comedy* (with illustrations) published for the medical profession by Winthrop Laboratories. See also *BMCT* 8.

"Go and Catch a Falling Remark," *Horizon* 15.3 (Summer 1973) 120.

Recollection of Nicholas Murray Butler. *Columbia Today* 2.1 (June 1976) 17.

See also entries without asterisks in the section of the bibliography on articles developed from his radio program.

REVIEWS OF A NONCLASSICAL AND MORE GENERAL
NATURE

J. Romains, *Verdun. New York Times* (December 31, 1939) section 6, p. 1.

H. A. L. Fisher, *Pages from the Past. New York Times* (February 25, 1940) section 6, p. 14.

M. Bishop, *Ronsard, Prince of Poets. Saturday Review* 22 (May 25, 1940) 8.

P. Chapman, *The Spirit of Molière. Saturday Review* 22 (October 5, 1940) 17.

J. Romains, *Aftermath: Men of Good Will. Saturday Review* 23 (February 8, 1941) 5.

N. Strelsky, *Saltykov and the Russian Squire. Russian Review* 1 (1941) 119–20.

B. Wason, *Miracle in Hellas. New York Times* (May 2, 1943) section 7, pp. 1 and 30.

Review of *The Greek White Book. New York Times* (June 13, 1943) section 7, p. 21.

E. Newton, *The Meaning of Beauty. New York Times* (November 5, 1950) section 7, p. 31.

Review of *Life's Picture History of Western Man. New York Herald Tribune* (November 18, 1951) section 6, p. 4.

R. M. Hutchins and M. J. Adler, *Great Books of the Western World. New York Times* (September 14, 1952) section 7, pp. 1 and 34.

"The New Reviewer," *Harper's* 205 (September 1952) 94–99.

"Some New, Some Perennial," *Harper's* 205 (October 1952) 101–5.

"Fiction, History, Fun," *Harper's* 205 (November 1952) 102–12.

"Enough for Everyone, Almost," *Harper's* 205 (December 1952) 96–106.

"Perspectives," *Harper's* 206 (January 1953) 95–100.

"People, Puppets, and Poetry," *Harper's* 206 (February 1953) 100–107.

"Wide Is the World," *Harper's* 206 (March 1953) 99–105.

"Hail and Farewell," *Harper's* 206 (April 1953) 100–107.

"Lines of Communication," *Harper's* 206 (May 1953) 96–103.

"Always Roaming with a Hungry Heart," *Harper's* 206 (June 1953) 100–106.

"Lower than the Angels," *Harper's* 207 (July 1953) 96–100.

[August 1953 column written by C. H. Grattan.]

"Moral Struggles," *Harper's* 207 (September 1953) 94–98.

"Reality, Satire, Romance," *Harper's* 207 (October 1953) 94–99.

"Voyages of Imagination," *Harper's* 207 (November 1953) 94–102.

"New Wine, Old Bottles," *Harper's* 207 (December 1953) 92–102.

"Now Flows from Then," *Harper's* 208 (January 1954) 95–100.

"Darkness and Light Divide the Course of Time," *Harper's* 208 (February 1954) 95–98.

[No special title, *Harper's* 208 (March 1954) 100–106.]

"Welcome Spring," *Harper's* 208 (April 1954) 93–100.

"Whales, Gypsies, Children," *Harper's* 208 (May 1954) 94–103.

"Cry Havoc," *Harper's* 208 (June 1954) 92–99.

"Life and Health, Disease and Death," *Harper's* 209 (July 1954) 93–99.

"Despotism and Liberty," *Harper's* 209 (August 1954) 96–101.

"Sound and Fury," *Harper's* 209 (September 1954) 98–105.

"The Alexandrians of Lawrence Durrell," *Horizon* 2.4 (March 1960) 113–18. Review of *The Alexandria Quartet*. See also *BMCN* (September 1958) 8 and *BMCN* (April 1960) 8.

"Life Behind the Ivy," *Horizon* 3.1 (September 1960) 117–19. Review of C. P. Snow, *The Affair*. See also *BMCN* (May 1960) 2–3.

"Only Yesterday: The Third Reich," *Horizon* 3.2 (November 1960) 119–21. Review of W. L. Shirer, *Rise and Fall of the Third Reich*.

"The Bible Is Given New Speech," *Horizon* 3.4 (March 1961) 94–97. Review of *The New English Bible*. See also *BMCN* (July 1961) back cover and *BMCN* (Special Spring Selection 1970) 3–8.

"Our Man in Purgatory," *Horizon* 3.5 (May 1961) 116–17. Review of G. Greene, *A Burnt-Out Case*.

"Poor Winnie in Pooh-Latin," *Horizon* 3.6 (July 1961) 112–15. Review of A. Lenard, *Winnie Ille Pu*.

"Uncommon Thoughts in a Common Place," *Horizon* 4.1 (September 1961) 114–15. Review of an assortment of commonplace books.

"Henry Miller's Stream of Self-Consciousness," *Horizon* 4.2 (November 1961) 104–5. Review of *Tropic of Cancer* and *Tropic of Capricorn*. See also *Explorations* 209–15.

"Paris at Five O'Clock," *Horizon* 4.5 (May 1962) 113–15. Review of C. Mauriac, *The Marquise Went Out at Five*. See also *BMCN* (May 1962) 9–10.

"To the Sound of Hollow Laughter," *Horizon* 4.6 (July 1962) 89–91. Review of V. Nabokov, *Pale Fire*.

"History by Another Name," *Horizon* 5.1 (September 1962) 112–14. Review of E. and J. Goncourt, *Journal*.

"A Diary from the Depths," *Horizon* 5.2 (November 1962) 108–10. Review of C. M. de Jesus, *Child of the Dark*.

"Dreamer of Light and Dark," *Horizon* 5.3 (January 1963) 109–11. Review of C. G. Jung, *Memories, Dreams, Reflections*.

"Greetings from Goethe's Land," *Horizon* 5.4 (March 1963) 111–13. Review of G. Grass, *The Tin Drum*.

"Liszt and Chopin," *Horizon* 5.5 (May 1963) 109–10. Review of F. Liszt, *Frederic Chopin*.

See also entries without asterisks in the section of the bibliography on reviews published by Book-of-the-Month Club.

ARTICLES DEVELOPED FROM HIS RADIO PROGRAM
(* = classical)

"Modern English Usage," *People* 3–12.   *Henry W. Fowler*

"Science and Humanism," *People* 13–21.   *Sir William Osler*

"An American Poet," *People* 22–28 and *Powers* 129–34.   *Robinson Jeffers*
"The Criticism of Edmund Wilson," *People* 29–36.   *Edmund Wilson*
"Lawrence in America," *People* 37–44.   *D. H. Lawrence*
"Poetry and Romance," *People* 45–52.   *John Masefield*
"Enigma with Variations," *People* 53–60.   *Sir Donald Tovey*
"The Poet and the Modern Stage," *People* 61–68.   *Christopher Fry*
"Dickens as a Dramatist," *People* 69–76.   *Charles Dickens*
"Mr. Eliot," *People* 77–85 and *Powers* 135–42.   *T. S. Eliot*
"The Autobiography of Shakespeare," *People* 86–93 and *Powers* 39–46.
    William Shakespeare
"The Old Gentleman," *People* 94–105. See also booklet (with illustrations) published as a Christmas keepsake by Oxford University Press (New York, 1952) 31 pages.   *George Washington*
"The West," *People* 109–16.
"Oxford and Its Press," *People* 117–29.
"From World to World," *People* 130–37   *C. S. Lewis*
"A Guide to Oxford," *People* 138–46.
"Sailing to Byzantium," *People* 147–55.
"Unpacking the Great Books," *People* 159–67.
"Science for the Unscientific," *People* 168–75.
"The Historian's Job," *People* 176–84.
"The Making of Literature," *People* 185–94.
"Crime and Punishment, Sometimes," *People* 195–202.
"Narcissus the Novelist," *People* 203–10.
"The Museum without Walls," *People* 211–18.
"The Art of Translation," *People* 219–31.
"The Pleasures of Satire," *People* 232–39.
"Books and Cooks," *People* 240–47.
"The Sense of Nonsense," *People* 248–55.
"The Case of the Disappearing Detectives," *People* 256–64.
"Prison Books," *People* 265–74.
"Perchance to Dream," *Clerk* 3–10.
"One Smith in a Billion," *Clerk* 11–19.   *Sydney Smith*
"Ice and Fire," *Clerk* 20–28.
"Looking Back on Today," *Clerk* 29–36.
"Books of Wisdom," *Clerk* 37–45.
"An Eminent Historian," *Clerk* 46–54.   *Lytton Strachey*
"Arms and the Woman," *Clerk* 55–61.
"The Outsider," *Clerk* 62–68.   *George Orwell*
"Words and Meanings," *Clerk* 69–76.
* "The Christians and the Lions," *Clerk* 77–83.
"The Gettysburg Address," *Clerk* 84–91.   *Abraham Lincoln*
"What Use Is Poetry? (I–II)," *Clerk* 95–109 and *Powers* 333–47.
"Seventeen Syllables," *Clerk* 110–16 and *Powers* 183–89.
"The Poet and His Vulture," *Clerk* 117–24 and *Powers* 82–90.   *Lord Byron*

"Melody in Poetry," *Clerk* 134–41 and *Powers* 3–10.

"The Madness of Hamlet," *Clerk* 142–48 and *Powers* 286–92.

William Shakespeare

"The Poet and the Musician," *Clerk* 149–55.

Johannes Brahms and Alfred Tennyson

* "A Drinking Song," *Clerk* 156–64 and *Powers* 174–82.

"The Old Wizard," *Clerk* 165–72 and *Powers* 122–28. *W. B. Yeats*

"Professor Paradox," *Clerk* 173–81 and *Powers* 114–21. *A. E. Housman*

"The Art of Invective," *Clerk* 185–93.

"Witches and Their God," *Clerk* 194–201.

"I to the Hills Will Lift Mine Eyes," *Clerk* 202–9.

"Kitsch," *Clerk* 210–19.

"A New Pleasure," *Clerk* 220–27.

* "The Philosopher of the Atom," *Clerk* 228–34. *Epicurus*

"The Small Flat World," *Clerk* 235–42.

"A Bouquet of Poison Ivy," *Clerk* 243–51.

"Perspectives of Science," *Clerk* 252–59.

"Escape," *Clerk* 260–68.

"A Symbolic Picture," *Talents* 26–33. *Hieronymous Bosch*

"Madam Cat," *Talents* 75–83. *S. G. Colette*

"The Immortal Journalist," *Talents* 126–34. *Samuel Pepys*

"The World My Prison," *Talents* 323–31.

"The Unsigned Letters," *Powers* 68–74. *Robert Burns*

"An Independent American," *Powers* 106–13. *Walt Whitman*

"The Wild Welshman," *Powers* 151–57. *Dylan Thomas*

"Scorn Not the Sonnet," *Powers* 190–96.

"An Unfinished Poem," *Powers* 293–300. *T. S. Eliot*

"Browning as a Painter," *Powers* 308–14. *Robert Browning*

"Man and the Devil," *Powers* 315–22. *J. W. Goethe*

"An Unwritten Book," *Explorations* 3–9. *Lord Acton*

"Ishmael," *Explorations* 187–93.

"The Final Words," *Explorations* 292–303.

"The First Few Words," *BMCT* 1 and *Talents* 222–30.

"A Poet in Italy," *BMCT* 2 and *Powers* 46–52. *William Shakespeare*

"The House High on the Hill," *BMCT* 3 and *Talents* 151–57. *Axel Munthe*

"Do You Talk Good?," *BMCT* 4.

"A Study of History (I–II)," *BMCT* 5–6. *Arnold J. Toynbee*

"The Psychology of Hate," *BMCT* 7. *Robert Browning*

"An Introduction to Dante," *BMCT* 8. See also commentary (with illustrations) published for the medical profession by Winthrop Laboratories (New York, 1972) 8 pages. *Dante Alighieri*

"Winged Words," *BMCT* 9.

"The Nobel Prizes," *BMCT* 10. *Alfred B. Nobel*

"A Face in the Mirror," *BMCT* 11 and *Talents* 255–61.

* "The Ruler of the World," *BMCT* 12 and *Talents* 174–80. *Hadrian*

"A Test of Good Writing," *BMCT* 13.

"The Fascination of What's Different," *BMCT* 14 and *Talents* 48–55.

                                                          Charles Ives

"Could It Be Verse?," *BMCT* 15 and *Powers* 212–20.

"Introduction to *Don Quixote*," *BMCT* 16.   *M. Cervantes*

"The Melancholy Astronomer," *BMCT* 17.   *Omar Khayyam*

"Bach," *BMCT* 18 and *Talents* 41–47.   *J. S. Bach*

"The Anatomy of Slang," *BMCT* 19.

"Kicking His Mother," *BMCT* 20 and *Powers* 167–73.   *W. H. Auden*

* "The Miraculous Jackass (I–II)," *BMCT* 21–22.   *Apuleius*

"The View from Marquand's Head," *BMCT* 23.   *J. P. Marquand*

"Adventures in Rhythm," *BMCT* 24, *Clerk* 125–33, and *Powers* 11–26.

"The Animal Kingdom," *BMCT* 25 and *Talents* 165–73.   *Konrad Lorenz*

* "The Trial of Socrates," *BMCT* 26 and *Talents* 117–25.   *Socrates*

"People of the Caves," *BMCT* 27 and *Talents* 10–17.

"The Art of Diplomacy," *BMCT* 28.

"The Unconscious Artists," *BMCT* 29 and *Talents* 3–9.

* "The Book of Miracles," *BMCT* 30 and *Powers* 264–70.   *Ovid*

"University Eccentrics," *BMCT* 31.

"Summer Reading," *BMCT* 32 and *Talents* 293–99.

"Compulsory Reading," *BMCT* 33 and *Talents* 269–76.

"The Shield of Achilles," *BMCT* 34.   *W. H. Auden*

"What's in a Name?," *BMCT* 35 and *Talents* 231–37.

* "The Biography of the Classics (I–II)," *BMCT* 36–37. See also *Horizon* 5.2 (November 1962) 74–95, *Light of the Past* (New York, 1965) 257–75, *Explorations* 341–65, and *Discovery of Lost Worlds* (New York, 1979) 290–311.

"Pictures of War," *BMCT* 38 and *Talents* 56–62.

"The Philosophy of History," *BMCT* 39.

"I'm Going to Write a Book," *BMCT* 40 and *Talents* 215–21.

"The Old West," *BMCT* 41.   *Buffalo Bill*

"Time Fiction," *BMCT* 42.   *J. R. R. Tolkien*

"The Decadent," *BMCT* 43 and *Talents* 92–99.   *J. K. Huysmans*

"History on the Silver Screen," *BMCT* 44 and *Talents* 191–98.

"The Doctor's Son," *BMCT* 45.   *John O'Hara*

* "The Republic and Its Inheritance," *BMCT* 46.

"The Look-It-Up-Shelf," *BMCT* 47 and *Talents* 285–92.

"Death of a Poet," *BMCT* 48, *Talents* 84–91, and *Powers* 158–64.

                                                          Dylan Thomas

"Scottish Words," *BMCT* 49 and *Talents* 199–206.

"English Shibboleths," *BMCT* 50 and *Talents* 207–14.

* "Housman's Prose," *BMCT* 51. See also CW 67 (1974) 363–68.

                                                 A. E. Housman

"The Age of Dirt and Splendor," *BMCT* 52.   *Louis XIV*

"The Magician," *BMCT* 53 and *Talents* 158–64.   *Somerset Maugham*

"Diminuendo," *BMCT* 54 and *Powers* 205–11.

"On Rereading *Bleak House*," *BMCT* 55.   *Charles Dickens*

"The Bird on the Gibbet," *BMCT* 56 and *Talents* 34–40.   *Pieter Bruegel*

"Men of Good Will (I–II)," *BMCT* 57–58.   See also *Saturday Review* 21 (April 6, 1940) 14–15 and 28–29.   *Jules Romains*

"Puss in Books," *BMCT* 59.

"The Letters of Jefferson," *BMCT* 60 and *Talents* 135–42.   *Thomas Jefferson*

"The Face and Form of Buddha," *BMCT* 61.

* "Olympian Spring," *BMCT* 62 and *Powers* 251–63.   See also *Antioch Review* 12 (1952) 338–46.   *Carl Spitteler*

"The Vergil of the Insects," *BMCT* 63 and *Talents* 109–16.   *Jean-Henri Fabre*

* "Speechmaking: A Lost Art (I–II)," *BMCT* 64–65.

"Inside Aubrey," *BMCT* 66 and *Talents* 100–108.   *John Aubrey*

[*BMCT* 67 is not on file at Columbia University, New York Public Library, Oxford University Press, Book-of-the-Month Club, Library of Congress, and University of California (Berkeley). I suspect, in keeping with the reasoning that I believe Dr. Highet would have used, that the person responsible for numbering the transcripts may accidentally have skipped this number. *Editor*]

"The Mystery of Zen (I–II)," *BMCT* 68–69 and *Talents* 308–22.

"The Immigrants," *BMCT* 70 and *Talents* 332–40.

* "Permanent Books," *BMCT* 71 and *Talents* 300–307.

"A Great Teacher," *BMCT* 72.   *William A. Neilson*

"Fair Greece, Sad Relic," *BMCT* 73.

"Greek Voices," *BMCT* 74.

* "Pandora's Box," *BMCT* 75.

"The Face of Italy," *BMCT* 76.

"An Unknown World," *BMCT* 77 and *Talents* 183–90.

"I Married an Author," *BMCT* 78 and *Talents* 262–68.   *Helen MacInnes*

"The Pleasures of a Naturalist," *BMCT* 79.   *Gerald Durrell*

* "Jolly Old Graves," *BMCT* 80 and *Talents* 18–25.

"The Poet and the Urn," *BMCT* 81 and *Powers* 236–43.   *John Keats*

"How Shelley Died," *BMCT* 82 and *Powers* 91–97.   *P. B. Shelley*

"Modern American Humor," *BMCT* 83.

"Secret Languages," *BMCT* 84 and *Explorations* 61–67.

"A Few Blue Notes," *BMCT* 85.

"The Birth of a Book (I–II)," *BMCT* 86–87 and *Talents* 238–54.

"The First Deadly Sin," *BMCT* 88 and *Talents* 143–50.   *Baron Corvo*

"Venice Observed," *BMCT* 89 and *Talents* 63–71.   *Mary McCarthy*

* "Desire and the Soul (I–II)," *BMCT* 90–91.   *Apuleius*

"Intelligent Cookery," *BMCT* 92.   *Peter Gray*

"Ourselves as Others See Us," *BMCT* 93.

"Criticoses," *BMCT* 94 and *Talents* 277–84.

"The Lady and the Poet," *BMCT* 95 and *Powers* 61–67.   *Alexander Pope*

"One Kind of Glory," *BMCT* 96.

"An American Naturalist," *BMCT* 97.   *E. W. Teale*

"Play and Life," *BMCT* 98 and *Explorations* 117–22.

"Artistic Forgeries (I–II)," *BMCT* 99–100. See also *Horizon* 1.4 (March 1959) 105–9.

"The Faster Fowler," *BMCT* 101.   *Margaret Nicholson*

"A Surrealist Memory," *BMCT* 102 and *Explorations* 171–77.   *Salvador Dali*

"Changing Words," *BMCT* 103 and *Explorations* 68–77.

"Pet Marjory," *BMCT* 104 and *Explorations* 156–63.   *Marjory Fleming*

"The Art of the Caves," *BMCT* 105.

"How to Torture an Author," *BMCT* 106 and *Explorations* 267–73.

* "Love among the Romans,"   *BMCT* 107. See also *Horizon* 1.2 (November 1958) 108–11, *Explorations* 257–64, and *Discovery of Lost Worlds* (New York, 1979) 312–15.

"The Reluctant Artist," *BMCT* 108.   *Leonardo da Vinci*

"Two Husbands," *BMCT* 109.   *S. G. Colette*

"The Stationary Man," *BMCT* 110 and *Explorations* 178–86.   *Gilbert White*

"On First Looking into *The Arabian Nights*," *BMCT* 111 and *Explorations* 51–57.

"Where Is God?" *BMCT* 112.

"The Man in the Gray Velvet Suit," *BMCT* 113 and *Explorations* 224–32.

                                                                                                         Erik Satie

"A Scholar's Life," *BMCT* 114. See also *The Immortal Profession* 145–74.

                                                                                                      Gilbert Murray

"The Third Sitwell," *BMCT* 115.   *Sacheverell Sitwell*

"Bird Watching as an Art," *BMCT* 116.

"Mass Culture," *BMCT* 117.   *Richard Hoggart*

"Chess Men," *BMCT* 118.

"The Pleasures of Gardening," *BMCT* 119.

"Education by Remote Control," *BMCT* 120.   *Lord Chesterfield*

"Barrie's Scotland," *BMCT* 121 and *Explorations* 20–26.   *James M. Barrie*

"The Memory Machines," *BMCT* 122.

* "The Epic of a Crime," *BMCT* 123 and *Powers* 271–77.   *Lucan*

"Lifetime Labels," *BMCT* 124 and *Explorations* 85–91.

"Horse Power," *BMCT* 125.

"The End of the World Is at Hand," *BMCT* 126 and *Explorations* 216–23.

"The Romancer," *BMCT* 127.   *Arthur Conan Doyle*

"I'm Not Scared," *BMCT* 128.   *Algernon Blackwood*

"How to Write an Essay," *BMCT* 129 and *Explorations* 304–10.

"The Bloomsberries," *BMCT* 130.

"The Beat Generation," *BMCT* 131.

"An Uncertain Smile," *BMCT* 132.   *Françoise Sagan*

"Prometheus at the Piano," *BMCT* 133.   *Abram Chasins*

"The Wild Preacher," *BMCT* 134.

"Speech for the Plaintiff," *BMCT* 135.   *Charles Dickens*

"Mad Maggie," *BMCT* 136. See also *Horizon* 1.3 (January 1959) 44–49.

                                                                                                      Pieter Bruegel

* "Ulysses," *BMCT* 137.   *James Joyce*
"Build Your Own Library," *BMCT* 138.
"Father and Son," *BMCT* 139 and *Explorations* 43–50.   *Edmund W. Gosse*
"Sense and Nonsense," *BMCT* 140–41. See also *Horizon* 1.1 (September 1958)
    129–31 and *Explorations* 274–91.
"A Young Man's Fantasy," *BMCT* 142 and *Explorations* 27–35.
                            George Meredith
"Learning a Language," *BMCT* 143 and *Explorations* 92–100.
"Courage," *BMCT* 144.   *Edward Le Comte*
* "Propaganda and Poetry," *BMCT* 145 and *Powers* 197–204.
                            Thomas B. Macaulay
"Mystics and Realists," *BMCT* 146.
"Saint Thomas Eliot?" *BMCT* 147.   *T. S. Eliot*
* "A Little Latin Lyric," *BMCT* 148 and *Powers* 221–27.   *Horace*
"American English," *BMCT* 149.
"Shakespeare's Dreams and Dreamers," *BMCT* 150 and *Powers* 301–7.
                         William Shakespeare
"The Adventurous Traveler," *BMCT* 151 and *Explorations* 10–19.
                       Alexander W. Kinglake
* "The Philosopher Enthroned," *BMCT* 152 and *Explorations* 194–203.
                        Marcus Aurelius
"Useless Speeches," *BMCT* 153 and *Explorations* 328–33.
"Peer Gynt," *BMCT* 154 and *Explorations* 36–42.   *Henrik Ibsen*
"The Voice of the Law," *BMCT* 155 and *Explorations* 334–40.
                       W. H. Davenport
* "Buried Treasures," *BMCT* 156.   *Heinrich Schliemann*
"The Ancient Mariners' Association," *BMCT* 157 and *Explorations* 311–20.
"The Magic-Maker," *BMCT* 158 and *Powers* 143–50.   *E. E. Cummings*
"The Life of a Yogi," *BMCT* 159 and *Explorations* 164–70.
* "The Hidden Language of Prehistoric Greece," *BMCT* 160.
"The Elegy in a Country Churchyard," *BMCT* 161 and *Powers* 278–85.
                         Thomas Gray
"The Mystery of Edwin Drood," *BMCT* 162.   *Charles Dickens*
"A Mouse and a Louse," *BMCT* 163 and *Powers* 74–81.   *Robert Burns*
"Lolita," *BMCT* 164.   *Vladimir Nabokov*
"The Language of Adam," *BMCT* 165 and *Explorations* 108–14.
                         Noah J. Jacobs
"New Year's Day with Mr. Pepys," *BMCT* 166 and *Explorations* 233–43.
                         Samuel Pepys
"The Personality of Joyce," *BMCT* 167 and *Explorations* 135–46.   *James Joyce*
"Tell Me a Story," *BMCT* 168.
"Arthur the King," *BMCT* 169.   *T. H. White*
* "A Modern Epic," *BMCT* 170.   *Nikos Kazantzakis*
"Name into Word," *BMCT* 171. See also *Horizon* 2.5 (May 1960) 126–28 and
    Explorations 101–7.
* "Shakespeare at Work," *BMCT* 172.   *William Shakespeare*

"The Lonely Philosopher," *BMCT* 173.   *L. J. J. Wittgenstein*
"The Harp That Once," *BMCT* 174.
"Heir of the Whole World," *BMCT* 175 and *Powers* 53–60.   *Thomas Traherne*
"Painter of the Miraculous," *BMCT* 176.   *Salvador Dali*
"Obscurity in Poetry," *BMCT* 177 and *Powers* 27–35.
"The Waste Land," *BMCT* 178 and *Powers* 323–29.   *T. S. Eliot*
"Foreigners Are Fools," *BMCT* 179 and *Explorations* 78–84.
"The Doctor's Life," *BMCT* 180.
* "Penetrating a Book," *BMCT* 181 and *Powers* 244–50.   *Vergil*
"Memories of Heaven," *BMCT* 182 and *Powers* 228–35.   *William Wordsworth*
"What the Greeks Did," *BMCT* 183.   *Arnold J. Toynbee*
"The Teacher's Life," *BMCT* 184.
"Hot Gospeler," *BMCT* 185 and *Explorations* 147–55.   *Aimée S. McPherson*
"Ten Commandments for the Translator," *BMCT* 186.
"A Neglected American," *BMCT* 187 and *Powers* 98–105.
                                                      Ralph Waldo Emerson
"A Personal Library," *BMCT* 188.

REVIEWS PUBLISHED BY BOOK-OF-THE-MONTH CLUB
(* = classical)

Z. Oldenbourg, *The Cornerstone*. BMCN (December 1954) 1–3.
A. Koestler, *The Invisible Writing*. BMCN (December 1954) 10.
M. Brand, *Some Love, Some Hunger*. BMCN (March 1955) 8.
J. M. Gironella, *The Cypresses Believe in God*. BMCN (April 1955) 5.
R. West, *A Train of Powder*. BMCN (April 1955) 8.
C. Fadiman, *Party of One*. BMCN (May 1955) 6.
R. Fülöp-Miller, *The Night of Time*. BMCN (May 1955) 9–10.
C. Dane, *The Flower Girls*. BMCN (June 1955) 2–3.
L. Yutang, *Looking Beyond*. BMCN (June 1955) 5.
M. Edelman, *A Dream of Treason*. BMCN (July 1955) 7.
E. Simon, *The Twelve Pictures*. BMCN (Midsummer 1955) 6.
W. Gaddis, *The Recognitions*. BMCN (Midsummer 1955) 8–9.
A. Huxley, *The Genius and the Goddess*. BMCN (August 1955) 7.
D. Johnston, *Nine Rivers from Jordan*. BMCN (August 1955) 8–9.
T. Mann, *Confessions of Felix Krull, Confidence Man*. BMCN (September 1955) 5–6.
I. Edman, *The Uses of Philosophy*. BMCN (September 1955) 7–8.
R. Bacchelli, *Nothing New under the Sun*. BMCN (September 1955) 10.
N. Dennis, *Cards of Identity*. BMCN (October 1955) 8.
R. Godden, *An Episode of Sparrows*. BMCN (November 1955) 4–5.

C. Fadiman, *The American Treasury (1455–1955)*. BMCN (November 1955) 7.

K. Lindemann, *The Red Umbrellas*. BMCN (November 1955) 11–12.

J. Masters, *Bugles and a Tiger*. BMCN (December 1955) 1–3.

J. O'Hara, *Ten North Frederick*. BMCN (December 1955) 5.

W. Buchan, *Kumari*. BMCN (December 1955) 8–9.

C. S. Lewis, *Surprised by Joy*. BMCN (February 1956) 8.

S. Chotzinoff, *Toscanini: An Intimate Portrait*. BMCN (March 1956) 2–3.

K. Amis, *That Uncertain Feeling*. BMCN (March 1956) 9.

S. K. Padover, *A Jefferson Profile*. BMCN (April 1956) 8.

H. Nicolson, *Good Behaviour*. BMCN (April 1956) 10.

E. Burdick, *The Ninth Wave*. BMCN (May 1956) 1–3.

G. M. Mardikian, *Song of America*. BMCN (June 1956) 7.

J. Clark, *Hunza: Lost Kingdom of the Himalayas*. BMCN (July 1956) 10–11.

H. Wendt, *In Search of Adam*. BMCN (Midsummer 1956) 1–3.

E. Crankshaw, *Gestapo: Instrument of Tyranny*. BMCN (Midsummer 1956) 8.

E. Pryor, *The Double Man*. BMCN (January 1957) 5–6.

M. Waltari, *The Etruscan*. BMCN (January 1957) 9.

W. Hill, *Onionhead*. BMCN (March 1957) 11–12.

J. P. Marquand, *Stopover Tokyo*. BMCN (March 1957). See separate circular.

C. Morgan, *Challenge to Venus*. BMCN (April 1957) 8.

H. Swiggett, *The Durable Fire*. BMCN (June 1957) 1–3.

E. M. Remarque, *The Black Obelisk*. BMCN (June 1957) 6.

T. Plievier, *Berlin*. BMCN (June 1957) 8–9.

J. Masters, *Far, Far the Mountain Peak*. BMCN (June 1957) 11–12.

T. Chamales, *Never So Few*. BMCN (July 1957) 8–9.

P. White, *Voss*. BMCN (Midsummer 1957) 1–3.

H. A. Kissinger, *Nuclear Weapons and Foreign Policy*. BMCN (Midsummer 1957) 6–7.

G. W. Brace, *The World of Carrick's Cove*. BMCN (August 1957) 6–7.

M. Shulman, *Rally Round the Flag, Boys!* BMCN (August 1957) 8–9.

A. Le May, *The Unforgiven*. BMCN (September 1957) 6–7.

C. B. Davis, *Unholy Uproar*. BMCN (September 1957) 9.

J. Kerouac, *On the Road*. BMCN (September 1957) 10–11.

J. Braine, *Room at the Top*. BMCN (October 1957) 11–12.

M. L. Coit, *Mr. Baruch*. BMCN (November 1957) 1–3.

P. H. Bonner, *Amanda*. BMCN (November 1957) 7–8.

C. N. Parkinson, *Parkinson's Law*. BMCN (November 1957) 12.

C. Wilson, *Religion and the Rebel*. BMCN (December 1957) 11.

J. Jones, *Some Came Running*. BMCN (January 1958) 9.

H. Fast, *The Naked God*. BMCN (January 1958) 12.

J. Maritain, *Reflections on America*. BMCN (February 1958) 6.

P. S. Feibleman, *A Place without Twilight*. BMCN (March 1958) 7.

R. Condon, *The Oldest Confession*. BMCN (May 1958) 8–9.

L. Durrell, *Balthazar*. BMCN (September 1958) 8. See also *Horizon* 2.4 (March 1960) 113–18.

N. Shute, *The Rainbow and the Rose*. BMCN (October 1958) 9.

J. R. Ullman, *The Day on Fire*. BMCN (October 1958) 10–11.

T. Berger, *Crazy in Berlin*. BMCN (October 1958) 11–12.

M. McMinnies, *The Visitors*. BMCN (November 1958) 1–4.

* H. Lamb, *Hannibal: One Man Against Rome*. BMCN (November 1958) 7.

P. Berton, *The Klondike Fever*. BMCN (November 1958). See separate circular.

Review of *The Travels of Marco Polo*. BMCN (November 1958). See separate circular.

E. Lipsky, *The Scientists*. BMCN (January 1959) 1–3.

J. Jones, *The Pistol*. BMCN (January 1959) 6.

J. Masters, *Fandango Rock*. BMCN (February 1959) 8–9.

S. Bellow, *Henderson, the Rain King*. BMCN (March 1959) 6–7.

E. T. Hall, *The Silent Language*. BMCN (April 1959) 6.

J. Thurber, *The Years with Ross*. BMCN (May 1959) 2–3.

A. Cordell, *The Rape of the Fair Country*. BMCN (May 1959) 9–10.

J. Kessel, *The Lion*. BMCN (June 1959) 1–3.

M. Cheke, *The Cardinal de Bernis*. BMCN (June 1959) 7–8.

R. L. Bruckberger, *Image of America*. BMCN (July 1959) 4–5.

W. Strunk Jr., *The Elements of Style*. BMCN (July 1959) 9.

I. Andric, *The Bridge on the Drina*. BMCN (Midsummer 1959) 6.

H. Wendt, *The Road to Man*. BMCN (Midsummer 1959) 10–11.

M. Harris, *Wake Up, Stupid!* BMCN (August 1959) 6.

G. Duffy, *Warden's Wife*. BMCN (August 1959) 8–9.

P. Fleming, *The Siege at Peking*. BMCN (September 1959) 8.

A. Huxley, *Collected Essays*. BMCN (September 1959) 13.

T. Williams, *Town Burning*. BMCN (October 1959) 6–7.

M. Lott, *Dance Back the Buffalo*. BMCN (October 1959) 8.

J. A. Shimer, *This Sculptured Earth: The Landscape of America*. BMCN (October 1959) 10.

M. M. Hunt, *The Natural History of Love*. BMCN (October 1959). See separate circular.

J. A. Michener, *Hawaii*. BMCN (November 1959) 1–3.

C. Ryan, *The Longest Day*. BMCN (November 1959) 8.

V. Nabokov, *Invitation to a Beheading*. BMCN (November 1959) 9–10.

G. Paloczi-Horvath, *The Undefeated*. BMCN (December 1959) 7.

S. Carrighar, *Wild Voice of the North*. BMCN (December 1959) 8.

S. Myrivilis, *The Mermaid Madonna*. BMCN (December 1959) 11.

J. Berry, *Krishna Fluting*. BMCN (January 1960) 5–6.

K. Waterhouse, *Billy Liar*. BMCN (January 1960) 7.

K. R. Greenfield, *Command Decisions*. BMCN (January 1960) 8–9.

G. Jenkins, *A Twist of Sand*. BMCN (February 1960) 5–6.

G. Swarthout, *Where the Boys Are*. BMCN (February 1960) 8.

L. Lee, *The Edge of Day*. BMCN (March 1960) 2–3.

E. Wilson, *Apologies to the Iroquois*. BMCN (March 1960) 7.

D. W. Sciama, *The Unity of the Universe*. BMCN (March 1960) 8–9.

E. Bowen, *A Time in Rome. BMCN* (March 1960) 12.

L. Durrell, *Clea. BMCN* (April 1960) 8. See also *Horizon* 2.4 (March 1960) 113–18.

M. Keon, *The Durian Tree. BMCN* (April 1960) 11–12.

C. P. Snow, *The Affair. BMCN* (May 1960) 2–3. See also *Horizon* 3.1 (September 1960) 117–19.

W. Styron, *Set This House on Fire. BMCN* (June 1960) 7.

L. Mosley, *The Glorious Fault. BMCN* (June 1960) 8–9.

P. S. Beagle, *A Fine and Private Place. BMCN* (June 1960) 12.

G. Ordish, *The Living House. BMCN* (Midsummer 1960) 7.

L. Eiseley, *The Firmament of Time. BMCN* (August 1960) 6.

J. D. MacDonald, *The End of the Night. BMCN* (August 1960) 8–9.

C. Fitzgibbon, *When the Kissing Had to Stop. BMCN* (August 1960) 10–11.

N. Kazantzakis, *The Last Temptation of Christ. BMCN* (September 1960) 7–8.

M. Irwin, *That Great Lucifer. BMCN* (September 1960) 9.

A. H. Lewis, *The Worlds of Chippy Patterson. BMCN* (October 1960) 11–12.

C. Coccioli, *The White Stone. BMCN* (October 1960) 13–14.

H. Tracy, *A Number of Things. BMCN* (October 1960) 15.

R. Stephan, *My Crown, My Love. BMCN* (November 1960) 6.

A. Schwarz-Bart, *The Last of the Just. BMCN* (November 1960) 10.

B. Mather, *The Pass beyond Kashmir. BMCN* (November 1960) 12.

J. Betjeman, *Summoned by Bells. BMCN* (December 1960) 10–11.

J. O'Hara, *Sermons and Soda-Water. BMCN* (December 1960) 13–14.

C. Gartner, *The Infidels. BMCN* (December 1960) 15–16.

B. Boyce, *Man from Mt. Vernon. BMCN* (January 1961) 5.

J. Stuart, *God's Oddling. BMCN* (January 1961) 6.

I. Stone, *The Agony and the Ecstasy. BMCN* (March 1961) 1–4.

J. Dos Passos, *Midcentury. BMCN* (March 1961) 7–8.

D. Holman-Hunt, *My Grandmothers and I. BMCN* (March 1961) 9–10.

H. and B. Overstreet, *The War Called Peace. BMCN* (March 1961) 11–12.

* O.-W. Von Vacano, *The Etruscans in the Ancient World. BMCN* (April 1961) 13–14.

A. Cowell, *The Heart of the Forest. BMCN* (April 1961) 15–16.

R. O'Grady, *O'Houlihan's Jest. BMCN* (May 1961) 9–10.

I. Murdoch, *A Severed Head. BMCN* (May 1961) 13.

D. Acheson, *Sketches from Life. BMCN* (June 1961) 5.

R. L. Taylor, *A Journey to Matecumbe. BMCN* (June 1961) 7.

Z. Oldenbourg, *Destiny of Fire. BMCN* (July 1961) 8.

Review of *The New English Bible. BMCN* (July 1961) back cover. See also *Horizon* 3.4 (March 1961) 94–97 and *BMCN* (Special Spring Selection 1970) 3–8.

J. M. Espinas, *By Nature Equal. BMCN* (Midsummer 1961) 8.

P. Quennell, *The Sign of the Fish. BMCN* (Midsummer 1961) 9.

J. R. Salamanca, *Lilith. BMCN* (Midsummer 1961). See separate circular.

H. Tracy, *A Season of Mists. BMCN* (August 1961) 5.

G. Griffin, *Master of This Vessel*. BMCN (August 1961) 6.

J. Steinbeck, *The Winter of Our Discontent*. BMCN (August 1961). See separate circular.

V. Peterson, *A Matter of Life and Death*. BMCN (September 1961) 10–11.

P. White, *Riders in the Chariot*. BMCN (October 1961) 9.

J. Berry, *Flight of White Crows*. BMCN (October 1961) 10.

R. Ingersoll, *Point of Departure*. BMCN (October 1961) 14.

M. Kantor, *Spirit Lake*. BMCN (November 1961) 5–6.

P. Dennis, *Little Me*. BMCN (November 1961) 8.

R. Ardrey, *African Genesis*. BMCN (December 1961) 7–8.

E. Waugh, *The End of the Battle*. BMCN (January 1962) 7.

R. C. Hutchinson, *The Inheritor*. BMCN (January 1962) 11.

* M. Renault, *The Bull from the Sea*. BMCN (February 1962) 1–3.

F. Duerrenmatt, *The Quarry*. BMCN (February 1962) 6.

* S. Perowne, *Hadrian*. BMCN (February 1962) 10.

J. Prebble, *Culloden*. BMCN (March 1962) 11.

L. Durrell, *The Dark Labyrinth*. BMCN (March 1962) 14.

E. Williams, *George*. BMCN (April 1962) 1–3.

A. Huxley, *Island*. BMCN (April 1962) 13–14.

R. Frost, *In the Clearing*. BMCN (May 1962) 5–6.

J. L. Dyson, *The World of Ice*. BMCN (May 1962) 8–9.

C. Mauriac, *The Marquise Went Out at Five*. BMCN (May 1962) 9–10. See also *Horizon* 4.5 (May 1962) 113–15.

A. Mosby, *The View from No. 13 People's Street*. BMCN (June 1962) 6.

R. Ruark, *Uhuru*. BMCN (July 1962) 1–3.

R. Linney, *Heathen Valley*. BMCN (July 1962) 8.

I. B. Singer, *The Slave*. BMCN (July 1962) 12–13.

W. Nigg, *The Heretics*. BMCN (Midsummer 1962) 7–8.

A. Nevins, *The State Universities and Democracy*. BMCN (Midsummer 1962) 9–10.

D. Robertson, *The River and the Wilderness*. BMCN (August 1962) 7.

L. L. Strauss, *Men and Decisions*. BMCN (August 1962) 10–11.

A. Drury, *A Shade of Difference*. BMCN (September 1962) 9.

J. Clavell, *King Rat*. BMCN (September 1962) 11–12.

R. Bradbury, *Something Wicked This Way Comes*. BMCN (October 1962) 6.

* P. MacKendrick, *The Greek Stones Speak*. BMCN (October 1962) 9.

B. Smith, *Portrait of India*. BMCN (November 1962) 7.

E. W. Teale, *The Strange Lives of Familiar Insects*. BMCN (November 1962) 11.

R. McKenna, *The Sand Pebbles*. BMCN (December 1962) 1–2.

H. Innes, *Atlantic Fury*. BMCN (December 1962) 6.

S. Jackson, *We Have Always Lived in the Castle*. BMCN (December 1962) 8.

E. Taylor, *The Fall of the Dynasties*. BMCN (January 1963) 4–6.

P. Farb, *Face of North America*. BMCN (February 1963) 1–5.

J. B. Priestley, *Margin Released*. BMCN (February 1963) 7–8.

J. C. Herold, *Bonaparte in Egypt. BMCN* (March 1963) 5.

M. Carter, *A Fortune in Dimes. BMCN* (March 1963) 7.

J. Y. Cousteau, *The Living Sea. BMCN* (April 1963) 2–5.

R. M. Watt, *Dare Call It Treason. BMCN* (April 1963) 8.

S. E. Morison, *The Two-Ocean War. BMCN* (May 1963) 12.

C. D. Bowen, *Francis Bacon: The Temper of a Man. BMCN* (June 1963) 9–10.

M. Jones, *A Buried Land. BMCN* (June 1963) 12–13.

I. Murdoch, *The Unicorn. BMCN* (June 1963) 14.

V. Mehta, *Fly and the Fly-Bottle. BMCN* (July 1963) 10–11.

J. A. Michener, *Caravans. BMCN* (Midsummer 1963) 1–3.

H. Arendt, *Eichmann in Jerusalem. BMCN* (Midsummer 1963) 5–6.

G. Gross, *Masterpieces of Murder: An Edmund Pearson True Crime Reader.*
    BMCN (Midsummer 1963) 8–9.

W. and A. Durant, *The Age of Louis XIV. BMCN* (August 1963) 1–3.

M. McCarthy, *The Group. BMCN* (September 1963) 7.

S. Mrozek, *The Elephant. BMCN* (October 1963) 11–12.

O. A. Bushnell, *Molokai. BMCN* (November 1963) 8–9.

D. D. Eisenhower, *Mandate for Change: 1953–1956. BMCN* (November 1963)
    9–10.

A. Dulles, *The Craft of Intelligence. BMCN* (December 1963) 8.

C. F. Gibbon, *Going to the River. BMCN* (December 1963) 13.

C. W. Thayer, *Guerrilla. BMCN* (January 1964) 11–12.

R. Collier, *The Great Indian Mutiny. BMCN* (February 1964) 8.

H. Schwartz, *Tsars, Mandarins, and Commissars. BMCN* (February 1964) 10.

B. Ballantine, *Horses and Their Bosses. BMCN* (February 1964) 11.

E. Baker, *A Fine Madness. BMCN* (March 1964) 8.

E. Ayrton, *Silence in Crete. BMCN* (March 1964) 11.

J. Kennaway, *The Bells of Shoreditch. BMCN* (April 1964) 8–9.

D. Storey, *Radcliffe. BMCN* (April 1964) 10.

S. Chotzinoff, *A Little Nightmusic. BMCN* (April 1964) 11–12.

M. Djilas, *The Leper. BMCN* (May 1964) 11.

W. A. Smith, *When the Lion Feeds. BMCN* (May 1964) 12.

L. Ross, *Reporting. BMCN* (May 1964) 13.

G. Millstein, *New York: True North. BMCN* (May 1964) 15–16.

V. Baum, *It Was All Quite Different. BMCN* (June 1964) 7.

I. Kirkpatrick, *Mussolini. BMCN* (June 1964) 9.

W. K. Zinsser, *The Haircurl Papers. BMCN* (June 1964) 10–11.

E. Hamilton, *The Ever-Present Past. BMCN* (July 1964) 5.

W. Golding, *The Spire. BMCN* (July 1964) 7.

J. W. Corrington, *And Wait for the Night. BMCN* (July 1964) 9.

W. Wetmore, *All the Right People. BMCN* (July 1964) 12.

*G. Vidal, *Julian. BMCN* (Midsummer 1964) 9.

E. Trevor, *The Flight of the Phoenix. BMCN* (Midsummer 1964) 11.

D. Howarth, *The Desert King: Ibn Saud and His Arabia. BMCN* (Midsummer
    1964) 13.

374 BIBLIOGRAPHY

J. Alsop, *From the Silent Earth*. *BMCN* (August 1964) 6–7.

E. Clark, *The Oysters of Locmariaquer*. *BMCN* (August 1964) 9–10.

L. Barzini, *The Italians*. *BMCN* (August 1964) 12.

P. B. Young, *Undine*. *BMCN* (September 1964) 9.

L. A. Harris, *The Fine Art of Political Wit*. *BMCN* (September 1964) 15.

P. Scott, *The Corrida at San Feliu*. *BMCN* (October 1964) 11–12.

J. P. Sartre, *The Words*. *BMCN* (October 1964) 13.

R. West, *The New Meaning of Treason*. *BMCN* (November 1964) 1–5.

E. Briggs, *Farewell to Foggy Bottom*. *BMCN* (November 1964) 10.

M. Bardos, *Night Light*. *BMCN* (November 1964) 12.

J. S. Carter, *Full Fathom Five*. *BMCN* (December 1964) 4–5.

V. Nabokov, *The Defense*. *BMCN* (December 1964) 9.

H. V. Morton, *A Traveller in Italy*. *BMCN* (December 1964) 13.

L. Bemelmans, *La Bonne Table*. *BMCN* (January 1965) 7.

R. C. Hutchinson, *A Child Possessed*. *BMCN* (February 1965) 9–10.

S. Carrighar, *Wild Heritage*. *BMCN* (March 1965) 1–5.

F. Lewis, *Red Pawn*. *BMCN* (March 1965) 10.

E. Burdick, *Nina's Book*. *BMCN* (March 1965) 15–16.

W. Eastlake, *Castle Keep*. *BMCN* (April 1965) 13.

W. Wilkinson, *Even in the Depths*. *BMCN* (April 1965) 14.

J. A. Michener, *The Source*. *BMCN* (May 1965) 1–3.

E. Wilson, *O Canada*. *BMCN* (May 1965) 11.

S. De Beauvoir, *Force of Circumstance*. *BMCN* (June 1965) 12–13.

G. Owen, *The Ballad of the Flim-Flam Man*. *BMCN* (June 1965) 15.

R. P. Warren, *Who Speaks for the Negro?* *BMCN* (July 1965) 8.

I. Andric, *The Woman from Sarajevo*. *BMCN* (August 1965) 12.

* G. Schmitt, *Electra*. *BMCN* (October 1965) 12.

G. Perrault, *The Secret of D-Day*. *BMCN* (October 1965) 14–15.

D. Acheson, *Morning and Noon*. *BMCN* (November 1965) 13.

G. Conchon, *The Savage State*. *BMCN* (December 1965) 11.

* L. Deuel, *Testaments of Time*. *BMCN* (December 1965) 15.

W. D. Davies, *Invitation to the New Testament*. *BMCN* (February 1966) 5.

* P. Green, *The Laughter of Aphrodite*. *BMCN* (February 1966) 8.

C. Ryan, *The Last Battle*. *BMCN* (March 1966) 2–6.

J. Stafford, *A Mother in History*. *BMCN* (March 1966) 9–10.

K. Rexroth, *An Autobiographical Novel*. *BMCN* (March 1966) 11.

J. Hersey, *Too Far to Walk*. *BMCN* (April 1966) 10.

E. A. Speiser, *At the Dawn of Civilization*. *BMCN* (April 1966) 12.

G. Griffin, *A Last Lamp Burning*. *BMCN* (May 1966) 11.

B. Haas, *The Last Valley*. *BMCN* (June 1966) 8.

I. B. Singer, *In My Father's Court*. *BMCN* (June 1966) 9.

R. Kipling, *Kim*. *BMCN* (July 1966) 5–6.

J. A. Smith, *John Buchan*. *BMCN* (July 1966) 12.

P. L. Fermor, *Roumeli*. *BMCN* (August 1966) 12.

J. Barth, *Giles Goat-Boy or, The Revised New Syllabus*. BMCN (August 1966) 13–14.

K. Amis, *The Anti-Death League*. BMCN (September 1966) 10.

A. Hiroshige, *The Fifty-three Stages of the Tokaido*. BMCN (September 1966) 13.

* M. Renault, *The Mask of Apollo*. BMCN (October 1966) 1–3.

V. Nabokov, *Speak, Memory*. BMCN (January 1967) 5–7.

R. Blake, *Disraeli*. BMCN (March 1967) 10.

H. Pu Yi, *The Last Manchu*. BMCN (March 1967) 14.

H. E. Burtt, *The Psychology of Birds*. BMCN (April 1967) 10.

W. S. Kuniczak, *The Thousand Hour Day*. BMCN (May 1967) 1–4.

D. Bloodworth, *The Chinese Looking Glass*. BMCN (July 1967) 2–6.

E. Bradford, *The Sundered Cross*. BMCN (July 1967) 14–15.

G. Griffin, *An Operational Necessity*. BMCN (Midsummer 1967) 1–3.

S. Gainham, *Night Falls on the City*. BMCN (August 1967) 1–3.

* R. Lattimore, *The Odyssey of Homer*. BMCN (October 1967) 9. See also BMCN (Midwinter 1977) for the separate circular.

W. S. Lewis, *One Man's Education*. BMCN (October 1967) 11.

F. Diaz-Plaja, *The Spaniard and the Seven Deadly Sins*. BMCN (October 1967) 13.

M. Ayrton, *The Mazemaker*. BMCN (Special Fall Selection 1967) 11–12.

H. C. Schonberg, *The Great Conductors*. BMCN (November 1967) 15–16.

D. Morris, *The Naked Ape*. BMCN (January 1968) 1–4.

J. A. Michener, *Iberia: Spanish Travels and Reflections*. BMCN (April 1968) 2–7.

V. Nabokov, *King, Queen, Knave*. BMCN (May 1968) 2–3.

L. Collins and D. Lapierre, *Or I'll Dress You in the Morning*. BMCN (July 1968) 1–6.

J. Kessel, *The Horsemen*. BMCN (July 1968) 12–13.

A. Myrer, *Once an Eagle*. BMCN (Midsummer 1968) 2–4.

R. Hardman, *Fifteen Flags*. BMCN (Midsummer 1968) 7.

B. and B. Gould, *American Story*. BMCN (August 1968) 10–11.

P. Horgan, *Everything to Live For*. BMCN (October 1968) 9.

T. Wolfe, *The Pump House Gang: The Electric Kool-Aid Acid Test*. BMCN (October 1968) 11–12.

A. I. Solzhenitsyn, *The First Circle*. BMCN (Special Fall Selection 1968) 2–6.

A. Drury, *Preserve and Protect*. BMCN (Special Fall Selection 1968) 11.

G. Plimpton, *The Bogey Man*. BMCN (December 1968) 10.

P. De Vries, *The Cat's Pajamas and Witch's Milk*. BMCN (December 1968) 12.

H. W. Chapman, *Fear No More*. BMCN (January 1969) 11–12.

J. Yaffe, *The American Jews*. BMCN (March 1969) 8–9.

J. Bruller, *The Battle of Silence*. BMCN (March 1969) 10–11.

W. Rayner, *The Last Days*. BMCN (March 1969) 12–13.

J. De Hartog, *The Children*. BMCN (Special Spring Selection 1969) 10–11.

J. Bainbridge, *Another Way of Living: A Gallery of Americans Who Choose to Live in Europe.* BMCN (Special Spring Selection 1969) 13–14.

H. Harrison, *Captive Universe.* BMCN (April 1969) 8.

J. Cheever, *Bullet Park.* BMCN (May 1969) 2–3.

H. Hesse, *Gertrude.* BMCN (May 1969) 13.

P. S. Buck, *The Three Daughters of Madame Liang.* BMCN (July 1969) 1–3.

D. G. Compton, *The Palace.* BMCN (July 1969) 10–11.

S. De Gramont, *The French: Portrait of a People.* BMCN (August 1969) 1–4.

W. Rayner, *The Knifeman: The Last Journal of Judas Iscariot.* BMCN (August 1969) 10.

S. Gainham, *A Place in the Country.* BMCN (September 1969) 8.

D. Morris, *The Human Zoo.* BMCN (October 1969) 1–4.

S. Alliluyeva, *Only One Year.* BMCN (Special Fall Selection 1969) 1–4.

R. C. Hutchinson, *Johanna at Daybreak.* BMCN (November 1969) 8.

L. Lee, *As I Walked Out One Midsummer Morning.* BMCN (December 1969) 12–13.

M. Mujica-Lainez, *Bomarzo.* BMCN (January 1970) 8–9.

S. Hook, *Academic Freedom and Academic Anarchy.* BMCN (March 1970) 10–11.

A. Moorehead, *Darwin and the Beagle.* BMCN (March 1970). See separate circular.

Review of *The New English Bible.* BMCN (Special Spring Selection 1970) 3–8. See also BMCN (July 1961) back cover and *Horizon* 3.4 (March 1961) 94–97.

G. Bibby, *Looking for Dilmun.* BMCN (Special Spring Selection 1970) 11–12.

K. Rose, *Superior Person.* BMCN (April 1970) 6.

A. H. Lewis, *Carnival.* BMCN (April 1970) 10.

E. Clark, *Baldur's Gate.* BMCN (June 1970) 1–3.

M. Copeland, *The Game of Nations.* BMCN (July 1970) 12.

I. Macalpine and R. Hunter, *George III and the Mad Business.* BMCN (Midsummer 1970) 9.

D. Jenkins, *The Dogged Victims of Inexorable Fate.* BMCN (Midsummer 1970) 11.

B. Mather, *The Break.* BMCN (Midsummer 1970) 12.

D. Bloodworth, *An Eye for the Dragon: Southeast Asia Observed (1954–1970).* BMCN (August 1970) 1–5.

K. Millett, *Sexual Politics.* BMCN (September 1970) 10.

H. Charrière, *Papillon.* BMCN (October 1970) 2–5.

K. Amis, *The Green Man.* BMCN (October 1970) 7.

R. Stewart, *The Possession of Joel Delaney.* BMCN (Special Fall Selection 1970) 9.

C. A. Lindbergh, *The Wartime Journals of Charles A. Lindbergh.* BMCN (November 1970) 7.

A. Schnitzler, *My Youth in Vienna.* BMCN (December 1970) 8–9.

M. M. Luke, *A Crown for Elizabeth.* BMCN (December 1970) 10–11.

D. Parker, *Constant Reader*. BMCN (January 1971) 11–12.

L. Eiseley, *The Invisible Pyramid*. BMCN (Special Midwinter Selection 1971) 6.

R. Payne, *A Portrait of André Malraux*. BMCN (Special Midwinter Selection 1971) 9.

J. Weidman, *Fourth Street East*. BMCN (February 1971) 6.

S. E. Morison, *The European Discovery of America*. BMCN (March 1971) 1–5.

T. Lilley, *The Officer from Special Branch*. BMCN (March 1971) 11.

P. P. Read, *Monk Dawson*. BMCN (March 1971) 12.

J. Houston, *The White Dawn*. BMCN (April 1971) 1–3.

K. R. Toole, *The Time Has Come*. BMCN (April 1971) 6–7.

A. Moorehead, *A Late Education*. BMCN (April 1971) 9.

U. O'Connor, *Brendan Behan*. BMCN (June 1971) 9.

F. Capra, *Frank Capra: The Name above the Title*. BMCN (July 1971) 1–4.

E. Hoffer, *First Things, Last Things*. BMCN (Midsummer 1971) 5.

Z. Oldenbourg, *The Heirs of the Kingdom*. BMCN (Midsummer 1971) 7–8.

T. Gallagher, *The X-Craft Raid*. BMCN (September 1971) 7–8.

H. Cole, *Fouché: The Unprincipled Patriot*. BMCN (September 1971) 10.

K. Scherman, *Two Islands: Grand Mananand and Sanibel*. BMCN (October 1971) center spread.

R. Sencourt, *T. S. Eliot*. BMCN (Special Fall Selection 1971) 7.

H. and J. Van Lawick-Goodall, *In the Shadow of Man*. BMCN (Special Fall Selection 1971) 11.

R. G. Martin, *Jennie: The Life of Lady Randolph Churchill. Volume II: The Dramatic Years*. BMCN (November 1971) 1–5.

F. D. Ommanney, *Lost Leviathan*. BMCN (November 1971) 9–10.

M. Rofheart, *Fortune Made His Sword*. BMCN (February 1972) 2–3.

M. Crichton, *The Terminal Man*. BMCN (March 1972) 4–5.

J. C. Masterman, *The Double-Cross System*. BMCN (March 1972) 7.

J. Wambaugh, *The Blue Knight*. BMCN (March 1972) 11.

M. Middlebrook, *The First Day on the Somme*. BMCN (Special Spring Selection 1972) 7–8.

E. Wiesel, *Souls on Fire*. BMCN (April 1972) 8–9.

E. Morgan, *The Descent of Woman*. BMCN (May 1972) 2–4.

S. Lenz, *The German Lesson*. BMCN (May 1972) 8–9.

W. Lord, *The Dawn's Early Light*. BMCN (June 1972) 2–4.

D. Acheson, *Grapes from Thorns*. BMCN (July 1972) 7.

P. Horgan, *Encounters with Stravinsky: A Personal Record*. BMCN (July 1972) 15.

H. Tracy, *The Quiet End of Evening*. BMCN (Midsummer 1972) 8–9.

F. Mowat, *A Whale for the Killing*. BMCN (August 1972). See separate circular for Canadian members.

P. Matthiessen and E. Porter, *The Tree Where Man Was Born: The African Experience*. BMCN (October 1972) 2–4.

R. Godden, *The Diddakoi*. BMCN (October 1972) 6.

C. Frankel, *A Stubborn Case*. BMCN (November 1972) 6.

M. Gray, *For Those I Loved*. BMCN (December 1972) 2–5.

* M. Renault, *The Persian Boy*. BMCN (January 1973) 6–7.

R. Payne, *The Life and Death of Adolf Hitler*. BMCN (April 1973) 1–5.

H. Böll, *Group Portrait with Lady*. BMCN (May 1973) 1–3.

J. F. Bernard, *Talleyrand: A Biography*. BMCN (May 1973) 5.

* M. Grant, *Cleopatra*. BMCN (May 1973) 7.

K. S. Davis, *FDR: The Beckoning of Destiny (1882–1928)*. BMCN (May 1973) 12.

A. Hall, *The Tango Briefing*. BMCN (Midsummer 1973) 1–3. See special issue for Canadian members.

M. West, *The Salamander*. BMCN (September 1973) 1–4.

L. Sanders, *The First Deadly Sin*. BMCN (October 1973) 1–4.

J. Gathorne-Hardy, *The Unnatural History of the Nanny*. BMCN (October 1973) 27.

G. Vidal, *Burr*. BMCN (November 1973) 2–3.

S. Birmingham, *Real Lace*. BMCN (January 1974). See separate circular.

M. M. Luke, *Gloriana: The Years of Elizabeth I*. BMCN (February 1974) 1–4. See special issue for Canadian members.

F. M. Brodie, *Thomas Jefferson: An Intimate History*. BMCN (Special Spring Selection 1974) 1–3.

J. Le Carré, *Tinker, Tailor, Soldier, Spy*. BMCN (June 1974) 1–3.

B. and M. Kalb, *Kissinger*. BMCN (August 1974) 1–3.

C. Ryan, *A Bridge Too Far*. BMCN (October 1974) 1–3.

M. Mayer, *The Bankers*. BMCN (January 1975) 1–3.

J. Wain, *Samuel Johnson*. BMCN (Special Spring Selection 1975) 3.

A. Dolgun and P. Watson, *Alexander Dolgun's Story: An American in the Gulag*. BMCN (May 1975) 1–3.

A. Smith, *Powers of Mind*. BMCN (October 1975) 1–3.

B. Woodward and C. Bernstein, *The Final Days*. BMCN (May 1976) 1–4.

E. Crankshaw, *The Shadow of the Winter Palace: Russia's Drift to Revolution (1825–1917)*. BMCN (October 1976) 2–3.

J. Keegan, *The Face of Battle*. BMCN (December 1976) 1–3.

* R. Lattimore, *The Iliad of Homer* and *The Odyssey of Homer*. BMCN (Midwinter 1977). See separate circular. See also BMCN (October 1967) 9.

L. Ullmann, *Changing*. BMCN (February 1977) 1–3.

P. Caputo, *A Rumor of War*. BMCN (Midsummer 1977) 1–3.

J. Le Carré, *The Honourable Schoolboy*. BMCN (Special Fall Selection 1977) 1–3.

INDEX